THE FOURTH WAY

T·H·E FOURTH WAY

A Theory of Knowledge

REINHARDT GROSSMANN

INDIANA UNIVERSITY PRESS
Bloomington and Indianapolis

The paper used in this publication meets the minimum requirements of American
National Standard for Information Sciences—Permanence of Paper for Printed
Library Materials, ANSI Z39.48-1984.

 ™

Manufactured in the United States of America

Library of Congress Cataloging-in-Publication Data

Grossmann, Reinhardt
  The fourth way : a theory of knowledge / Reinhardt Grossmann.
    p. cm.
  Includes bibliographical references.
ISBN 0-253-32654-0
  1. Knowledge, Theory of. 2. Empiricism. 3. Realism. I. Title.
BD161.G745 1990
121—dc20   89-45921
                                                                          CIP

I 2 3 4 5 94 93 92 91 90

5,27-92

Contents

Preface

In his commentary on *Kant's Critique of Pure Reason,* Vaihinger considers the four possible views which result if one combines the epistemological distinction between rationalism and empiricism with the ontological distinction between realism and idealism. He claims that until Kant, rationalism was always connected with realism, empiricism always with idealism. But Kant discovered a new combination: The marriage of rationalism with idealism. And then Vaihinger mentions in parentheses that the fourth possible combination, empiricism with realism, has always been considered to be impossible (see H. Vaihinger, *Kommentar zu Kants Kritik der reinen Vernunft,* vol. I, p. 52). It is this "impossible" view which I shall defend. That is why I called this book "The Fourth Way."

Empiricism means different things to different people. I have in mind the view that our knowledge of the external world rests entirely on perception, and that knowledge of our own minds is solely based on introspection. I hold that there is no special faculty of the mind, no Platonic "contemplation," no Cartesian "understanding," no Husserlian "eidetic intuition," by means of which we know external objects. My version of empiricism may be called "radical," for it insists, not only that we know the familiar objects around us by perception, but also that we know numbers and other abstract entities by means of perception. I hold that the truths of arithmetic ultimately rest just as much on perception as the truths of physics.

It is in regard to this contention that my view differs most profoundly from other theories of knowledge. While many contemporary philosophers accept empiricism in regard to the "natural sciences," hardly anyone agrees with me that logic, set theory, and arithmetic are a matter of empirical knowledge. But empiricism cannot stand on one leg. An empiricism that claims exception for logic, set theory, and arithmetic is no empiricism at all. Arithmetic, in particular, is the touchstone for any serious attempt to defend empiricism. I shall therefore have to discuss arithmetic knowledge in great detail.

Realism, too, has many meanings. I mean the view that there are such perceptual objects as apples, that these things consist of smaller things like molecules, and that these in turn consist of even smaller objects like elementary particles (or of whatever else the physicist may discover). None of these things is mental. Nor do they depend for their existence or nature on there being minds. But my realism, too, is of a radical sort, for I also hold that there are sets and numbers, and that these things as well do not depend for their existence or nature on minds. Just as an empiricism in regard to science alone can be no more than a paltry evasion of the rationalist's challenge, so realism only in regard to ordinary perceptual objects can be nothing but a worthless response to the idealist's taunt. The realist's work is only half done after he has refuted Berkeley. That an apple is not a collection of ideas is fairly obvious. "That number is entirely the creature of the mind," however, seems to be an unshakable conviction of even the most realistic philosophers.

But even if we rid ourselves of this idealistic bias, even if we accept numbers and sets as part of the furniture of the world, there remains the formidable task of placing these entities somewhere in the hierarchy of categories. Granted that numbers are nonmental, to what category do they belong? Are they sets? Or are they perhaps properties of properties? This task, I believe, has been so futile up to now because the proper category for numbers was simply not a part of standard ontologies. Philosophers have for generations tried in vain to squeeze numbers into one of the familiar and traditional categories. Until very recently, there was very little to choose from: Numbers had to be either individual things or else properties of individual things. For an idealist, they could only be either intuitions or concepts. A third possibility finally appeared with the reluctant acceptance of the category of set. But this acceptance posed a new challenge: How to reconcile the existence of sets with empiricism.

Vaihinger, as I said, claims that Kant discovered a new combination: the compatibility of rationalism with idealism. I do not think highly either of Kant's rationalism or of his idealism. But Kant discovered—and proudly insisted on—one crucial truth: arithmetic is necessary and yet synthetic. With this discovery, he challenged all empiricists as well as all rationalists. Empiricists have to explain how arithmetic can possibly be necessary; rationalists, how it can possibly be synthetic. This challenge, I believe, has not been met.

I would like to thank my colleague Romane Clark, who read part of the manuscript and made many helpful suggestions.

One

Knowledge of the External World

PERCEPTION

And who does not see that philosophy must make a very ridiculous figure in the eyes of sensible men, while it is employed in mustering up metaphysical arguments, to prove that there is a sun and a moon, an earth and a sea.

—Thomas Reid, *Essays on the Intellectual Powers of Man,* p. 231

A. Historical Perspectives

ONE

Descartes's Realism

On the Brink of Disaster

a) The Scholastic Background

Descartes's "new way of ideas" breaks decisively with the Aristotelian tradition. But it also leads inevitably to both skepticism and idealism. It is ironic that the supreme attempt to refute skepticism should make skepticism all but inevitable. And it is tragic that the modern features of Descartes's philosophy should unavoidably lead to skepticism and idealism. The tragedy lies in the fact that modern philosophers seem to be faced with an inescapable dilemma: either they have to reject Descartes's innovations, or else they have to pay for embracing his revolution by succumbing, sooner or later, to skepticism and/or idealism. What precisely is responsible for this malaise of modern theories of knowledge?

According to the Aristotelian tradition, a perceptual object, for example, an apple, is a combination of matter and form. This combination, the so-called substance, has certain properties, the so-called accidents of the substance. For example, the apple may be green. When one perceives the apple, let us call it "Oscar," a complicated causal process takes place. The gist of this part of the traditional theory is that the apple, through a medium, causes a material impression on the sense organ; in our case, on the eye. This impression is considered to be a material image of the perceived object. Next, the so-called active intellect goes to work on the material image and extracts from it the substantial form of the perceived object. As a result of this mental process, the form of Oscar comes to exist in the mind of the perceiver. The perception of Oscar thus simply consists in that his form exists in a mind. The form is then both "in" the apple and "in" the mind. One and the same thing, to emphasize, thus exists both in the mind and in the apple: the form, as it is usually put, exists materially in the apple and immaterially in the mind. Some philosophers conclude that the form has two kinds of existence: it has material existence in Oscar and mental existence in the mind of the perceiver.

There are three parts of this analysis which I wish to stress for future reference. Firstly, the Tradition assumes that in perception the mind does not "reach out" to make direct contact with Oscar. It is directly related only to what is *in* it, namely, the form of Oscar as it exists mentally. I shall call this all-important assumption "the principle of immanence," and I shall sum it up in the slogan: *The mind knows (directly) only what is in it*. This principle, I shall argue, is the source of the skepticism invited by Descartes's philosophy.

Secondly, even though the mind can only know what is in it, the mind nevertheless knows the form of Oscar; for this form is literally in the mind. The mind, therefore, has really no need to "reach out" and touch the apple. The form of Oscar comes to the mind, so to speak. Let us call the form of Oscar, as it exists in the mind, a "concept." In having the concept of Oscar in his mind, the perceiver knows Oscar. The relationship between the concept and its object, between the form as it exists in the mind and as it exists in the substance, is one of identity. I shall call this "the thesis of identity."

Thirdly, the matter of this particular apple, Oscar's matter, does not exist in the mind of the perceiver. Now, some philosophers of the Tradition have held that it is the matter of a substance which materially distinguishes between one substance and another. If so, then it is Oscar's matter which accounts for his individuality. It is Oscar's matter which accounts for his "thisness." But since his matter never exists in a mind, we cannot perceive Oscar in his individuality. It follows that we cannot really perceive the individual apple Oscar but merely his form.

b) Knowledge by Way of Ideas: The Inevitability of Skepticism

Descartes's epistemological revolution consists in a rejection of the thesis of identity. What is in the mind when you perceive Oscar is not *his form,* but something else, namely an *idea* of him. This idea is neither identical with any property of Oscar's nor with the property of being an apple. This idea, far from being identical with the form (essence) of Oscar, does not even resemble Oscar's form. The Cartesian idea, unlike the concept of the Tradition, is not in any sense, shape, or form like the apple. This rejection of the identity thesis follows straight-forwardly from Descartes's conception of the mind as a substance which is essentially different from material substances. Nothing which is "in" a material substance can also be "in" a mind, and conversely. Mind and matter have nothing in common.

But Descartes, like almost every other philosopher of his time (and many philosophers of our time), accepts the calamitous principle of immanence. He agrees with Arnauld that "we can only have knowledge of what is outside us through the mediation of ideas in us" (A. Arnauld, *L'Art de penser; la Logique de Port-Royal,* p. 63). In Leibniz's words, human souls "perceive what passes without them by what passes within them" (*The Leibniz-Clarke Correspondence,* p 83).

It is the combination of the rejection of the thesis of identity with an acceptance of the principle of immanence that condemns Descartes's philosophy to fall before the skeptical argument. Since the mind can only know what is in it, it can only know the idea of the apple. Knowledge of Oscar, if it is possible at all, must therefore be mediated by this idea. But since this idea of the apple is no more like Oscar than the word 'Oscar' is, Oscar can only be known as *the thing which is represented by the idea*. The relationship between the idea and its object is neither identity nor resemblance. Let us call it "representation." What kind of relation is representation? Some of Descartes's opponents claimed that representation is inconceivable. Descartes's view, they said, is simply unintelligible. Surprisingly, some Cartesians agreed with this verdict. Representation, they conceded, is a miracle. Yet they preferred the miracle to a rejection of their revolutionary new insight that ideas are not like their objects. The idea of Oscar, they kept on insisting, is not at all like Oscar (cf. R. A. Watson's *The Downfall of Cartesianism*). An old way of thinking thus clashed in their minds violently with a new-found conviction. We shall see that the representation relation is not at all inconceivable. It is perfectly reasonable to assume that there exists a unique and indefinable relation between every idea and its object. The idea of Oscar, for example, is an idea of Oscar, and of nothing else, because it represents (intends) Oscar and nothing else.

No, the problem with Cartesianism lies somewhere else. The principle of immanence is the true culprit. It is this principle which provides the skeptic with his decisive argument against Cartesianism. The argument goes as follows (see, for example, John Sergeant, *Solid Philosophy, Asserted against the Fancies of the Ideaists . . .*). In order to know what a given idea I_1 represents, we must be able to compare the idea with what it represents. But in order to compare I_1 with an object O_1, so that we can find out whether or not O_1 stands in the representation relation to I_1, we must obviously know both the idea and the object, but in addition we must know the object other than by means of the idea. However, according to the principle of immanence, we cannot know an object other than by means of an idea. Therefore we cannot compare an idea with an object and hence cannot find out what objects correspond to which ideas. We do not know, therefore, what objects our ideas represent. And thus we do not know what there is in the way of an external world.

Since I believe that the skeptic's argument is valid, let me reformulate it in a different way in order to bring out what I take to be its fundamental structure. The question is again: What object is represented by a given idea I_1? We can only answer this question if we can establish a fact of this sort: I_1 stands in the representation relation to O_1. This fact must somehow be presented to the mind. But in order to have this fact present to the mind, both I_1 and O_1 must be present to the mind. But, according to the principle of immanence, O_1 cannot be present to the mind; for the mind can only be presented with what is in it, and O_1 is not in it. Hence we cannot find out what object I_1 represents. The situation is quite different when it is a question of relations between ideas. If we want to know whether or not I_1 stands in the relation R to I_2, we can apprehend the fact that I_1 stands in R to I_2; for we can have present to the mind both I_1 and I_2 (and, we have assumed, also R). But in the case of I_1 and an object, the object can only "be known by description" since, according to the principle of immanence, it cannot be present to the mind. But such knowledge is useless in our case. If we ask whether or not I_1 represents "the object which I_1 represents," the answer is obvious but does not tell us what specific object I_1 represents. And if we ask whether or not I_1 represents "the object which I_2 represents," the answer is obviously negative.

I have tried to give as clear a version of the skeptic's argument as I can, because it has also been applied to sensations and has been accepted in that context by philosophers from Locke to Russell. It alleges there, as we shall see, that we cannot know the true degree of warmth of a bucket of water or the true shape of a table top. All we can ever know are our own sensations of warmth and of shape.

In whatever context the skeptic's argument may appear, it is clear from our analysis how we must attack it. We cannot give up Descartes's brilliant insight that ideas do not resemble their objects. The idea of Oscar is not at all like Oscar: it has no color, it has no shape; it is neither hard nor soft; it has no smell, nor has it size. The idea of Oscar is as different from Oscar as anything can be. Yet it represents Oscar. There is a unique (intentional) relation which connects every idea with its object. This part of Cartesianism is sound. What has to be abandoned is the principle of immanence. It is not true that the mind only knows what is in it. Quite to the contrary, as we shall see: the mind never knows what is *in* it; it only knows what is *before* it! As I see the dialectic, skepticism can only be averted if we refute the principle of immanence. In order to refute it we shall have to unearth the motives for the principle and attack these motives. And we shall have to show how a rejection of the principle agrees with the phenomenology of perception. This is the main task of the second section of this book.

Cartesianism, by combining a rejection of the thesis of identity with an acceptance of the principle of immanence, leads to skepticism. But this combination is almost always part of a representational theory of knowledge. Representationalism, therefore, almost always falls prey to skepticism. But Cartesianism also leads to idealism. In this case, the fault lies not with the Tradition but with modern science. Cartesianism, as has often been remarked, has one foot in the Tradition and one foot in modernity. Since it retains the principle of immanence, it is too old-fashioned to escape from skepticism. Since it embraces the distinction between primary and secondary qualities, it is too modern to avoid idealism.

c) Secondary Qualities: The Inevitability of Idealism

The distinction between primary and secondary qualities, it should be emphasized, is not an essential part of the Cartesian revolution. Rather, it is forced upon philosophy in general and the Cartesians in particular by the scientific revolution of the 17th century. Galileo, for example, makes the distinction in these words:

> Now I say that whenever I conceive any material or corporeal substance, I immediately feel the need to think of it as bounded, and as having this or that shape; as being large or small in relation to other things, and in some specific place at any given time; as being in motion or at rest; as touching or not touching some other body; and as being one in number, or few, or many. From these conditions I cannot separate such a substance by any stretch of my imagination. But that it must be white or red, bitter or sweet, noisy or silent, and of sweet or foul odor, my mind does not feel compelled to bring in as necessary accompaniments . . .
>
> Hence I think that tastes, odors, colors, and so on are no more than mere names so far

as the object in which we place them is concerned, and that they reside only in the consciousness. Hence if the living creature were removed, all these qualities would be wiped away and annihilated. [*The Assayer,* in *The Philosophy of the* 16*th and* 17*th Centuries,* R. H. Popkin, ed. (New York: The Free Press), 1966, p. 65]

One can hardly say it more clearly: colors exist only in minds, and if there were no minds, colors would not exist. Before there were minds, ferns were not green, sunsets were not red, and the sky was not blue! What an invitation to apply *modus tollens!* If it were true that colors exist only in minds, then the sky wouldn't be blue without minds. But the sky would obviously be blue, even if there were no minds. Therefore, it cannot be true that colors exist only in minds. I am perfectly willing to rest my case against the distinction between primary and secondary qualities on this argument. But, as usual, the philosophical situation is more complicated; though, I think, not more sophisticated, and we must return to Descartes to fill in the rest of the story.

Extension, according to Descartes, is a modification of material substance and, as such, is known by ideas. This means among other things, I take it, that the shapes of things are known by way of ideas. Shapes are therefore represented by ideas which do not resemble them. Color, on the other hand, is not a property of material substances. It does not exist in the external world at all; it is merely a sensation in minds. Sensations, in distinction to ideas, though they are *caused* by material substances, do not *represent* such substances (or their properties). The color olive green, a certain determinate shade of green, is merely a sensation in the mind. Thus the mind contains both ideas and sensations, and both ideas and sensations are caused by material substances. But ideas, unlike sensations, are not merely caused, they also represent.

I think that this is an accurate description of Descartes's view. But we must realize that his view is less clear than this brief description may make it appear. For example, both sensations and ideas are said to be in minds. But *how* are they in minds? What kind of relation do they have to minds? As far as ideas are concerned, an answer is close at hand: Ideas are *modifications* of mental substances. They are "in" mental substances in precisely the same way in which shape is "in" a material substance. The relation between a mind and its ideas is the relation between a substance and its accidental modifications. But what about sensations? If olive green were a modification of the mind, then the mind would have to be olive green! But surely minds are not colored. Nor, of course, are they hot or smelly. Notice that this problem does not arise for shape. Shape is not a property of the mind. It exists in the mind only as an idea. Notice also that a similar problem already arises in the Tradition. The form or essence of the apple Oscar, as we saw, is supposed to be present in the mind of the person who perceives Oscar. But it is clear that it cannot be "in" the mind in the same way in which it is "in" Oscar. By being in Oscar, it makes Oscar what Oscar is, namely, an apple rather than, say, a snake. But by being in the mind of the perceiver, it does not make the perceiver into an apple. Returning to Descartes, we must assume that while ideas are modifications of minds, sensations are in some other, not further specified, way in the mind. But this implies that we cannot give a univocal explication of what it means for a mind to know what is in it. If to know an idea is to be modified by it, then sensations must be known in some other fashion. Or else they cannot be known at all.

Another difficulty appears in connection with Descartes's famous wax example in the second Meditation. According to our interpretation of Descartes, a certain idea, I_1, represents a certain shape, say, squareness. Now, in connection with the wax example, Descartes claims that we recognize that the piece of wax before us is the same as the one we saw earlier, even though all of its sensible properties have changed, *including its shape* and color. Here he seems to be treating shape and color alike as sensations in the mind, known, as he says, "by means of the senses." But what is then known, not by means of the senses, but by way of ideas (by the understanding)? If we reject everything that does not belong to the piece of wax, Descartes asserts, then nothing is left "but something extended, flexible, and movable." What is this notion of *something extended?* Is this the notion of something square, or of something rectangular, or of something round? Obviously not, Descartes answers, for he would not conceive clearly and truthfully what wax was, if he did not think that this bit of wax were capable of receiving more variations in extension than he had ever imagined. Thus, when Descartes conceives of the wax as something extended, he does not conceive of it as having this or that particular shape.

The wax example seems to show that Descartes treats particular shapes exactly like particular colors, namely, as sensations. But he also says that we know the piece of wax as something extended, not by means of the senses, but through the understanding. How can we reconcile these two views? Well, it could be that particular shapes are sensations, but that the *property of having shape* is not a sensation but is known by means of an idea. According to this possibility, what the wax really and truly has is not this or that particular shape, but the property of having shape. The distinction between primary and secondary qualities is then, not, as we have assumed, the distinction between squareness and olive green, but the distinction between having shape, on the one hand, and being square or olive green, on the other. However, this interpretation runs immediately into difficulties. If the distinction between primary and secondary qualities is the distinction between having shape and squareness, then it must also be the distinction between having color and olive green. And then being colored would be just as much in the material substance as extension, that is, as the property of being shaped. And the same would hold for all other sensible properties. Galileo's distinction would be destroyed. Nor does this interpretation make much sense on other grounds. What sense could it possibly make to assert that a material substance has the property of having shape, but does not have any particular shape, that it is colored, but does not have any particular color?

One thing is certain: Descartes's wax example throws our neat distinction between shapes as primary qualities and colors as secondary qualities into a cocked hat. Perhaps the facts are rebelling against theory, as so often happens in philosophy. This is a most pleasing thought. For is it not preposterous to believe that the wax really has a shape but has no color? Does not the wax change its shape just as much as its color when it is held to the fire? No, the reason for Descartes's distinction between primary and secondary qualities cannot be found in enlightened common sense. We know of course where it comes from. Physics tells us that the "atoms" of which the wax consists have shape but have no color. Scientifically-minded philosophers conclude, therefore, that "out there," in the nonmental world, color is not to be found. And since it is not "out there," where else could it be but "in" the mind?

TWO

Berkeley's Idealism

The Price for Avoiding Skepticism

a) The Main Argument

Berkeley shows ingeniously how to avoid the skepticism within the heart of Cartesianism. But he fails miserably because he accomplishes this miracle only by succumbing to the idealism that lies at its soul. His strategy is very simple. Firstly, he denies the existence of Cartesian ideas, that is, of *representational* mental things. This is the point of the *Introduction* of the *Treatise*. His attack on Cartesian ideas appears there in the form of an attack on abstract (general) ideas. Secondly, he renames Cartesian sensations (and images) "ideas." And, thirdly, he identifies perceptual objects with bundles (collections) of Berkeleyan ideas, that is, with bundles of Cartesian sensations. The problem of how the mind can know external objects disappears! In accordance with the principle of immanence, the mind knows its own (bundles of) sensations; and since these sensations are the perceptual objects of the external world, the mind automatically knows the external world. We might say that Berkeley, like the Tradition, rejects representationalism. According to the Tradition, what is in the mind, the essence of the thing known, does not *represent* anything, but *is* the very thing known or, rather, *is* its essence. It is true that what is in the mind is not identical with the substance without the mind, but only with its essence or form. But everything knowable about the external substance is truly in the mind. Berkeley, of course, has no material substances. Oscar, the apple, is for him merely a bundle of properties. Thus there is no distinction between matter and essence (form). All of Oscar, not just his essence, can therefore be in the mind. But what is in this sense "in" the mind, is mental. Oscar is therefore a mental thing. This is Berkeley's idealism.

A while ago, I said that either shape and color are both properties of the wax, or else neither is, and they are both mere sensations in the mind. Of course, I believe that the wax has a color and a shape. Berkeley, on the other hand, accepts the second alternative. He acknowledges joyfully what the Cartesian tries to hide, namely, that idealism is inevitable, once colors are relegated to the status of secondary qualities. Berkeley's argument is as simple as it is powerful:

(1) A material object is nothing but a bundle of sensible properties.

(2) Sensible properties are nothing but ideas (read: sensations).
Therefore:

(3) A material object is nothing but a bundle of ideas.

It is the power of this argument that made it all but impossible for modern philosophers to mount a defense of realism. There even exists what may be called a philosophical "superstition" to the effect that Berkeley is irrefutable. I call this a superstition because it seems to me to be as obvious as anything can ever be in philosophy that Berkeley's argument is proven to be unsound by the fact that the conclusion is false. But we cannot be content with merely pointing out that apples do not exist in minds. We must show precisely where and how Berkeley's argument goes wrong.

Two simple steps lead from Descartes's professed realism to Berkeley's defiant idealism. In the first place, Berkeley attacks the notion of material substance, using ammunition provided by Descartes himself as well as by Locke and others. And, in the second place, he argues that whatever speaks for the contention that colors are mere sensations in minds, also shows that shapes are such sensations. In short, he argues that all sensible properties are mere sensations.

b) The Attack on Material Substance

I mentioned earlier that the Tradition has a problem about how individual things as individuals are known (perceived). What is in the mind, we saw, is the form or essence of Oscar. But this essence is the same for all apples. What distinguishes Oscar from other apples, therefore, must be his matter. But this matter cannot be known, for it does not enter into the mind of the knower. Hence, Oscar, this *particular* apple, cannot be known. Platonists, by contrast, have precisely the opposite problem: They have a difficult time explaining how the mind knows, not the particular, but the universal, the form. According to this tradition, what comes through the senses is the particular, what belongs to the world of becoming. What is sensible, to say it concisely, is what is in space and/or time. How then do we know the forms, denizens of the world of being? The Platonist usually invents a special mental faculty in answer to this question. The mind has two eyes, he claims, the eye of the senses and the eye of understanding (contemplation). Thus while the Aristotelian has to explain how we know particulars, the Platonist has to explain how we know universals. But let us return to Berkeley or, rather, to Descartes.

Descartes's solution to the Aristotelian problem, we can now see, is "Platonistic" in kind: he simply postulates a special faculty of the mind, the understanding, which is supposed to acquaint us directly with material substances. Sensible properties, he holds, are known through the senses; the material substances in which they inhere, on the other hand, are known by the understanding. But this solution will not do. Descartes is mistaken: there is no such faculty as what he calls "understanding." If there were, then we should be able to recognize the piece of wax as the same, even if we have not continuously observed it. But we are not. Assume that I show you a white billiard ball, a while later show you another white billiard ball, and then ask you whether the one I am now showing you is the same as the one I showed you earlier. Obviously, you can only guess. But if Descartes were right, and if there existed a special faculty which "grasps" the material substance directly, as it were, then you would be able to tell whether or not the one billiard ball is the other, irrespective of how similar they may look. It is simply a fact that we can only recognize perceptual objects as the same by means of their properties and relations to other things.

But one may also draw quite a different conclusion from Descartes's wax example. One may argue that it shows that there can be no such thing as a material substance. If there were such a thing, one could reason, then one would have to be able to recognize it directly, as Descartes claims we can. But we have just seen that we do not, as a matter of brute fact, recognize perceptual objects directly, but only through their properties and relations. Hence there are no material substances. In this manner, the wax example contains a powerful argument against the existence of material substances. Berkeley, however, attacks the notion of substance from a different direction. He follows in the footsteps of Locke. He simply asserts that we are never acquainted with material substances; that we perceive nothing but sensible properties (see, for example, the beginning of the first dialogue of G. Berkeley's *Three Dialogues between Hylas and Philonous*). Nor is he the only philosopher who holds this strange view. Locke, we remember, speaks of material substances as things we do not know. Reid claims that it is a *metaphysical principle* that "the qualities which we perceive by our senses must have a subject, which we call a body, . . ." (Reid, *Essays on the Intellectual Powers of Man*, p. 650). And Hume asserts that there is no impression of a material substance; and since there is no impression of it, there can be no idea of it either. It seems to be a dogma of the empiricists that the mind does not perceive individuals but only properties. And yet what could be plainer than that we see apples as well as their colors, that we perceive individual things as well as their properties and relations? Both the Tradition and empiricism fail because they deny this fact.

In regard to the question of whether or not material substances (particular things) are knowable, we must make several distinctions. It must be admitted that individual things cannot be *directly recognized*, but only through their properties and relations. We can recognize a white billiard ball as the same as one we have seen earlier because it has a small red spot on one side. Or we can be sure that it is the same because we have observed, uninterruptedly, its spatio-temporal path. But we cannot directly recognize it to be the same. In this sense of 'knowing', individual things cannot be known. But this is not the important sense of the word. There are two such important senses. According to one, to know an individual thing is to know things about it. It is to know what properties it has and in what relations it stands to other things. We know an apple, in this sense, when we know what shape and color it has, how much it weighs, what kind of apple it is, where it comes from, who sold it to us, etc., etc. It seems quite obvious to me that we know individual things in this fashion, for we can know all of the things I just mentioned about Oscar.

It has been said that to know things about an individual means to know things about it when it is considered in isolation, stripped of its properties and relations, as a mere, naked, particular thing. And since we cannot know what an individual is when we consider it bare of all of its properties and relations, one has argued, we cannot know individual things. But is it not silly to ask what properties an individual has when considered devoid of all properties? If we adopt this notion of what it means to be known, then it follows that nothing whatsoever can be known. Properties, for that matter, can then not be known either; for what is a property when considered devoid of all properties and relations? No, we know individual things just as well as we know other kinds of things, for we know their properties and relations. We even know some of their *categorial* properties which distinguish them from all other kinds of existents. An individual thing, for example, stands in temporal relations to other individual things; no other category is temporal in this sense. This is one of the fundamental theses of my ontology.

In another important meaning of the word, we know an individual thing when we are acquainted with it. In this sense, I know the Eiffel Tower, but do not know the Kremlin; I know the color shade olive green, but a blind person does not. I believe that it is in this sense of acquaintance that Berkeley denies knowledge of anything other than sensible properties. At the beginning of the first dialogue of the *Three Dialogues,* Hylas concedes without the slightest protest what is quite obviously untrue, namely:

> that sensible things are those only which are immediately perceived by sense. You will further inform me whether we immediately perceive by sight anything besides light and colors and figures; or by hearing, anything but sounds; by the palate, anything besides tastes; by the smell, anything besides odors; or by touch, more than tangible qualities.
>
> (Berkeley, 1965)

We would want to protest that we immediately perceive by sight such things as apples, and that apples, though they *have* colors, *are* not colors, and though they *have* shapes, *are* not shapes. We want to object that we can smell roses, taste lobsters, and touch lips, and that none of these things is a property.

It is easy to turn the table on Berkeley. Since you do not deny that there are apples, we may ask, how do you think we are acquainted with them, if not by sight, touch, etc.? He may reply that we are acquainted with them because they are nothing but bundles of sensible properties, and we are, admittedly, acquainted with such properties. But this answer will not do. What is a *bundle* of sensible properties? There are only two plausible answers: a bundle is either itself a sensible property or something other than a sensible property. But it cannot be the former for ontological reasons; a property must be a property of something, and an apple is not "of something." (Berkeley, I take it, does not believe that everything is a property of the absolute!) And it cannot be something other than a sensible property, for then we could not be acquainted with bundles of sensible properties, according to Berkeley's own view. To put it bluntly, Berkeley contradicts himself when he holds both that nothing comes through the senses but sensible properties and also that we are acquainted in perception with such individual things as apples.

Nothing, but nothing, can shake our conviction that we perceive individual things as well as their properties and relations. Nor can we doubt even for a moment that we know what kinds of properties and relations individual things have. On this matter, as at many other crucial junctures of our inquiry, common sense rules supreme. The Aristotelians and the modern empiricists are both wrong. But the Platonists do not do much better, as we shall see later. They go wrong by postulating a mysterious faculty, whether it be called "contemplation" or "eidetic intuition," which is said to acquaint us with universals. Here, too, we take our stand with common sense. We see not only individual apples, denizens of the world of becoming, but also their properties and relations, citizens of the realm of being. Perception, "the senses," acquaints us with individuals as well as their properties and relations. How can perception accomplish this miraculous feat? By being propositional! Both Aristotelianism and Platonism in regard to perception can be overcome if we hold fast to the fundamental insight that what we perceive are such states of affairs as that this apple, Oscar, is green. In perceiving that Oscar is green, we perceive both the individual apple and its universal color. This is the most important thesis of our theory of knowledge: Perception is propositional.

c) The Identification of Sensible Properties with "Ideas"

I believe that the first premise of Berkeley's main argument is false. But the argument would still be devastating if the second premise alone, that a material object is nothing but a bundle of sensations, were true. It is this second thesis, to the effect that sensible properties are nothing but sensations in minds, that opens the door to idealism. A mind-independent individual thing whose properties are not the sensible properties we know, is no more an apple than Kant's *Ding an sich* is. A realism worth defending cannot be the pitiful view that there are nonmental things "we know not what." What motivates this kind of last-ditch realism, one suspects, is nothing more than a fit of defiance. The idealist has already won the argument, but one last gesture is left: prove to me, one challenges, that there really is nothing at all out there. But realism does not consist in this futile gesture. Realism holds that there are dogs and apples, clouds and mountains, elements and electrons; that these things have an existence distinct from being perceived; and that we know by means of perception and inference from perception what some of their properties and relations are.

Sensible properties, contrary to what Berkeley claims, are properties of perceptual objects; they are not sensations in minds. The apple before me is green; and it would still be green if nobody looked at it or had ever looked at it. If there were no minds, sunsets would be red, clouds would be white, and the sky would be blue. What is "out there" is not just "extension," but color as well. Berkeley, of course, accepts the Cartesian belief that color is a mere sensation. But he also insists that the so-called primary qualities are not any different from color, as far as their mental status is concerned. He argues that whatever speaks for the mental nature of color speaks for the mental nature of primary qualities as well. In order to defend realism, we must resist the very first step of the dialectic. Berkeley has got it right: What holds for color, holds for shape as well. But he is wrong about color: It is not a mere sensation in a mind. What we must refute is what I shall call "the argument from physics."

Berkeley also alludes to another argument (see, for example, par. 14 and 15 of his *Treatise Concerning the Principles of Human Knowledge*). I shall call it "the argument from the relativity of sensing." Let me remind you of Locke's version of it, involving three buckets of water, each one having a different temperature. However, Berkeley very astutely remarks that this argument does not prove that warmth is only a sensation in a mind, but rather that we cannot know the true degree of warmth of the water or the true color of apples. The argument from the relativity of sensing is really an argument, not for idealism, but for skepticism. It is a version of the skeptical argument which I outlined earlier. In this particular form, the question is not how we know that certain objects correspond to certain ideas, but how we know that certain properties correspond to certain sensations. This version naturally arises from the original argument when one identifies, in the Berkeleyan vein, ideas with sensations. Properly analyzed, as I said, the argument is not an argument for idealism, but rather an argument for skepticism.

Berkeley avoids skepticism in regard to perceptual objects by paying the price of idealism. But skepticism is a hydra with many heads. Having cut off one of these heads, Berkeley is immediately confronted with another. According to Berkeley, there are other minds, and the question immediately arises of how these minds are known. It is evident that other minds are not *in* our minds as apples presumably are. The principle of immanence once again steps forward and announces the imminent arrival of skepticism! Berkeley can only close his eyes and refuse to acknowledge defeat. Other minds, he says, are known not by way of ideas (sensations), but by way of *notions*. These notions in our minds are not identical with the things (minds) of which they are notions. Rather, they *represent* those things. But this kind of representationalism, as we have seen, must fall before the skeptical argument. We can now appreciate the full extent of Berkeley's failure: skepticism, even at the price of idealism, has merely been postponed. In order to escape from it for a second time, Berkeley would have to pay the ultimate price: he would have to embrace solipsism.

I mentioned earlier, in connection with Descartes's classification of color as a sensation, that there is a problem of precisely how sensations are *in* minds. If a sensation is an accidental modification of a mind, and if olive green is a sensation, then it follows that the mind of someone with an olive green sensation must be olive green. But how could a Cartesian mind, this extensionless substance, possibly be colored? On the other hand, if sensations are not accidental modifications of minds, in what specific relation do they stand to minds? This problem becomes particularly urgent in Berkeley's philosophy, for according to this philosophy, not just colors but whole apples are supposed to be *in* minds. Berkeley clearly sees that there exists a problem. Sensations (his ideas) cannot be properties of minds. However, he does not solve the problem. He merely declares (in par. 49) that color, extension, etc., are in the mind "not by way of *mode* or *attribute,* but only by way of *idea*." Of course, this does not answer the question of how an idea is *in* the mind.

But, as I just said, not only colors but whole apples are supposed to be in Berkeleyan minds. And this complication raises a host of further questions. The apple in Berkeley's mind is said to be a *bundle* of ideas (sensations). What, precisely, is a bundle? To what category do bundles (collections) belong? If we had a plausible answer to this question, we could perhaps figure out how such bundles are supposed to be *in* minds. There is one plausible answer, as I pointed out earlier: A bundle is a complex property, consisting of the properties which Berkeley identifies with sensations. But if the bundle that is Oscar is a complex property, what could it possibly be a property of, except the mind in which it exists? It will not do to say that it is not a property of anything, for a property which is not a property of anything is an ontological absurdity. But if a bundle is not a (complex) property, what else could it be? It cannot be a substance, for, according to Berkeley, there are no material substances, and it is not a mind. The bundle that is Oscar is thus neither a substance nor a modification of a substance. It must therefore belong to a category unknown to the Aristotelian (and Cartesian) tradition. And herein lies the importance of Berkeley's philosophy: Unlike Descartes's, it does not merely try to improve on the Tradition within the Traditional ontology, but completely breaks with that ontology. After Berkeley, the ontology of substance and modification of substance is supplanted by an ontology of whole and part. (For a contemporary version of the latter, see *Parts and Moments: Studies in Logic and Formal Ontology,* B. Smith, ed.)

d) Sensations Distinguished from Sensible Properties

The question of how sensations are *in* minds depends on a prior question: To what category do sensations belong? Cartesians, as well as many other philosophers, seem to have taken for granted that sensations are properties. A certain shade of color, olive green, is said to be a sensation. But this color is obviously a property of things. Therefore, the sensation must be a property. And, indeed, what else but a property could a sensation be, given the framework of a substance-modification ontology? It could hardly be a mental or a material substance. Nor does Berkeley's bundle ontology open up new possibilities. But sensations are not properties. To believe that they are is one of the most fatal mistakes of modern philosophy; a mistake that has pervaded most theories of knowledge from Descartes to G. E. Moore. We cannot possibly hope to escape from the twin scourges of skepticism and idealism until we have exposed this mistake. And now, at the beginning of our inquiries, is as good a time as any to distinguish sharply between sensible properties on the one hand and sensations on the other.

If the visual sensation (sense impression) which we under normal circumstances experience when we look at a green apple were identical with the color of the apple, then the sensation would have to be a property. The so-called sensation green would be (a) a property, insofar as the color of the apple is a property, and it would also be (b) something mental, insofar as a sensation is supposed to be something mental. It would follow, please note, that the apple has a mental thing as a property. This conclusion should suffice, in my opinion, to discredit the identification of the color with the sensation. But be that as it may, I hold that the sensation is not a property at all, neither of the apple nor of anything else, but is an individual thing. This sensation, like all sensations, has a certain temporal location. It is also spatial, unlike some but not all other sensations. But in my ontology, these are characteristics of individual things: What is in time and/or space is an individual thing. When I look at the apple, I experience, among other things, a certain individual sensation. The apple causes me to have this visual sensation. How does the color green (a certain shade of green) enter into the picture? Under normal circumstances, when I look at a green apple, my visual sensation is also green. What I experience is quite literally a green sensation. The sensation *has* this color in the same sense in which the apple *has* it. By the way, the sensation is also round, just like the apple. Some sensations have shapes, just like apples. Under normal circumstances, therefore, when we look at a green apple, both the apple and the sensation are green. Under these circumstances, the apple and the sensation literally *share* a common property. By a "green sensation" or a "sensation of green" we may therefore mean two quite different things. We may mean, firstly, a sensation which is *caused* by a green object. Or we may mean, secondly, a sensation which *is* green. That these are not the same thing can be seen from the fact that a sensation caused by something green need not be green. If you wear tinted glasses, a green apple may cause you to have a grey sensation. Nor is it impossible for something which is not green to cause you to experience a green sensation. If you wear green glasses, a white wall causes you to experience a green sensation.

One way of summing up my view is to say that there is no such thing as a "sensation green." There is such a thing as a green sensation (that is, a sensation which is green) and there is also such a thing as a sensation of green (that is, a sensation caused by something green). If we make these important distinctions, namely, the distinction between a sensation and its properties and also the distinction between the properties of the sensation and the properties of the object which causes the sensation, many of the traditional confusions can be avoided.

Under normal conditions, when you see a green apple, in what sense is the color green *in* the mind? This color shade is literally *in* the mind because it is a property of something mental, namely, of a sensation. But this sensation is *in* the mind in quite a different way, namely, by being experienced by a mind. Thus a color is *in* the mind in the sense that it is the property of something, a sensation, which is experienced by a mind. We shall have to explain this matter in greater detail later, but it should already be clear what our answer is to the question of whether or not colors are mental. This question, we can now see, misses the mark. In our ontology, it makes little sense. The apple is nonmental; it is a perceptual object. The sensation, on the other hand, is a mental individual. Some individuals are mental, others are not. But colors are not individual things; they are properties of individual things. As such, they are neither mental nor nonmental. Or, if you prefer, they are both mental and nonmental. It does not matter what we say as long as we keep in mind that they are not individual things, and that they can be properties of both mental and nonmental things. What holds for color, holds for other sensible properties as well. Roundness, for example, is a property of both the apple which you see and the visual sensation which you experience. Does this mean that the mind is green and round when you see something green and round under normal conditions? It all depends on what you mean by "the mind." Since the mind is not identical with any one of its sensations, it does not follow from the fact that any one of its sensations can be green, that it can be green.

The color of Oscar is not identical with the visual sensation which we experience when we look at Oscar. The color and the sensation do not even belong to the same category: the first is a property, the second is an individual thing. Yet, philosophers, as I have already said, are prone to identify the two. Reid, for example, tells us that when smelling a rose, the agreeable odor which he experiences is a sensation. But he is not only experiencing this sensation; he is also perceiving an external object:

> . . . and the object of my perception in this case, is that quality in the rose which I discern by the sense of smell. Observing that the agreeable sensation is raised when the rose is near, and ceases when it is removed, I am led, by my nature, to conclude some quality to be in the rose, which is the cause of this sensation.

> (Reid, p. 243)

Reid is a hair's breadth away from idealism. In order to cling to a realism of sorts, he "postulates" a property of the rose which somehow corresponds to (causes) the experienced sensation. This property is not the "agreeable odor" which he experiences. The rose does not have this odor. It has some mysterious property, a property which is only known (by description!) as the property which causes a certain sensation. Skepticism waits around the corner. The familiar pattern emerges: Idealism avoided means skepticism embraced. We escape from the horns of this dilemma because we do not identify the smell of the rose with a sensation in the mind. According to our view, when smelling the odor of the rose, we experience a sensation which has a certain odor, namely, the odor of the rose. We smell the odor of the rose and we experience a sensation with the same odor. No mysterious property hides behind the familiar odor.

Even near-contemporary philosophers make the mistake of identifying sensations with their properties. G. E. Moore, for example, makes this mistake in his *Some Main Problems of Philosophy* (pp. 48, 52, 54, and 67). It is clear that his infamous question of whether or not sensations (sense-data) are parts of the surfaces of perceptual objects must appear in a different light as soon as we distinguish between a sensation and its properties. When I look at Oscar, is the green sensation which I experience part of his surface? Obviously not, for this sensation no longer exists when I turn my head. When I turn away, it is the sensation which disappears, not a part of the surface of the apple. Is it then the color green which is part of the surface of Oscar? Obviously not, for the color is not a spatial part of the surface of the apple. Rather, it is a property of that surface. The color of the sensation is the same as the color of (the surface of) the apple.

Or consider what Russell says in connection with the argument from the relativity of sensing. Commenting on Berkeley's conclusion from this argument, Russell states:

> Our previous arguments concerning the color did not prove it to be mental; they only proved that its existence depends upon the relation of our sense organs to the physical object—in our case, the table. That is to say, they proved that a certain color will exist, in a certain light, if a normal eye is placed at a certain point relatively to the table.

> (B. Russell, *The Problems of Philosophy,* p. 41)

But colors, according to Russell, are universals and hence exist timelessly (Russell, p. 100). Thus the existence of a color could not possibly depend on normal light and a certain eye's position. What does so depend on the light, the position of the eye, and on many other things as well, is the existence of the corresponding sensation. More precisely, it is the existence of a sensation with certain properties. Under different circumstances, a different sensation with different properties would exist. Russell has carelessly identified an individual sensation with its properties.

Let us return to the main line of our inquiry. The Cartesian philosophy, I have claimed, contains the seeds both of idealism and of skepticism. The seed of idealism is the distinction between primary and secondary qualities; the seed of skepticism is the principle of immanence. We have seen how Berkeley manages to avoid skepticism by embracing idealism. But surely "houses, mountains, rivers, and, in a word, all sensible objects" do exist outside of minds. Is there no other way to avoid skepticism? And, leaving skepticism aside, what is the proper way to guard against idealism? Perhaps a look at Reid, brilliant critic of Berkeley and Hume, will show us the way.

THREE

Reid's Revolt

The Elusiveness of Realism

a) A Correct Analysis of the Cartesian Quandary

To study Reid after having read Descartes, Locke, Berkeley, and Hume, is to step out of Plato's cave into a bright spring morning. On page after page, Reid illuminates the origins of the Cartesian predicament and castigates the follies of its idealistic consequences. He clearly sees that it is the principle of immanence that pushes the Cartesian into skepticism. And he never tires of ridiculing the idealistic claim that we perceive nothing but our own ideas (sensations, impressions). What we perceive are the ordinary objects around us: trees and flowers, houses and mountains, people and animals, clouds and rainbows. No philosophical argument, no matter how sophisticated or how convincing it may appear at first, can possibly be sound, if it denies this truism. This is the spirit of Reid's philosophy. It is, in the words which he uses to describe the Cartesians, "a more important acquisition to mankind than any of its particular tenets" (T. Reid, *Essays on the Intellectual Powers of Man*, p. 150), and for exercising this spirit so zealously, Reid deserves our grateful attention.

But what Reid observes about Descartes, namely, that he rejected only a part of the ancient theory concerning the perception of external objects, holds just as well for Reid himself. While Reid rejects the principle of immanence, he does not escape from the argument based on the relativity of sensing. Even more devastating, in my eyes, is his acceptance of the distinction between primary and secondary qualities: It forces him to the very edge of idealism. Reid fully realizes the shortcomings of the Cartesian system. And he also resists the temptations of idealism. But he does not find his way out of the maze created by Descartes. He cannot find his way out because he accepts both the argument from physics and the argument from the relativity of sensing. It is a measure of the strength of these two arguments that not even Reid dared to reject them. Small wonder, therefore, that so many recent and contemporary philosophers surrender to them.

Descartes, according to Reid, shed only part of the Aristotelian theory. This theory, he explains, "may be divided into two parts: the *first,* that images, species, or forms of external objects, come from the object, and enter by avenue of the senses to the mind; the *second* part is, that the external object itself is not perceived, but only the species or image of it in the mind" (Reid, p. 150). Descartes rejects the first part but accepts the second. But Reid not only sees that it is the principle of immanence that gives Descartes trouble, but he also uncovers the reasons for accepting it. There are, he says, two such reasons or, as he puts it, "prejudices" (Reid, 406). The first is the conviction that the mind can only act on what is part of it; there can be no interaction between what is outside and what is inside the mind. The second is the belief that if a mind has an object, this object must exist; the mind cannot *be about* things which are not.

I must confess that I am not sure what to make of the first of these two prejudices. Reid quotes a Dr. Porterfield in this connection: "How body acts upon mind, or mind upon body, I know not; but this I am very certain of, that nothing can act, or be acted upon, *where it is not;* and therefore, our mind can never perceive any thing but its own proper modifications, . . ." (Reid, p. 217; my italics). What are we to make of this "where it is not"? When I perceive a tree in the distance, I am not where the tree is. Neither my body nor my mind is in the proximity of the tree. It does not even make sense to think of my mind as being near to the tree or far from it. My mental act of seeing the tree in the distance, though it causally depends on my brain which is spatially located, is not at any particular place. It is neither where the tree is, nor is it at a certain distance from the tree. Is the objection that interaction presupposes spatial contiguity? But how, if this is the point, can the mind be said to perceive its own ideas, since neither the idea nor its perception is spatially located? And how can any interaction between body and mind then be possible?

I understand much better the second reason for the principle of immanence. This reason also buttresses the so-called argument from hallucination. The mind, one maintains, can only be related to things which exist. If you see a pink elephant in one of your hallucinations, a pink elephant cannot really be the object of your act of seeing, for there exists no such thing in this situation. Something else must truly be before your mind, something which does exist. One view has it that this something is a sense-datum (a bundle of sensations). Thus, what we perceive in hallucinations are not perceptual objects but sensations. But this conclusion proves that the argument cannot be sound. Whatever we may be said to perceive in hallucinations, it is certainly not our sensations. Shall we then give up the idea that the mind can only relate to existents? But how can we? How can there possibly exist a *relation* between something (the mind, the mental act) and nothing?

The Cartesians may have added a third reason for accepting the principle of immanence: The mind only knows what is in it because the mind can know *for certain* only what is in it. Knowledge, in the Cartesian spirit, is identified with certitude. Nothing less deserves to be called knowledge. And then one argues that one can have certain knowledge only of what is in the mind.

At any rate, whatever the reasons for accepting the principle of immanence may be, Reid clearly saw that the principle leads to idealism.

b) Tricks of the Idealistic Trade

A moment ago, I spoke of the *conclusion* that what we perceive are always our own ideas (sensations, sense-impressions). But this is usually presented as a self-evident *axiom* of the idealistic system. Berkeley, you may recall, starts out by claiming that it is evident to anyone who takes a survey of the *objects* of human knowledge that they are *ideas* of three different kinds. Or take the first sentence of Hume's *Treatise:* "All the perceptions of the human mind resolve themselves into two distinct heads, which I shall call impressions and ideas." How can philosophers get away with starting their inquiries with such an obvious falsehood? You mean to say, George Berkeley, that when we study molecular bonding, we study our ideas? You hold that when we study the causes of earthquakes, we study ideas? You maintain that when we study the feeding habits of orangutans, we study ideas? What is it that prevents the idealist from realizing the absurdity of his position? What is it that protects his view from the ridicule which it deserves? It is a way with words! Words serve as a smokescreen to hide the clash with common sense. Reid has no equal when it comes to blowing away this smokescreen. His criticisms of the terminological contortions of Locke, Berkeley, and Hume are masterpieces.

Speaking very generally, the idealist plays with the meaning of words like 'idea', 'sensation', 'object', etc. Locke, of course, is famous for using 'idea' for anything under the sun. He apologizes for his lack of precision, but this very apology perpetuates the idealistic sleight of hand:

> It [idea] being that term which, I think, serves best to stand for whatsoever is the *object* of the understanding, when a man thinks, I have used it to express whatever is meant by *phantasm, notion, species,* or *whatever it is which the mind can be employed about in thinking;* and I could not avoid frequently using it.
>
> I presume it will be easily granted me, that there are such *ideas* in men's minds: every one is conscious of them in himself; and men's words and actions will satisfy him that they are in others.

(J. Locke, *An Essay Concerning Human Understanding.* Introduction, p. 8)

We cannot but grant Locke "that there are such ideas in men's minds." But these ideas, we protest, are not the only objects of the understanding. Every idealist, I submit, has to perform this particular trick: he has to convince himself and us that it is really ideas which we perceive, think of, understand, or compare, when we perceive, think of, understand, or compare the things in the world around us. The price for failing the performance is an application of *modus tollens* to his theory.

Berkeley, too, is aware that he uses the word 'idea' in a very peculiar sense: "But, say you, it sounds very harsh to say we eat and drink ideas, and are clothed with ideas. I acknowledge it does so—the word *idea* not being used in common discourse to signify the several combinations of sensible qualities which are called things; . . ." (G. Berkeley, *A Treatise Concerning the Principles of Human Knowledge,* par. 38). But then he goes on to defend this unfortunate choice of terminology: ". . . but this does not concern the truth of the proposition which, in other words, is no more than to say we are fed and clothed with those things which we perceive immediately by our senses" (Berkeley, 1957, par. 38). Again, we cannot but grant Berkeley that we are fed and clothed with those "things which we perceive immediately by our senses," but those things are certainly not ideas.

We have just come across another trick of the idealist, a trick most masterfully employed by Berkeley and greatly perfected by contemporary phenomenalists and other "reductionists." Whenever we are outraged by the idealist's fast and loose way with words, he assures us that our indignation is unjustified. We are told that the idealist really does not wish to deny anything we believe; that he is completely on the side of common sense or, as Berkeley puts it, on the side of the vulgar. Berkeley is a master of this ploy. He is so successful that there are philosophers who believe that he is a common–sense realist! Please, have a look at the third dialogue of the *Three Dialogues between Hylas and Philonous*. Philonous there assures Hylas that his philosophical (idealistic) view comes down to this:

> If by material substance is meant only sensible body, that which is seen and felt, and the unphilosophical part of the world, I dare say, means no more, then I am more certain of matter's existence than you or any other philosopher pretend to be. If there be any thing which makes the generality of mankind averse from the notions I espouse, it is a misapprehension that I deny the reality of sensible things; . . .

(Berkeley, Three Dialogues between Hylas and Philonous)

Did Berkeley really believe that his view that an apple is nothing but a collection of ideas in a mind is in accordance with the universal sense of mankind? Or was he merely trying to convince himself and others not to apply *modus tollens* to his view? We must never underestimate the stubbornness of philosophers. In this respect, philosophers are not so different from the vulgar: Having finally, after much toil and trouble, arrived at their views, they are loath to give them up, no matter how silly they are. But in addition philosophers have a more perverse streak: They delight in shocking accepted opinion. Some philosophers, it seems, are only happy if they have arrived at absurd conclusions. Berkeley, at any rate, tried to conceal the clash between his conclusions and common sense.

Things go from bad to worse when we turn from Berkeley to Hume. Look at this famous pronouncement:

> We may divide all the perception of the human mind into two classes or species, which are distinguished by their different degrees of force and vivacity. The less lively and forcible are commonly dominated thoughts or ideas. The other species want a name in our language, and in most others; let us therefore use a little freedom, and call them *impressions*. By this term, *impression,* then, I mean all our more lively perceptions, when we hear, or see, or feel, or love, or hate, or desire, or will.

(Quoted from Reid, p. 11)

Reid, analyzing this quotation, points out the many confusions it contains. One of these deserves special attention. Hume's list of so-called impressions appears to be a list of mental acts: An act of hearing, an act of seeing, of feeling, of loving, of hating, etc. But it could also be a list of the objects of such acts: of what is seen, of what is heard, what is loved, what is hated, etc. Nowhere in Hume does this most important distinction between a mental act and its object receive the attention that it deserves. Reid complains: "And when I read all that he has *written* on that subject, I find this word *impression* sometimes used to signify an operation of the mind, sometimes the object of the operation; but for the most part, it is a vague and indetermined word that signifies both" (Reid, p. 11).

Contemporary phenomenalists continue this tradition of trickery. The terminology has changed. Ideas are supplanted by sense-impressions. But the claim is the same: Even though sense-impressions are mental things, it is not absurd, but perfectly compatible with common sense, to believe that ordinary perceptual objects *consist* of them. One pretends that these mental sensations may quite naturally be thought of as "parts of the surfaces of perceptual objects." But we must object: If by "sense-impression" we mean a mental sensation, something that would not exist if there were no minds, then it is the received opinion of all mankind that perceptual objects do not, in any sense, shape, or form, consist of sense-impressions. On the other hand, if we mean by this expression something that could conceivably be a part of a perceptual object, then a sense-impression could not possibly be mental. Sensations are sensations, perceptual objects are perceptual objects, and there is no reason at all to confuse the two.

c) Reid's First Mistake: The Nature of Sensations

It is one thing to recognize the absurdity of idealism, but quite another to dismantle the idealistic arguments. Reid was never taken in by the idealistic legerdemain. But he did not know, alas, how to break off the point of the idealistic spear. He reminds one of G. E. Moore, whose commitment to realism never wavered, but who never found a convincing answer to the idealistic arguments. The crucial test for Reid, as for any realist, is his treatment of the arguments from physics and from the relativity of sensing. He must fail because he accepts the argument from physics and, therefore, the fatal distinction between primary and secondary qualities. Let us look at this part of his philosophy first, and at the argument from the relativity of sensing in the next section.

Reid does not distinguish between a sensation and the act of experiencing the sensation. This is one of the very few parts of his analysis of the contents of the mind with which I disagree. It becomes important for our present concern because this mistake prevents him from realizing how futile it is to distinguish between primary and secondary qualities. Reid, of course, is not the only philosopher who refuses to make the act—object distinction for sensations. But this refusal has always been rather poorly motivated. When you see a tiger, everyone admits, there is the seeing and there is the object seen, the tiger. And the seeing is not the same as its object; the seeing is not the tiger. But when you feel a pain, some say, there exists no corresponding distinction between the feeling and the pain. Why not? It seems to me to be quite obvious that just as the seeing is not the tiger, so the feeling is not the pain. May I not also feel something else, something other than a pain? And if so, does it not follow that the mental act cannot be identical with a pain? Perhaps the word "feeling" is to be blamed, since we have to speak of feeling a feeling. But this can be avoided if we agree to speak of *experiencing* a pain, a desire, a memory. I hold, in accordance with this terminology, that there exists a certain kind of mental act, experiences, which has objects of different sorts. Of course, what I experience when I experience a pain or when I experience a desire is just as mental as the act of experiencing itself is. This marks an important difference between these examples and our earlier example of seeing a tiger. But I fail to see how this important difference makes a difference in regard to the act-object distinction. Why, then, do so many philosophers insist that there is no act-object distinction for sensations? Why, in particular, does Reid reject the distinction? Here is what he says:

> Sensation is a name given by philosophers to an act of mind, which may be distinguished from all others by this, that it hath no object distinct from the act itself. Pain of every kind is an uneasy sensation. When I am pained, I cannot say that the pain I feel is one thing, and that my feeling it is another thing. They are one and the same thing, and cannot be disjoined, even in imagination. Pain, when it is not felt, has no existence. It can be neither greater nor less in degree or duration, nor any thing else in kind, than it is felt to be. It cannot exist by itself, nor in any subject, but in a sentient being. No quality of an inanimate insentient being can have the least resemblance to it.
>
> (Reid, p. 27)

Notice that Reid says that sensations *are* acts, but acts without objects. This is a truly amazing remark. A mental act without an object, according to Brentano's celebrated thesis, is an ontological absurdity. But perhaps Reid means to say, not that the act of feeling (a pain!) has no object, but rather that it is its own object. But this assertion is no less absurd: how could a mental act have no other object than itself? We must keep in mind that this is not Brentano's view, according to which every act has two objects, a primary object (its ordinary object, so to speak) and, as its secondary object, itself. According to Reid's radical view, there is no primary object at all. But this is not all. Even more amazing than the claim that the feeling of a pain is an act without an object, is Reid's identification of the pain with the feeling of the pain. According to his view, therefore, it would be more nearly correct to say that there are no pains but only feelings of pain than to maintain that there are no feelings of pain but only pains. The act-object distinction disappears for pain, not because there is no act in this case, but because there is no object.

Let us turn to Reid's arguments. He says, firstly, that a pain has no existence when it is not felt. I agree with him completely: Just as a desire which is not experienced does not exist, so does a pain which is not felt (experienced) does not exist. In general, it holds for all mental things, with *one exception,* that to be experienced and to exist are equivalent. The exception is the act of experiencing itself: It exists, even when it is not itself experienced. Notice also that I said that to be experienced is *equivalent* to existence, not that it is the same thing. Berkeley's slogan thus is true for all mental things save one: To be is to be experienced. But it is most certainly false for perceptual objects and their perception: To be is not to be perceived. But how does the agreed upon equivalence show that there is no distinction between the act of experiencing, on the one hand, and what is experienced, on the other? Surely, from the fact that the pain exists if and only if its experience exists it does not follow that the pain *is* the experience or that the experience *is* the pain.

I shall also agree with Reid that a pain cannot be other than what it is felt to be. But here, too, I must add a caveat. I do not mean to endorse the common view that knowledge of sensations (and other mental things) is infallible, absolutely certain, indubitable. Rather, I agree with Reid, not because I think that we cannot be mistaken about pains (and other mental things), but because experience is the kind of act which is neither correct nor incorrect. This is a longer story, and we shall come back to it later. For the moment, let us set aside certain questions and reservations and simply agree that pains are what they are experienced to be. But again, I do not see how this fact proves Reid's contention that a pain is the same thing as its experience. Nor, finally, does this contention follow from the fact that a pain cannot exist by itself, or from the fact that it must exist in a mind.

Turn from pain to a "color sensation." If Reid is right, then the "sensation olive green" is a mental act! Now, if there is one thing that rubs common sense the wrong way, then it is certainly the notion that the color of the olive in my Martini is a mental act. But this does not prevent Reid from exploiting his identification of act and object by treating sensations sometimes as acts and sometimes as objects, that is, as sensible properties. And this brings us to Reid's second fundamental mistake, his acceptance of the distinction between primary and secondary qualities.

d) Reid's Second Mistake: Secondary Qualities

When I read chapter XVII of Reid's *Essays,* I am reminded of the uncomfortable truth that philosophical catastrophe lies in wait for even the most reasonable, most thoughtful, and most careful of philosophers. Extension, according to Reid, is a primary quality of bodies. Color, on the other hand, is a secondary quality. Let us compare the shape square with the color shade olive green. According to Reid, our senses give us a direct and distinct notion of the primary quality squareness, but of the secondary quality olive green, our senses give us only a relative and obscure notion. However, this is misleading, for it is not really olive green which is the secondary quality of which we are said to have a relative and obscure notion, but rather a property, not further specified, which causes us to have the sensation olive green. It would be more correct to describe Reid's view by saying that perceptual objects have two kinds of quality: certain primary qualities like shape, and certain secondary qualities which are known only as the causes of certain sensations. It is not really olive green, therefore, which is the secondary quality, but rather some unknown quality which causes the sensation olive green. We are dealing with *three* things: a primary quality (squareness), a secondary quality (the cause of the sensation olive green), and the sensation olive green. We shall see later on how this distinction plays havoc with Kant's philosophy.

I see no reason, other than the argument from physics, why shape should be favored in this manner over color. May it not just as well be asserted that there is a quality of the perceptual object, otherwise unknown, which causes the sensation square? Conversely, may one not with equal justification hold that the color is a primary quality, directly and distinctly known? Of course a shape is not a color, but I know both for what they are and equally directly. Reid tries desperately to convince us that color is not a property of the perceptual object. His example is the smell of a rose rather than its color. Our position is firm and clear, backed by the awesome power of common sense: the rose has a certain smell, this smell exists independently of any person or mind that notices the smell, and we know this smell "directly and distinctly." Against this, Reid remarks that he is at a loss to say what that quality is in the rose which we call its smell. How quaint! Surely, that quality is the smell of the rose. We happen to have few words for distinct smells, so that we describe a smell usually as the smell of a certain kind of thing. But this does not negate the fact that we *know* smells directly by acquaintance, and not just by description, as the smells of certain objects. A person without the sense of smell may know the smell of a rose only as a property which the rose has, but we are acquainted with that smell.

Reid continues by claiming that he has a distinct notion of the sensation which the unknown quality of the rose, its smell, produces in his mind. We cannot quarrel with this assertion as far as it goes. But then comes the punch line: There can be nothing like this sensation in the rose, he says, because the rose is insentient. Here is the heart of his argument. Here, his contention that sensations are mental acts pays off. For, if the sensation is a mental act, then it cannot exist in the rose, since the rose is not a mind. From our point of view, Reid has committed two mistakes. Firstly, he has mistakenly identified a property (the smell) with an individual thing (the sensation). Secondly, he has mistakenly identified this sensation with the act of experiencing it. By the same path, one can of course easily prove that color cannot be a property of the rose, cannot be "in" the rose: The color is a sensation in the mind; this sensation is a mental act; and since mental acts only exist in minds, not in roses, the color cannot exist in the rose. But the smell of the rose is not a sensation. It is a property of the rose and also a property of the sensation. It exists "in" the rose and "in" the sensation. But even if we follow the pernicious custom of thinking of the property as a sensation, it does not follow that this sensation (since it is the property) cannot exist in the rose. This is why Reid needs his peculiar assumption that sensations are mental acts.

This assumption also allows him to pretend that his view does not really clash with common sense. Reid is aware that the clash exists: "But there seems to be a contradiction between the vulgar and the philosopher upon this subject, and each charges the other with a gross absurdity. The vulgar say that fire is hot, and snow cold, and sugar sweet; and to deny this is a gross absurdity and contradicts the testimony of our senses" (Reid, p. 258). Is it not ironic that the champion of common sense is forced to take the side of the philosopher against the side of the vulgar on this matter? But Reid manages to convince himself, by practicing the familiar philosophical self-deception, that the contradiction is "more apparent than real." As usual, the self-deception requires a verbal bridge. Like some philosophers before him and many more after him, Reid claims at this point that when we say so-and-so, we do not really mean what we say, but mean such-and-such instead. When the philosopher says that there is no heat in the fire, he means, according to

Reid, that the fire has no *sensation of heat*, that is, that there does not occur a mental act of a certain sort in the fire. And since he means precisely this and nothing more by saying that heat is not in the fire, the vulgar will agree with him as soon as his meaning becomes clear to them. On the other hand, the philosopher agrees with the vulgar that heat is in the fire, if by "heat" is meant that unknown quality which causes the sensation in us. Thus the vulgar and the philosopher really agree, and the former do not contradict the latter.

What a piece of sophistry! We should expect this kind of assurance from Berkeley, not from Reid. It should be clear to everyone that Reid does not resolve the contradiction between the opinion of common sense and the theory of the philosopher. Of course, the fire does not contain a mental act of experiencing (sensing) heat. The philosopher has common sense on his side with this remark. But why does he insist on expressing this truism by saying that the fire is not hot (that "heat is not in the fire")? Surely this is not what we ordinarily mean by saying that fire is not hot. Obviously, what we do mean to assert by saying that fire is hot is that it has a certain quality of hotness; that it has this property; that it has this characteristic. In short, we ascribe a certain property to the fire, not a mental act. The issue is not whether or not fire *feels heat*, but whether or not it *is* hot. The philosopher, according to Reid, also agrees with us vulgar people that there is really a property hotness in the fire, that the fire really has this property. But it is clear that the property which the philosopher has then in mind is not the property which we have in mind. When we speak of heat, we mean heat, not some quality, we know not what, which causes us to have certain sensations. We mean a property with which we are acquainted. Again, there really is no agreement between the vulgar and the philosopher, contrary to Reid's claim. And this shows us, in the end, that the philosopher must be mistaken.

If squareness, unlike color, is a true property of bodies, we may ask, what is the corresponding sensation? According to Reid, there is such a sensation and it is a mental act. But what is this sensation? I cannot think of a plausible answer. Reid, however, assures me that I am hard pressed for an answer only because I pay no attention to this sensation: "When a primary quality is perceived, the sensation immediately leads our thought to the quality signified by it, and is itself forgotten. We have no occasion afterward to reflect upon it; and so we come to be as little acquainted with it, as if we had never felt it" (Reid, p. 257).

If Reid were correct, the color olive green would be comparable to the feeling of a toothache. One could also say that it is comparable to a toothache; for the feeling of a toothache and the toothache are, according to Reid, one and the same thing. At any rate, do we not say that we *feel* a toothache, but *see* the color of the rose? If color really were a sensation like a pain, would we not say that we *feel* the color of the rose? Reid invokes the familiar ploy according to which what is not there, is really there, but not attended to. When we feel a toothache, he says, we also perceive a disorder in the tooth. Thus we find sensation and perception conjoined both in the case of color and in the case of pain. There is this important difference between the two cases: "But, in the toothache, the sensation being very painful, engrosses the attention; and therefore we speak of it, as if it were felt only, and not perceived; whereas, in seeing a colored body, the sensation is indifferent, and draws no attention. The quality in the body, which we call its color, is the only object of attention; and therefore we speak of it, as if it were perceived, and not felt" (Reid, p. 268). According to Reid, in the case of pain, we pay attention to the pain, this sensation, but do not pay attention to something else that occurs simultaneously with it, namely, a *perception* of some disorder or other. Well, I do not think that any such *perception* occurs when I have a toothache. There is no seeing, hearing, smelling, etc. of any disorder in the tooth. But this is not the strangest part of Reid's view. As you just read, he goes on to say that when we perceive a colored body, we pay no attention to its color; the color, this sensation, we are told is indifferent. But surely, if there is one thing to which we pay attention when we see a colored body, it is its color. Of course, we must not be misled by Reid's phrase "the quality in the body, which we call its color." We saw earlier that this quality is *not* what *we* would call its color. If we called it anything, we would speak of "that property of the surface of the body which is responsible for our experience of a sensation of such-and-such a color" or of something similar.

We feel a pain in a certain tooth. But if the pain is the feeling of the pain, if it is a mental act, then it cannot possibly be in the tooth, and common sense must again be mistaken. Here, then, is another problem for Reid. This time, he grants that we say something that is neither obscure nor false when we say that the ache is in the tooth. But he claims that it is really the disorder which is in the tooth and that the pain is, properly speaking, nowhere. Common sense simply confuses the perceived cause of the pain with the pain itself. But, we are immediately reassured, common sense is nevertheless not mistaken, because it never makes the distinction and means by 'pain' both the sensation and its cause. Speaking once again on behalf of the vulgar, I categorically deny that we confuse the pain with its cause and that we thus mean both by "pain." Since we do not confuse the pain with the decay in the tooth, we do not mean to say that that particular tooth is decayed when we say that it hurts. Once again it is obvious that Reid's view cannot be reconciled with common sense, no matter how hard he tries.

Why is it, we may want to know at this point, that philosophers continuously tell us that we cannot mean what we say, but must mean something else? And why is it that they keep insisting that we must mean what they say we mean, rather than what we know we mean? Should we not be the best judges in these cases? And why do they constantly claim that we would cheerfully admit that their absurdities are our truisms, if only we would make the proper distinctions, when in reality we make precisely these distinctions? Let it be granted, once and for all, that we mean by 'olive green' a certain color shade and not an unknown quality; that we mean by 'toothache' a pain and not the decay in the tooth; and that we mean by 'feeling' a pain the feeling of a pain and not the pain itself.

So much for Reid's contention that color is a sensation, while shape is a property of bodies. The reason for this contention, we already know, does not come from philosophy proper. There is no phenomenological argument to the effect that color is in the mind while shape is in the world. No, the contention comes from misunderstood physics. Reid alludes to this background in connection with a remark about the atomists: "That the atoms, which they held to be the first principles of things, were extended, solid, figured, and moveable, there was no doubt; but the question was, whether they had smell, taste, and color . . ." (Reid, p. 259). So-called primary qualities are simply those properties, not to be discovered by philosophical reflection, but by physics, which the ultimate particles have; secondary qualities, then, are all of the rest of the properties which perceptual objects seem to have. "Out there," so the reasoning goes, only elementary particles and their properties exist. If there are any other properties at all, they must then be "in the mind." Hence they must be sensations. In this manner is born the absurd view that a color like olive green is some kind of mental phenomenon. Reid, we have just seen, holds that it is a mental act. Brentano, we shall see later, denies that it is a mental phenomenon, precisely because it is *not* a mental act. But he agrees with the received opinion of almost all philosophers that it is not a physical phenomenon either. Thus he comes to the conclusion that it does not exist at all!

Reid faces still another problem. Secondary qualities, precisely speaking, are properties in bodies which are known only as the causes of certain sensations. But this cannot really be true, according to Reid's theory. "It has been discovered," he says, "that the sensation of smell is occasioned by the effluvia of bodies; that of sound by their vibrations. The disposition of bodies to reflect a particular kind of light occasions the sensation of color" (Reid, p. 256). Thus it seems that we know these secondary qualities after all. We can say a number of positive things about them. We know them clearly and distinctly, just as we know the so-called primary qualities of figure, motion, number, etc.

e) Reid's Third Mistake: Acquired Perception

One of the great virtues of Reid's philosophy is that he admits the existence of mental acts of perception. And it is to his everlasting credit that he clearly sees that perception is not a matter of inference. Yet, when he analyzes the crucial argument from the relativity of sensing, he cannot shake off traditional philosophical wisdom and escape from error. He possesses the means to counter the argument, but does not, at the crucial moment, employ them effectively.

Perception, according to Reid, has three important ingredients (Reid, p. 111). Firstly, it involves a conception or notion of the perceived object. Secondly, it contains a strong and irresistible conviction and belief in the existence of the object. Thirdly, this belief in the existence of the object is immediate and not a matter of reasoning. In short, an act of perception, according to Reid, *is* an act of believing in the existence of a certain perceptual object, but this belief is not arrived at by inference. I hold that perception is propositional. One perceives, for example, *that* (the apple) Oscar is green. I am therefore willing to grant without further ado that perception involves a conception of the perceived object. It is the second feature of perception, pointed out by Reid, which is of concern to me.

I am not sure whether Reid holds that one cannot perceive what does not exist, or merely that one is always convinced that what one perceives exists. At one point, he says, "I acknowledge that a man cannot perceive an object that does not exist;

. . ." (Reid, p. 419). But at other places he merely states, "When I perceive any external object, my belief of the real existence of the object is irresistible" (Reid, p. 404). Of course, there is no conflict between these two views. Reid may have held both. But for my purposes it is necessary to distinguish between them. I think it is clearly false that all objects of perception exist; just as clearly as that all beliefs are true or that all desires are fulfilled. I take it to be a matter of common sense that one can *see* a pink elephant in one's hallucination, or that one can *hear* the devil whisper obscenities, while *smelling* his hellish odor. Under certain abnormal circumstances, there occur perceptual acts whose objects do not exist. These acts, and this is the crucial point, are perfectly good acts of perception: the seeing of the pink elephant is in precisely the same way a seeing as the seeing of a real elephant in a circus; it is not just a mere judging, or believing, or surmising. What is abnormal about such situations is precisely this, that a perfectly "normal" act of perception has a nonexistent object. This is in my opinion, as we shall see later, the proper response to the argument from hallucination. You can see how important it is for me to distance myself from Reid's view, if his view implies that all objects of perception exist.

What about the second view, the view that there is always an irresistible belief in the existence of the perceived object? It is true that one may believe in the existence of an object, even if that object does not exist. Why, otherwise, would a person follow the advice of the devil who speaks to him? But does one always believe in the existence of the perceived object? Can there be no perception with the simultaneous conviction that what one perceives does not exist? Is it not possible to know that one is hallucinating and, therefore, not to believe in the existence of the perceived objects? I think that it is. But we must be careful at this point. When we believe in the existence of the perceived object, or when we doubt its existence, the belief or doubt is *not* a constituent of the perceptual act. In my view, perception does not consist, even in part, of believing. Perception is not a form of believing. An act of perception, that is, an act of seeing, or of hearing, etc., is an indefinable, unanalyzable mental act, as different from an act of believing as it is from an act of desiring or an act of remembering. The adage "Seeing is believing" does not mean that seeing is the same thing as believing. Rather, it expresses the truth that one believes what one has seen with one's own eyes. Belief, we may perhaps say, follows in the wake of perception. It is based on perception. It accompanies perception. But it is not the same mental phenomenon as perception.

Reid's third characteristic of perception is the crucial one for our immediate purpose. Our conviction of the existence of the perceived object, Reid tells us, is immediate; it is not derived from a train of reasoning and argumentation (Reid, p. 116). We do not *infer* that the perceived apple exists, but *perceive* it. With this insight, Reid breaks the spell of the principle of immanence. Let me describe the situation in my own words. When you see that Oscar is green, you neither *infer* that there is an apple before you nor do you *infer* that it is green. In particular, we do not infer these things from our visual sensations. *Perception is not sensation plus inference.* As Reid clearly sees, it is precisely this assumption that perception somehow consists of sensation plus inference that the skeptic needs for his argument

(Reid, p. 666). Such an inference must be based on knowledge of a specific connection between certain sensations and certain perceptual objects. But this knowledge can be gained only if we can be acquainted with perceptual objects independently of sensations. Such acquaintance, however, is impossible according to the principle of immanence.

According to one accepted view, when you *see* that Oscar is green, you *experience* certain visual sensations, and you *infer* from these sensations that there is a green apple in front of you. By means of this inference, as it is sometimes put, you *acquire the belief* that there is a green apple in front of you. It is this acquired belief which is your perception. Or perhaps it is the acquisition of the belief (together with the acquired belief?), that is, the process of inference, which is the perception. In either case, you reason from the experienced sensations, according to certain principles, to the existence and nature of a perceptual object. The skeptic argues that you could not possibly have acquired the necessary principles of inference. Assuming the truth of the principle of immanence, as I have said before, he is right. Well, what is the correct analysis of the perceptual situation? One thing is certain: In perception, no inference takes place. There occur certain sensations and there occurs an act of perceiving. But no mental process of inference takes place, either consciously or unconsciously, either explicitly or implicitly, either deliberately or habitually. What, then, is the connection between the experienced sensations and the act of perception?

According to Reid, the sensation is a *natural sign* which signifies the property of the external body. But this connection between sign and property is not itself perceived. Thus we cannot infer the property from the sign on the basis of our knowledge of the connection. As Reid describes the situation, "When I grasp an ivory ball in my hand, I feel a certain sensation of touch. In the sensation, there is nothing external, nothing corporeal. The sensation is neither round nor hard; it is an act of feeling of the mind, from which I cannot, by reasoning, infer the existence of any body. But, by the constitution of my nature, the sensation carries along with it the conception and belief of a round hard body really existing in my hand" (Reid, p. 638). I disagree with Reid, of course, about the nature of the sensation: It is not a mental act. And though it is true that there is "nothing external, nothing corporeal" in it, it is not true that the sensation is not round and hard. But these disagreements do not matter for the moment. What matters, rather, is the following agreement. Reid says that by the constitution of his nature the sensation carries along with it the relevant perception. When he has the sensation, he also has the perception. I think that this is essentially correct, but I would express it in a different way. Roughly, the experienced sensations are a *(partial) cause* of the act of perception. Since you experience certain sensations, and given that certain other conditions are fulfilled, you also experience a certain act of perception, that is, you see that Oscar is green. Thus the act of perceiving does not occur as a result of a process of inference. It is not caused by a thought or reasoning process, but is caused directly, as it were, by the sensations.

Human nature is such that we have certain perceptions whenever we experience certain sensations *(and certain other conditions are fulfilled)*. This bond is a matter of our constitution. In principle, an organism could have all of our sensations, but none of our perceptions. An organism could even experience acts of perception without the corresponding sensations! Reid sees this too: "Nor can we perceive any necessary connection between sensation and the conception and belief of an external object. For anything we can discover, we might have been so framed as to have all the sensations we now have by our senses, without any impressions on our organs and without any conception of any external object. For any thing we know, we might have been so made as to perceive external objects, without any impressions on bodily organs, and without any of those sensations which invariably accompany perception in our present frame" (Reid, p. 289). Needless to say, the causal relationships between sensations and corresponding perceptions are extremely complicated. And I must emphasize once again that many other factors determine just which perceptions occur. Expectations play a role, and so do feelings and emotions, past experiences, and learning. Most importantly, the perceptual objects themselves influence what we perceive. This is such an important fact because it clashes with the customary picture of the causal chain in perception.

According to this customary picture, certain physiological processes occur in the sense-organs, the nervous system, and in the brain, as a consequence of certain external stimuli (the perceptual object, etc.). These physiological processes eventually cause certain sensations to be experienced. The mind somehow goes to work on these sensations and, as a result, arrives at a certain belief about a perceptual object. The mind somehow reasons from the sensations to what there is in front of one's nose. Sensations furnish the only basis for one's perceptual beliefs. The way to the perceptual belief leads causally as well as inferentially through the sensations. Now, Reid does away with the notion that the perceptual belief is arrived at by means of an inference from the sensations. But this leaves us still with the causal chain. What I wish to point out is that this connection as well is tentative. We must change our preliminary characterization of the relationship between sensations and perception. The physiological processes which take place in the brain as a consequence of the stimulation of the sense-organs, and of past experience, expectations, etc., cause *both* the experience of certain sensations and the experience of certain acts of perception. The occurrence of a certain act of perception, in other words, does not causally depend on the sensations alone, although it may look that way, since the two usually occur together. Rather, we cannot perceive without sensations because the processes in the brain which cause us to perceive, inevitably (as a matter of fact) also cause us to have certain sensations. Can we have sensations without perceptions? The traditional answer assumes that the dependency has one direction: perceptions are caused by sensations, but sensations can occur without perceptions. According to the customary picture, one somehow learns to interpret one's sensations. These interpretations are one's perceptions. A baby merely experiences sensations; a buzzing, booming, confusion of sensations. Only later does it learn slowly, by inference, what there is in front of its eyes and mouth. Or perhaps this learning takes place rather quickly, once the baby has grasped the basic rules of inductive and deductive logic. What really happens is of course quite different from this philosophical picture. At a very early age, the baby perceives perceptual objects and experiences sensations. If there ever is a time when it merely experiences sensations and does not perceive, then this is undoubtedly due to the fact that its nervous system has not yet reached a certain degree of maturity.

We are finally ready to evaluate Reid's reply to the argument from the relativity of sensing. He considers Hume's version of the argument: "The table, which we see, seems to diminish as we remove further from it; but the real table, which exists independent of us, suffers no alterations. It was therefore nothing but its image which was present to the mind" (Hume, as quoted by Reid, p. 221). The crucial assumption is that we *see* a smaller table, as we move away from it. Since the real table does not get smaller, so Hume argues, what we *see* cannot be the actual size of the table, but only, as he puts it, an "image." Here is Reid's response:

> We learn by experience to judge of the distance of a body from the eye within certain limits; and from its distance and apparent magnitude taken together, we learn to judge of its real magnitude. And this kind of judgment, by being repeated every hour, and almost every minute of our lives, becomes when we are grown up, so ready and so habitual, that it very much resembles the original perceptions of our senses, and may not improperly be called *acquired* perception.
>
> (Reid, p. 225)

It seems to me that we have here the precise kind of picture of how we "learn how to perceive on the basis of our sensations" which I criticized earlier. I say cautiously "it seems to me," because the case is not as clear for magnitude (size) as it is for other properties of perceptual objects. But what Reid says about size in this passage, he also seems to assert, for example, for shape: ". . . open your eyes and you shall see a table precisely of that apparent magnitude, and that apparent figure, which the real table must have in that distance, and in that position" (Reid, p. 227). Allow me therefore to switch from size to shape, and let us consider the shape of the table top. Hume's argument then becomes: The shape of the table top *which you see* when you approach the table changes from trapezoidal to rectangular. But the actual shape of the table top does not change. Hence, what you see when you approach the table is not the actual shape of the table top, but only the shape of an impression in your mind.

Berkeley already noted in the *Treatise* (para. 15) that this argument is not valid. In truth, the argument does not show that we cannot see the shape of the table top, but only, assuming that the premises are true, that we cannot know which of the seen shapes is *the* shape of table top. Granted that what we *see* from different angles are different shapes, the question arises: Which of the seen shapes is the real shape of the table top? Is it trapezoidal, for example, or is it rectangular? The skeptic claims that there is no reason why we should prefer one of the seen shapes to all the others.

We shall return to the argument and give it a more precise formulation. However, the gist of it is clear enough that we can evaluate Reid's response. Reid says that we *learn* to judge the true shape of the table top by taking into consideration our distance from the table, our elevation relative to it, etc. This learning takes place in childhood. After a while, the inference becomes so "ready and so habitual" that we no longer notice it. It then resembles ordinary perception which, as we saw, is not a matter of inference. I think that there are two things wrong with this account. First of all, it is simply not true, as experience plainly shows, that children infer the shapes of things in this manner. It is absurd to believe that they use the rather complicated geometric laws required for such inferences. Anyone who has tried to teach geometry to older children can only scoff at the thought that tiny tykes should constantly and accurately deduce the shapes of things by means of the laws of geometry. Nor is there any introspective evidence for the existence of such a process of inference. I am convinced that nobody can recall practicing in early childhood inferences about the true colors of things (with the help of the laws of optics?), about their true shapes, etc. Or do these inferences lie so far back that no memories can reach them? But then how plausible is the claim that even small babies use the laws of geometry and optics?

Nor, secondly, does Reid's explanation really come to grips with the skeptic's argument. The skeptic wants to know how we can possibly select the real shape of the table top from all the shapes we see when we walk around the table, when none of them wears a label saying "I am the true shape." Obviously, we need some kind of principle of selection, for example, the truth that if, from a certain definite point of view, you see the table top with such-and-such a shape, then it actually is rectangular. But we can never discover such a principle, according to the skeptic, for we could only discover it if we could compare the seen shape with the actual shape; and this comparison is only possible if either you can directly see the actual shape or else infer what it is by means of a principle which is different from the one we are trying to discover. The first possibility is excluded by the nature of the situation: it is assumed that none of the shapes which you directly see stands out as *the* shape of the table. The second possibility is also eliminated because it would involve us in a vicious infinite regress. It follows that we cannot compare the apparent with the real shape. But since we cannot compare them, we cannot discover the required principle of inference. And without such a principle, we cannot know the actual shape of the table top.

I believe that the skeptic's line of reasoning, given the premises which Reid grants him, is sound and convincing. If we accept Reid's view that the shape of the table top can only be known through an inference, then it follows that it cannot be known at all. But it is rather astonishing that Reid adopts this view, for he could hold instead that we know the shape directly through perception. Perception, we noted, is for him not a matter of inference. However, he would then have to reject Hume's first premise, namely, that we see different shapes from different points of view. Perhaps he was under the spell of the traditional picture according to which babies learn to infer the properties of the things around them from their sensations.

Be that as it may, I think that Reid's failure to overcome idealism and his capitulation to skepticism are not so much signs of a lack of philosophical acumen, as they are proof of the power of the distinction between primary and secondary qualities and of the principle of immanence. I know of no philosopher from Descartes to Moore who could withstand this power.

FOUR

Kant's Transcendental Idealism

Disaster Extolled

a) A Berkeleyan Perspective

In connection with Reid's philosophy, I spoke of stepping out of Plato's cave into a bright spring morning. To enter Kant's philosophy is not like returning to the cave. It is like getting lost in a fog. To the famous "der Kant hat sie alle verwirret," we must add: "weil er so verwirret war"! (H. Vaihinger, *Kommentar zu Kant's Kritik der reinen Vernunft,* vol. 2, p. 502).

Kant, it seems, was not too familiar with Berkeley's philosophy. Yet, I shall start our inquiry by reminding you of Berkeley's basic contention, namely, that the so-called primary qualities (size, shape, motion, rest, and number) are just as much mere ideas (sensations) in minds as the so-called secondary qualities. Shape is no better off than color. This means that all of the sensible properties of perceptual objects are mere ideas. Add to this the ontological thesis that a perceptual object is but a bundle or collection of sensible properties, and you get what I have called Berkeley's main argument for idealism. Idealism thus follows straightforwardly from two quite simple assertions.

One can look at Kant's philosophy from many different perspectives. From one, a less historical and more structural perspective, Kant can be seen to provide a further argument, and quite a powerful one, for Berkeley's contention that primary qualities are just as "subjective" as secondary ones. Berkeley pointed out that shape suffers just as much from the relativity of sensing as color. Kant's argument is of an entirely different sort. Roughly, it states that primary qualities are just as "subjective" as secondary ones because we have synthetic knowledge a priori about them. Space and time, Kant holds, are merely "subjective." They are the *forms* of our sensibility. Since they are the forms of our sensibility, they apply automatically to the objects formed by them. This line of thought is so familiar that I need not spell it out in detail. But let me add that I do not wish to deny that there is an important difference between space and time, on the one hand, and "ordinary" sensations, on the other. Nor do I wish to belittle the difference between Berkeley's task and the completely different problem which Kant poses in terms of these forms of intuition. However, the fact remains that the primary qualities of shape, size, number, etc., that is, spatial, temporal, and numerical attributes, are placed in the mind.

The situation is quite different in regard to Berkeley's ontological thesis. Far from rejecting the category of (material) substance, Kant emphasizes its importance for the formation of objects. The category of substance, in connection with the forms of intuition, produces out of the manifold of sensations a perceptual object. Berkeley's apple is not just a bundle of sensations given to the mind as a finished bundle, but is the product of an elaborate mental process. Nevertheless, the material and the form of this product is purely mental. Kant's apple, just like Berkeley's, is a mental thing. Kant's theory merely adds a very complicated and rather nebulous mental process of production to Berkeley's simple idealism. The facts, of course, rebel in either case: An apple is neither a simple collection of sensations, nor is it a most elaborate construction out of such sensations.

But there is, as we know, a joker in Kant's deck: the *Ding an sich. The Ding an sich,* from our structural rather than historical point of view, is what remains if we abstract from the perceptual object all of its perceptual properties, namely, a bare substance. It is the wax, as conceived of by Descartes, divorced from all of its sensible properties. As such, it cannot be known by the senses, but only by the understanding. But Kant also stresses the causal role of this "substance behind the sensible properties." He sometimes talks as if the *Ding an sich* were somehow the cause of our sensations. The unknown substance which supports sensible properties does not play this causal role; it does not cause its properties, but merely props them up. Kant's *Ding an sich* is more like Berkeley's God who is ultimately responsible for our experiencing the particular bundles of sensations which we do experience.

From our Berkeleyan perspective, we get the following picture of Kant's philosophy. Firstly, Kant confirms Berkeley's contention that primary qualities are as mental as secondary ones. He adds a whole new dimension to the grounds for this contention by claiming that space and time are the forms of our intuitions. Secondly, as a result, Kant agrees with Berkeley's view that perceptual objects are mental things. In this respect, he is a Berkeleyan idealist. However, and thirdly, while Berkeley thinks of the mental thing as a given collection of sensations, Kant assumes that it is the product of a great deal of mental activity. The so-called primary qualities play an important epistemological role in this activity. They have an epistemological function as (a) the forms of intuition (shape, size, duration, etc.), and (b) the categories (substance, force, divisibility, etc.). Fourthly, while Berkeley holds that the flow of bundles of sensations is caused by God, Kant assumes that the mind receives the raw material for its productivity from an unknown *Ding an sich.*

If this perspective illuminates Kant's basic system, then it follows that a realist must not only turn back the Berkeleyan arguments for the mental nature of primary qualities, but also refute Kant's arguments for the synthetic a priori nature of our knowledge of space and time. He must, in other words, address himself to the problem of mathematical knowledge as Kant conceives of it. It is part of the genius of Kant's philosophy that in it idealism cannot be divorced from this problem.

How did Kant view his relationship with Berkeley? Kant agrees that "all bodies, together with the space in which they are, must be considered nothing but mere presentations in us, and exist nowhere but in our thoughts" (*Prolegomena,* par. 13, remark ii). But Kant goes on to point out that, according to his philosophy, there really exist in the nonmental world certain *Dinge an sich:* "Consequently I grant by all means that there are bodies without us, that is, things which, though quite unknown to us as to what they are in themselves, we yet know by the representations which their influence on our sensibility procures us" (Kant, 1957). And then he turns the table on us by pointing out that Locke and others have held that the secondary qualities are mental, without having been called, for that reason, idealists. The only difference between Locke and himself, Kant says, is that he, in distinction to Locke, claims that "all the properties which constitute the intuition of a body belong merely to its appearance" (Kant, 1957). This view, Kant claims, does not destroy the existence of the thing which so appears to the senses, as genuine idealism does. Hence, so Kant seems to conclude, his view is no more idealistic than Locke's.

There is no point arguing about the word 'idealism'. Kant's view is quite different from Locke's and Berkeley's. There is, we must always remind ourselves, the much maligned *Ding an sich* in Kant's philosophy. Yet, Kant's appeal to Locke does not touch upon the real issue. No view, no matter how similar or dissimilar it may be to Berkeley's or Locke's views, can be correct if it denies the non-mental nature of perceptual objects and their properties. From our point of view, Kant's "realism" is a sham. It substitutes for the exciting fullness of the perceptual world the arid realm of unknown *Dinge an sich*. If weighed on the scale of truth, it does not beat Berkeley's undisguised idealism by much.

What is at issue is not the quality of semantic acrobatics with the term 'idealism', but rather what Kant himself clearly describes in the following paragraph from the same place:

> I should be glad to know what my assertion must be in order to avoid idealism. Undoubtedly, I should say that the representation of space is not only perfectly comfortable to the relation which our sensibility has to objects—that I have said—but that it is quite similar to the object—an assertion in which I can find as little meaning as if I said that the sensation of red has a similarity to the property of cinnibar which excites this sensation in me.

> (Kant, 1957)

What Kant here pronounces to be meaningless is precisely the view which I have defended, although not quite in the way in which he formulates it. The red sensation is indeed "similar" to the property of cinnibar which causes me to have it. In fact, it is this very same property, namely, a certain shade of the color red. Similarly, some of the spatial relations among perceptual objects are roughly the same, under normal circumstances, as the spatial relations among my sensations; sensations which are caused by those perceptual objects. We may speculate that Kant does not share our understanding of the situation because he, like many other philosophers, thinks of a shade of red as a sensation and not, as we do, as a property of a sensation. Nor does he believe that the property of cinnibar, which causes us to experience the sensation, is the shade of red just mentioned. Rather, he holds that this property of cinnibar is some kind of "physical" quality of the cinnibar which causes us to have the sensation *of* [sic] red. This insidious conception of the situation is by now so familiar to us that we need not dwell on it. But something else deserves special emphasis. Notice that Kant here compares the sensation of red, not with an unknown quality of the *Ding an sich,* but with a physical property of cinnibar. What suddenly appears here on the philosophical stage is something we have not encountered before, namely, a "middle thing" located somewhere between sensations and their combinations, on the one hand, and the *Dinge an sich,* on the other. We shall return to this phantom of the philosophical theater in a moment.

There are two further references to Berkeley in the *Critique of Pure Reason.* In B 69–70, Kant defends himself against the accusation that his conception of intuition as mere appearance transforms the world into mere illusion. He tries here, as in the *Prolegomena,* to make a sharp distinction between appearance and illusion. Much of what he says at this point is not clear (cf. Vaihinger, vol. 2, pp. 486–94). Fortunately, we need not try to make sense of it. From the perspective we have chosen, it is clear that what matters is not the distinction between appearance and illusion, but the distinction between the mental and the non-mental. The question is not whether or not Kant transforms the world into mere illusion, but whether or not perceptual objects are transformed into mental constructions. In regard to Berkeley, Kant remarks that it is no wonder that Berkeley turned bodies into mere illusion, since he started out by thinking of space and time as belonging objectively to bodies. Kant repeats here his standard claim that any conception of space and time as mind-independent entities must lead to contradictory conclusions about their natures. Needless to say, we do not accept this claim. Berkeley's apple has certain spatio-temporal attributes (properties and relations) just as "objectively" as it has certain other perceptual properties (color, taste, etc.). The assumption that the shape of Oscar is just as much a mind-independent property of it as its color leads neither to contradiction nor to confusion.

b) The Special Nature of Space

From our Berkeleyan perspective, Kant's view about space comes down to the claim that such alleged primary qualities as size and shape are just as mental as the secondary qualities of color, taste, etc. Shape, we may sum it up, is just as mental as color. However, Kant rejects this assimilation in the *Critique of Pure Reason* (A 28–29, B 44–45), and we must take a look at the following important passage:

> (A 28) With the sole exception of space there is no subjective representation, referring to something *outer,* which could be entitled [at once] objective [and] *a priori.* This subjective condition of all outer appearances cannot, therefore, be compared to any other. The taste of a wine does not belong to the objective determinations of the wine, not even if by the wine as an object we mean the wine as appearance, but to the special constitution of sense in the subject that tastes it. Colours are not properties of the bodies to the intuition of which they are attached, but only modifications of the sense of sight, which is affected in a certain manner by light. Space, on the other hand, as condition of

outer objects, necessarily belongs to their appearance or intuition. Taste and colors are not necessary conditions under which alone objects can be for us objects of the senses. They are connected with the appearances only as effects accidentally added by the particular constitution of the sense organs. Accordingly, they are not *a priori* representations, but are grounded in sensations, and, indeed, in the case of taste even upon feeling (pleasure and pain), as an effect of sensation. Further, no one can have *a priori* a representation of a colour or of any taste; whereas, since space concerns only the pure form of intuition, and therefore involves no sensation whatsoever, and nothing empirical, all kinds and determinations of space can and must be represented *a priori*, if concepts of figures and of their relations are to arise. Through space alone is it possible that things should be other objects to us.

(Kant, 1965)

Kant's first sentence asserts that space is the only subjective representation which is (a) objective and (b) a priori. Color, we take it, is neither. Kant argues that space is objective while color is not by asserting that colors are not properties of the bodies to the intuition of which they are attached, while space necessarily belongs to their appearance or intuition. Colors, I take him to be saying, do admittedly not belong to perceptual objects, but are merely sensations in minds. Space, on the other hand, is a property of perceptual objects; even as appearances, such objects have spatial attributes (shape, size, spatial relations). In other words, Kant here invokes the distinction between primary and secondary qualities to make his point. It is as if he had simply forgotten his whole philosophy, falling back to the level of what passes for scientific common sense. Everyone knows, he seems to be arguing, that color is only in the mind, while shape and size are really properties of "outer" non-mental things. Thus while the latter are objective, the former are merely subjective. But the distinction does not fit into Kant's philosophy. Or, rather, as I shall argue in a moment, it can only be made to fit if we turn his philosophy into a Rube Goldberg type of contraption with layers of unknown things and levels of unconscious processes. What I wish to call attention to at this point is the incredible power which the distinction between primary and secondary qualities has had over the minds of philosophers, including Kant's.

Color, in distinction to space, is supposedly not an a priori representation. This assertion leads into the thicket of Kant's philosophy, and a full discussion of it would lead us too far astray. But a few remarks are in order. Firstly, what is at stake is the Kantian dogma that there can be no sensations of space (and time), a dogma to which we shall return in a moment. Secondly, we must note that what Kant here contrasts with each other is not shape with color, but rather space with color. And this raises the all-important question of what this space is. He says that it is something that "concerns only the pure form of intuition." Is it then a pure form of intuition? Well, I shall not get lost in Kant's fog, but merely note that we can distinguish among at least three notions of space in Kant: (1) Space as *form* of intuition, (2) space as (pure) *intuition* (content of intuition; this is the space of geometry; it is one individuum), and (3) space in the form of *spatial properties* and *relations*. Perhaps these three notions can somehow be combined in the following picture, keeping in mind that this picture does not agree with many of Kant's pronouncements. The mind has the ability to order things spatially; this is a function of space as a form of intuition. What results from this arrangement of intuitions is the empirical, relative space of perception; things are perceived as having certain shapes and as standing in certain spatial relations to each other. When the mind goes to work on this product of the spatial form, it abstracts from it the one absolute space. This abstraction is the space of physics (cf. Vaihinger, vol. 2, p. 230). However, this interpretation leads immediately to difficulties for Kant's philosophy. Where does this leave the space of mathematics (geometry)? Furthermore, and more importantly, if the space of geometry is said to be gotten in the way in which the space of physics is abstracted, then geometry is no longer known a priori! It is then a matter of experience.

Space, in our view, consists of and is exhausted by spatial properties, such as size and shape, together with the various spatial relations. Kant is very vague about these obvious spatial features of the world. It has been noted, for example, that he never tries to explain why a particular perceptual object is perceived to be round while another is perceived to be square. Obviously, the alleged fact that intuition is spatial, that it must pass through the spatial filter, does not explain why we perceive a particular perceptual object as round rather than square. Nor is this circumstance explained by the presumed fact that we have a pure intuition of an infinite space. Be that as it may, it is at any rate clear that Kant says very little about the particular problem which has our attention, namely, the problem of how shape compares with color in regard to the distinction between primary and secondary qualities.

Let us next look at the relevant passage in the second edition of the *Critique:*

(B 45) The above remark is intended only to guard anyone from supposing that the ideality of space as here asserted can be illustrated by examples so altogether insufficient as colors, taste, etc. For these are rightly regarded not as properties of things, but only as changes in the subject, changes which may, indeed, be different for different men. In such examples as these, that which originally is itself only appearance, for instance, a rose, is being treated by the empirical understanding as a thing in itself, which, nevertheless, in respect of its color, can appear differently to every observer. The transcendental concept of appearances in space, on the other hand, is a critical reminder that nothing intuited in space is a thing in itself, that space is not a form inhering in things in themselves as their intrinsic property, that objects in themselves are quite unknown to us, and that what we call other objects are nothing but mere representations of our sensibility, the form of which is space. The true correlate to sensibility, the thing in itself, is not known, and cannot be known, through these representations; and in experience no question is ever asked in regard to it.

(Kant, 1965)

Kant claims that the ideality of space is not the ideality of color; for while color is merely subjective, even for the empirical understanding, space is not. While the color of Berkeley's apple is a mere sensation in the mind, we could say, its shape is not. In short, in order to guard against a confusion of the ideality of space with the ideality of color, Kant appeals to the distinction between primary and secondary qualities. He seems to base this distinction on the argument from the relativity of sensing. The color of the rose, he claims, can appear differently to different observers. In the spirit of Berkeley, we would wish to point out to Kant that the same can be said about the shape and the size of the rose. Of course, Berkeley's spirit is not the spirit of our philosophy. We do not even accept the premise that the perceived color of the rose must vary from observer to observer. But if we accepted this fundamental premise of the argument, then we would also have to insist that the spatial characteristics of the rose vary in the same fashion. Even in the second edition of the *Critique of Pure Reason*, Kant appeals to the traditional distinction between primary and secondary qualities and to one of the traditional arguments for it.

Notice, lastly, the unequivocal commitment to idealism: "what we call outer objects are nothing but mere representations of our sensibility." The German word is of course *Vorstellungen*. A perceptual object, therefore, is nothing but a *Vorstellung*. It is true that there is also the *Ding an sich*. But this part of Kant's view rests on nothing more than blind "Humean" belief. From a systematic point of view, the *Ding an sich* is merely an appendage of the body of Kant's philosophy.

Kant tries to defend his blend of idealism in the well-known second remark of paragraph 13 of the *Prolegomena* which we have mentioned before. What is so remarkable about this passage is that Kant does not invoke the distinction between primary and secondary qualities, but, quite to the contrary, treats space on a par with color, taste, etc. Kant, following in the footsteps of Berkeley, tries to put a reasonable face on the absurd view that a perceptual object, Berkeley's apple, for instance, is a representation in a mind. We see here the same idealistic trick at work which we have exposed on earlier occasions. "Look," Kant says to us, "you have already admitted that color is a mere sensation in the mind. Yet you also believe that there are perceptual objects and, hence, you are not an idealist. Now, I hold that other properties as well—shape, size, etc.—are mental. Yet I too believe that there are 'external things.' So I deserve to be called an idealist no more than you do." Kant has a point, but the point is not what he believes it to be. What his line of reasoning shows, if it shows anything, is that Berkeley's contention is correct: If you admit that color is only in the mind, you may as well also admit that shape is only in the mind. But to admit either, we must emphasize against Kant, is to be an idealist or, more cautiously, it is to make an idealistic view inevitable. "External objects" without colors, tastes, etc., are simply not the perceptual objects which a realist defends. And perceptual objects without colors, tastes, etc., and also without shapes, sizes, etc., are even less like them.

Let us now pause for a moment in our main discussion and touch upon a more peripheral issue, an issue which, nevertheless, has played a major role in the history of philosophy. I have in mind Kant's dogma "That in which alone the sensations can be ordered, cannot itself be sensation" (Kant, 1965, A 20, B 34). In other words, the dogma that there are no spatial sensations. If Kant were correct, then there would indeed exist quite a difference between color, on the one hand, and space, on the other. But is he? Why does he accept the dogma? Since Kant does not argue for it explicitly, we can only speculate about his reason.

But first we must remind ourselves of how our conception of sensations differs from the commonly accepted one. A color shade, for instance, the color olive green, is commonly said to be a sensation. But the color is clearly a property, and this raises the question of what it is a property of. If one believes in Berkeley and assumes that an olive, for example, is nothing but a bundle of properties, and that these properties are sensations, then we have an answer: The sensation olive green is a property of an olive. Sensations turn out to be properties of perceptual objects. But assume that we do not accept the bundle view of individual things. What then is this color a property of? This question is seldom if ever raised by those who think of colors (and other perceptual properties) as sensations. No wonder, for it is obvious that there is no plausible answer to it. Olive green cannot very well be a property of the mind (mental substance), for this would imply that the mind is colored (and has a taste, etc.). Nor can it be a property of olives, for this would imply that olives have "mental" properties. But if so-called color sensations are properties neither of minds nor of nonmental individuals, what are they properties of? According to our view, the dilemma does not appear. Colors are not sensations at all, for sensations are individual (mental) things, while colors are not. Colors are properties of certain sensations, and they are also properties of certain perceptual objects. Olive green is a property of olives, and also a property of certain sensations which we experience when we look at olives under ordinary conditions. Thus it is, properly speaking, neither mental nor nonmental. But there are mental things, sensations, which have this color, and there are also nonmental things, perceptual objects, which are olive green.

Having refreshed our memory of this important point, let us return to what a moment ago I called Kant's dogma. Why can there be no sensation of space? Well, we have already noted that Kant has at least three different conceptions of space. There is, first of all, space as the form of outer intuition. I can make some sense of this phrase "form of outer intuition," if I translate it into "spatial intuition," that is, if I assume that there is a *kind* of intuition which is spatial. So-called outer intuition is presumably of this sort. We may call this notion of space, tongue in cheek, the "adverbial view." I shall concede that space, so conceived, cannot be a matter of sensation. We simply do not have sensations of (properties of) acts of intuition. Mental acts, of whatever kind, are not the sort of thing which causes us to experience sensations. This leads us to the second conception of space, space as an absolute, infinite, individual thing. (For passages from Kant, see Vaihinger, vol. 2, pp. 71–72.) Space as an empty container to be filled with sensations does not seem to be the sort of thing of which we can have sensations. Thus I am willing to agree, again, that there are no sensations of space so conceived.

But what about spatial properties and relations? Consider shape first. It seems to me to be obvious that a sensation may have a shape just as well as a color. In this straightforward sense, there are "shape sensations" just as there are "color sensations." Of course, what we really mean by these common but misleading expressions is that there are shaped sensations just as there are colored sensations. And there are also, we should add, sensations *of* shape just as there are sensations *of* color. That is, there are shaped sensations caused by shaped perceptual objects, just as there are colored sensations caused by colored perceptual objects.

But sensations do not just have shape and color, they also stand in spatial relations to each other. A green and round sensation, for example, may be *between* two red and square sensations. And just as we have somewhat perversely agreed to speak of a round sensation when a sensation is round, so we could speak of a between sensation when a sensation is between two other sensations. Thus we come to the conclusion that Kant is mistaken. There are spatial sensations just as there are color sensations; for there are round sensations and between sensations. There are also, as should be clear, sensations of space in the sense that there are sensations of spatial objects.

However, we must keep in mind that the case for spatial relations is quite different from the case for spatial properties. Until very recently, it has been philosophical dogma that relations are not part of the furniture of the world. Of relations, Berkeley tells us, we have not ideas but notions. And the reason is that knowledge of relations, as distinct from knowledge of (ordinary) properties, requires an activity of the mind. Relations, according to the traditional view, are created by mental acts of comparison. What is given, on the level of sensations, are certain properties, but no relations. Only if the mind goes to work on these given sensations, do relations come into being. According to this hazy picture, the mind orders and arranges the sensations presented to it and, by doing so, creates the relations among them.

Perhaps it is this kind of picture which moved Kant to say that "that in which alone the sensations can be ordered, cannot itself be sensation." It may rest ultimately on the conviction that while sensations are given to the mind, their order is not. But we insist that just as the colors and shapes of sensations are not created by the mind, so is their arrangement and order not produced by the mind. Sensations are experienced as having certain properties and as standing in certain relations to each other.

Sensations are mental. Yet, they can have shapes and stand in spatial relations to each other. It follows that some mental things "are in space." Our view contradicts a version of Descartes's assertion that the mind is not extended. More precisely, it contradicts the widespread view that mental things cannot be spatial. However, Descartes's view is true of mental acts. A wish or a desire, it is clear, cannot appear between two other things. If a mind consisted of nothing else but of mental acts, if it were nothing but thought, to speak with Descartes, then it would indeed be true that mental things (a mind) are not spatial. But a mind also contains sensations, and insofar as it contains them, it is spatial in the sense which we have explained above.

c) The Double Affection Interpretation

I have painted a picture—some would undoubtedly say a caricature—of Kant as a sophisticated Berkeleyan idealist who (a) postulates a *Ding an sich,* (b) holds a confused and confusing view of space, and (c) poses an enduring challenge to theories of mathematical knowledge. But there is also a more realistic side to Kant's philosophy. This realism appears in the later stages of Kant's philosophical development. What I have so far discussed, one might say, is the early Kant, the Kant of the *Inauguraldissertation* and of the first edition of the *Critique of Pure Reason*. What emerges in his later philosophy is a new kind of entity, a "Mittelding," a thing situated somewhere between the *Ding an sich* and the perceptual object conceived of as a mental construction. What emerges with time is, to use our terminology, a *physical object,* distinct both from the *Ding an sich* and the perceptual object. This emergence is signaled by Kant's distinction between primary and secondary qualities in the passages quoted earlier as well as in other places (see Erich Adickes, *Kants Lehre von der doppelten Affektion unseres Ich,* pp. 67–74).

In the passage from A 28, for example, Kant says that "Colors are not properties of the bodies to the intuition of which they are attached, but only modifications of the sense of sight, *which is affected in a certain manner by light*" (my italics). What affects the sense of sight is thus not the *Ding an sich,* but light. One may therefore conclude that Kant holds that in addition to the unknowable *Ding an sich* and the perceptual object, which is constructed out of color, taste, etc., there also exists a physical entity, light, which is identical neither with the former nor with the latter. In B 45 we read, similarly, that colors and taste "*are rightly regarded,* not as properties of things, but only as changes in the subject, changes which may, indeed, be different for different men" (my italics). When they are so regarded, Kant continues, then the perceptual object, a rose, "is being treated by the empirical understanding as a thing in itself, a thing which, nevertheless, in respect of its color, can appear differently to different observers." Kant seems to accept here, too, the distinction between primary and secondary qualities and, with it, the rose as a "Mittelding" somewhere between the *Ding an sich* and the perceptual object.

How seriously shall we take these passages? It all depends on what we wish Kant had held. I have already indicated that I do not believe there is such a thing as *the* Kantian philosophy, *the* Kantian system. There are, rather, Kantian themes, themes which often are not clearly stated and which may even contradict each other. But if one cannot resist the temptation to find the one and only true Kantian philosophy—and it is surely amazing how many brilliant people have succumbed to this temptation—then one may read into Kant's allusions to the primary-secondary distinction the makings of an idealism infinitely more sophisticated than Berkeley's. One may then see one's way clear to make peace between Kant's philosophy, on the one hand, and the teaching of modern science, on the other. The distinction between primary and secondary qualities, I have emphasized, is a child of modern science. While color and taste are only in the mind, the Cartesian scientist holds, shape, number, motion, etc. are real properties of physical objects (atoms). Now, if Kant had made this distinction, he would have been in tune with science; he would have been in tune with the conviction that even though color and taste are only in the mind, "out there," in the nonmental world, there really exist certain physical things in genuine space. Kant, one could then assert, was no Berkeleyan idealist, for although he holds that *perceptual* objects are only mental, he also holds that there are nonmental *physical* objects. This interpretation of Kant kills two birds with one stone: It avoids the charge that Kant was a Berkeleyan idealist and it brings Kant into harmony with physics.

Adickes has worked out such an interpretation. He takes the point of view of "scientific realism":

> According to scientific realism, however, what affects us are not the colored, sounding, hard or soft objects of sense which surround us. Rather, philosophers and scientists have agreed since Kepler's, Galileo's, and Descartes's time that all qualities of sense are only subjectively founded properties, not belonging to the things themselves, but originating in our mind as its reaction and, hence, only existing in the form of contents of consciousness. Bodies were conceived of as collections of atoms or corpuscles, and the whole world around us was thought of as diffused into a series of continuous motions, be it of the bodies themselves or of their smallest mass parts.
>
> (Adickes, p. 37)

Adickes argues brilliantly that the usual interpretations of Kant clash with scientific realism, for according to these interpretations what affects us is the *Ding an sich,* not the physical object. But if "one eliminates the empirical affection [by the physical object] and retains only the transcendental one, then the world of experience would lose all genuine objectivity and reality. There would be no real connections, no real mutual influence among bodies; the only causes would be the things in themselves" (Adickes, p. 40). In short, Adickes rejects the view that the nonmental world consists exclusively of *Dinge an sich.* Instead, he develops the so-called double affection interpretation, according to which the things in themselves affect, not the empirical self, but the so-called I in itself. The result of this over-arching interaction is the creation of the world of physics and of the empirical self. But the latter interact too, just as common sense and physics proscribe. For example, certain physical forces interact with a human body which, in turn, acts on the mind and thus causes a red sensation. What Adickes's interpretation of Kant's philosophy amounts to is a scientific realism, as described above, which is suspended between two unknowable poles and which involves an unknowable process. The unknowable poles are the *Ding an sich* and the *Ich an sich.* The unknowable process is the creation of the physical world and the empirical self.

What a strange and fascinating view! I have no doubt whatsoever that it is just as false as the view usually ascribed to Kant. But I think that it would be a mistake to dismiss Adickes's interpretation for this reason alone. Quite to the contrary, I think that he catches an important undercurrent in Kant's philosophy. Kant, I believe, was indeed under the spell of "scientific realism" and quite often allowed this spell to dictate his choice of example and terminology. So-called scientific realism, and this is the point I wish to make, was and still is a pervasive dogma, a dogma which has had everyone under its spell. Even though Kant's philosophical arguments led into quite a different direction, he could not but heed its force. Ever so often in Kant's philosophy, the physical object appears suddenly on the scene, like a ghost that will not be laid to rest. Kant could not rid his philosophy of this ghost. Adickes cannot believe that a philosophy deserves our respect, unless it embraces the dogma.

But the dogma is false. It is false not because it insists, against the idealist, that there are physical objects, but because it denies that the perceptual objects around us are nonmental. It puts the sweet, red, round apple in the mind. And it does so because it takes for granted that these qualities are nothing but sensations in minds. The truth is, though, that the sweetness of the apple, its color, its smell, are just as much part of the objective (nonmental) world as are the molecules of which the apple consists. As Whitehead puts it, "For us, the red glow of the sunset should be as much part of nature as are the molecules and electric waves by which men of science would explain the phenomenon" (A. N. Whitehead, *The Concept of Nature,* p. 29).

The distinction between primary and secondary qualities serves Adickes's purpose of inserting a physical object between the *Ding an sich* and the merely mental perceptual object. True enough, he reasons, the red, sweet, round apple is merely a construction in the mind. But physics tells us in undeniable terms that "out there," in addition, certain other things exist, things which, though they have no color, no taste, etc., are not unknowable *Dinge an sich*. Adickes remarks at one point that the distinction between primary and secondary qualities "presupposes that there are objects which have only the primary qualities and not the secondary ones, but which in regard to the latter only have certain properties to which (more precisely, to the influence of which) our I answers with its subjective reactions: the secondary qualities" (Adickes, p. 69). But what are those primary qualities? Philosophy once again gets in the way of physics: "If one thinks about the distinction between primary and secondary qualities more thoroughly, then one must conclude that everything that constitutes matterness, that is, the occupation of space by matter . . ., stands or falls with the secondary properties. What remains are forces . . . Really free from secondary qualities one becomes if and only if one traces back the occupation of space to an interaction of forces" (Adickes, p. 71). The physical objects saved from Berkeleyan idealism, in the end, thus turn out to be philosophical chimeras, not the esoteric particles of modern physics. Adickes's attempt to reconcile Kant with physics is a case of love's labor lost. There is an important lesson in all of this for us. The philosophical arguments for the distinction between primary and secondary qualities lead, not to *scientific* realism, but to a *philosophical* realism according to which the things "out there" are neither the familiar perceptual objects around us nor the strange physical objects of the physicist's theory.

FIVE

Brentano's Idealism

Disaster Undisguised

a) The Distinction between Mental and Physical Phenomena

Descartes makes a sharp distinction between bodies and minds: Bodies are extended, minds think. To think, Descartes tells us, is to doubt, to understand, to conceive, to affirm, to deny, to will, etc. In short, to think is to have mental acts. Brentano tries to improve on Descartes's distinction. If what distinguishes the mind from the body are mental acts, then we must ask next how mental acts are different from bodies. Mental acts and only mental acts, according to Brentano's famous answer, are intentional. Mental acts and only mental acts are directed toward objects. Ultimately, what distinguishes a mind from everything else is its direction toward objects, its intentionality. This insight, resurrected if not discovered by Brentano, has been the foundation of most recent philosophies of mind. It is a cornerstone of Meinong's theory of objects as well as Husserl's phenomenology. It has echoes in Heidegger's philosophy, and it appears in Sartre. Moore uses it to refute idealism, and Russell bases his distinction between knowledge by acquaintance and knowledge by description on it.

Let me interrupt for a moment and clarify a distinction which I have presupposed. Descartes speaks of material substances; Brentano, of physical phenomena. I have talked about perceptual objects as well as of physical objects, and I have distinguished between the two. Chairs, mountains, clouds, apples, people, etc., are examples of perceptual objects; molecules, atoms, electrons, and quarks are examples of physical objects. Perceptual objects consist of physical objects. An apple, for example, consists of atoms and, ultimately, of the most elementary particles the physicist has discovered. With this distinction in mind, the realism-idealism issue concerns the existence of perceptual objects: Are apples mental or not? It is clear, firstly, that if there are no perceptual objects, then there are no physical objects either; for the former are supposed to consist of the latter. It is also clear, secondly, that if perceptual objects are mental, then so are the physical objects of which they are supposed to consist. Finally, and thirdly, granted that perceptual objects are nonmental, it is an open empirical question of what sorts of ultimate physical object they consist.

Brentano, I said, speaks of physical phenomena, and he asks how they differ from mental phenomena. He presupposes that this distinction is exhaustive: some thing is either a mental phenomenon or else it is a physical phenomenon; there is no third possibility. This assumption, as we shall see in a moment, leads Brentano into trouble. Brentano starts out by giving examples of mental phenomena:

> Every idea or presentation which we acquire either through sense perception or imagination is an example of a mental phenomenon. By presentation I do not mean that which is presented, but rather the act of presentation, thus hearing a sound, seeing a colored object, feeling warmth or cold, as well as similar states of imagination are examples of what I mean by this term. I also mean by it the thinking of a general concept, provided such a thing actually does occur. Furthermore, every judgment, every recollection, every expectation, every inference, every conviction, or opinion, every doubt is a mental phenomenon. Also to be included under this term is every emotion: joy, sorrow, fear, hope, courage, despair, anger, love, hate, desire, act of will, intention, astonishment, admiration, contempt, etc.

(F. Brentano, Psychology from an Empirical Standpoint, pp. 78–79)

What a difference there is between this list and Descartes's! Descartes mentions such "intellectual" mental acts as doubting, affirming, understanding, and conceiving. There is no mention of emotions. Brentano, on the other hand, lists joy and sorrow, despair and anger, love and hate. Or compare Brentano's inventory of the furniture of the mind with Hume's assertion that "All the perceptions of the human mind resolve themselves into two distinct kinds, which I shall call *impressions* and *ideas*" (D. Hume, *A Treatise of Human Nature,* Book I, Part I, Section I).

But there is also something strange about Brentano's list. He mentions hearing a sound, but also seeing a colored *object*. Hearing and seeing are mental acts of perception. What we perceive are perceptual objects, their properties and relations. We see tomatoes and their colors, we taste steaks and their flavors, we hear bells and their tones. At this point, Brentano does say that seeing a colored *object* is an example of a mental phenomenon, but it is clear from other places that this is a slip of the pen. According to Brentano, we cannot really perceive perceptual objects, but only their properties. For example, we cannot really perceive a tomato, but only its color. But this is not quite correct either. According to his view, perception somehow reduces to acts of sensing, the having of sensations. What we "perceive," consequently, are not even properties of perceptual objects, but are properties of sensations. What we perceive, to be most faithful to Brentano's view is *something red,* for instance, where the something is not a perceptual object but a sensation.

When we turn to Brentano's examples of physical phenomena, we find another slip of the pen. He mentions "a color, a figure, a landscape which I see, a chord which I hear, warmth, cold, odor which I sense; as well as similar images which appear in the imagination" (Brentano, pp. 79–80). The example that does not fit is the landscape. A landscape is not a property of a sensation like color, shape, warmth, cold, etc. are. Of course, from my point of view, only the landscape belongs to the list. Only the landscape is a perceptual object, properly to be contrasted with mental phenomena. But Brentano sees things quite differently from us. A color, warmth, an odor, these are to his mind examples of physical phenomena. Even if we substitute the term 'nonmental' for Brentano's 'physical phenomenon', his list sounds weird. Obvious examples of nonmental things are, rather, tomatoes, the Empire State Building, and a hair on Napoleon's head.

But we are even more surprised when we read that images are examples of physical phenomena. What could be more obvious than that images are mental things? Would there be images, if there were no minds? Surely, something is fundamentally wrong with Brentano's division. And it is not difficult to discover what this something is. Brentano has divided the world up, not into mental and nonmental things, but into mental acts and the rest of things. *Brentano identifies mental phenomena with mental acts.* As a result, whatever is not a mental act turns out to be a physical phenomenon. Since an image, as distinguished from an act of imagination, is not a mental act, it must be a physical thing. Since a sensation, something red, as distinguished from an act of sensing, is not a mental act, it must be a physical phenomenon. Even a pain, as distinguished from the act of feeling a pain, must be classified as a physical phenomenon. Brentano's identification of the mental with mental acts leads to philosophical catastrophe.

Another thought may also have played a role. Perhaps Brentano was convinced that nothing spatial could possibly be mental. Since sensations can have spatial properties and stand in spatial relations to each other, as we explained in the last section, he may have concluded that they cannot be mental. Since they cannot be mental, they must be physical. And a similar argument may have convinced him that images are physical things.

We can easily separate Brentano's important insight from his catastrophic mistake. Intentionality, the direction toward an object, we must realize, is not the essential characteristic of the mental, but of mental acts. Mental acts and only mental acts have objects. But there are also mental things which are not intentional and, hence, which are not mental acts. An image, for example, is obviously a mental thing; yet it is not intentional in the way in which an act of imagination is. A pain, as distinguished from the act of feeling it, has no object. Nor do sensations have objects. A mind consists of many things. Some of these are mental acts, others are not. And only the former are intentional.

Sensations, according to Brentano's division, are physical phenomena. This is the bizarre corollary of his assertion that all mental phenomena are intentional. But something even stranger is yet to come. Brentano also subscribes, like almost everyone else, to the view that a color, warmth, cold, etc. are not to be found in the world of the physicist. He accepts, in other words, some version of the distinction between primary and secondary qualities. According to this distinction, color, warmth, cold, etc. are said to be mental things. Thus we have now the following situation: According to Brentano's definition of the mental, these things (properties) cannot be mental but must be physical. According to his belief in the primary-secondary quality distinction, however, they cannot be physical. Thus they can be neither mental nor physical. They belong neither in the mind, nor in the nonmental world. They are in limbo. They are nowhere. This means that there really are no such things! The dialectic of the situation is obvious. Color, for example, is first shunted into the mind because it is not a primary quality of physical objects. When it is so relocated, it is called a sensation. But Brentano also thinks that mental things must be intentional, and color is obviously not an intentional thing; it is obviously not a mental act. Therefore, it cannot be mental either; it cannot really be a sensation in the mind. In desperation, Brentano concludes that there is no such thing at all as color.

Brentano is a Berkeleyan without ideas (sensations)! His philosophy transcends idealism. In his ontology, there are mental acts and nothing but mental acts. There are no colors, no smells, no pains, no images, etc. Beyond mental acts, there may or may not exist a world of physical objects, but our belief in such a world is mere conjecture. Is it not surprising that the student of Aristotle and opponent of Kant should end up with an idealism more extreme than Berkeley's? Two important lessons can be learned from Brentano's plight. Firstly, we must not accept Brentano's characterization of the mental: There are mental things which are not mental acts. Secondly, once again we are made aware of the pervasiveness of the primary-secondary quality distinction. Brentano may have been an Aristotelian at heart, but his mind belonged to the "empiricistic" tradition of modern science. According to this tradition, color does not exist in the "external" world.

But color is not in limbo. It belongs to the world. However, it is neither exclusively a part of the external world, nor is it exclusively mental. As a property of sensations, it may be said to be "in the mind." As a property of perceptual objects, it may be said to belong to the "external" world.

b) The Thesis of Intentionality

Every mental act (though not every mental thing) is directed toward an object. I shall call this "the thesis of intentionality." Once pointed out, the thesis is a truism. There is no idea which is not an idea of something; there is no desire which is not a desire for something; there is no belief which is not a belief in something; and so on. No philosophical argument could persuade us otherwise. But the consequences of this truism have great philosophical significance.

Mental acts have objects. But in what, precisely, does this "having" of objects consist? There is an obvious and to my mind correct answer: Every mental act is *related* to an object. There is a unique relationship—let us call it "the intentional nexus"—which holds between every mental act and something else, the so-called object. Without the intentional nexus, there would be no world *for* a mind. But this obvious answer runs immediately into a most intractable difficulty. Sometimes, what we see does not exist, what we desire does not come to pass, what we believe is not the case, and so on. In short, sometimes the objects of our acts do not exist, are not facts, are not the case. Some acts, as I shall put it, have nonexistent objects. But how can a relation, the intentional nexus, possibly hold between a mental act and something that does not exist? Must not a relation always establish a connection between existents? How can there exist a connection to something that is not there? Is not a relation with a nonexisting term, as some philosophers have claimed, an absurdity? On the other hand, if the intentionality of mental acts does not consist of a relationship between the act and its object, what does it consist of? How else can we possibly understand the "directedness toward an object"? What else can we make of the fact that every mental act "has" an object? I really see no alternative to the relational interpretation of the thesis of intentionality. But irrespective of whether I am right or wrong, the dialectic of the situation is clear: While a relational account of intentionality must face the problem of nonexistent objects, a nonrelational account must explain the directedness of mental acts.

But it is not only the problem of nonexistent objects that has moved philosophers to throw themselves upon the second horn of the dilemma. A relational account presupposes the ontological recognition of relations. One who rejects the existence of relations, for whatever metaphysical reason, cannot explicate intentionality in relational terms. Brentano, I think, could never shake off an Aristotelian prejudice against relations. His students Meinong and Husserl freed the theory of intentionality from the burden of this prejudice.

Recall the Cartesian mystery of how representation is possible without identity or similarity. The intentional nexus solves this mystery. An idea is neither identical with nor similar to its object. This is the Cartesian insight. Yet, it represents its object in that it intends it. This is the insight of Brentano and his students. For an idea to *represent* an object is to *have* that object; and to have an object, is to be related to it by means of the intentional nexus. You may think that this is no solution at all, but merely an invitation to accept the Cartesian mystery. And you are right, up to a point. We have here a situation quite common in philosophy. We have the question: How is such and such possible? And the answer seems to be nothing more enlightening than: Well, it just is! How is it possible for the body to interact with the mind? Well, it just does! We must take a closer look at the question in order to understand the true nature of the situation. The question really is: How is it possible for the body to interact causally with the mind, if such interaction must be thought of as taking place in space, and minds are not spatial? The answer is, not trivially that such interaction takes place as a matter of fact, but rather that it can take place *because* causal interaction must not be thought of as taking place necessarily in space. The mystery arises because of an assumption, and the answer claims that this assumption is false. Causal interaction must be understood not as spatial interaction, but as lawfulness. This is the enduring lesson of Hume's analysis.

In our case of intentionality, the mystery arises because it is similarly assumed that there are no other relations than similarity and (its limit) identity. The Cartesians were faced with a mystery because they could not conceive of any other relations between ideas and their objects than those of similarity and identity. What we have, therefore, is not just a stubborn insistence that ideas do represent their objects. There is philosophical progress. A fundamental philosophical prejudice has been destroyed. In the case of causality, what has been abandoned is the "push-pull model" of causality. In our present case, what has been removed is a pervasive prejudice against relations other than those of similarity and identity. It is not by chance that Brentano's students arrived simultaneously at a better understanding of the nature of intentionality and of the importance of relations. In order to accept a relation as peculiar as the intentional nexus, one must first acknowledge, cheerfully and without reservation, the existence of the category of relation.

It was another student of Brentano's, K. Twardowski, who introduced the by now familiar distinction between a mental *act,* its *content,* and its *object* (K.

Twardowski, *On the Content and Object of Presentations).* An act of presentation, for example, is a mental individual thing. It is not spatial, but it is temporal. This act has two important properties which I shall call "kind" and "content." It has, firstly, the property of being an act of representation; this is its kind. This property distinguishes it from acts of judgment, for example. An act of judgment would have the property of being a judgment. It would be of a different kind. It has, secondly, a content, that is, a property which determines its object. For example, the presentation of a certain tree is different from the presentation of a certain elephant. And this difference, according to the distinction under discussion, is not just an "external" difference between the objects, but is an "internal" difference between the two acts. The acts themselves are qualitatively different. Since it is possible for different kinds of acts to have the same object, there are all kinds of possible combinations. Someone may believe while someone else doubts that Mt. Everest is the highest mountain on earth. In this case, we have acts of different kinds, but with the same object and, hence, with the same content. Or it may be the case that someone believes that Mt. Everest is the highest mountain on earth, while someone else believes that Salzburg is the birthplace of Mozart. In this case, the two acts are of the same kind, but the contents differ and hence, the objects. And so on.

As one can see from these last examples, the term 'object' has to be taken in a wide sense. The object of a belief is not an individual thing, but a circumstance, a state of affairs. The kind of mental act which intends such states of affairs I shall call "propositional." One of the most important theses of this investigation is that perceptual acts are propositional. Acts of seeing, for example, intend states of affairs. The importance of this thesis will become clear when we discuss how we are acquainted with abstract entities, that is, with things which are neither spatial nor temporal.

A second point to note is this. The content of an act varies with its object, and conversely. Content and object determine each other. It is therefore the content, not the act as an individual thing, which stands in the intentional nexus to the object. The intentional nexus thus holds between a property of the act and the act's object. In the case of propositional mental acts, the intentional nexus obtains between a property and a state of affairs.

The so-called content of an act of presentation is, I believe, what some philosophers have called an "idea," a "concept," or a "notion." The idea of the moon, for example, as it is supposed to exist in the mind, is a certain property of all of those acts which are acts of presentation of the moon. Thus my idea of the moon is identically the same as yours, even though my act of presentation differs numerically from yours. It is clear that ideas must be distinguished from sensations. An idea is nothing "sensible." It does not have a color, a shape, or a size. The idea of an equilateral triangle, for example, is neither equilateral nor is it triangular. It has no shape at all. But the sensation which is under normal circumstances caused by the perception of an equilateral triangle has a shape. Our sensations may or may not resemble the things which cause them, our ideas never do. This, of course, is the heart of Descartes's contention that ideas represent without similarity. It is also the view which Berkeley attacks in the *Introduction* to the *Treatise.*

Both ideas and sensations must be further distinguished from images. Images, like sensations, can resemble what they are images of. They, like sensations, are individual things rather than properties. The mental image of an equilateral triangle, for example, has a shape. Ideas represent their objects because they intend them, even though they do not resemble them. Sensations do not represent anything, but they may resemble their causes. Images are like sensations in that they do not intend anything but resemble the things of which they are images. However, what makes an image of the Eiffel Tower into an image of the Eiffel Tower is not solely its resemblance to the Eiffel Tower, but a mental act of imagining or of remembering. When you imagine a mermaid, there occurs a certain kind of mental act as well as an image. It is this mental act of imagining which "connects" the image with some object; in this example, with a mermaid. In imagination, we imagine something by means of something else, the image. Imagining is a more complicated kind of mental act than, for example, believing or desiring. It resembles the two fundamental kinds of mental act that make language possible, namely, *meaning something by something* and *understanding something by something*. For example, we mean a certain shape by the word 'square' and a certain shade of color by the expression "olive green." In these two cases, the words (certain shapes or noises) correspond to the image, what is meant to what is imagined. In memory, too, the memory image gets its direction toward an object through a mental act, namely, an act of remembering.

So much for the important distinction between concepts (ideas), sensations, and images; a distinction that was often hidden under the blanket term "idea."

c) In the Footsteps of Brentano: Moore's Refutation of Idealism

According to Twardowski, the content of an act is *part* of the act, but its object is not. According to our analysis, the content is a *property* of the act, its object is not. While the object of a given mental act may or may not exist, the content always exists. If you conceive of Mt. Everest, then the object as well as the content of your conception exist. But if you conceive of the golden mountain, then only the content of your conception exists. Philosophers have said such things—and Brentano was one of them—as that Mt. Everest exists, not only in your mind, but also in reality, while the golden mountain only exists in your mind. In terms of the distinction between content and object, we can make sense of this kind of talk. There are really not two kinds of existence, existence in reality and existence in the mind. There is only one kind. The golden mountain does not exist, period. Only its idea exists.

Brentano speaks of the "immanent objectivity" of mental acts and of the "mental inexistence of objects" (Brentano, p. 88). When you conceive of the golden mountain, the golden mountain is the immanent object of your conception; it has mental inexistence. As we use these terms, an immanent object is a contradiction in terms. The object of an act is always extraneous to the act. What is immanent is the content.

The content of a mental act could not exist without the act, while its object does not depend on the act for its existence. Mt. Everest, for example, does not depend for its existence on your conceiving it. It would exist even if there were no mental acts at all; even if nobody had ever seen it or thought of it. But the idea of Mt. Everest would not exist if there had never been a mental act of which it is the content. This simple truth forms the basis of Moore's famous attempt to refute idealism (G. E. Moore, "The Refutation of Idealism," pp. 1–30). Moore distinguishes between the sensation blue (notice, not blue sensation!) and the awareness of this sensation. He argues that since the sensation blue is an object of the act of awareness and not a part of it, the sensation could exist without the awareness. In our words, since the sensation blue is the object of an awareness, not one of its properties, the existence of the sensation does not necessarily depend on the existence of the act. Berkeley's *esse est percipi* is therefore not necessarily true, and idealism has been refuted.

The first thing to notice is Moore's insistence that the idealist must treat the *esse est percipi* principle as a necessary truth. What kind of necessity is here involved? It is clear from Moore's argument that it must be ontological necessity. We may agree that it is a law of ontology that a property of mental acts can only exist if mental acts exist. It follows then that the sensation blue, if it is a property of mental acts, cannot exist unless the acts exist. It is then necessarily true that a sensation cannot exist unless it is experienced, that is, unless it is the property of an experience. By pointing out that the sensation blue is not a property of acts of experiencing, not a "content" of mental acts, but the object of such acts, Moore shows that the ontological law does not apply to sensations. He thus shows that one argument for the necessity of Berkeley's principle, as applied to sensations, is not sound.

But he does not show that this principle is false. And, indeed, I think that the principle is true for sensations, not as a matter of some kind of necessity, but simply as a matter of fact. Sensations occur only "in minds", they do not float around all by themselves. But to occur "in a mind" is the same as to be experienced. This, as we shall see, follows from our conception of what a mind is. Therefore, there are no sensations which are not experienced. And if Berkeley were correct in claiming that perceptual objects are nothing but bundles of sensations, then the idealist's conclusion that such objects cannot exist unperceived would indeed follow. This shows, I think, that Moore's main argument hardly touches on the issues. The important question is not whether Berkeley's principle is necessarily true for sensations, but whether it is true. Moore merely shows, if he shows that much, that unsensed sensations are ontologically possible, not that there are any.

But it should also be obvious that the truly important question is not even the question of whether or not there are unsensed sensations, but whether or not there are perceptual objects. The question is not whether or not a blue sensation can exist when it is not experienced, but whether or not there are apples. Only if we identify apples with bundles of sensations, as Berkeley does, do the two separate issues get conjoined. And it is precisely this identification which the realist must reject. For the realist, sensations are mental and do not exist unsensed, while perceptual objects are not mental and can exist unperceived. When Berkeley identifies perceptual objects with bundles of sensations, he invites the obvious objection that this identification must be mistaken because an apple can exist unperceived, while a bundle of sensations cannot exist unsensed. I think that this objection is the most decisive refutation of Berkeley's idealism. I also think that Berkeley was quite aware of the force of this reply, but could not think of a way to avoid it. Be that as it may, it is somewhat ironic that Moore's refutation of idealism threatens to disarm our most telling objection to Berkeley. If Moore holds that sensations actually exist unsensed, then we can no longer argue that they are in this respect quite different from perceptual objects and hence cannot be identified with them.

At the end of his paper, Moore claims to have shown that there is no question of how we are to get outside the circle of our own ideas and sensations. "Merely to have a sensation," he says, "is already to *be* outside that circle. It is to know something which is as truly and really *not* a part of *my* experience, as anything I can ever know" (Moore, 1970a, p. 29). His claim is of course only true if he means by "ideas and sensations," not Berkeley's ideas, but mental acts of having ideas and sensing sensations. To sense a sensation, we can agree, is to "transcend" the sensing toward the sensation. But with this meaning, a Berkeleyan can be perfectly comfortable. He claims that we do not get outside the circle of Berkeleyan ideas, that is, of sensations; and Moore has done nothing to refute this claim. The important question is: How do we get outside the circle of mental things to the perceptual objects? Moore turns to this question in the very last paragraph of his paper. There he maintains that we make contact with perceptual objects by means of the same peculiar relation of awareness through which we are acquainted with sensations. Berkeley is mistaken when he claims that we can be directly aware only of our own ideas. And then Moore states: "The question requiring to be asked about material things is thus not: What reason have we for supposing that anything exists *corresponding* to our sensations? but: What reason have we for supposing that material things do *not* exist, since *their* existence has precisely the same evidence as that of our sensations?" (Moore, 1970a, p. 30).

This may not be a refutation of idealism, but it is a step toward realism. Our acquaintance with perceptual objects, Moore tells us, is as *direct* as our acquaintance with sensations. It is not mediated by sensations. This takes care of the skeptical devil. Furthermore, material things in space are sharply distinguished from sensations; the former do not consist of the latter. This takes care of the idealistic deep blue sea. After such a splendid beginning, we may wonder, why does Moore so desperately try in later papers to stick sensations to the surfaces of perceptual objects? Was it because he could not see his way clear to defend this sort of realism? Was it because he never really believed in it in the first place? We only know that in the end he frankly admitted that although he believed in realism, he did not know how to defend it. My essay is an attempt to succeed where Moore and many others have failed. I follow in Moore's footsteps, trying to show that they lead eventually to a solid realism that can be defended against all skeptical and idealistic objections.

B. Systematic Considerations

The Argument from Physics

a) An Outline of the Argument

Idealism and its contemporary version, phenomenalism, has two main sources. I have already identified one of these, namely, the distinction between primary and secondary qualities. This division, I pointed out, rests on the argument from physics. But there is also a second source which I have not as yet mentioned and which deserves a chapter of its own. This is the argument from hallucination. The present chapter deals with the argument from physics; the next one, with the argument from hallucination. Finally, there is the principle of immanence which threatens the theory of knowledge with skepticism. It is the basic premise of the argument from the relativity of sensing. In the third chapter of this section, we shall discuss this argument. But an analysis of the principle of immanence will have to wait until we turn to the second main part of this book, namely, to our knowledge of the mind.

The three important arguments just mentioned combine and reinforce each other in strange ways, so as to render succor at times to idealism, at times to skepticism, and at times to both. And whenever one of them seems too weak to destroy realism, another one will jump into the breach.

Modern physics, so it has seemed to many philosophers from Galileo through Descartes to Kant, Sellars, and Armstrong, has chased such perceptual properties as colors, shapes, odors, etc. from the "external" world. This seems to leave us only with two possibilities: Either these properties merely exist in the mind, or else they exist nowhere, that is, they do not exist at all. Berkeley, we saw, opts for the first possibility; Brentano, I have maintained, accepts the second. But to hold that there are no colors, neither in the external world nor in the mind, is, not to present a philosophical position that can be discussed, but to violate common sense to such a degree that argument is made impossible. As Moore used to emphasize, what premises could one possibly hope to share with a philosopher who holds that there are no colors, no shapes, no odors? Philosophical views that deny the common ground from which all disputes must start are not merely false, but are absurd. The view that there are no colors, whether held by Brentano or by Goodman, is absurd (see N. Goodman, "Predicates without Properties").

Berkeley's view, on the other hand, is not absurd in this sense, but merely false. Color is indeed in the mind, that is, it is indeed a property of mental sensations. But Berkeley denies, and this is where he goes wrong, that there are apples in the nonmental world which are green. He denies that the color has an existence "outside of the mind." We need not be misled by the spatial metaphor. Berkeley denies that there are apples as mind-independent perceptual objects. And it is precisely this proposition which a stout-hearted realist must defend. How, then, does physics undermine this proposition?

Things have not changed very much philosophically from the days of Galileo to the days of Gell-Man. Atoms, one used to say, have figure, number, size, and they are in motion or at rest. But they have no color, no odor, etc. Elementary particles (or else quarks, psy-functions, or what-have-you) we now believe, have a number of esoteric qualities like mass, spin, electric charge, etc. But they are still not colored. What these ultimate building blocks of the universe are, and what properties they have, it must be conceded at once, is a matter for the physicist to discover. Philosophical speculation is out of place. Thus I shall not, even for a moment, lock horns with the physicist by claiming that elementary particles are colored. No, elementary particles do have the properties that the physicists have discovered; and color is not among them. But we also insist on, and shall not move one inch away from, the common-sense truth that the perceptual objects around us are colored. Berkeley's apple is truly green. And we shall rebuff even the most sophisticated attempt by the most famous physicist to convince us otherwise. Apples are green, and no theory proves that they are not. The argument from physics, however, tries. It starts from the true premise that elementary particles are not colored and concludes mistakenly that apples cannot be colored. Obviously, there must be hidden premises. What are they?

Well, since elementary particles are not colored, and since apples *consist* of elementary particles, apples cannot be colored either. We must assume, in order to keep the argument going, that perceptual objects ultimately consist of elementary particles. This premise is as unobjectionable as the first premise. But it obviously does not suffice to get to the conclusion. Some kind of principle is needed to the effect that things have only those properties which their constituents (parts) have. Let us call a principle of this sort "a principle of reduction." The idea is that the properties of complex things (of wholes, of structures) are somehow "reduced" to the properties of their constituents.

b) The Principle of Reduction

Sellars, who has devoted much time to this topic, formulates a principle of reduction in this manner: "If an object is *in a strict sense* a system of objects, then every property of the object must consist in the fact that its constituents have such and such qualities and stand in such and such relations or, roughly, every property of a system of objects consists of properties of, and relations between, its constituents" (W. Sellars, *Science, Perception and Reality,* Routledge and Kegan Paul, London, p. 27. See also his later "The Structure of Knowledge," pp. 298–300).

Notice that Sellars speaks of an object which is "in a strict sense" a system of objects. He implies that the principle is only true for certain systems of objects. A certain structure, consisting of pieces of wood, for example, is a ladder, even though none of its parts is a ladder, as he points out. A ladder, a car, or a typewriter is in the strict sense a system of objects, and that is why the property of being a ladder is reducible. Being a ladder, he says, "is [being] made up of being cylindrical (the rungs), rectangular (the frame), wooden, etc." (Sellars, 1963, p. 26). What Sellars is driving at, I think, is that being a ladder is a *complex property*. He seems to be reasoning that the ladder can have the complex property of being a ladder, even though none of its parts is a ladder, because the complex property of being a ladder is not really anything in addition to the properties of which it consists. Notice that Sellars slips when he lists the properties of which "being a ladder" is made up of: He mentions being cylindrical and rectangular; but these are properties, not of the ladder, but of parts of the ladder. What we want are properties of which the complex property of being a ladder consists, and these must be properties of the ladder. Let us therefore change the example and talk about Berkeley's apple. Oscar, we shall assume, is green and round. Let us introduce the expression 'ground' as an abbreviation for the longer 'green and round'. We can then say that the sentence 'Oscar is ground' means nothing more nor less than that Oscar is green and round. The "property" ground, one can claim, is defined in terms of the two properties green and round. I put 'property' in quotes because, strictly speaking, there is no such property. There is only the word 'ground'. What there is in the way of property are the two properties green and round. Similarly for the word 'ladder'. I interpret Sellars to mean that there really is no such property as that of being a ladder; there is only the word 'ladder'. What there are, in reality, are certain wooden parts, their properties, and the relations among them. To say that this is a ladder is then merely a short way of saying something quite complicated about those wooden parts, their properties, and their relations.

What about the property of being olive green? If we apply Sellars's principle of reduction to this property, we come to the conclusion that there really is no such color shade "out there." What there is instead are the various properties of and relations among the ultimate constituents of olive green perceptual objects. There are no colors "out there" because colored objects are in a strict sense systems of elementary particles, and such systems have no properties of their own. Color words are mere abbreviations for complicated expressions describing properties of and relations among elementary particles.

How plausible is this view? Not very. It is obvious to me that the word for a color shade is not an abbreviation of this sort; it is not an abbreviation in the sense in which 'ground' is an abbreviation for 'green and round'. How, otherwise, could Caesar have asked for *green* olives in his diet? No, 'olive green' is an expression for a certain color shade and not an expression that describes the properties of and relations among elementary particles. Sellars agrees with this conclusion. But he arrives at a different lesson. A color shade, he argues, unlike the property of being a ladder, cannot be a complex property: "Pink does not seem to be made up of imperceptible qualities in the way in which being a ladder is made up of being cylindrical (the rungs), rectangular (the frame), wooden, etc." (Sellars, 1963, p. 26). Since it is not a complex property, the pink ice cube cannot be in a strict sense a system of elementary particles. Thus there is a clash between what Sellars calls the "scientific image," according to which "out there" are elementary particles without colors, and the "manifest image," according to which "out there" are pink ice cubes. I see no clash (cf. my "Perceptual Objects, Elementary Particles, and Emergent Properties"). The ice cube of the manifest image *is identical with* the complicated structure of elementary particles of the scientific image. And the ice cube is truly and literally pink, even though its ultimate constituents have no color. It is simply not true, as Sellars assumes, that complicated structures of elementary particles can have no properties of their own.

What the argument from physics shows, from our perspective, is that the principle of reduction is false: Structures (wholes) have many properties which their parts do not have, and which cannot be reduced, in the precise way described earlier, to the properties and relations of their constituents.

c) Laws and the Complaisant "Identification" of Properties

There is no such property as ground; there are only the two properties of green and round. In Sellars's example, there is no such property as that of being a ladder; there are only the properties of and relations among the parts of the ladder. The word "ground" is a mere linguistic convenience, according to Sellars's view; and so is the word 'ladder'. The case is clear for 'ground'. I do not think that it is obvious for 'ladder', but I shall not argue. As far as color is concerned, the view is obviously false. There are colors and not just color words. But we must be very careful at this point and must keep apart two quite different notions of reduction or definition. There is, on the one hand, the notion of reduction just discussed, according to which a property is reduced to other properties, if it can be shown that only these other properties exist. But there is, on the other hand, also the notion that a property is reduced to other properties, if its occurrence can be deduced from these other properties and certain laws. A property that cannot be reduced in this sense of the term is often called an "emergent property." The following quotation gives a precise form to this notion of reduction: "the occurrence of a characteristic W in an object w is emergent relative to a theory T, a part relation Pt, and a class G of attributes, if that occurrence cannot be deduced by means of T from a characterization of the Pt-parts of w with respect to all the attributes in G" (C. G. Hempel and P. Oppenheim, "Studies in the Logic of Explanation", p. 336).

According to this criterion, the color of the ice cube as well as the color of Berkeley's apple are not emergent properties, for their occurrence can be deduced from certain laws of physics. Roughly, a surface has a certain color if and only if its atomic structure is in a certain state. It should be perfectly obvious, but apparently is not, that to claim that colors are or are not emergent is not the same as to claim that colors exist or do not exist. What sense could it possibly make to assert in one and the same breath that the occurrence of property P is lawfully connected with the occurrence of properties Q and R, but that there really is no such property as P? The lawful connection between properties presupposes the existence of the properties so connected.

Yet, the discovery of the laws which connect the colors of surfaces with the states of the atoms which form the surfaces has led many scientists and quite a few philosophers to say such things as that "out there, in the physical world, there are no colors at all." But is it not perfectly obvious that the inference from

(1) A surface has color C if and only if its atomic structure is in state S

to (2) C does not exist; only the state of the atomic structure does,

is invalid? This version of the argument from physics, too, must somehow fill the gap between (1) and (2) with plausible premises. And since I do not believe that this can be done, I have maintained that the argument is not sound.

It is customary among many contemporary philosophers to say that what the physicist has discovered is that the color of the surface, C, is *identical with* a certain physical property, P, of the (constituents of) the surface. But the physicist has *discovered* no such thing. What he found out is, rather, that the surface has the property C *if and only if* it has P. Since this issue has played such an important role in the philosophy of science—it is at the heart of the dispute over materialism—I shall pedantically ask, firstly: Can you distinguish between a state of affairs of the form:

Property P is the same as property Q

and a state of affairs of the form:

Property P occurs if and only if property Q occurs?

For example, if every green thing in the universe were round, and conversely, would it not be the case that whenever something is green it is round, and conversely, without it being the case that the color is the same as the shape? If you profess not to be able to distinguish between these two states of affairs, then I must confess that I do not know how to proceed. But if you grant the distinction, then I assert, secondly, that what the scientist discovered is a fact of the second kind, an equivalence. He may have looked at a certain surface, determined its color with the naked eye, and then measured the physical state of the surface; to the color pink, for example, he may have discovered in this fashion, corresponds a certain state S_1, while to the color olive green, there corresponds a different state S_2. What the physicist definitely did not do was to compare the properties of the color and of the state in order to determine whether or not they are the same, as one would have to if one were to ask whether the color is the same as the state. The physicist did not try to determine whether or not the state of the surface can be more or less saturated like a corresponding color. No physicist, I believe, unless he has a philosophical ax to grind, seriously contemplates the possibility that the states he studies are the same as the colors he sees. His situation is quite different from the situation of an astronomer who tries to find out whether a certain heavenly body, observed at a certain place at a certain time, is the very same as a body observed at a different place at a different time. This astronomer *would* ask whether or not the "two" bodies have the same properties, including the same spatio-temporal ones.

I conclude that the physicist discovered that there is a certain lawful connection between the occurrence of colors, on the one hand, and the occurrence of certain atomic states, on the other. Now, it has been claimed, for example by Armstrong, that the discovery of such a law is a prima facie case both for the identity of colors and states and for their equivalence. Both possibilities are open, so to speak. Not really: The second alternative is not a mere possibility, but a fact. We know that colors and states are equivalent. We also know that this equivalence does not preclude the possibility of their identity. But is there any reason to suppose that the identity is more than a logical possibility? Is there any reason at all? It seems to me that, quite to the contrary, there is conclusive evidence that colors are not states, for colors have many properties which states do not have, and conversely. Surely, it is disingenuous at this point to reply: "But if colors are states, then they do have all their properties in common." It is as disingenuous as is the reply, when the identity of elephants and mice is at stake, that if elephants are mice, then an appetite for peanuts simply is an appetite for cheese.

The "physicalist," as I shall call my opponent, usually "identifies" the colors with the states. He is hell-bent on getting rid of colors, by hook or by crook, that is, by argument or by decree. What is his motive? Before I try to answer this question, one thing needs to be emphasized. Physicalists often claim to have "theoretical-scientific" objections to positions like mine. They presume to speak in the name of science against my philosophical, allegedly antiscientific, view. Nothing could be further from the truth. I warmly embrace the scientific spirit as well as the scientific method. I see no conflict between science and my way of doing philosophy. Nor do I feel any animosity toward the successes of science, an animosity that has sometimes been expressed by an "identification" of science with technology. I therefore know that my opponent's view rests neither on superior scientific knowledge nor on a deeper admiration for science. It seems to rest, rather, on a metaphysical urge, an urge that is cloaked in the mantle of science. It rests on the urge to be rid of mind and all that goes with it; for what goes with it are colors and all the other "secondary qualities."

Is it not in perfect harmony with both common sense and physics to say, as I do, that surfaces have colors and that they have these colors because they consist of atoms which are in certain states? I have been told by Armstrong that philosophers like J. J. C. Smart object to my view by claiming how "badly such laws sit with the fundamental laws of physics, which seem likely to be *the* laws of natural science" (letter from Armstrong). "The laws Grossmann wants to postulate," Armstrong writes, "would be a sore thumb on the corpus of science, nomological danglers as Herbert Feigl put it. The natural solution for the scientifically minded . . . is that the equivalence marks not a law, but an identity. The perceived color *is* the atomic structure" (letter from Armstrong). But I do not *postulate* any laws. I merely accept, in the scientific spirit, the laws which the scientist *discovers*. It is the physicist, not the philosopher or the common man, who discovered these fascinating laws. And it is philosophers like Smart, Feigl, and Armstrong who misuse the physicist's discovery in order to justify a strictly *metaphysical* move, namely, the "identification" of colors with states. It cannot be repeated often enough that what motivates these and other philosophers is not a defense of science against metaphysical speculations, but a metaphysical conviction of their own, a conviction so deep that science cannot reach it.

What about the objection that the equivalence sits badly with the fundamental laws of physics; that it is a nomological dangler? Call it what you wish, dislike it as much as you want to, the fact remains that laws like this are scientific achievements of the highest order. They are shining jewels in the crown of science. For they explain to us the world around us, the world in which we live every minute of every hour of every day, with all its wonders and puzzles, all its delights and horrors. They explain to us why the perceptual world is what it is in terms of its underlying structure. Of course, these laws are not *the* laws of physics. They are not laws about elementary particles. But it would be an argument with a very tight circle if one were to reason that laws other than *the* laws of physics are unacceptable, and that they are unacceptable because they are not *the* laws of physics. Or have we here another metaphysical belief of the physicalist, namely, the belief that there can be no laws other than *the* laws of physics?

Finally, would it not be *simpler* just to go ahead and "identify" the colors with the states? Well, the world is as complicated as it is, and to make it simpler than it is, is to misconceive it. Simplicity alone counts for nothing. Otherwise, we may as well identify everything with everything else and be content with contemplating the absolute. The question is not one of simplicity, but one of truth: Are colors the same as atomic states? I argued that the answer is negative. As I see the dialectic, this is not an open question to be decided by considerations of simplicity. The fact is that colors are not atomic states. And this fact points at another facet of the dialectic. If the "scientific minded" physicalist were really scientific minded, he would try to show, in the true scientific spirit, that colors are the same as atomic states in the only way in which we can ever show that a thing A is the same as a thing B, namely, by showing that colors have the same properties and stand in the same relations as states. At the very least, he would ask his physicist friends to do the job for him. But of course he does neither. Instead of rolling up his sleeves and tackling the task of proving that his hunch is correct, that colors really are atomic states, he keeps on talking about "identifying" the two. Astronomers, by contrast, truly scientific minded as they are, did not just talk about "identifying" the morning star with the evening star. They found out that the two heavenly bodies are the same by discovering that the morning star has the same properties and spatio-temporal relations as the evening star.

Berkeley's apple is green. Nothing in modern physics proves otherwise. That it cannot be green follows neither from the fact that elementary particles are colorless nor from the fact that its surface is in a certain atomic state. It does not follow from the former, because the principle of reduction is false. It does not follow from the latter, because colors are not atomic states. Does it not make sense to adopt our view which so effortlessly combines common sense with the latest discoveries of physics? Must one go on to insist that there is a clash between common sense and physics, not for scientific reasons, but from metaphysical motives?

■

The Argument from Hallucination

a) An Outline of the Argument

The argument from hallucination is supposed to show that we never see perceptual objects but see only sensations (sense-impressions). This conclusion is so obviously false that we know that the argument cannot possibly be sound. The value of the argument consists, in my opinion, in the fact that it highlights a very important ontological puzzle. As an argument for idealism or phenomenalism, it is doomed from the start.

The argument has two parts. The conclusion of the first part is that in a hallucination, a person sees sensations rather than perceptual objects. Let us follow Ayer's formulation of the argument for the details (A. J. Ayer, *The Problem of Knowledge,* pp. 98-99). Macbeth had a hallucination in which he saw a dagger. But, of course, there was no dagger before him. Since there was no dagger in front of him, he could not really have seen one. So, what did he see? Ayer answers: "if we are to say that he saw anything, it must have been something that was accessible to him alone, something that existed only so long as this particular experience lasted; in short, a sense-datum." What we see in hallucinations, therefore, are sense-impressions.

In the second part of the argument, we are supposed to be convinced that what is true for hallucinations holds for all perceptual situations: In all perceptual situations, we perceive sense-impressions. The crucial premise is that ordinary perceptual situations do not differ phenomenally from hallucinations and must, therefore, yield under analysis the same ingredients. It follows presumably from this assumption that even in normal situations, we perceive nothing but sense-impressions. For example, when you see a dagger before you on the table, you, just like Macbeth, are seeing not a perceptual object, but merely a visual sensation. What we consider to be a real dagger, in distinction to Macbeth's imaginary one, is therefore really a sense-impression (or a bundle or family of sense-impressions).

It is clear that the phenomenalist who accepts this argument faces the same urgent problem as Berkeley: If the real dagger is just another sense-impression, how *does* veridical perception differ from hallucination? And the only half-way plausible answer is Berkeley's answer: These two kinds of situation can only differ in the degrees of their coherence. But this answer is quite obviously false. We know that in the case of veridical perception there is a dagger in front of you on the table, while in the hallucination there is no dagger before you. And this proves again that the argument from hallucination cannot possibly be sound.

There can be no doubt that Macbeth sees a dagger. There can be no doubt that he experiences an act of seeing a dagger. And there can also be no doubt that there is no dagger before him to be seen. The first part of the argument from hallucination challenges us to resolve this apparent contradiction. The proponent of the argument resolves it by claiming that the act of seeing does indeed have an object, but that that object is not a dagger. It is true, so he reasons, that Macbeth sees something. But it is also true that what he sees is not a dagger. What is it? It is a sense-impression (or a family of sense-impressions). From our point of view, quite independently of the rest of the argument, this conclusion is an absurdity. According to our view, one can no more see a sense-impression than one can see a pain. And what holds for seeing, holds for perception in general: One can only perceive perceptual objects, never sensations. What Macbeth sees, therefore, cannot possibly be a sense-impression. Does he then see a perceptual object? In one sense he does, in another, he does not. But there is no mystery. Since we do not want to mislead someone who does not know the story, we cannot just say that he saw a dagger and let it go at that. There was no dagger; Macbeth had a hallucination. But there occurred a seeing of a dagger and not, for example, an experience of a shrill auditory sensation or the seeing of a pink rat. How, precisely, we make clear to someone that even though there occurred the seeing of a dagger, there was no dagger before Macbeth, depends on the situation. What is important is the fact that we all know that Macbeth could have seen a dagger, even when there was no dagger. We know that one can see a dagger when there is none to be seen. We know that this kind of experience can occur. But does not our insistence that Macbeth experienced an act of seeing imply that some object or other must have been seen, even though this object cannot be a dagger? No, it does not! A mental act of seeing can occur, even when its object does not exist. "It is only if we artificially combine the decision to say that the victim of a hallucination is seeing something," Ayer correctly observes, "with the ruling that what is seen must exist, that we secure the introduction of sense-data" (Ayer, 1956, p. 99).

From the first part of the argument we learn the profound lesson that even though every mental act has an object, not all of these objects exist. Macbeth sees something, a dagger. His act of seeing, we say, has an object. But this object does not exist. There is no dagger in front of him. Could anything be plainer than that *what* he sees, the object of his seeing, does not exist? Is it not a mere truism that what we see on certain occasions is not there; that what we believe is sometimes not the case; that what we desire often does not come to pass? The proponent of the argument from hallucination denies these truisms.

According to our analysis, there occurs a mental act of seeing a dagger, but there is no dagger. What about a veridical situation? Well, in this case, too, there is the seeing of a dagger. The person in this situation experiences a mental act of seeing a dagger, just as Macbeth does. But now there also exists a dagger. The two situations, we may say, agree phenomenally but differ ontologically. If we describe the two minds, there is no difference. But the two perceptual situations consist not only of a mind: There is also extra-mental reality to be considered. And in regard to this reality, the two situations differ as day differs from night. In the one case, there is no dagger; in the other, there is one.

What gives strength to the argument from hallucination is the contention of its first part that Macbeth must be seeing sense-impressions, since there is no dagger to be seen. We have exposed the hidden premise of this line of reasoning, namely, the assumption that the objects of mental acts must exist. Put differently, the assumption is that acts cannot have nonexistent objects. But we cannot let matters rest by denying this assumption. There is more to the story of nonexistent objects. We have to face a genuine ontological dilemma.

b) The Nexus of Intentionality

There are at least two distinct reasons why it has been held that the objects of mental acts always exist; one profound, the other rather shallow. The shallow one is that we would not tell an unsuspecting person that Macbeth saw a dagger when he merely hallucinated. From the fact that we would mislead a person by telling him that Macbeth saw a dagger when he had a hallucination, one somehow concludes that Macbeth could not really have seen a dagger, but must have *thought that he saw a dagger*. It does not take a great amount of ingenuity to untangle this small problem of communication. We merely have to tell the third person that Macbeth had a hallucination, that *what he saw* did not exist. That he saw something is then quite obvious to the third person.

The profound reason goes back to the proper analysis of the nature of intentionality. This analysis presents us with two tough dilemmas. When you see a real dagger before you, then you are somehow related to the dagger; when you believe that the earth is round, you are related to this fact; and when you are afraid of spiders, you are related in some fashion to spiders. There is a very strong suggestion that the intentionality of mental acts is relational in character. All mental acts, one may conclude, are somehow related to their objects. Brentano's thesis of intentionality, the thesis that every mental act *has* an object, is but the thesis that every mental act is *related* to an object. Let us call this peculiar relation "the intentional nexus." However, this obvious analysis of the nature of intentionality runs immediately into the problem of nonexisting objects. How can there possibly obtain a relation between Macbeth's act of seeing, on the one hand, and a dagger, on the other, if there is no dagger that can serve as the second term of the relation? How can there be a relation between a mental act and something that does not exist? Is not a relation between an existent, the act, and something that is not there at all, the object, an ontological absurdity? These rhetorical questions arise from the conviction that a relation cannot have nonexistent terms.

But if it is a law of ontology that all relations have existent terms, then we must search for a nonrelational account of intentionality. It will not do to say, as some philosophers have, that the intentional nexus holds in veridical perception, but not in Macbeth's case. This would not be an account of the feature of intentionality with which we are concerned. Macbeth's seeing has an object in the very same sense in which a veridical seeing has an object. In the relevant sense, every act has an object. Every seeing is a seeing of something; every belief is a belief in something; and every desire is a desire for something. Our task is to make ontological sense of this common feature of all acts. What other possibility is there? I do not believe that any account other than the relational one is plausible. But I cannot show this here (see my *The Categorial Structure of the World,* pp. 189–203; and also my "Nonexistent Objects Versus Definite Descriptions," pp. 363–77). I shall mention, though, that I am convinced that a nonrelational analysis of intentionality must lead to solipsism. If the mind is not related in some fashion or other to the world, then it cannot know the world. Nor, it seems to me, can it even know itself unless it is so related to itself. Here then is the first of the two dilemmas I mentioned earlier, a dilemma as threatening as any I know of: A relational assay of intentionality confronts us with the problem of nonexistent objects, while a nonrelational one leads to solipsism.

I embrace the first horn of this dilemma. Thus I have to face the problem of nonexistent objects. What is at stake, we have already seen, is the truth of the ontological hypothesis that all relations, including the intentional nexus, have existing terms, that all relations are "normal." Now, this hypothesis is either true or it is false. If we accept a relational analysis of intentionality, we are therefore faced with a second dilemma. If we assume it to be false, as I do, then we must admit that there are "abnormal" relations, relations which can connect existents with nonexistents. On the other hand, if we accept the hypothesis, then we have to say that Macbeth's hallucinatory dagger, all appearance to the contrary, really exists. Since I cannot bring myself to believe that hallucinatory objects exist, I prefer to be impaled by the first horn of the dilemma: I must reject the alleged law about relations. I hold that the intentional nexus is different from ordinary, "normal," relations. Spatial, temporal, and other relations are normal: They hold only between existents. If A is to the left of B, then both A and B exist. If A occurs later than B, then both A and B exist (but not, of course, at the same time). And if A is the father of B, then both A and B exist. But when Macbeth sees the dagger, then only his seeing exists, the dagger does not. More precisely, since I hold that all perception is propositional, when Macbeth sees that there is a bloody dagger dangling in front of him, then his act of seeing exists, the state of affairs seen, however, does not exist.

The great strength of the argument from hallucination derives from its hidden premise that there are no abnormal relations and, in particular, that the intentional nexus is not abnormal. Macbeth sees something. There can be no doubt about this point. What he apparently sees, a dagger, does not exist. There can be no doubt about this point either. Since his act of seeing is related to its object by a normal relation, it must have an existing object, and what could that possibly be under the circumstances except a bundle of sense-impressions? In this situation, what else exists and is "private"?

One may try to rob the argument of its force by inventing a diluted kind of being. Macbeth, one might argue, does not see a bundle of sense-impression, but sees a dagger. However, this dagger, though it does not exist, has being of a lesser sort. It is not just nothing. Since the dagger has some sort of being, the intentional nexus is not "abnormal." It holds between two beings. We seem to have escaped from both horns of the dilemma: We have to hold neither that the intentional nexus is abnormal nor that what Macbeth sees is a bundle of sensations. But this impression is mistaken. It is created by a semantic trick. An abnormal relation, we must recall, is a relation which does not connect existents. The intentional nexus between Macbeth's act of seeing and the dagger with diluted being is therefore not normal but abnormal. The view under discussion does not escape from the fate of having to assume the existence of an abnormal relation. It merely tries to hide the weirdness of the intentional nexus by the purely gratuitous introduction of a new kind of being.

We can see what is not there and believe what is not so. These are the facts. The argument from hallucination, we have seen, denies these facts. We accept them. But we have also seen that a difficult dilemma may force one to take the other side. Common sense triumphs in the end, but not without having paid some respect to philosophical sophistication.

c) Nonexistent Perceptual Objects

Perceptual acts are propositional. This is one of the most important theses of my view. Precisely speaking, when Macbeth sees the hallucinatory dagger, there occurs an act which intends some such *state of affairs* as: This is a bloody dagger. It is true, of course, that Macbeth sees a dagger. I am not trying to deny this truism. But I wish to insist that he sees a dagger because he sees *that* there is a dagger in front of him or *that* this is a dagger. It is true that Johnny sees an elephant when Johnny sees, for example, that an elephant is balancing himself on his hindlegs, or that an elephant is entering the ring, or that an elephant is splashing water over his back. What holds in this sense for seeing, holds in my opinion for all acts of perception.

I could have said that all perceptual acts are judgments. But this would have been misleading. A judgment, one usually explains, is something that can be true or false. A mere "presentation" (idea, notion, concept), on the other hand, cannot be true or false. And neither can a wish or a desire, even though these mental acts are propositional. But a perception is either true or it is false. When Macbeth sees that there is a dagger in front of him, he is mistaken. There is no dagger before him. And when Johnny sees that the elephant is balancing on his two hindlegs, his perception is correct. Yet, a perception is not a judgment, although they share this feature of being true or false. Perceptions and judgments form two distinct kinds of mental act. When you see that the elephant is eating peanuts, you experience a mental act which is totally different from the one you experience when you merely think (judge) that he is eating peanuts.

It is important to emphasize this difference because it has often been held that a perception is nothing but a judgment which is based on sensations (sense-impressions). The difference between seeing the elephant eat peanuts and merely thinking about it is not just that in the first case there occur certain visual sensations which are absent in the second situation. No, the crucial mental acts are different in the two situations: In one situation, there occurs an act of seeing, and in the other, an act of judging (asserting, assuming, etc.). We have already pointed out how the mistaken view that perception consists of sensations plus judgment invites skepticism. We can now understand why it has been so popular. Since perception is propositional and, moreover, true or false, it is easily confused with judgment. But it is also clear that perception somehow involves the senses. Perception, one erroneously concludes, consists both of judgment and the experience of sensations.

Macbeth sees a dagger when there is no dagger in front of him. What he sees is not so, it is not the case, he is mistaken. Put philosophically, the state of affairs which his act of seeing intends is not a fact. In general, a perceived state of affairs may or may not be a fact. Let us say, equivalently, that it may or may not exist. The intentional nexus is abnormal, as I put it earlier, in that the perceived state of affairs may not exist. The "object" intended, a certain state of affairs, may not exist. When we first talked about Macbeth's hallucination, though, we called the dagger the nonexistent object of his seeing. We must keep these two notions of object apart. In one meaning, the object of a mental act is whatever is intended by the act; whatever the intentional nexus connects with the act. In perception, this object is always a state of affairs. But this object, the state of affairs, may involve a perceptual object. In the case of Macbeth's hallucination, this second object is of course the dagger. In his case, the state of affairs seen does not exist, and neither does the object seen. The dagger does not exist, because the state of affairs seen, that this is a dagger or that there is a dagger, does not exist. The elephant, on the other hand, exists because what Johnny sees is a fact: There is an elephant balancing on two legs.

These considerations lead us to distinguish between hallucination and mere illusion. In Macbeth's case, there was nothing in front of him at all at the place where he saw the dagger. But assume that he had mistaken a candle for a dagger. He thinks he sees a dagger in front of him when in reality there is a candle at that place. In this case, too, his perception is mistaken. But it is mistaken, not because there is nothing in front of him where he sees a dagger, but because he mistakes something that is in front of him for a dagger. A perception that this is a dagger can be false either because this is not a dagger but something else, or because there is nothing there at all. The state of affairs *This is a dagger* may not be a fact, either because this is *not* a dagger, or else because there is no *this* at all. In the former case, one usually speaks of an illusion; in the latter, of a hallucination.

And this brings us back to the argument from hallucination. It is claimed that there really is a *this* which Macbeth sees, and that this *this* is a sense-impression. But Macbeth is mistaken, for he believes that this sense-impression is a dagger. What he sees, therefore, is in a sense there, and, in another sense, not there. The sense-impression exists; the dagger does not. According to this analysis, Macbeth's hallucination is more like an illusion, as we have explained it. But notice that this analysis does not fully escape from the problem of nonexistent objects. Macbeth comes to believe, mistakenly, *that this is a dagger* when in reality it is a sense-impression. (Have we here one of the sources of the popular philosophical view that perception is nothing but acquired belief?) Now, what does this act of believing intend? Obviously, the nonexistent state of affairs that this is a dagger. In this case, the intentional nexus connects a belief with a state of affairs which does not obtain, which is not the case, or, in short, which does not exist. Thus one cannot escape from the problem of nonexistent objects as long as one admits that there are false beliefs, false assertions, false judgments or, given our conception of perception, that there are false perceptions.

We insist, as I have said before, that sensations (sense-impressions) cannot be seen. Macbeth cannot possibly be *seeing* a sense-impression when he hallucinates the dagger. Of course, at that moment, he *experiences* a certain sensation of a certain shape, size, and color. And he probably experiences also a great number of other sensations. But what he experiences, in our sense of the term, is not what he sees; and what he sees is not what he experiences. Neither in veridical perception nor in hallucination do we ever see sensations.

What one perceives may not be so; what one perceives may not be there. Perception raises the same problem as false belief: How can the mind be related to what is not the case? But it also raises an additional problem. How can the mind be related to things that do not exist? In perception, something is directly given to us; something appears in person before us, so to speak. This makes perception quite different from mere belief or mere assumption. You cannot, precisely speaking, believe that *this* is a dagger. You can only see it. But you can believe, for example, that *there is a dagger* before you. Individual perceptual objects appear only in perception directly, in person, before us. What cases of hallucination teach us is that even though individual things may be directly presented to us in perception, these things may not exist.

The Argument from the Relativity of Sensing

a) An Analysis of the Argument

The argument from the relativity of sensing is one of the most convincing arguments in the history of philosophy. From Locke to Meinong and Husserl, from Berkeley to Russell and Moore, no philosopher has been able to resist its spell. Reid, as we have seen, tried to resist, but even he succumbed in the end. What precisely is the argument, and how is it treated in a contemporary setting? I have chosen two examples, one from Russell, the other from Husserl.

Russell begins the argument in this way:

> Although I believe that the table is 'really' of the same color all over, the parts that reflect the light look much brighter than the other parts, and some parts look white because of reflected light. I know that, if I move, the parts that reflect the light will be different, so that the apparent distribution of colours on the table will change. It follows that if several people are looking at the table at the same moment, no two of them will see exactly the same distribution of colours, because no two can see it from exactly the same point of view, and any change in the point of view makes some change in the way the light is reflected.

> (B. Russell, *The Problems of Philosophy*, pp. 8–9)

The most important part of this description of a familiar situation is Russell's claim that of several people, no two will *see* exactly the same distribution of colors. This claim, I think, is false. All of the people who are looking at the table (at the same time, from different points of view) will see that the table is, let us say, light brown. Russell's mistake is not apparent because he also talks about what the table *looks like;* for example, that parts of it look white. And he also talks about a change, not of the color of the table, but of the *apparent distribution* of colors on the table. While we agree that parts of the table may look white and that the apparent distribution of colors may change, we also insist that what the persons see is a light brown table.

Next, Russell draws the first ominous conclusion from his description: "It is evident from what we have found that there is no colour which preeminently appears to be *the* colour of the table, or even of any one particular part of the table—it appears to be of different colours from different points of view, and there is no reason for regarding some of these as more really its colour than others"

(Russell, 1977, p. 9). This conclusion is false. The table is seen to be light brown. Every observer agrees on that. What color is this table? One look from any point of view suffices: it is light brown. Repeat the test with another observer and you get the same result.

Russell now goes on to reason that since the colors which we "see" vary with our points of view, they cannot be colors of the table: "This colour is not something which is inherent in the table, but something depending upon the table and the spectator and the way the light falls on the table" (Russell, 1977, p. 9). We must deny, Russell maintains, that the table in itself has any one particular color. What holds for color, holds of course for texture, shape, etc. "Thus it becomes evident," Russell concludes, "that the real table, if there is one, is not the same as what we *immediately experience* by sight or touch or hearing. The real table, if there is one, is not *immediately* known to us at all, but must be an inference from what is immediately known" (Russell, 1977, p. 11; the first italics are mine). With these last words, Russell has opened the door to skepticism. The skeptic can now argue, soundly in my opinion, that there can be no such inference which is grounded on experience. Hence we cannot know whether or not there is a table and, if there is one, what properties it has.

I called the argument from the relativity of sensing convincing. From the description of an ordinary situation one arrives in two swift steps at the conclusion that we do not "immediately experience by sight" the table and its color. But notice that in the process the perfectly good and normal 'see' has been replaced by the strange and awkward 'immediately experience by sight'. Imagine that Russell had instead concluded that we do not see the table and its color. (Notice also the 'real' in front of 'table'; such are the tricks of the philosophical trade.) Even a student of philosophy might then not have been impressed by the argument. "Lord Russell," he may have said, "Let us go over the premises again; since the conclusion is obviously false, at least one of the premises must be false (or else, the argument must be invalid)." Russell and many other sophisticated philosophers, on the contrary, accepted the conclusion and then tried, ever more desperately, to discover the kind of inference that would lead from the immediately given, the sense-data, to the perceptual object, the table.

Russell speaks of sense-data and means by this expression "the things that are immediately known in sensation: such things as colours, sounds, smells, hardness, roughness, and so on. We shall give the name 'sensation' to the experience of being immediately aware of these things. Thus whenever we *see* a colour, we have a sensation *of* the colour, but the colour itself is a sense-datum, not a sensation" (Russell, 1977, p. 12; the first italics are mine). By a sensation Russell thus means the mental act of sensing. What is sensed is the sense-datum. A color is a sense-datum; for example, the color shade light brown is said to be a sense-datum. We find here the same mistake as in earlier philosophers: The sense-datum (sensation), which is an individual thing, is confused with one of its properties. The sense-datum, we repeat, *has* a color, a shape, etc., but it *is* not a color, shape, etc. It is clear that Russell uses "sensation" quite differently from us. We use it for the sense-datum; he uses it for the mental act of sensing the sense-datum. But this difference need not confuse us. My criticism of Russell's version of the argument aims at the way in which he replaces talk about seeing a color by talk about sensing a color. He supplants the mental act of seeing by the quite different act of sensing. No wonder that the table and its properties disappear from the world of "experience," for experience is confined to sensing. What is sensed, I agree with Russell, is a sense-datum and its properties, and not the table and its properties. Thus if all there were to "immediate experience by sight" is sensing, then we could indeed not know the table and its properties by "immediate experience by sight". And how but by inference could we then know the table and its properties? But there is more to "immediate experience by sight." There is seeing! And what is seen is not the sense-datum and its properties, but a table and its properties. When you look at the table, you see a light brown table, and you sense (experience) a certain sense-impression (sensation). It is not a question at all of *inferring* the color of the table from the color of your sense-datum. You *see* the color of the table.

Let us take another look at Russell's argument. We would describe the situation in this way. When you look at the table, you *see* its color; it is light brown. There occurs an act of seeing which is neither a sensing of a sense-datum nor an inference from a sense-datum. You also experience a certain sense-impression which has a certain shape and a "distribution of colours." If you pay attention to this sense-datum, you will notice, for example, that parts of it are almost white while others are light brown. You will also notice that this distribution of colors changes when you move around the table. Of course, the color of the table does not change when you move around it. Nor does your perception of the color change: you see that the table is light brown, no matter where you stand. What changes as you move are the colors of your sense-impressions, not the color which you see. Russell therefore describes, as he depicts the situation, the changing colors of our sense-impressions, and not the color which we see. One could say that he confuses the color seen with the colors sensed. Or one might say that he simply does not recognize that there is a color seen; all he acknowledges are the colors sensed.

As a result of this mistake, he thinks that no color appears to be *the* color of the table. This is quite true as long as we only consider the sensed colors. However, we must also keep in mind that from a certain point of view the color seen coincides with the color sensed. Perhaps the example of shape is clearer. If you were to look at the table top while suspended from the ceiling, straight down, you would see that it is rectangular. Furthermore, your sense-impression would also be rectangular. Under this condition, the shape which you see and the shape which you sense coincide. We may therefore call it "the normal situation."

Since the colors which we sense vary with lighting conditions, position, and even with the state of the nervous system, these colors are not the colors of the table. The table, we know, does not change its color when we walk around it. But this does not mean that only the sense-impressions are colored, that color is not "something inherent" in the table: the table does have a particular color. And we know this color, because we see it.

Let us turn to Husserl:

The perceived thing in general, and all its parts, aspects, and phases, whether the quality be primary or secondary, are necessarily transcendent to the perception, and on the same grounds everywhere. The color of the thing seen is not in principle a real phase of the consciousness of color; it appears, but even while it is appearing the appearance can and *must* be continually changing, as experience shows. The *same* color appears 'in' continuously varying patterns of *perspective color variations.* Similarly for every sensory quality and likewise for every spatial shape.

(E. Husserl, *Ideas,* par. 41)

The table, we agree with Husserl, transcends our perception of it. It is not a part of our perceiving, but its object. And the same holds for the color of the table. But it is not true, as Husserl then goes on to claim, that we know the color of the table *through or by means of* perspective color variations, that is, through the colors of our sense-impressions. The table's color is not transcendent in the sense that it transcends what is "directly before the mind" when we look at it. The color of the table is "directly before the mind" because it is seen.

As I said before, most modern philosophers have accepted the argument from the relativity of sensing. But this argument, as I also pointed out, leads directly to skepticism. The skeptic correctly argues that if we can know the color of the table only by inference from the colors which we sense, then we cannot know it at all. For, in order to know the table's color, you must know something to the effect that the experience of a yellow sense-impression indicates under certain conditions that the table is light brown. But how could we possibly discover a regularity of this sort? There is only one way: We must *compare* the color of the sense-impression with the color of the table. We must "take a look," first at the color of the sensation, noting that it is yellow, and then at the color of the table, noting that it is light brown. But if Russell and Husserl are correct, then we cannot "take a look" at the color of the table. We can only look at the color of our sense-datum. Therefore, we cannot compare the color of the sense-impression with the color of the table. Hence we cannot discover the required regularity. Therefore we cannot know the color of the table.

Let me formulate the argument more generally in order to show how powerful it is.

(1) We assume that we know the colors of our sensations under certain conditions.

(2) We also assume that we know the color of the table, not by acquaintance, but only by means of the following description: The color of the table is *the* color which causes us under certain conditions to experience sense-impressions that are, say, white, light brown, etc. More generally, we know the color of the table only as the color which stands in a certain relation, R, to the colors of our sensations. I take this assumption to be the conclusion of the argument from the relativity of sensing.

(3) But to know the color of the table in this manner is not to know what color the table has. We do not know, for example, whether it is light brown or dark brown, or whether it is green or navy blue.

The skeptic's argument thus rests on the principle that to know something merely as the A which stands in R to B, is not to know what properties A has. Assume that you want to know who murdered the Dean of Women (assuming that just one person committed the foul deed). If you are told that it was the brother of the president of the university, then you still do not know what particular person killed the Dean, unless you also know what particular person is the president's brother. Assume that the president's brother has been introduced to you at a cocktail party as Mr. Henry Miller, and that you had a pleasant conversation with him. Since you are acquainted with Mr. Miller, you know the person who killed the dean, and you could pick the person out of a line-up. But obviously you could not do so if you were not acquainted with the person who killed the dean.

We know something about the color of the table if we know that it is the color which causes us, under certain circumstances, to experience a white sensation. We know, to be specific, that it stands in a certain relation to the color of our sensation. However, we do not know which of several colors it is. But this is not what ordinarily happens. Ordinarily, we claim to know what particular color the table has, what shape it has, etc. The table is light brown, the top is rectangularly shaped, etc. Thus we know that the skeptic's conclusion is false. Since we accept its first premise, and since we accept the principle about knowledge by relational description mentioned above, we must reject the second premise. It is not true that we can know the color of the table only by relational description. We know it by acquaintance. We know it by sight.

b) The Appearance of Appearances

In his response to Hume's version of the argument from the relativity of sensing, Reid speaks of the *appearance* of a perceptual object: "In a word, the appearance of a visible object is infinitely diversified, according to its distance and position" (T. Reid, *Essays on the Intellectual Powers of Man*, p. 227). Appearances have played a large role in more recent discussions of the argument and we shall now take a look at them.

The first premise of the argument from the relativity of sensing states that the table *looks different* from different angles and distances. It has been said that it *appears* to have different colors from different angles and distances. Both expressions hide the implausibility of the first premise. When you look at the table from one point of view, you see that it is light brown; and when you look at it from another point of view, you see again that it is light brown. Imagine that the first premise had been formulated in this way: When you look at the table from one point of view, you see that it is dark brown; from another point of view, you see that it is white; from still another point of view, you see that it is light brown; and so on. We would immediately object that these perceptual mistakes do not ordinarily occur. But if you say that the table looks dark brown from one angle and white from another, or that it appears to be dark brown from one point of view and white from another, then you may get away with it.

To say that the table looks dark brown from one point of view and white from another, or that it appears dark brown from one point of view and white from another, is simply false. When we say that the table looks dark brown, we mean that we *see* it to be dark brown, but have some doubt that it really is dark brown. As Vesey puts it: "What an object looks like to somebody is what, on looking at it, that person would take it to be, if he had no reason to think otherwise" (G. N. A. Vesey, "Seeing and Seeing as," p. 69). In our example of veridical perception, the person would take the table to be light brown from every angle and distance.

In a classic discussion of the argument, C. D. Broad talks about a penny, lying on a table, and viewed from different positions: "We know, e.g., that when we lay a penny down on a table and view it from different positions it generally looks more or less elliptical in shape" (C. D. Broad, "The Theory of Sensa," p. 86). It is a *certain fact,* he claims, that the penny does look different as we move about. I claim that this is neither certain nor even a fact. When we view the penny it does not look more or less elliptical: it looks round. And as we move about, the penny does not look different (in shape): it looks the same. Broad realizes that something is wrong with his description of the perceptual situations. He knows that a person looking at the penny would never say: "This is elliptical" or "I see that this penny is elliptical." "When I judge that a penny looks elliptical," Broad explains, "I am not mistakenly ascribing elliptical shape to what is in fact round. Sensible appearances may *lead* me to make a mistaken judgment about physical objects, but they *need* not, and, so far as we know, commonly do not. My certainty that the penny looks elliptical exists comfortably alongside of my conviction that it is round" (Broad, 1965, p. 87). Broad here uses "looks like" and "appears" not in the ordinary way. In his sense, you may say that the penny looks oval even when you see it to be round. What is this sense?

When you look at the penny, you see that it is round. But you also have, according to our view, an elliptical sense-impression. This suggests that Broad is talking about your sense-impression when he says that the penny looks elliptical to you or that it has an elliptical appearance. You may be reporting, not the shape of the penny, not the shape you *see,* but the shape of your sense-impression. On many ordinary occasions, there may be no reason for you to notice the properties of your sensations. But occasionally the shape or color of one of your sense-impressions may become important. H. H. Price gives the example of someone looking at the sun as it approaches the horizon on a winter evening. He knows of course that the sun is round, and he also sees that it is round. But he may be struck by the fact that under those conditions he experiences an oval sense-impression. And he may express his astonishment by saying: "Look at that sun, it looks oval, almost like an egg." In short, the sensible appearances of Broad's example are sensations and their properties: "Thus when I look at a penny from the side, what happens, on the present theory, is at least this: I have a sensation whose object is an elliptical, brown sensum; and this sensum is related in some special intimate way to a certain round physical object, viz., the penny" (Broad, 1965, p. 89). In our words, I sense (experience) an elliptical, brown sensation, and this sensation is caused by a round penny.

Broad uses the appearance terminology in order to "introduce" sense-data. This has become a favorite practice in response to a spreading rejection of sense-data. One seems to reason like this. Nobody can object to the appearance terminology; we all use it in ordinary discourse. If we can therefore introduce the sense-data terminology as a mere variant of the appearance terminology, we have secured the existence of sense-data. Or, at least, nobody can then object to the use of a sense-data terminology. But this kind of reasoning seems to me to have things backward. That there are sensations, visual sensations, auditory sensations, etc. is a fact that requires no philosophical argument. To deny that there are sensations is as silly as to deny that there are perceptual objects. Sense-data, therefore, need no philosophical introduction. They need not be made palatable to philosophers. If a philosopher cannot swallow them, the worse for the philosopher. When we look at the penny, we have an elliptical sense-impression, as everyone can prove by drawing the penny in perspective. And perhaps, just perhaps, we can also express this fact by using expressions like "looks like" or "presents an elliptical appearance" in an unfamiliar way.

But I must add a word of caution. To hold that there are sensations is not the same as to hold that there are sense-data in all of the many meanings which philosophers have given to this term. Sensations are "ordinary, everyday types of things." Sense-data, on the other hand, are often philosophical props. How else can one explain, for example, Moore's quite serious question of whether or not sense-data are parts of the surfaces of perceptual objects? Or how else can one explain the ridiculous claim that there are unsensed sense-data? While there can be no doubt that there are sensations, I am sure that there are no "sense-data" of that sort.

While Broad uses the appearance terminology in order to introduce sense-data, other philosophers have used it in order to introduce a special sense of "being appeared to." They say that the penny appears elliptical to you, but deny that there is an elliptical appearance (see, for example, Roderick M. Chisholm, *Perceiving,* pp. 115–25). It is a fallacy, they claim, to conclude that there is an elliptical appearance, if the penny appears elliptical to you. I shall be brief and go to the heart of the matter, since this view is by now well-known. The heart of the matter is that these philosophers acknowledge acts of sensing but no sense-impressions. But to reject sensations, is as silly as to reject perceptual objects. What reasons are there in this case for denying the obvious?

It is usually maintained that there are a number of puzzling questions about sensations which do not arise for the corresponding acts of sensing (see, for example, James W. Cornman, *Perception, Common Sense, and Science,* pp. 78–89). For example, one claims that the question of whether one can be mistaken about the properties of one's sensations is particularly troublesome. Cornman asks: "Does anyone fail to experience a property that one of his sensa has?" I think that the answer is straightforward and not difficult at all. As the question is phrased, the answer is negative: Nobody can fail to *experience* a property of a sensation which he experiences. This is a mere truism. It amounts to no more than that one cannot fail to experience what one experiences. Sensations cannot have properties which are not experienced, for a sensation cannot be other than it is. But perhaps Cornman means to raise a different and more important question, namely: Can a sensation have a property which one does not *notice?* But to this question the answer is clear-cut as well: Of course, it can. There is no difference between sensations and perceptual objects in this regard. To take Cornman's example, assume that a tiger appears at the edge of the jungle a few yards away from you. He stands there for a second or two and then vanishes back into the jungle. Assume also that the tiger has exactly twenty stripes on the side which was turned toward you. Did you notice that the tiger has twenty stripes? Of course, not! You were much too excited to count his stripes. You saw a striped tiger, but you did not see that the tiger had twenty stripes. What about your visual sense-impression of the tiger? Cornman thinks that this question presents us with a dilemma. Presumably, neither the view that the sense-impression has twenty stripes nor the view that it does not is satisfactory. But there is no dilemma. Your sense-impression had twenty stripes, just like the tiger. But you did not pay any attention to your sense-datum and did not count its stripes. Thus you did not notice that it had twenty stripes. If you are really in doubt about the number of stripes of your sense-impression, you merely have to lure the tiger back out of the jungle and then pay attention to your sense-impression.

Why are we supposed to be impaled by this answer? Cornman states that "it is quite unreasonable to say that the sensum someone briefly experiences because of a quick glimpse of a tiger, has a definite number of stripes, although he does not experience it to have some definite number of stripes" (Cornman, p. 81). Notice the 'experience' here. We must again correct the expression: It is not unreasonable at all to hold that a sensum which is only briefly *experienced* should have properties which are not *noticed*. By now it is clear that the alleged difficulty revolves around the problem of whether or not our knowledge of sense-impressions is infallible. And it should be obvious that we come down squarely on the side of those philosophers who have held that we can and do make mistakes about our sensations. Not only do sensations have properties which we do not notice when we experience them, we can even make mistakes about their properties when we pay attention to them. We shall return to this topic in the next main section and then explain in what sense all knowledge of mental things is fallible.

Another reason why sensa are taken to be suspect is contained in the question of where sensa are spatially located (Cornman, pp. 84–85). Again, I fail to see the difficulty. It is clear that sensa are not located in perceptual space, since they are not perceptual objects. But this says nothing more, we must quickly add, than that they are not spatially related to perceptual objects. The oval sensation caused by the tilted penny is neither to the left of the penny nor to its right. Nor does it stand in any other spatial relation to the penny. But it does stand in spatial relations to other sense-impressions. For example, it may be to the left of a yellow sensum which is caused by a pencil. Visual sensations have spatial properties (size and shape) and stand in spatial relations, just as perceptual objects do. They share these spatial features with perceptual objects, just as they share colors with them.

So much for two of the alleged difficulties with sensations. It remains to emphasize how peculiar this kind of attack on sense-impressions is. One denies the existence of sensations on the sole ground that they raise certain problems. But so do perceptual objects. And so do physical objects. Should we then also deny the existence of apples and electrons, and switch to talking about "seeing applely" and "measuring electronly"?

But we have strayed from our main topic: The nature of appearances. Appearance is often contrasted with reality, and thereon hangs another interesting tale. If you mistakenly think that the penny looks oval to you just because you experience an oval sensum, then you may also make a second mistake. Calling the sensations "appearances of the penny," you may think of the properties which the penny *appears to have* as properties which your sensations *really have*. And then it follows, as Broad puts it, "that sensa cannot appear to have properties which they do not really have" (Broad, 1965, p. 93). For, if sensa could appear to have properties which they do not have, then we would have to conclude that there are "super-sensa" which really do have the properties that the ordinary sensa merely appear to have. And this reasoning would lead to an infinite series of sensa. But we must protest: It is not the function of sensations to solve the appearance-reality problem, which consists in the fact that a penny, though round, may appear to be oval. It is false that the sensation caused by the penny always has the shape which the penny appears to have. The penny may appear to be round, even if its sensation is oval. The appearing terminology, we insist, is not ordinarily a sense-data terminology. When you look at the tilted penny, it does not appear to be oval at all. You see that it is round; you are certain that it is round. And if you were to use the word "appear," you would say: "It appears round to me." On the other hand, if, for philosophical reasons, you use the appearance terminology as a replacement for the sense-data terminology, then you can no longer play with the appearance-reality distinction. Then to say that the penny presents an oval appearance is to say nothing more nor less than that it causes an oval sense-impression. And then it follows that sensations cannot have appearances, but it does not follow that they cannot appear to be other than they are, in the ordinary sense of this phrase. They cannot have appearances, because sensations do not cause you to have sensations of sensations in the way in which perceptual objects cause you to have sensations. But this fact does not imply that it is impossible to make mistakes about them.

The appearing terminology, to sum up, is not a natural way of talking about sensations. Quite to the contrary. Sensations are not appearances. To believe that they are may lead one to the mistaken conclusion that we cannot make mistakes about them. Nor need we be defensive about talking about sensations. That there are sense-data is a matter of common sense. But this fact has been hidden behind the shifting clouds of philosophical confusion. If one studies recent discussions about the existence and nature of sense-data, then it becomes clear why some philosophers are tempted to escape from all that heat by jumping into the fire of the adverbial view.

c) The Causal Theory

What is "immediately given by sight," according to the argument from the relativity of sensing, is not the real table. If the real table is known at all, then it is known only mediately, indirectly. Thus there is a gap between what we know directly, sense-impressions, and what we know only indirectly, namely, perceptual objects. I do not think that this gap can be closed and, therefore, I believe that the skeptic will triumph. But there have been attempts to close it and thus to close the door to skepticism. We shall now take a look at the most famous of these attempts, the so-called "causal theory of perception" (see, for example, H. H. Price, *Perception,* pp. 66–102).

Return with me to Russell in order to take a measure of his philosophical plight. Why should we believe that there is a "real" table "out there" that causes our sense-impressions? We are told that the assumption that there are perceptual objects (and that they have the properties which we think they have) is the *most simple hypothesis* which explains the behavior of our sense-impressions: "If the cat appears at one moment in one part of the room, and at another in another part, it is natural to suppose that it has moved from the one to the other, passing over a series of intermediate positions. But if it is merely a set of sense-data, it cannot have been in any place where I did not see it; thus we shall have to suppose that it did not exist at all while I was not looking, but suddenly sprang into being in a new place" (Russell, 1977, p. 23). I have felt since my undergraduate days that this is one of the most flimsy of all of Russell's arguments. I "see" a bundle of sense-impressions at one place; a little later I "see" a similar bundle at a different place. Am I supposed to explain how they got from one place to the other? Of course, if I assume that there is a cat that causes my sense-impressions, then nothing is more natural than to assume that the cat that caused the first bundle of sense-impressions has moved across the room and now causes the second bundle of sense-impressions. Nor is it clear to me what Russell's argument has to do with simplicity. A thoughtful skeptic, I think, would respond to Russell with the question: "What cat?"

But the fatal and obvious objection to Russell's line of reasoning is that we do not know of cats *by inference* to the simplest hypothesis. We *see* the cat, first in one corner, then in another. Russell does not feel too comfortable with his explanation and adds: "Of course it is not by argument that we originally come to our belief in an independent external world. We find this belief ready in ourselves as soon as we begin to reflect: it is what may be called an *instinctive* belief" (Russell, 1977, p. 24). Thus it turns out that we do not, after all, infer the existence of an external world, but are born with an instinctive belief in it. But Russell, to his credit, does not feel happy with the instinct theory either. So he confuses the situation by pointing out, quite correctly, that a web of beliefs forms a hierarchy that must rest on some basic beliefs. He tailors this fact to his particular purpose: "All knowledge, we find, must be built up upon our instinctive beliefs, and if these are rejected, nothing is left" (Russell, 1977, p. 24). But our knowledge of the external world is not based on instinctive beliefs. Instinct has nothing to do with it. It is built on perception. We know that there are perceptual objects and what they are because we can see them, hear them, smell them, etc.

All right, let us assume that we instinctively believe that there are perceptual objects. But how do we know what they are like? Is there also an instinctive belief that apples are red and that elephants like peanuts? Of course not. But, then, there really are no perceptual objects in Russell's so-called external world. "Out there,"

Russell believes with the majority of philosophers and physicists, are elementary particles and the like. And these physical objects have no colors and do not eat peanuts. How does this "scientific world view" jibe with the instinct theory just mentioned? Do we instinctively believe that there are cats that move from place to place or do we instinctively believe that there are elementary particles? If we believe the former, is not our instinctive belief false? And what then happens to the system of knowledge built upon this and other such instinctive beliefs? On the other hand, how plausible is the view that we instinctively believe in electrons?

According to Russell, there are sense-data with which we are directly acquainted and there are the physical objects science talks about. The gap, we see, is between knowledge of sense-impressions and knowledge of physical objects. How is this gap to be bridged? Well, there is presumably the instinctive belief in "external causes" for our sense-impressions. But this merely assures us of the existence of a Kantian *Ding an sich*. Surely science claims to know more than that there are unknown causes of our sensations. At this point Russell invokes two new devices. Firstly, there is *knowledge by description*. Secondly, there is *knowledge by isomorphism*. Knowledge by description, as we have all learned from Russell, explains how we can know things with which we are not acquainted. We may know a perceptual object, for example, as the object which causes us to experience a certain sense-impression under certain circumstances. There is nothing wrong with Russell's famous distinction between knowledge by acquaintance and knowledge by description. Unfortunately, knowledge by description is not able to close the skeptical gap, as I pointed out. Even if we grant what a skeptic need not grant, namely, that we are somehow justified in making a causal inference from our sense-impressions to "external objects," there remains the fatal objection that we do not know the external world by causal inference. Russell, as we just saw, concedes this point.

Secondly, there is knowledge by way of isomorphism. This is a most spellbinding bridge over the skeptical gap. The basic idea is that even though we cannot infer the properties of the external world from the properties of our sensations, we can know the *structure* of the external world, because that structure is isomorphic to the structure of the realm of sense-data. For example, Russell says that "we may assume that there is a physical space in which physical objects have spatial relations *corresponding* to those which the corresponding sense-data have in our private spaces" (Russell, 1977, p. 31; my italics). And similarly for time: "Thus, in so far as time is constituted by duration, there is the same necessity for distinguishing a public and a private time as there was in the case of space. But in so far as time consists in an *order* of before and after, there is no need to make such a distinction;" (Russell, 1977, p. 32). And Russell concludes with these words: "Thus we find that, although the *relations* of physical objects have all sorts of knowable properties, derived from their correspondence with the relations of sense-data, the physical objects themselves remain unknown in their intrinsic nature, so far at least as can be discovered by means of the senses" (Russell, 1977, p. 34). Brentano, in the same vein, describes the task of physics in this fashion: "Physical science is the science which tries to explain the succession of physical phenomena of normal and pure . . .

sensations by assuming that it is the effect on our sense organs of a world which is space-like extended in three dimensions and time-like running in one direction" (F. Brentano, *Psychology from an Empirical Standpoint*, vol. I, p. 138).

The same appeal to knowledge by way of isomorphism is used by Meinong to escape from skepticism and idealism (see A. Meinong, *Ueber die Erfahrungsgrundlagen unseres Wissens*). According to Meinong, there exists a noumenal world beyond the phenomenal world of our mental phenomena. This noumenal world is *similar* to the phenomenal world in that it contains things and their properties. In addition, however, these noumenal entities stand in the same relations ("relations of comparison") of difference, similarity, and equality in which their phenomenal counterparts stand. One can therefore surmise, for example, that if two sensations have similar properties, then their noumenal counterparts have similar properties. Furthermore, number is a projectible feature: If we hear two tones, then there correspond to these sensations an equal number of noumenal objects in the noumenal world.

What principle distinguishes between projectible and nonprojectible features? Russell does not give a straightforward answer, but Meinong does:

> It is the wide, even unlimited, field of application of those two kinds of ideal object [relations of comparison and numbers]. One cannot think of a pair of objects which are not different in the extended sense just used; as little [can one think] of objects which do not form a complex with a determinate number of parts. Under such conditions, an application to what is not phenomenally given, that is, to noumenal objects, is naturally completely unobjectionable. The situation is quite different for complexes like melodies which are only applicable to tones. . . .

(Meinong, p. 103)

Any two objects of the phenomenal world are different from each other, and any kind of object of this world can be numbered. Therefore, Meinong argues, these features must also occur in the noumenal world. What is projectible are the features which every possible phenomenal world must have. The noumenal world may have quite a different "content" from the phenomenal world, but it must share its *categorial structure*.

But what reason is there for believing that the two worlds must share the same categorial structure? From the fact that something is a categorial feature of the phenomenal world it simply does not follow that it must also be a categorial feature of the noumenal world. Nor can we argue that we can only conceive or imagine the noumenal world in terms of the categorial features of the phenomenal one and that it, therefore, must have these features. It may well be the case that the noumenal world, if there is one, is beyond our conception and imagination. I think that we are left with Russell's "instinctive belief": The only reason we can have for believing that the noumenal world must be isomorphic to the phenomenal world is blind instinct, and that of course is no reason at all.

Notice, finally and most importantly, how badly this talk about a noumenal world behind the mental world jibes with the professed belief in the world of physics. Compared to the world of physics, Russell's and Meinong's "external world" is as bloodless as a skeleton. Open a textbook on physics and you will be impressed and perhaps even enchanted by the colorful properties elementary particles are said to have. No uncertainty here. No ignorance. We know, within the bounds of scientific certainty, what the features of the physical world are. The "external world" of Russell and Meinong, it turns out, is not the world of physics at all. If there were such a world, then it would have to transcend the world of physical objects. We have just witnessed a most amazing turn of events: The causal argument and the thesis of isomorphism do not bridge the gap between the mental and the physical realms, but lead, at best, from the mental world to a strange world of noumenal objects.

The real world, we are told, is not the world of perceptual objects, not the world of apples and colors, but the world of physics. In the name of science, the perceptual world must be exorcised. We protested that such a drastic measure is unnecessary, that apples and elementary particles dwell harmoniously in the non-mental world. But in vain. And then something incredible happened. Philosophy raised its wise old head and introduced the argument from the relativity of sensing. Suddenly, those who insisted that the "external world" is the world of physics found themselves at a total loss: knowledge of the physical world becomes impossible. The very best they can come up with is an instinctive belief in a noumenal world. The best they can do is to postulate an isomorphic world of noumena. Thus the physical world is lost to them as well. "Out there," in the end, are neither apples nor elementary particles. "Out there" are unknown things with unknown features.

But we know better. We can explain how we know of elementary particles and their properties. We do not lose the world of physics for the shadowy world of noumenal objects, because for us the physical world is firmly tied to the perceptual world. Is it not ironic that those who believe that they have to choose between the perceptual world and the physical world end up with neither? What shall it benefit a philosopher to dump the world of perceptual objects into the mind, if he will lose the fascinating world of physics?

d) "Parts of the Surfaces of Inkstands"

Russell's version of the argument from the relativity of sensing concerns the color of a table. What holds for color, holds for shape and other properties as well. The true properties of the table are presumably hidden behind a veil of appearances. But this is not the only curtain that shields the table from the mind. Even if we could see its color and its shape, it is argued, we could not see the "whole table," but only a spatial part of it. *The* table, according to some philosophers, is hidden from mental view in a complicated twofold manner. We cannot perceive *it,* but only parts of *it;* and these parts are not really perceived either, but are hidden behind appearances (sensations, sense-data). This, in my opinion, is the gist of Husserl's famous theory of aspects. He describes the perspectible feature of perception in these words:

It is not an accidental caprice of the Thing nor an accident of "our human constitution" that "our" perceptions can reach the things themselves only and merely through their perspective modifications. On the contrary, it is evident, and it follows from the essential nature of spatial thinghood (and in the widest sense inclusive of "visual illusion") that Being of this species can, in principle, be given in perception only by way of perspective manifestation.

. . . it is an essential necessity to be apprehended as such with apodeictic insight that spatial Being in general can be perceived by an Ego actual or possible only when presented in the way described.

(Husserl, 1962, par. 42)

I shall not discuss Husserl's theory of aspects, but consider Moore's version of this theory. Moore's discussion is interesting for two reasons. Firstly, he connects the perspectible feature of perception with the problem of how to close the skeptical gap. He tries to convince himself that sense-impressions are parts of the surfaces of perceptual objects, namely, of those parts that are turned toward the perceiver. He may have asked himself: Since a spatial aspect of a perceptual object is obviously not identical with the object, why not identify this aspect with a sense-datum? Secondly, it is instructive and humbling to observe how the great champion of common sense, once he has strayed from the path, takes one wrong philosophical turn after another. Here is a paradigm of how a most cautious and astute philosopher can arrive at an absurd conclusion by starting from what he considers to be obvious and certain premises. Whenever I am inclined to believe that a line of reasoning in this book runs smoothly and in the right direction, I remind myself of Moore's paper, "Some Judgments of Perception."

Moore considers the perceptual judgement, *This is an inkstand,* and claims that it seems to him "so very certain" that:

in all cases in which I make a judgment of this sort, I have no difficulty whatever in picking out a thing, which is, quite plainly, in a sense in which nothing else is, *the* thing about which I am making my judgment; and that yet, though this thing is *the* thing about which I am judging, I am, quite certainly, not, in general, judging with regard to it, that *it* is a thing of that kind for which the term, which seems to express the predicate of my judgment, is a name.

(Moore, 1970b, p. 229)

In plain words, when Moore asserts that this is an inkstand, he is *not* asserting that what the 'this' represents is an inkstand. He is not making this judgment, because the *this* of his judgment is *not* an inkstand. Far from being "so very certain," this claim is plainly false. What Moore asserts is either true or else it is false. Now, he obviously means for his judgment to be true. But if it is true, then the *this* of his judgment must be an inkstand. How, otherwise, could the assertion that this is an inkstand be true?

Why is Moore so certain that the *this* of his judgment is *not* an inkstand? This is where perspective enters into the considerations: "Nobody will suppose, for a moment," Moore says, "that when he judges such things as 'This is a sofa,' or 'This is a tree,' he is judging, with regard to the presented object, about which his judgment plainly is, that it is a *whole* sofa or a *whole* tree; he can, at most, suppose that he is judging it to be a part of the surface of a tree" (Moore, 1970b, p. 230; my italics). Once again, in plain English, since Moore sees only part of the sofa, the *this* of his judgment cannot be the whole sofa, but must be the part that he sees. What sets Moore's tortuous train of thought in motion is the assumption that he cannot possibly see a "whole" perceptual object, but can see only a part of it.

Next, Moore identifies the part of the surface of the inkstand which he sees with a sense-impression: "The object of which I have spoken as *the* object, about which, in each particular case, such a judgment as this always is a judgment, is, of course, always an object of the kind which some philosophers could call a sensation, and others would call a sense-datum" (Moore, 1970b, p. 231). Notice the "of course"! Hardly any philosopher, and certainly not I, would call a part of the surface of a perceptual object a sensation. Any temptation to call it a sensation would be immediately quenched by the realization that this would turn surfaces of perceptual objects into mental things.

Moore, then, is quite certain (1) that the *this* of his judgment is not the inkstand before him, (2) that it is part of the surface of the inkstand, and (3) that this part of the surface is a sensation. I think that all three of these propositions are false.

What might have moved Moore to assert the near-contradiction that in the true judgment *This is an inkstand,* the *this* is not an inkstand? The little word 'whole' in 'whole inkstand' is the clue. Moore seems to reason that the *this* cannot be the whole inkstand because he does not see the whole inkstand, but does see the *this*. Why does Moore believe that he does not see the whole inkstand? A whole, of course, has parts. The whole inkstand has many spatial parts. Moore, I surmise, adopted the principle that one cannot be said to have perceived a whole perceptual object unless one has perceived all of its parts. Listen to Kant's version of this principle: "When we see a house in the distance, we must necessarily have a representation of the different parts of the house . . . For if we did not see the parts, we would not see the house either. But we are not conscious of this presentation of the manifold of its parts" (I. Kant, *Logik,* p. 34).

It cannot be denied that Moore cannot see the back of the inkstand as long as he looks at it from the front. It is therefore true that he does not see all of the spatial parts of the inkstand when he looks at it from the front side. Thus if the just announced principle were true, it would follow that we cannot see (whole) inkstands (in one glance, from one point of view). It would be true, as Husserl puts it, that "our perceptions can reach the things themselves only and merely through their perspective modifications." But the principle is false: perceptual objects are presented to us "directly" and not through their parts or perspective modifications. The fault lies with the phrase "seeing a whole inkstand." I suppose that one may only be said to have seen the *whole* inkstand if one has walked around it, looked at it from all sides, and looked inside as well. In this sense, Moore has not seen the whole inkstand as long as he looks only at its front. But it does not follow from this fact that what he sees is part of the surface of an inkstand. The expression could also mean something else, namely, something like "not just seeing part of an inkstand." Assume that an apple has been cut into halves and that you see one half of it before you on the table. In this case, what you see is not the whole apple, but merely a part of it.

To sum up, I have argued that just as we see the properties of perceptual objects "directly," so do we see the objects themselves "directly," and not through or by means of their spatial parts. My argument rests on a rejection of the principle that one can only see a perceptual object if one sees all of its parts.

My analysis applies not only to spatial parts, but also to temporal parts of perceptual objects. Broad, after he has concluded that "The perceptual situation contains as a constituent something which is in fact part of the surface of the bell," goes on to claim in the same vein that "at most we can say that it contains as a constituent a short event which is in fact a slice of a longer strand of history, and that this longer strand is the history of a certain bell" (C. D. Broad, *The Mind and its Place in Nature*, p. 149). But just as we do *not* see part of the surface of the inkstand when we see the inkstand, so do we not see a temporal slice of the bell when we see the bell. And this for the same reason. The bell has temporal parts; it has a temporal history. But to see the bell is not the same as to see these temporal parts. In the spatial as well as in the temporal case, a certain type of argument is at work:

(1) An inkstand has (consists of) many spatial and temporal parts.

(2) Therefore, to see an inkstand is to see all of these parts.

(3) But we cannot see all of these parts (from a point of view, at a moment).

(4) Therefore, we cannot see the inkstand.

I have said that premise (2) of this argument is false. We can now see clearly why it is false. Assume that the inkstand has a scratch at the bottom, and let us express this fact awkwardly by saying that the inkstand has the property of having a scratch. Now, it is clear that from the fact that the inkstand has the property, it does not follow that you see that it has this property when you see the inkstand. For example, when you see that the inkstand is half full of ink, you do not see that it has a scratch at its bottom. The description "the half full inkstand in front of Moore' describes the very same thing as the description 'the inkstand in front of Moore with a scratch at its bottom'. But it does not follow from this fact that the two expressions can be substituted for each other *salva veritate* in all contexts. The inkstand before Moore is identical with the inkstand consisting of such and such spatial parts. But it obviously does not follow that when you see that the inkstand before Moore is half full, you see that the inkstand with such and such spatial parts is half full. In short, the principle adopted by Moore for spatial parts and by Broad for temporal parts is false, because the so-called principle of extensionality is false (see my *The Categorial Structure of the World*, pp. 375–380). Formulated linguistically and tailored to our case, the principle states that description expressions which describe the same thing can be substituted for each other *salva veritate* in all contexts. The principle of extensionality is so obviously false that one can only wonder why it has ever been adopted. Surely, when I believe that the earth is round I do not ipso facto believe that two plus two equals four, even though the sentences 'the earth is round' and 'two plus two equals four' are both true. Similarly, for the case illustrated above, when two expressions describe the same thing. It must be emphasized that the principle of extensionality is not the same as the Leibnizian law of substitutivity, according to which expressions which represent the same thing can be substituted for each other *salva veritate*. Perhaps the principle of extensionality has sometimes been accepted because it was confused with the law of substitutivity.

If Broad were correct in that the "most that we can grant is that a small spatio-temporal fragment of the ontological object is literally a constituent of the situation," then we can construct another skeptical argument, similar to the argument from the relativity of sensing (Broad, 1960, p. 150). In a nutshell and in Broad's terminology, how do we come by the conviction that this fragment is "not isolated and self-subsistent . . .; but that it is spatio-temporally a part of a larger whole of a certain characteristic kind . . ."? (Broad, 1960, p. 151). Broad sees clearly that we do not come by this conviction through inference, and he also admits that it cannot be justified by inference (Broad, 1960, p. 151–152). What is left, then, is the skeptical conclusion that this conviction is nothing more than "instinctual belief." But we know how to avoid this conclusion. We have defended the view that, contrary to Moore and Broad, we see perceptual objects and not just spatio-temporal parts of them.

Two

Knowledge of Our Minds

INTROSPECTION

ONE

Experience versus Inspection

a) Rejection of the Principle of Immanence

We shall now return to the source of the skeptical triumph over Cartesianism, namely, the principle of immanence. According to this principle, the mind knows only what is *in* it. It cannot reach out and make direct contact with perceptual objects. The Cartesians added a special twist to this traditional dogma by stressing the issue of certainty. To know, they insisted, is to know for certain; and the mind can only know for certain what is in it. These two themes reinforce each other. One may argue on independent grounds that certain knowledge is possible only of the contents of one's mind. But if certain knowledge is the only kind of knowledge that deserves to be called knowledge, then the principle of immanence follows. On the other hand, one may argue, beginning at the other end, that since the principle of immanence holds, and since knowledge of one's own mind is the only certain knowledge, that all true knowledge is certain knowledge. I believe that both of these principles are false.

Let me illustrate the Cartesian problem by means of a diagram. In figure 1, the Cartesian mind is represented by a circle. Within the circle is an idea. This idea is known by the mind in some way. That it is known by the mind is represented by the arrow that aims at the idea. The question is: How does the mind know the external perceptual object? That the perceptual object can be known only indirectly follows from the principle of immanence. But in what this indirect knowledge consists is the puzzle the Cartesian cannot solve.

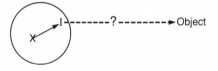

Figure 1

And this is not the only problem with the Cartesian view. As we mentioned earlier, the nature of the small arrow within the mind is not explained. But we shall leave all of the other problems aside and concentrate on the skeptical argument. The skeptic asks, as we remember, how we can possibly know what object is presented by which idea. And he goes on to claim that the Cartesian cannot answer this question, because he cannot compare a given idea with its object. He cannot compare the idea I with the object O because such a comparison requires that we know directly not only I, but also O. But the principle of immanence, accepted by the Cartesian, does not allow for direct knowledge of O.

What is our analysis of the situation? In order to concentrate only on the important points, I shall simplify to the point of distortion. Assume that someone sees a certain perceptual object O. According to our account, this person experiences a certain mental act of seeing. This act has a certain content, and the content stands in the intentional nexus to O. Figure 2 gives the gist of this situation.

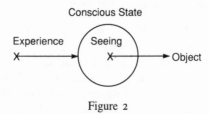

Figure 2

The small crosses represent the mental acts of experiencing and of seeing. The contents of these acts are not diagrammed. The arrow depicts the intentional nexus. The circle represents not a mind, as in our previous diagram, but what I shall call a "conscious state." By a conscious state I mean the sum total of what a mind experiences at a given moment. It is the (complex) object of the act of experiencing. At a given moment, a mind experiences not only a mental act of seeing, but also various sensations, feelings, emotions, images, etc. In order to keep the diagram as simple as possible, I have left out all of these things and put only the mental act of seeing into the conscious state.

A mind is not identical with a conscious state, for it also consists of the act of experiencing. Thus a mind at a moment has two essential parts. It always consists of an experience and what is experienced. It always consists of an act of experiencing and of a conscious state.

There is some similarity between our mind and the Cartesian mind, even though the diagrams look quite different. This similarity appears if we imagine, for just a moment, another circle drawn around both the act of experiencing and the conscious state, as in figure 3.

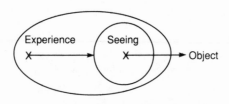

Figure 3

What corresponds to the mysterious arrow in the Cartesian mind is our act of experiencing. Instead of an idea in the mind, we have the mental act of seeing or, more precisely, the content of this act. And finally and most importantly, the puzzling relationship between the idea and its object is explicated by the intentional nexus between the content of the act of seeing, on the one hand, and the perceptual object, on the other.

What happens when we try to apply the skeptical argument to our analysis? The crucial question becomes: How do we know what perceptual object corresponds to which content? Well, we know what perceptual object we are seeing when the mind is in the state depicted by figure 2, say, an elephant. But we do not know what kind of content we are experiencing in this situation. In order to find out what kind of content it is, what it "feels like" to see an elephant rather than something else, we must turn our attention away from the elephant and concentrate on the act of seeing and its content. This switch in attention results in a different mental state from the one of figure 2. It requires, I submit, that we experience not an act of seeing, but rather an act which intends the act of seeing. It requires that we experience an act of reflection whose object is the act of seeing, as shown in figure 4.

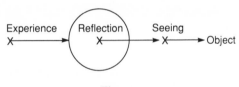

Figure 4

This then is our answer to the skeptic. We know what perceptual object corresponds to which content by, firstly, seeing the perceptual object, as shown in figure 2, and, secondly, by inspecting the content of the act of seeing, as shown in figure 4. In this fashion, we can compare the one with the other.

Notice how radically the dialectic of the situation has shifted. For the Cartesian, the problem is how he can know the perceptual object. For us, it is how we can know the content. To see an object, according to our view, is to know it in the sense of being acquainted with it. And to see an object is to experience a mental act of seeing. There is no problem of how we know the object which we see. To know a perceptual object is, not to *know* the content of the act of seeing, but to *experience* this content. *Experience is not knowledge.* Quite to the contrary: What is experienced is, ipso facto, not known. In order to know the content, one must shift one's attention away from the elephant to the content. And this is achieved by reflection on one's act of seeing. Nothing is easier than to know what one is seeing. What is difficult is to find out what the contents of one's mind are. The Cartesian has exactly the opposite problem. He presumably knows what is *in* his mind, but does not know what is *before* it. He assumes that to know something is to experience it. And the skeptic then argues that since one cannot experience perceptual objects, one cannot know them. But the skeptic cannot attack our view. We do not accept the principle of immanence. Quite to the contrary: We hold that the mind never knows what is *in* it. The mind can only know what is *before* it. More precisely, the mind only knows the objects of those acts which are part of the conscious state. Perhaps Hegel makes the same point in paragraphs 84 and 85 of the *Introduction* to his *Phenomenology of Spirit:*

> For consciousness is, on the one hand, consciousness of the object, and on the other, consciousness of itself; consciousness of what for it is the True, and consciousness of its knowledge of the truth. Since both are *for* the same consciousness, this consciousness is itself their comparison; it is for this same consciousness to know whether its knowledge of the object corresponds to the object or not. The object, it is true, seems only to be for consciousness in the way that consciousness knows it; it seems that consciousness cannot, as it were, get behind the object as it exists for consciousness so as to examine what the object is *in itself,* and hence, too, cannot test its own knowledge by that standard. But the distinction between the in-itself and knowledge is already present in the very fact that consciousness knows an object at all. Something is *for it* the *in-itself;* and knowledge, or the being of the object for consciousness, is, *for it,* another moment. Upon this distinction, which is present as a fact, the examination rests.

(G.W.F. Hegel, Phenomenology of Spirit, p. 54)

The Cartesian has a different concept of knowledge from ours. According to him, knowledge resides in experience. According to our view, knowledge resides in the mental acts which are experienced. Experience, we hold, is blind. Only the mental acts which are experienced can know.

Let us add an illustration in order to drive this point home. When you desire something, you "know" not your desire, but the object of your desire, for your desire is merely experienced; it is merely in your mind. In order to inspect your desire, you must not experience it, but must experience instead an act of reflection whose object it is. Similarly, to fear something is to "know" what you fear, but not to "know" your fear. In order to inspect your fear, you must experience an act of reflecting on the fear. And similarly for other mental acts.

b) Another Look at the Argument from the Relativity of Sensing

Having reversed the Cartesian turn, we shall take another look at the argument from the relativity of sensing. In Russell's version of the argument, the true color of a certain table is in doubt. Russell asserts that if you look at the table from different angles, you will see different colors. And he concludes that the table in itself has no particular color, since there is no reason why we should ascribe one rather than any other of those colors to the table.

We have seen why and where Russell's argument fails. But we can now take a more informed look at the relevant mental states. When you look at the table from a certain point of view, you experience a certain colored sensation, S_1, and you see that the table is light brown, as in figure 5.

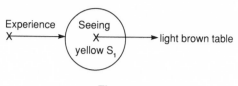

Figure 5

We shall assume that the sensation is not light brown, but yellow. Next, you walk around the table and look at it from a different angle, so that you experience a sense-impression which is not yellow, but grey, as in figure 6.

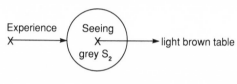

Figure 6

Notice that even though the color of your visual sensation has changed, what you see (as you see it) has not changed: You still see that the table is light brown. Thus what is true is not, as Russell assumes, that you see different colors from different angles, but rather that you *experience* different colors from different angles. Russell further assumes, and thus opens the door to the skeptic, that you know the different colors which you (allegedly) see, but have no reason to attribute a particular one to the table as such. From our analysis it follows that you do not "know" these colors, for these colors are colors of your sensations and therefore experienced but not known. What you know in this situation is the table and its color: you know that the table is light brown because you see it to be light brown. In order to know the sensations and their colors, you have to inspect them. But you can only inspect them if you turn your attention away from the table and pay attention to the sensations instead. You must reflect on the sensation rather than merely experience it, as shown in figure 7.

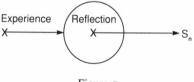

Figure 7

When you see that the table is light brown, you experience a yellow sensation. But you do not know that your sensation is yellow. To realize that the sensation is yellow, to notice its color, to become aware of its color, you must attend to the sensation rather than to the table. You must stop seeing the color of the table and inspect your visual sensation. You must turn inward, so to speak, and reflect on your sensation. There is no problem of how we know the color of the table: we simply see what color it has. If anything is difficult, it is to discover the features of our sensations. Their inspection requires a special mental attitude, a mental attitude which is difficult to induce and even more difficult to maintain. These are of course psychological difficulties, not philosophical problems. As far as the argument from the relativity of sensing is concerned, we have no philosophical problem. We know the colors of perceptual objects by perception, and we know the colors of our visual sensations by inspection. Neither is known only indirectly, that is, by inference. But they are known by different kinds of mental acts. We *see* the colors of perceptual objects, but we cannot *see* the colors of our sensation. On the other hand, we can *reflect* on the colors of our sensations, but we cannot *reflect* on the colors of perceptual objects.

c) Reid and the Nature of Attention

Our distinction between experience and reflection was anticipated by earlier philosophers. Reid, for example, distinguishes between consciousness and reflection. It will shed further light on our view if we compare it briefly with Reid's.

"Consciousness," Reid says, "is a word used by philosophers, to signify that immediate knowledge which we have of our present thoughts and purposes, and, in general, of all the present operations of our minds" (T. Reid, *Essays on the Intellectual Powers of Man*, p. 10). But consciousness, Reid explains, is not the same as paying attention, for "we are conscious of many things to which we give little or no attention" (Reid, p. 34). Attention resides in another kind of mental act:

> It is in our power, however, when we come to the years of understanding, to give attention to our own thoughts and passions, and the various operations of our minds. And when we make these the objects of our attention, either while they are present, or when they are recent and fresh in our memory, this act of the mind is called *reflection*.

> (Reid, p. 35)

This act of reflection, according to Reid, is like the act of seeing in that "it gives a like conviction with regard to internal objects, or things in the mind, as the faculty of seeing gives with regard to objects of sight" (Reid, p. 35). The main difference between Reid's and our account seems to be that he conceives of consciousness as giving us knowledge about the workings of the mind, while we insist that only reflection gives us such knowledge. Experience, which seems to correspond to Reid's consciousness, we have maintained, is not knowledge. But we agree with Reid that reflection is to mental things what perception is to perceptual objects. Just as we know perceptual objects by means of perception, so do we know mental things by means of reflection. However, there are also passages in Reid which demand a different interpretation. On page 551 of the *Essays*, he states that consciousness "gives the like immediate knowledge of things in the mind,. . . . as the senses give us of things external." At this place, it is not reflection that is compared to perception, but rather consciousness. And here reflection, too, seems to acquire a different function:

> Consciousness, being a kind of internal sense, can no more give us distinct and accurate notions of the operations of our minds than the external senses can give of external objects. Reflection upon the operations of our minds is the same kind of operation with that by which we form distinct notions of external objects. They differ not in their nature, but in this only, that one is employed about external and the other about internal objects; and both may, with equal propriety, be called reflection.

> (Reid, p. 552)

According to our view, reflection is a unique mental act that cannot intend external objects. It is not some kind of "thinking about" or "contemplating." As I said before, it is to mental things what perception is to perceptual objects.

Perhaps these quotations from Reid can be reconciled with each other. Perhaps, his view can be summarized in the following three theses. (1) There is an inner sense, consciousness, which yields knowledge of the operations of the mind, just as the outer sense, perception, yields knowledge of external objects. (2) In addition to this inner sense and this outer sense, in addition to consciousness and perception, there exists a different kind of mental act, namely, reflection. (3) To reflect is to pay attention either to an object of inner sense or to an object of perception. If this is Reid's view, and I am not at all sure that it is, then we disagree with him on the following important points.

Firstly, experience is not to mental things what perception is to external objects; for to perceive something is to pay attention to it, while we do not pay attention to the mental things which we experience. Rather, what corresponds to perception in regard to outer objects is reflection on mental things. There is a fundamental asymmetry between "inner sense" and "outer sense." *This asymmetry is of the essence of the mind.* It consists in the fact that mental things are "given to us" in two completely different ways, while perceptual objects are only "presented to us" in one way. A desire, for example, can be *experienced* or it can be *reflected upon,* while an apple can only be *perceived.*

Secondly, there exists no mental act of reflection on perceptual objects. Of course, one may reflect upon the fate of mankind, that is, one may think about it. But what we have here is not a particular kind of act, but a certain kind of mental process. This mental process consists of many kinds of mental acts: one may judge things, remember circumstances, wish for things, regret sorry states of affairs, and so on.

Thirdly, and for our immediate purpose most importantly, attention does not consist of a special kind of mental act. Attention, it should be pointed out, has posed a dilemma to introspective psychologists. It either consists of a mental act of paying attention or else it does not. If it is not a mental act, what could it possibly be? It is not a sensation or an image; nor is it a feeling or a mood. Thus we are moved to consider the first possibility. But attention does not seem to be a mental act either.

For if we perceive something, and thus pay attention to it, then there occurs an act of perception, but a *separate* act of paying attention cannot be found. When we think of something, there occur acts of judgment (assertion), acts of remembering, acts of assuming, etc., but again, no act of paying attention can be discovered. And similarly for desires, hopes, questions, and other kinds of mental acts: No separate act of paying attention occurs. Therefore, attention seems to have to be a mental act, and yet no such separate act of paying attention can be found.

It may well be that the problem of attention led to Reid's claim that in addition to the perception of perceptual objects there is also a reflection upon them. He must have noticed that to have a desire is not the same as to pay attention to it. Thus he distinguished between consciousness and reflection, and identified reflection with paying attention. But since he also believed that consciousness is an inner sense, comparable to the outer sense of perception, he concluded that just as the mere consciousness of a mental thing is not the same as paying attention to it, so the mere perception of an external object is not the same as paying attention to it. Therefore, he postulated reflection for external objects. He invented a special act of paying attention, reflection, which, when directed toward mental things, would yield knowledge of mental things, and when directed toward perceptual objects, would yield knowledge of external objects. But there is no such separate act of paying attention. This is clearly shown in the case of perception: to perceive something is to pay attention to it.

The problem of the nature of attention finds an easy answer in our view. It is true that there is no separate mental act of paying attention. And it is also true that it is not a sensation, feeling, image, etc. To pay attention to something is to have it "before" the mind. To be more precise, what one pays attention to is always the *object* of a mental act which is part of one's conscious state, that is, which is experienced. What is merely experienced, what is *part* of the conscious state, is not an object of attention. When you experience a desire, you do not pay attention to the desire, but to its object. When you inspect your desire, when you pay attention to it, your desire is the object of an act which is experienced, namely, of an act of reflection. When you pay attention to your desire, as shown in figure 8, you do not pay attention to the object of your desire, because this object is not the object of an act which is experienced. Rather, it is the object of an act which is reflected upon. In this situation, therefore, you do not pay attention to (a) the experience of the act of reflection, (b) the act of reflection, and (c) the object of your desire. You only pay attention to the object of the act which is part of your conscious state, which is experienced, that is, to the object of the act of reflection, that is, to the desire.

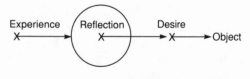

Figure 8

d) Brentano and the Doctrine of Secondary Objects

Brentano distinguishes between inner perception and inner observation (F. Brentano, *Psychology from an Empirical Standpoint,* vol. 1, book 1, chap. 2). Just as in Reid's case, there is some similarity between his distinction and our own between experience and reflection. But Brentano, as so often in his philosophical investigations of the mind, adds a special twist to his characterization of "inner perception." In order to fully understand this feature of his theory, we must briefly consider a traditional argument against the existence of mental acts.

According to this argument, we can show that if there exists a mental act, A_1, then there exist also an infinite number of further mental acts, A_2, A_3, A_4, etc. But experience shows that there never exists such an infinite series of acts in one mind. It follows, therefore, that no mental act at all exists. In detail, the argument proceeds like this. Assume that A_1 occurs in a mind. When A_1 occurs in a mind, the mind is conscious of A_1; for to *occur* in a mind is for the mind *to be aware of what occurs in it*. But this means that there must be a second mental act, A_2, which is the consciousness of A_1; for to be conscious of something is the same as for a mental act of consciousness to occur. But if A_2 occurs in the mind, the mind must also be conscious of it. Hence there must occur another act, A_3, which is the consciousness of A_2. And so on.

It is clear that this argument uses two crucial assumptions:

(1) A mind is conscious (aware) of every mental act that occurs in it. There are no "unconscious" mental acts. To speak with Berkeley: For mental acts it holds that to be is to be experienced.

(2) The consciousness of a mental act always consists of a different mental act. I think that the infinite regress is unavoidable if one accepts both of these assumptions. Since I am also convinced that there never occurs an infinity of mental acts in a mind, I must argue that (at least) one of the two assumptions is false. Brentano shares this assessment of the situation. He therefore accepts (1) and rejects (2). I, on the other hand, do just the opposite: I reject (1) and accept (2).

According to Brentano, the consciousness of a mental act does not consist of another act. Rather, every act is its own consciousness. This is the fascinating twist I announced earlier: The inner perception of a mental act A_1 is furnished by the act A_1 itself. A_1, as Brentano puts it, is its own *secondary* object. Assume that there occurs the hearing of a tone. This act, according to Brentano, has the tone as its primary object. But it also has a secondary object, namely, the act of hearing itself. See figure 9 for a diagram of this view.

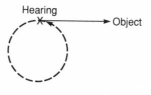

Figure 9

Like a snake with two heads, the act of hearing points simultaneously at two different objects: It points at the tone, but it also bites its own tail, as indicated by the broken looping arrow in figure 9. In this way, every mental act is its own "perception."

Brentano's rejection of (2) avoids the infinite regress. If A_1 occurs, then it is true, as (1) says, that the mind is conscious of A_1. But this consciousness does not consist in another mental act. A_1 is its own consciousness. Thus there need not occur a second mental act A_2. But as brilliant as this thesis about the peculiar interlacing of an act with its own consciousness is, it seems to me to be false. If Brentano's thesis were true, then it would follow that one hears not only tones, melodies, pitches, and the like, but also acts of hearing. If his thesis were true, then one would not, properly speaking, be *conscious* or *aware* of the act of hearing, but *hear* it. And this I take to be false. An act of hearing, I submit, cannot be heard. What does it sound like? What is its pitch? Clearly mental acts have no sound and no pitch. And just as one cannot hear an act of hearing, so can one not see an act of seeing.

In contrast to Brentano, I reject the first premise of the argument, the premise that a mind is conscious of every act that belongs to it. This rejection was implied earlier by my characterization of a mental state. A mental state, I said, has two essential parts: An act of experience and what is experienced, the conscious state. It follows that at any given moment, part of the mind is not experienced, that is, that the mind is not conscious, not aware, of this part. This part, of course, is the act of experience itself. By means of it, the mind experiences what it experiences, but it does not experience this experiencing. Using a different terminology to say the same thing, the mind always consists of a conscious part, the conscious state, and an "unconscious" part, the act of experiencing. Needless to say, this notion of the unconscious is completely different from Freud's. We shall see later how the Freudian conception fares, according to our analysis of the structure of the mind.

By the way, Sartre, in his inimitable way, goes a step farther than Brentano and reduces Brentano's doctrine of the self-consciousness of every act to absurdity. According to Sartre, the ego appears only before reflective consciousness, that is, the ego appears only before a mental act whose object is another mental act; for example, if one remembers a past perceiving (see Jean-Paul Sartre, *The Transcendence of the Ego*). How do we know that the ego does not also appear before unreflective consciousness? We cannot possibly "take a look" at unreflective consciousness, for if we do, we turn unreflective consciousness into reflected upon consciousness. But if we cannot "take a look," how are we to answer our question? Sartre sees the problem for his analysis and tries to solve it by invoking the self-consciousness of every mental act. Since every mental act is its own consciousness, he claims, there is also a memory which does not consist of a separate act (Sartre, 1988, p. 46). He maintains that, say, an act of seeing is not only a consciousness of itself, but also a memory of itself. He seems to argue that just as there is a consciousness of the act of seeing without there being a separate act of consciousness, so there is a remembering of the act of seeing without there being a separate act of remembering. I must confess that this view makes even less sense to me than Brentano's peculiar doctrine. Nor am I persuaded of his view when I read how Sartre proposes to reflect upon consciousness without reflecting upon it:

> That consciousness [for example, the act of seeing] must not be posited as object of a reflection. On the contrary, I must direct my attention on the revived objects [the seen landscape], but without losing sight of the unreflective consciousness, by joining in a sort of conspiracy with it and by drawing up an inventory of its content in a non-positional manner.

(Sartre, 1988, p. 46)

What a typically Sartrian solution: The mind conspires with itself against itself!

The Nature and Limits
of Introspection

a) Classic Introspection

With a firm grasp of the distinction between mere experience and reflection, we are able to explicate what the classic introspectionist psychologists meant by introspection. I shall start with three examples of the *inspection* of mental things other than mental acts.

(1) Someone is shown an apple. She is instructed to describe what she sees. She recognizes the object before her as an apple. She states that it is light green. Next, she is asked to describe not the perceptual object, but rather her visual sense-impression of the apple. What she is asked to do is, roughly, to forget that there is a green apple before her and to concentrate instead on her visual sensation. If she understands these instructions and if she has been trained to follow them, she will be inspecting her visual sensation.

(2) Assume that someone is instructed to imagine a mermaid, and that there occurs on this occasion the mental image of a mermaid. Then he is asked to concentrate on this image and to describe certain features of it, for example, whether or not it is colored and if so, what color the mermaid's hair is. In order to furnish this description, the person must inspect the mental image of the mermaid.

(3) Lastly, suppose that someone is in the process of composing an important letter to his best friend. While he is writing the letter, he feels a slight pain in his abdomen. After the letter is finished, having gotten worried about the persistent pain, he consults his wife, who happens to be a physician. She asks him to localize the pain and describe it in detail. He now realizes that the pain is "stabbing" rather than "dull and continuous." His description presupposes that he inspects the pain carefully.

These three examples, merely outlined here, allow us to make some general observations about the nature of inspection.

First. In each example, someone's *attention* was concentrated on the object of inspection. I have already described this feature and explained the nature of attention. According to this explanation, the object inspected is in each case the object of a mental act which belongs to the conscious state of the person.

Second. The three examples were so chosen that in each case inspection was preceded by a *conscious intention* to inspect. In each case, the person had, as the psychologists say, a *set* to inspect (cf., for example, G. E. Mueller's "Zur Analyse der Gedaechtnistaetigkeit und des Vorstellungsverlaufs," and J. J. Gibson, "A Critical Review of the Concept of Set in Contemporary Experimental Psychology"). However, inspection can also occur without a prior set to inspect. For example, a person may pay attention to a pain when it suddenly gets worse, and he may do so without any prior intention to inspect his pain more closely.

Third. The intention to inspect occurred in our examples as a consequence of a specific *task*. [Concerning the importance of tasks for introspection see, for example, H. J. Watt, "Experimentelle Beitraege zu einer Theorie des Denkens," and O. Selz's article in *Archiv fuer die gesamte Psychologie,* 27 (1913): 367–80.] Such a task usually has three effects. It brings about a shift in mental set. It brings about a shift in conscious states, for example, from perceiving an apple to inspecting a sense-impression, or from imagining a mermaid to inspecting the image. And it determines what particular things or features of things are to be inspected and described.

Fourth. In the description of the first example, I mentioned that the person in question has to be trained to follow the instructions. Some inspective conscious states are notoriously hard to induce and even harder to maintain. In ordinary life, we perceive things, imagine things, and feel things rather than scrutinize sensations, images, and pains. And even if inspection occurs in ordinary life, it usually lasts only for brief periods. What we find most often, even in controlled experimental situations, is a rapid shift back and forth between inspective and non-inspective conscious states.

Fifth. What is inspected in the three situations is not the seeing of an apple, the imagining of a mermaid, or the feeling of a pain, but rather such things as sense-impressions, images, and feelings. The objects of inspection are not mental acts, but what I shall call for the moment "mental contents."

Return to our first example: the perception of an apple followed by the inspection of a visual sensation. Does the person inspect her conscious state of perceiving the apple when she inspects the visual sense-impression caused by the apple? Obviously not. At first, her conscious state contains, among other things, an act of perception and a visual sensation. But at that moment she is not introspecting her conscious state, but is perceiving the apple. When she shifts from perceiving the apple to inspecting her sensation, her conscious state contains an act of reflecting on the sensation. She now experiences not an act of perception, but an act of reflecting. In this later situation, there no longer occurs an act of seeing the apple. This clearly shows that the inspection of sense-impressions is not the same as the inspection of conscious states of perceiving. Even if one were to inspect one's sense-impressions and, in addition, all kinds of kinesthetic sensations, images, feelings, and the like, one would not be inspecting a conscious state of perceiving. Yet, the classic theory of introspection claims that one does just that. According to this theory, a conscious state is said to be *analyzed* into its *introspective elements,* if all of the mental contents have been listed which can be discerned after a shift from the original conscious state to one of inspection. A conscious process is said to be analyzed if all of the mental contents have been listed which can be made out during introspective intervals. In either case, the original conscious state or process is said to consist of the mental contents listed. This conception of introspection simply denies the existence of mental acts. The mind of the classic introspectionist consists of nothing but sensations, images, and feelings.

According to the classical notion of introspection, therefore, introspection of conscious states and processes can be nothing more than the inspection of *mental contents*. To claim that one can introspect one's conscious states and processes is to claim merely that one can inspect mental contents after a shift has taken place from a certain conscious state to one of reflecting on mental contents. In this sense of the term, introspection is certainly possible. But notice how far this sense strays from what one expects from the meaning of the term. In the case of perception, for example, what is inspected by means of this kind of introspection is neither the perceptual conscious state *when it occurs,* nor the *act of perceiving after the introspective shift has taken place,* but it is merely the mental contents which, before the shift, were part of the conscious state.

b) Systematic Introspection

Classic introspection is possible. But what about the systematic introspection of conscious processes, that is, of a temporal series of conscious states? I shall again give three examples.

(1) The subject of a psychological experiment has been trained to search for a certain associated word whenever he hears a particular stimulus word. Hearing the stimulus word, searching for the associated word, and uttering the word constitute what may be called "the natural conscious process" in this situation. Such a natural conscious process is simply a process that is neither brought about nor influenced by a mental set to introspect. After a while, the subject is told to describe what goes on in his mind while he is searching for the appropriate associated word. He is to report, in other words, on his mental contents. If he understands the instructions and if he has been trained to follow them, the subject will now be set to inspect as soon as the next stimulus word appears. For a moment, he will search for the associated word. But then, as a consequence of his instructions, a shift in conscious states will occur, and he will inspect mental contents. After another moment, the subject will again turn to the task of finding the associated word. And so on. This procedure will therefore have some or all of the following effects on the natural conscious process of finding the associated word: (a) certain natural conscious states either will not occur at all, or (b) they will occur later than usual, or (c) they will not be noticed as clearly as usual. This shows how a set to introspect interferes with a natural conscious process, and since systematic introspection cannot be achieved without such a set, it shows how difficult if not impossible it is to introspect natural conscious processes systematically.

(2) Suppose that the subject frequently catches himself having a certain thought when he hears a particular stimulus word. He is therefore instructed to watch

himself carefully on later trials to see whether or not the particular word evokes that particular thought. The next time he hears the word, he is in a very curious position. It seems to be entirely up to him whether or not he thinks that thought. And irrespective of what he finally does, he cannot help viewing whatever he does as being somehow influenced by a factor which does not normally belong to the situation.

(3) Finally, let us suppose that the subject considers several ways of going about searching for the associated word, before he is presented with the first stimulus word, but after he has been instructed to introspect. When the first stimulus word appears, he follows one of these contemplated methods, even though he would not have chosen this particular method without the instruction to introspect. As a result of the set to introspect, a conscious process occurs that is different from the one that would normally take place.

The first example shows that a set to introspect interrupts a natural conscious process by introspective intervals. And it is clear from the other two examples that it may lead to conscious processes other than those which would take place without a set to introspect. This kind of influence led many psychologists to the conclusion that the *systematic* introspection of natural conscious processes is impossible (see, for example, A. Messer, "Experimentell-psychologische Untersuchungen ueber das Denken," p. 9; and G. E. Mueller and F. Schumann, "Experimentelle Beitraege zur Untersuchung des Gedaechtnisses" p. 306). But they also noted that something like introspection can occur without such a set. This is the reason why I distinguish between introspection and systematic introspection.

Sometimes, when we remember something, we notice suddenly that we have a more or less vivid memory image. In such cases, there occurs a sudden *unintended* shift in conscious states. Such an unintended shift also occurs when we *catch ourselves* daydreaming or thinking of Paris. Some psychologists held that a trust-worthy description of introspective contents can only be given if the subject experiences such a sudden unintended shift without any previous intention to introspect. They argued that only on these occasions can one be sure that the natural conscious process was not influenced or disturbed by a set to inspect mental contents. [see, for example, Mueller, p. 69, and an article by J. I. Volkelt in *Zeitschrift fuer Philosophie und philosophische Kritik* 90 (1887)]. Be that as it may, it is true that one can catch oneself experiencing certain conscious states. Ryle made much of the fact that we can also catch ourselves scratching and that, therefore, what we catch ourselves in need not be a mental process (G. Ryle, *The Concept of Mind,* p. 166). Of course it need not be mental. But I doubt that the psychologists who thought that reliable introspective reports are only possible in cases where one catches oneself undergoing a certain conscious process believed that catching oneself is a criterion for the mental nature of what one catches oneself doing. Rather, what they were talking about was a sudden unintended shift in conscious states. Such a shift occurs even in the case of catching oneself scratching rather than, say, daydreaming. When you suddenly notice that you have been scratching yourself behind the ear, your conscious state has changed. Catching oneself is a "mark of the mental," of the mental which is so distasteful to Ryle, not because what one catches oneself in has to be mental, but because catching oneself is itself a mental phenomenon. It is a sudden shift in conscious states.

Let me sum up some of our results. We saw that one can undoubtedly inspect mental contents, that is, such mental things as sensations, images, pains, and the like. We also saw that one can therefore "introspect" conscious states and processes. As the term was used, the introspection of a conscious state consists of the inspection of its mental contents. But we noted that there are good reasons why we may doubt that one can systematically introspect natural conscious processes without disturbing them one way or another. It must be emphasized here that most introspective psychologists were well aware of these features and limitations of their method. And it must also be stressed that much of the criticism of the program of introspective psychology fails to appreciate the distinctions we have drawn between inspection, introspection, and systematic introspection. Only if one fails to make these distinctions will one be tempted to deny the possibility of any kind of introspection. But if one makes them, then it becomes obvious why introspective psychologists did so well in some fields of inquiry and so poorly in others.

c) Reflection on Mental Acts

Classic introspection consists of the inspection of mental contents. Mental acts simply do not exist for the classic introspectionist. It was a psychological revolution when the Wuerzburg School discovered "imageless thought." Can you conceive of a mind without acts of perceiving, desiring, imagining, remembering, without acts of love, without questions, etc.? How could any reasonable psychologist have believed in such a mind? But, then, to put things in the proper perspective, we must also remember the mind of Hume, consisting of nothing but impressions and ideas. And, of course, some contemporary philosophers have no minds at all.

Is introspection of mental acts possible? One thing is clear: according to our analysis, such introspection cannot mean that an act is its own object. But this is not, at any rate, what happens when we inspect our fears and desires, our hopes and doubts. Introspection of mental acts consists of the inspection of mental acts. Such an inspection requires that its object be the object of attention. And to be an object of attention, as we have seen, is to be an object *before* the mind. This means that one must experience a mental act whose object is the inspected mental act. Put differently, there must occur in the conscious state a mental act which intends the act that is inspected. From our analysis it follows that one cannot inspect one's conscious states; for conscious states are not their own objects.

You see that there are two red pencils on the desk before you. According to our view, you experience a conscious state which, among other things, contains certain sense-impressions and an act of seeing. What you pay attention to, through the act of seeing, are not the contents of your conscious state, but rather the two red pencils on the desk. Now, how would one go about switching from paying attention to the pencils to paying attention to one's conscious state? It is obvious that as soon as one tries to pay attention to one's conscious state of seeing the pencils, one is no longer in this conscious state, one no longer perceives the pencils. And this shows that, in general, any attempt to inspect a conscious state inevitably destroys the conscious state. One cannot inspect the conscious state which one experiences, because in order to inspect it one would have to experience quite a different conscious state.

We cannot inspect an act of seeing when we experience it, when it is part of the conscious state. But can we not switch from seeing something to paying attention to our seeing something? Of course we can. But now another difficulty arises. A mental act of seeing is not something that lasts for a while. Properly and phenomenally speaking, it has no duration at all. You cannot be half-way through seeing the two red pencils on your desk. As soon as you *see* that there are these two pencils on the desk, you *have seen* it. And what holds for an act of seeing holds for all perceptual acts. More than that, it holds for all mental acts. Therefore, one cannot really switch one's attention to a mental act when one experiences it; for as soon as one experiences it, it is gone. But you can pay attention to it by remembering it. When you remember that a little while ago you saw two red pencils on your desk, the previous act of seeing is an object of your conscious state, not a part of it. It is before the mind, through the remembering. What is experienced is not the act of seeing, but the act of remembering, as shown in figure 10.

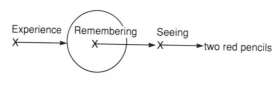

Figure 10

Thus we can pay attention to mental acts by remembering them.

But memory is not the only way in which we can pay attention to mental acts. There is also reflection. It seems to me that when you are aware that you just saw two red pencils on your desk, you do not, properly speaking, remember your seeing. You do not remember it in the way in which you remember a desire you had two years ago. There is, in my opinion, an immediacy to our "knowing what goes on in our minds" when it goes on which is quite different from memory. This "immediacy" is characteristic of what I have called an act of *reflection*. In short, I think that there are two quite different kinds of mental acts, memory and reflection, and that by means of reflection, we can constantly and immediately monitor what goes on in our conscious states. By reflection, we can pay attention to mental contents that last, as well as to mental acts that do not. I chose the term 'reflection' for this unique mental act because of Locke's terminology: "By reflection then, in the following part of this discourse, I would be understood to mean, that notice which the mind takes of its own operations, and the manner of them, by reason whereof there come to be ideas of these operations in the understanding" (J. Locke, *An Essay Concerning Human Understanding*, Book II, Chapter 1, 2).

d) A Word about Emotions and Moods

Mental acts, I said, have no phenomenal duration; they do not last for some time. How does this fact agree with the view that fear, for example, is a mental act?

There is a woman who for several hours lives in terrible fear that her neighbor will break into her house and shoot her. At one point, at the beginning of this time period, she experiences an act of fear that her neighbor will break into her house and shoot her. Afterwards, numerous other mental acts occur. She thinks of locking all her doors; she remembers a movie in which a person was in a similar situation; she wishes she could move the heavy dining room table against the door; she imagines what it would be like to be shot; she regrets having sent her husband out to shop for a new lawnmower; she wonders what kind of gun her neighbor may actually use when he shoots her; she hopes it will not be a shotgun; and so on. This, of course, is the stuff exciting movies are made from. The point I wish to make is that the act of fearing is not present all of the time while she is afraid. It only occurs sporadically, punctuating her fear, but not constituting it. Yet, the woman is obviously afraid all that time. Thus there are two facts which are undeniable. Firstly, mental acts of being afraid occur only intermittently in this situation. Secondly, the woman is afraid for hours on end.

I think that these facts call for a distinction between acts of fearing, on the one hand, and the emotional state of fear, on the other. While the acts occur only sporadically, the emotional state lasts uninterruptedly for a certain length of time. The *emotional state of fear,* as I shall use the expression, is not itself a mental act; it has no object. This emotional state can be experienced even at times when the act of fearing is not present. But the emotional state gets its "direction" from the mental act. The mental act makes this emotion a fear of being shot rather than, say, a fear of dying of cancer. Now, this distinction between the act of fearing and the emotional state of fear leads to a distinction between the introspection of the act and the introspection of the emotional state. The mental act of fearing to be shot can be remembered and it can be the object of reflection. Years later, the woman may remember those horrible hours and her fear of being shot by her neighbor. But she can also tell you at the time of her ordeal what it is she is afraid of: she can reflect on the mental act of fear which she just experienced. On the other hand, the emotional state of fear lasts for hours and can be inspected during that time. She experiences this emotional state and can intermittently reflect on it. The crucial difference between the reflection on the act of fear and the reflection on the emotional state is that the state lasts, while the act does not. As a consequence, the state can be inspected when it is present, while the act cannot. More accurately, the emotional state can be inspected while it is experienced, but the act cannot.

But even this way of describing the situation is not quite accurate. It follows from our analysis that the emotional state is not a part of the conscious state when it is inspected; it is the object of an act of reflection, and it is this act which is part of the conscious state. In other words, it follows from our analysis that the emotional state is not experienced when it is inspected; rather, the act of reflection is experienced. Yet, when we reflect on a present emotion, the emotion is not "gone"; it has not "disappeared from the mind"; it is still present. Thus we have to improve on our picture of what is "in the mind" at a given time. A mind, we realize, consists not only of an experience and what is experienced, the conscious state, but, under certain circumstances, also of what is reflected upon. To use our previous suggestive terminology, what is *before* the mind at a given time, the emotional state when reflected upon, can be *part of* that mind. What this means is, roughly speaking, that the emotion is still there when reflection ceases. The unfortunate woman of our example experiences the emotion of fear. Then, at a certain moment, she pays attention to it rather than to what she fears. She now reflects on her emotion. What she experiences is the act of reflection, not the emotion. But a moment later, she switches again to an unreflective attitude, and now once again she experiences the emotion. The emotion, we say, did not disappear while she reflected upon it; it was there and it is still there.

The picture of introspection which has so far emerged, I admit, is rather complicated. Perhaps this is another reason why so many have despaired of achieving for the mind what so clearly has been achieved for the world around us, namely, a careful and measured description of the phenomena. But the truth of our analysis can only be tested if we are willing to consider additional problems in the light of it.

If I am correct, then an "emotion" like fear or jealousy is really a complex phenomenon: it consists of an act as well as the emotional state. The act of fearing has an intentional object. One cannot fear, as Brentano would say, without fearing something. The emotional state, on the other hand, has no intentional object. It gets its object through the corresponding act. Furthermore, the act of fearing, like an act of seeing or an act of desiring, has no duration. It appears and is gone before one can interrupt it. The emotional state, on the other hand, lasts for some time. Some emotions may last for minutes; others, for hours. During all this time, the emotion is punctuated and reinforced by the corresponding act which gave birth to it and keeps it alive. Just as the fear is about to disappear, the act is experienced again, and the emotion gets a new lease on life. On another occasion, one cannot get rid of the emotional state, try as one may. No distraction will work. Quite to the contrary, one must compulsively dwell on one's jealousy, with the result that it gets worse as time goes on. Of course, the act of fearing which occurs intermittently may not always have the same object. With one fear, other fears are created. A whole network of related fears may thus give sustenance to the emotional state.

While the emotion lasts, I said, one can inspect it, just as one can inspect a memory image or a sensation. But I do not wish to imply that the inspection of an emotion has no influence on the emotion. It is obvious, for example, that one's anger may decrease if one takes a step back and takes a good look at it. By reflecting on one's anger, one puts some distance between oneself and the object of one's anger. The object of one's anger is no longer before one's mind. One lives, not in the object of one's anger, but in the anger itself. Thus there are emotions which can be influenced by acts of reflection, which can be gotten rid of by reflection; and there are emotions which resist all attempts to extinguish them by putting them into perspective. Anger is of the first kind, jealousy, of the second. Jealousy, as the German pun has it, "ist eine Leidenschaft, die mit Eifer sucht, was Leiden schaft."

A mood is in some respects like an emotion: it lasts for some time, and it colors all the ingredients of the mind. But in contrast to an emotion, it lacks the direction-giving mental act. When one is depressed, one is not depressed about something in particular; and when one is elated and happy, one is just happy in general. Like a strong emotion, a mood pervades one's mental life. The mental contents of one's conscious state are colored by it. If we had to depict a mood in our by now familiar diagram, we would have to color the conscious state a certain shade of grey; dark grey, or even black, for the bleaker moods; light grey or white for the happier moods. A mood, like an emotion, is not a separate constituent of the conscious state, like a sensation or an image, but is something that determines the quality of one's conscious state. (The distinction between emotions and moods has been especially well described by Otto Friedrich Bollnow in *Das Wesen der Stimmungen*.)

I claimed that a mood, in distinction to an emotion, has no act that gives it a direction toward an object. However, this does not mean that a mood may not be triggered by a specific experience or a certain thought. You may get depressed, for example, when reminded of your mortality by the death of a close friend. But even though your depression is caused by this reminder, your mortality is not its object. You may be afraid of dying, but you are not depressed about it. Of course, there are *reasons* why you are depressed, and part of the reason is that you thought about your friend's sudden death. But there are no "*objects*" of depression, as there are "objects" of mental acts.

Moods are even harder to change than emotions. It is well known that a depressed person cannot change her state by thinking cheerful thoughts, or by remembering better times, or by being assured that things are not all that gloomy. In order to come out of a depression, one must change one's behavior, rather than one's conscious state. The depressed person cannot talk herself into getting out of bed, taking a shower, having breakfast, and going to class. Someone else may force her to do these things, literally dragging her out of bed, etc.; and lo and behold, after breakfast, the depression is gone. Another day can be faced. Of course, the same result can be achieved through the miracles of chemistry. And there are depressions which cannot be treated any other way.

What I have said about emotions and moods, I am afraid, is standard fare and hardly controversial. Furthermore, novelists have given us detailed and profound descriptions of these mental phenomena. But I have had a philosophical motive. I wish to make a philosophical point in the next section. This point touches on the question of whether or not anxiety is a mood. I shall argue that the common view that anxiety is a mood is mistaken.

I think that we must distinguish between "feelings," "emotions," and "moods." Feelings are the various degrees and variations of pain and pleasure. Emotions like fear, anger, envy, jealousy, etc., are characterized by consisting both of a mental act, which gives a "direction" to the emotion, and the emotion proper (the emotional state) which lasts for some time. Moods, finally, are the various degrees of happiness and sadness, ranging from ecstasy to deep depression. In distinction from emotions, they have no direction-giving mental acts. These are not all the differences between feelings, emotions, and moods, but they may serve to indicate a broad distinction among these three kinds of mental phenomena.

THREE

████████

The Alleged Infallibility
of "Inner Sense"

a) Infallibility and Inspection of "Mental Contents"

There is a long and strong philosophical tradition, reaching from St. Augustine to the present, according to which knowledge of the contents of the mind is infallible. It will be our next task to highlight this tradition and to refute its thesis.

Descartes's method of doubt, you may recall, has three steps. Firstly, Descartes argues that the perception of ordinary objects is not infallible. A tower seen in the distance, for example, may appear to be round when it is really square. We may mistake the person across the street for our neighbor. And so on. Secondly, Descartes maintains that not even "near-perceptions" are infallible. Descartes believes that he is sitting by the fireplace, in his room, thinking about the fallibility of knowledge, but he may really be asleep in his bed, merely dreaming that he is awake and philosophizing. Thirdly and finally, an evil demon may be manipulating his mind so that he believes, as he of course does, that two plus three is five and that a square has four sides, even though these propositions may actually be false. Not even our knowledge of mathematical propositions, therefore, is infallible. Descartes then proceeds to show that at least one proposition is exempted from this systematic doubt. This is the proposition that he exists.

Two things are of special interest for our purposes. Firstly, the knowledge shown to be doubtful is not knowledge of mental things, of the contents of the mind, but of the external world. Our perceptions of the things around us, of towers in the distance, of persons across the street, are shown to be fallible. And so are our perceptions of our own bodies, their locations in space and in time. Even knowledge of mathematical propositions is shown to be doubtful. But nothing is said about knowledge of our minds. Perhaps Descartes could assume that the skeptic who was to be refuted shares with him the assumption that knowledge of the contents of our minds is not open to skeptical doubt.

The second point concerns Descartes's criterion for infallibility. The first two steps of the method of doubt seem to yield a clear and obvious answer: A *kind* of knowledge is deemed to be fallible if and only if we have made mistakes in regard to this kind in the past. Since we have made mistakes about things seen in the distance, the shape of the tower, for example, perception of distant objects is fallible. Since we have mistakenly believed that we are in one place when we merely dreamed that we were at that place, our perceptions of this sort are fallible as well. But this criterion would equally show that mathematical knowledge is fallible; for it is clear that we have made mistakes about mathematical matters as well. Who has not added up wrongly when trying to balance her check book? Even brilliant mathematicians accept false theorems as true. Why, then, does Descartes believe that he must introduce the evil demon when he takes the third step of the method of doubt? Why does he think that it is necessary to switch to a different criterion of infallibility, a criterion that may be summed up in this way: A kind of knowledge is infallible if and only if we could not make mistakes in regard to this kind of knowledge, even if a powerful demon were to try to deceive us? It would be pleasant to pursue this question, but we must not stray from our path. Let us adopt as our criterion for infallibility the one Descartes applies in the first two steps of the method of doubt. This is our question: Do we make mistakes about the contents of our minds?

Notice that I have not mentioned certainty. Certainty, I hold, is a matter of firmness of belief. It is a quality of belief. People can be certain about the most dubious propositions. I shall not reveal my prejudices by giving examples of those beliefs which I hold with certainty. But it can be said that I am as certain that I am now sitting at my desk as I am about some mathematical propositions. Certainty, it seems to me, can attach to our beliefs about the world around us, even to beliefs about the realm beyond the world around us, just as easily as to the statements of mathematics and logic. It can attach itself even to the propositions of metaphysics! On the other hand, there are propositions of set theory, for example, about which some of us are not certain at all. And many of the philosophical propositions which I tentatively advance in this work seem to me to be somewhat uncertain.

Can we make mistakes about what occurs in our own minds? Do we make mistakes, to take the obvious case first, about the sense-impressions which we experience? Some philosophers have argued that we cannot. Look at the following famous passage from H. H. Price:

> When I see a tomato there is much that I can doubt. I can doubt whether it is a tomato that I am seeing, and not a cleverly painted piece of wax. I can doubt whether there is any material thing there at all. Perhaps what I took for a tomato was really a reflection; perhaps I am even the victim of some hallucination. One thing however I cannot doubt: that there exists a red patch of a round and somewhat bulgy shape, standing out from a background of other colour patches, and having a certain visual depth, and that this whole field of colour is directly present to my consciousness.
>
> (H. H. Price, *Perception*, p. 3)

We grant immediately that the perception of the tomato is not infallible. But in regard to the red round patch, we wish to pause for a moment. I shall take for granted that this patch is what I have called a "visual sense-impression" or a "visual sensation." And I shall also assume that Price knows that this sense-impression is red rather than blue, round rather than square, and so on, because he has inspected it. If so, then Price is claiming that the inspection of visual sense-impressions is indubitable, that is, infallible. But this seems to me to be mistaken. It seems to me that we can make mistakes about the properties of our sense-impressions. For example, we may believe that a given sense-impression is round, but find out, after closer inspection, that it is really sort of pear-shaped. We may assert at first that it is uniformly red, but then notice that parts of it are darker than others, and so on. And what holds for visual sense-impressions holds equally well for auditory and olfactory ones: we can and do make mistakes about their properties and relations. Furthermore, we can and do make mistakes about feelings and emotions. The properties of a pain may at first not be obvious to us; an emotion may be mistaken for quite a different one. And such examples can be multiplied. Why, then, have so many philosophers insisted, in the face of common sense and introspective psychology, that our knowledge of mental contents is infallible?

Some may have reasoned that unless there are infallible truths, the skeptic cannot be refuted. And since they cannot bear the thought of skepticism's victory, they bury their heads, like philosophical ostriches, in the sand of ignorance. But surely this is a poor reason. If all knowledge is fallible, so be it! No amount of wishful thinking will change the fact. *I do believe that all knowledge is fallible.* But in distinction from those philosophers, I do not believe that this fact means the triumph of skepticism or, at least, the triumph of the kind of skepticism one needs to fear.

I think that there is also another, more profound, reason for believing that knowledge of sense-impressions is infallible. Take a look at this passage from Chisholm:

> If for any such characteristic F, I can justify a claim to knowledge by saying of something that it *appears* F (by saying of the wine that it now *looks* red, or *tastes* sour to me), where the verb is intended in the descriptive, phenomenological sense just indicated, then the *appearing* in question is self-presenting and my statement expresses what is directly evident. The claim that I thus justify, by saying of something that it appears F, may be the claim that the thing *is* F, but as we have seen, it may also be some other claim. To the question "What justification do I have for thinking I know, or for counting it as evident, that something now *looks* red to me, or tastes sour?" I could reply only by reiterating that something does now look red or tastes sour.

(R. M. Chisholm, *Theory of Knowledge,* pp. 32–33)

It is clear from the context that the appearing terminology is doing duty for the sensation terminology. Chisholm states that we could say "I am experiencing a red appearance" or "I have a sour taste" instead of "the wine appears now red to me" and "the wine now tastes sour to me," respectively. Chisholm is therefore talking about visual and other kinds of sense-impression. But notice the 'now' that appears in Chisholm's sentences; for example, in the expression 'the wine now looks red'. This suggests that he is not really talking about a lasting sense-impression but about one of his acts of reflection on the sense-impression. Right now, he seems to be saying, my reflection upon the sense-impression shows that it is red. In other words, Chisholm tells us what one particular act of reflecting on the lasting sense-impression yields. He is telling us that, according to this particular act, the sense-impression is red. But this kind of report must be distinguished from reporting on the color of the sense-impression as established by (thorough) inspection. The latter may involve a number of acts of reflection.

Next, Chisholm proposes to dispose of sense-impressions in favor of kinds of sensing, a move that has become popular under the heading of "the adverbial theory of sensing." Instead of talking about red sensations, he proposes to talk about sensing redly. Note that this is not supposed to mean that the sensing, the mental act, is red, but rather that it is a peculiar kind, not further specified, of sensing. Now, I think that an adverbial view of sensing makes no more sense than an adverbial theory of perceiving would, according to which one may be said to "see airplanely." But this is not the point I wish to make. Rather, I propose to accept his view for a moment in order to call attention to the fact that his introspective report is about a mental act and not about the object of this act, that is, about a visual sense-impression. When he states that he is now sensing redly, he is telling us that he is now experiencing a mental act of sensing of a certain sort. Looking at the subject matter from this perspective, we are faced with the possibility that some of those who claim infallibility for introspective reports about sense-data may in actuality claim infallibility for reports about acts of reflection.

This impression is reinforced when we turn to another class of statements which Chisholm takes to be "directly evident":

> Thinking and believing provide us with paradigm cases of the directly evident. Consider a reasonable man who is thinking about Albuquerque, or who believes that Albuquerque is in New Mexico, and suppose him to reflect on the philosophical question. What is my justification for counting it as evident, or for thinking that I know, that I am thinking about Albuquerque, or that I believe that Albuquerque is in New Mexico?

> (Chisholm, 1966, p. 28)

The first sentence is misleading. It is not thinking and believing in general which are directly evident, but rather thinking or believing that one is thinking or believing. What is supposedly infallible is not the thought that Albuquerque is in New Mexico, but the thought (judgment, assertion) that one is now thinking that Albuquerque is in New Mexico. Obviously, I can make a mistake about where Albuquerque is located, but presumably I cannot make a mistake about what I am now thinking. This interpretation of Chisholm's view raises the question of whether or not knowledge about acts of reflection and acts of believing (judging, asserting, etc.) are infallible.

b) Infallibility and Reflection on Mental Acts

Reflection, I claimed earlier, is a unique mental act which allows us to inspect mental contents and to monitor mental acts. It is the source of most of our knowledge about mental things. It provides us with most of the knowledge which we have of our own minds. In every case of reflection, the act of reflection is part of the conscious state, and its object is the object of one's attention. If one reflects on a desire, for example, the situation looks like figure 11.

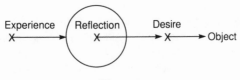

Figure 11

To have a mental act is to be able to reflect upon it. But this is not to say—and I cannot stress this point too strongly—that the act of experiencing itself is an act of knowing. I have devoted much time to arguing that experience is *not* reflection. And let me also stress once again that this turning of one's attention to mental acts in reflection is not a case of memory proper. Reflection has an immediacy, it seems to me, which acts of remembering do not have. It is like a shadow that accompanies all of our experienced mental acts.

Is reflection on mental acts infallible? Can we be mistaken about now thinking that Albuquerque is in New Mexico, now seeing an elephant standing on two legs, now having a desire for the boy next door? It may seem to be impossible to make mistakes in these matters. What would it be like to be mistaken about thinking that Albuquerque is in New Mexico? Well, there are two possibilities: one could be mistaken about what it is that one thinks, or else one could be mistaken about the mental act that occurs. For example, one may really be thinking that Albuquerque is in *Mexico;* or one may not really be *thinking* that Albuquerque is in New Mexico, that is, asserting it, but may merely suppose it to be in New Mexico. You could be mistaken about the object of the act or about the nature of the act itself.

There is no doubt that reflection is the basis, and the only basis, for all of our tests of our perceptions, beliefs, emotions, etc. You see a tower in the distance and perceive it to be round. When you reach it, you see that it is really square. You realize that you made a mistake earlier. You discover this mistake because you trust your memory: you remember now that a while ago it looked round to you. But this means that you now trust your reflections concerning (a) your remembering of what you perceived to be the case earlier, and (b) your present seeing that the tower is square. Only because you take these reflections for granted do you discover that you made a perceptual mistake. In general, there is no way of checking, no test, no discovery of mistakes, that does not rest ultimately on accepting the testimony of reflection. But though it is true that in the end we cannot but trust reflection, this does not imply that reflection is infallible. Nor does it follow, of course, that we can never discover that we have been mistaken. Reflection, though it is the last court of appeal, is nevertheless fallible. A person may not be sure whether just now he saw something or merely thinks that he saw it; a person may convince herself that she is not afraid of something when she really is; a person may come to believe that he despises his mother when he really desires her; and a person may insist that she believes something when she really believes something else. Reflection on mental acts, it seems to me, is no more infallible than inspection of mental contents.

This claim must appear so obviously mistaken, if not utterly wrongheaded, that we should look more carefully at a paradigm case of allegedly infallible knowledge.

Ayer contrasts the assertion "that is a bunch of grapes," made while he is sitting in a vineyard, with the assertion "I am now seeing what looks to me like a bunch of grapes," and then asks: "How in that case could I possibly be wrong?" (A. J. Ayer, *The Problem of Knowledge,* pp. 59–60). Even if there are no grapes there, even if he is hallucinating, Ayer points out, his statement would be true. That is undoubtedly so. But it does not follow, as he seems to think, that Ayer could not be mistaken in "describing the character of the experience" which he has, that is, in describing the character of the act which he experiences. It may be the case that Ayer's act of seeing does not really intend a bunch of grapes, whether or not there really is anything in front of him at all. Even as a mere report about the act of seeing and its object, his assertion can be false. There is a scene in Orwell's 1984 that forcefully proves my point. The interrogator O'Brien holds up his hand in front of his prisoner Winston, with four fingers extended and the thumb hidden. He asks Winston how many fingers he is holding up, and Winston answers: "Four." O'Brien turns a dial and Winston feels incredible pain. The next time, Winston answers the question with "Five." But O'Brien is not satisfied: "No, Winston, that is no use. You are lying. You still think there are four. How many fingers, please?" Winston screams: "Four! Five! Four! Anything you like. Only stop it, stop the pain." After more torture and more interrogation, the scene ends like this:

"Just now I held up the fingers of my hand to you. You saw five fingers. Do you remember that?"

"Yes."

O'Brien held up the fingers of his left hand, with the thumb concealed.

"There are five fingers there. Do you see five fingers?"

"Yes."

And he did see them, for a fleeting instant, before the scenery of his mind changed.

He saw five fingers, and there was no deformity.

The gist of this horribly repugnant scene is that a person can be forced, because of the threat of unbearable pain, to misreflect upon his perceptions. The lesson is that a person, in extreme circumstances, *may learn to be mistaken* about his perceptual acts. Let me emphasize that such mistakes are very rare. But even though they are rare, they prove that reflection is not infallible.

I chose Ayer's example of perception because it seems to me to make the strongest case for the infallibility of reflection. As soon as we turn to a different kind of example, my contention is strengthened. I have in mind emotions, desires, fears, etc. Reflections on acts of this sort are quite often mistaken. Freud's theory of the unconscious is merely a theoretical elaboration of this well-known fact. We can kill several birds with one stone if we take a brief look at Freud's view.

c) Infallibility and the Freudian Unconscious

Freud had an uncanny knack for expressing his views in a most inappropriate terminology. His use of the word 'unconscious' is a prime example of this tendency. Some of the misunderstandings of his theory could have been avoided had he chosen a more felicitous terminology. On the other hand, it may also be true that part of his fame rests precisely on this provocative use of language. Freud, we must keep in mind, is one of the greatest writers of German prose, and his style is, on the whole, admirably clear and concise. Why, then, does he time and again forge a technical vocabulary which is bound to distort his views and provoke antagonism to them? May his own unconscious have been at work for reasons that are quite clear to some of his admirers?

We shall discard Freud's idiosyncratic terminology and attempt to fit his theory into our emerging picture of the structure of the mind. The first thing to stress is that our notion of a conscious state has no connection with Freud's notion of the unconscious. One may be tempted to call anything "unconscious" which is mental but does not belong to the conscious state. The act of experiencing the conscious state would then be unconscious. Following the temptation further, we would then say that a mind consists at any given moment of a conscious and an unconscious part, namely, of a conscious state and the act of experiencing the conscious state. But I prefer not to talk this way; in part, at least, because I wish to avoid as best as I can any confusion with Freud's theory.

What does the Freudian notion of the unconscious come down to? In one sentence: An unconscious desire, for example, is a desire which, though it is *experienced,* is not *recognized* for what it is. The person who experiences the desire has *learned* to misidentify it. This learning process is called "repression."

Let us consider an example. Assume that a girl called Anna enters her father's bedroom one hot summer morning in order to ask him a question. Her father is just about to get out of bed and, since it is summer, he is completely nude. Suddenly, Anna feels a strong sexual desire for her father. She recognizes her desire, is terribly ashamed of it, and feels guilty for having it. But she also suddenly remembers that the night before, at the dinner table, her family had bemoaned the fact that a girlfriend of hers had suffered a sudden heart attack; and she wonders whether the terrible state she is finding herself in may not be due to a similar affliction. Perhaps she is mistaken: her agitation is caused, not by a desire for her father, but rather by a similar heart attack. With this thought, she runs from her father's room, goes to her bedroom, and starts taking her pulse. All of this happens in a flash.

The thought that something may be wrong with her heart reduces Anna's feeling of shame and guilt: she cannot help having a weak heart; it is not her fault. Of course, the thought that something is wrong with her heart is not a pleasant one, but it is like nothing compared to the recognition that she wants to sleep with her father. The reduction in shame and guilt is a most powerful reward for coming to believe that her heart may be weak. Anna thus learns to believe that there is something wrong with her heart. Whenever she feels from now on a desire for her father, or even feels a desire for another man (perhaps, someone who reminds her of her father), she immediately concludes that her heart is acting up again and starts taking her pulse. The counting of her heartbeat distracts her from having erotic feelings; it requires great attention. She complains to her mother about these frequent attacks and is sent to the family doctor. By now, these "attacks" have spread to other situations. She has an attack when she is alone with her boy-friend;

when she is in a crowded elevator, pressed against an attractive male; when she sorts her father's underwear for the washing. The family doctor, of course, finds nothing wrong with Anna's heart and sends her to a specialist. The specialist finds nothing wrong either and sends her to a colleague. Finally, one decides that Anna is neurotic, and she is put in the care of a psychoanalyst.

Anna's sad story illustrates the process of repression. The desire for her father is said to become unconscious because it is repressed. At first, when she entered her father's bedroom, her desire was conscious. She realized it for what it is when it first occurred. She (a) experienced the desire, (b) reflected upon it, and (c) recognized it for what it was. This recognition made her feel most awful. But then another possibility occurred to her, and the thought that there may be something wrong with her heart, in the blinking of an eye, removed her terrible guilt and shame. Thus the thought gets powerfully reinforced. Anna *learns to think* that her agitations are due to a weak heart rather than a desire for her father. She learns not to recognize her desire for what it is. The desire has now been *repressed* and has become *unconscious*. There is nothing mysterious about this process of repression and the resulting unconscious. It is a straightforward learning process. Anna's desire for her father, we must stress, is still there; it is still experienced; it is still a part of her conscious state, it has not disappeared. A repressed unconscious desire is just as much part of the conscious state as an unrepressed conscious desire. But Anna has learned to *misidentify* what she experiences. An unconscious desire, therefore, is simply a desire which is experienced but misidentified.

Unconscious desires, fears, wishes, etc., are prime examples of mistaken reflection. But it must be emphasized that there is an important difference between an "ordinary" mistake of reflection and a "neurotic" mistake. Anna's mistaken reflection *serves a purpose*. It is possible for you to think that you dislike someone intensely at first sight when, in reality, you are attracted to that person. But this may be an honest mistake; you simply have not sorted out your feelings too carefully. As soon as you reflect on what you really feel toward her, you realize that you find her attractive. The neurotic's mistake, by contrast, is systematic and functional. It always serves a purpose, and the purpose is to reduce guilt, shame, horror, and so on. What is fascinating about Freud's insight is not the bare fact that we can make mistakes about our desires, fears, hopes, etc., but that we can learn to perpetuate such mistakes because they serve a purpose.

To return to Anna, her troubles are just beginning after she has learned to believe that there is something wrong with her heart. The doctors now assure her that she is as healthy as an ox. She "knows," of course, that they must be mistaken, but why would they lie to her? Are they hiding something from her, something even more fearsome than a weak heart? Or are they right after all; is she really imagining things? Anna will have to invent further stories, make up new hypotheses. She may have to repress other fears. The point is that a neurotic's work is never done: the truth continuously threatens to destroy the web of misconceptions which the neurotic has so carefully spun. That is the reason why neurotics are miserable, why they cannot relax, and why they cannot concentrate on anything else. It is the task of the psychoanalyst to relieve the neurotic of this burden. The principle of Anna's cure is clear: the process of repression has to be reversed. She has to unlearn her misidentification of her desire for her father. Only the truth will make her free of neurosis. Most likely, she will only be able to face the truth if she can be made to feel less ashamed and guilty about her desire. However this is accomplished, her hypochondria will disappear as soon as she realizes that what agitates her is the desire for her father.

A neurotic, it may be said, hides the truth about her desires, fears, hopes, etc. from herself. Every neurotic lives a lie. But we must be careful not to take this talk of lying too literally. Otherwise, it is easy to arrive at Sartre's view that a Freudian view of repression is absurd (see Jean-Paul Sartre, *Being and Nothingness,* pp. 90–96). Sartre believes that Freud's theory splits consciousness into two parts, so that it becomes impossible to account for the fact that it is one and the same thing that does the lying and is lied to. He constructs the following dilemma. Either it is one and the same consciousness that lies and is lied to, or else it is not. According to Sartre, Freud chose the second alternative: Consciousness is split into two parts, the ego and the id. But this will not do, Sartre argues, for "the very essence of the reflexive idea of hiding something from oneself implies the unity of one and the same psychic mechanism and consequently a double activity in the heart of unity . . ." (Sartre, 1966, p. 94).

But the first alternative, as Sartre sees it, is not acceptable either. Assume that person X deceives person Y into believing P. In this case, X does not believe that P is the case. Y, on the other hand, does believe that P is the case. Now, if Y is the same person as X, if Y is the same consciousness as X, then X does not believe in P, insofar as X is the deceiver, and X also and at the same time believes in P, insofar as X is the deceived. But this is a contradiction. It is impossible for one and the same person, at the same time, to believe P and also not to believe P. According to Sartre, it is indeed one and the same consciousness which in "bad faith" deceives and is deceived. Does this mean, then, that Sartre believes in a contradiction? I do not know the answer. However, I also believe that Sartre would not be greatly disturbed by our question. Bad faith, he might well have replied, is by its very nature contradictory.

Our story of Anna's neurosis clearly shows in what precise sense she is both a liar and also lied to. She clearly realizes at first that she desires her father. Only because of this realization does she feel shame and guilt. Later, she thinks that she has a heart ailment, because this thought comforts her. She does not believe at one and the same time both that she desires her father and also that she does not desire her father. Rather, even though she believed at one time that she desires her father, she no longer does. Now she believes that something is wrong with her heart. She no longer believes that she desires her father; and if it were suggested to her that she does, she would respond with righteous indignation. Thus there is no contradiction.

There is a small lesson. One may come to think that there is a contradiction if one starts with the mistaken assumption that one cannot possibly have a desire without knowing that one has it. Since we have agreed that Anna still desires her father, even after she has convinced herself that there is something wrong with her heart, we would have to conclude, based on this assumption, that she still knows that she has the desire. And since she knows it, she believes it. Thus she would later on both believe and also not believe that she desires her father. It is precisely this point which I have argued earlier: To have a desire and to know that one has it, are two quite different things. I have even claimed that merely to have a desire is *not* to know that one has it. Experience is not knowledge. In order to find out what one experiences, one must reflect on what one experiences. And reflection, we have just seen, may not yield the correct answer. Anna gives the wrong answer, because the truth is unbearable.

d) A Word about Anxiety

I distinguished between emotions and moods. There can be no doubt that emotions and moods are essential parts of the furniture of the human mind. What would a mind be without fear and anger, without love and lust, without joy and sadness? But the importance of emotions and moods extends further. Without emotions, I believe, there would be no knowledge of the difference between right and wrong. Our knowledge of what is morally good and evil rests, ultimately, not on perception and reason, but on our emotional responses. This is a long story, and I have to be content here to point out that "knowledge of the external world" encompasses more than common sense and science. Morality lies at its center.

Moods, too, play an important role in our understanding of the world. Bollnow describes it well:

> Perception itself, therefore, is already thoroughly a matter of mood [gestimmt], and even the apparently excepted theoretical attitude has not freed itself from the mood, but, quite to the contrary, presupposes a certain mood, namely, that of "quiet lingering". The same holds immediately for all of the achievements of understanding life and the world. In every mood, the world is already interpreted in a very specific way, and all understanding is already guided by this basic interpretation of life and world through the mood.

(O. F. Bollnow, *Das Wesen der Stimmungen,* p. 57)

Bollnow goes on to show in detail how different moods, from ecstasy to deepest sadness, color our experience of people, of time, and of the world.

We undoubtedly owe the emphasis on the importance of moods to the existentialists. Heidegger in particular derives his analysis of human existence from a consideration of moods as the ground of this existence. But here we notice a curious phenomenon. Although existentialists stress the importance of all moods, it is one mood in particular that has caught their fancy: "The unique importance of anxiety is the common uniting presupposition of all existentialism, whose far-reaching consequences appear in ultimate clarity in Heidegger. All other moods are from the very beginning related to anxiety" (Bollnow, p. 67). Bollnow does not share this prejudice of the existentialists in favor of anxiety. His investigation deals with the influence of sadness and despair on our experience of reality, with the nature of Nietzsche's dionysical ecstasy, and even with Proust's conception of time in happiness. Yet, Bollnow shares the existentialists' view that anxiety is a fundamental mood. I shall argue that this view is mistaken. Anxiety is not only not the most important of all moods, but not a mood at all. Existentialists, therefore, are doubly mistaken. Their first mistake is, as Bollnow convincingly argues, that they think of anxiety as being of the essence of human existence. But they are also, secondly, mistaken, as I shall argue, on even deeper grounds; for anxiety is not a mood at all.

Bollnow almost stumbles on the truth when he at one point realizes that anxiety has no place in the spectrum from happiness to sadness which is characteristic of moods:

> On the one hand, they [anxiety and despair] are close to the dejected [gedrueckten] moods, are themselves forms, nay, enhanced forms of depression. On the other hand, however, they are so different from them that a common treatment would distort the essential nature of these two groups. Happiness and sadness are two poles between which human life fluctuates in a regular or irregular manner, and even though seriousness has its proper opposite in fun, these new moods [anxiety and despair] lie outside of such a polarity. They have no genuine opposite . . . One could therefore consider to remove them from the circle of customary moods, and to contrast them with the latter as being "in bad humour" [Verstimmungen].
>
> (Bollnow, pp. 48–49)

Indeed, anxiety does not fit the pattern characteristic of moods. In order to see where the existentialists—and even such an astute observer as Bollnow—go wrong, we shall take a brief look at Kierkegaard's notion of anxiety and then return to Anna's neurosis.

In his *The Concept of Dread*, Kierkegaard develops (at least) four theses about the nature of anxiety (dread):

(1) *Anxiety is a defining characteristic of human beings*. Human beings, and only human beings, can experience anxiety. Animals, for example, can be afraid, but they cannot be anxious. Kierkegaard states: "One does not therefore find dread in the beast precisely for the reason that by nature the beast is not qualified by spirit" (S. Kierkegaard, *The Concept of Dread*, p. 38; see also p. 47 and p. 139).

(2) *Anxiety is not the same as fear:* "One almost never sees the concept dread dealt with in psychology, and I must therefore call attention to the fact that it is different from fear and similar concepts which refer to something definite, whereas dread is freedom's reality as possibility for possibility" (Kierkegaard, p. 38).

(3) *The object of anxiety is nothingness*. This nothingness is sometimes said to be fate and sometimes said to be guilt. Here is a representative quotation: "If then we ask further what is the object of dread, the answer as usual must be that it is nothing" (Kierkegaard, p. 86; see also p. 55 and p. 69). Just as I have taken the liberty to use the translator's 'dread' in the quoted text, so I shall take the liberty to speak of 'nothingness' where the text contains 'nothing'.

(4) Anxiety reveals the possibility of freedom: "Thus dread is the dizziness of freedom which occurs when the spirit would posit the synthesis, and freedom then

gazes down into its own possibility, grasping at finiteness to sustain itself" (Kierkegaard, p. 55; see also p. 99).

Anxiety is undoubtedly a mental phenomenon, but it does not seem to have an object. That contradicts Brentano's thesis of intentionality, according to which every mental phenomenon has an object. Now, we could just admit, as we have already done, that Brentano's thesis is false, that there are exceptions to it; and we could then say that anxiety is one of these exceptions. Or else we could search for an object for anxiety. If we adopt the second possibility, we could reason—I am tempted to say "in Hegelian fashion"—as follows. (1) Anxiety has no object. (2) That is, nothing is the object of anxiety. (3) Therefore, the object of anxiety is nothing. (4) Thus anxiety has an object after all, namely, nothing. And to emphasize that nothing is an object, we could speak of *nothingness:* The object of anxiety is nothingness. In this fashion, Brentano's thesis of intentionality is saved and Kierkegaard's third thesis is vindicated.

I have indulged in this fanciful reconstruction of the way that may lead to nothingness, because I want to contrast it with quite a different way of securing an object for anxiety. According to this approach, anxiety does have an object, our first impression is mistaken, but this object (as well as the corresponding act) has been *repressed.* According to this Freudian interpretation, *anxiety is nothing but fear, but fear whose act and object have been repressed.* There exist not two distinct mental phenomena, fear and anxiety, but only one, namely, fear. There are not two kinds of mental acts, fear and anxiety, but only one kind, namely, fear. But a person may either know that his emotion is fear and what it is he is afraid of, or else he may merely experience the emotional state without recognizing its direction-giving mental act of fear and its object. In the latter case, it must seem to him that he is agitated, disturbed, nervous, etc., but that all of this turmoil has neither a direction nor an object. Of course, we know from our analysis of repression that the fear is still experienced by the anxious person; it is still part of the conscious state. There is the emotional state, and there is the direction-giving act of fearing a specific object (situation). But the person has learned not to recognize the act of fearing or its object. The repression may be more or less strong or extensive. Perhaps the person realizes that she is afraid, that what she experiences is "somewhat like fear," but she has no idea what she is afraid of. Or perhaps the person does not even know that it is the emotional part of fear that he experiences. In either case, what the person suffers from is constant and overwhelming fear without its act and object. Anyone who has ever been truly afraid knows what a horrible feeling it is. Now imagine the plight of the neurotic: he is overwhelmed by fear without knowing what he is afraid of, or even that he is afraid.

We saw earlier how Anna's desire becomes unconscious by the process of repression. The same learning process occurs when fear is turned into anxiety. Anna, we must now add to our story, not only realizes at first that she desires her father, but she is also terribly afraid that she may act upon her desire, that she may do something to fulfill her desire. Not only is she afraid that she may act in a certain way, she also recognizes this fear for what it is. As a consequence, she is not only ashamed of her desire, but also ashamed of what she might do. And just as she learns to misidentify her desire, because this misidentification is rewarded by a reduction of shame and guilt, so does she learn not to recognize her fear, for this non-recognition is rewarded in the same way. In order to reduce her shame and guilt, it is necessary that she not only not recognize her desire for what it is, but also not recognize her fear for what it is. Furthermore, there is the added complication that she could not keep on believing in her heart ailment and at the same time be fully aware of her fear of approaching her father in a provocative way. The recognition of her fear would lead to a recognition of her desire.

From our Freudian point of view, there is some truth to Kierkegaard's thesis that nothing is the object of anxiety. Anxiety has no object in the sense that the anxious person can no longer identify the object of his fear. In reality, though, it has an object; for it is nothing but fear whose object has been repressed. Our point of view also sheds some light on the rest of Kierkegaard's theses. It is clear that anxiety must be distinguished from fear just as his second thesis claims. But here, too, we must be cautious. Anxiety, I have emphasized, does not form a separate kind of mental act, distinct from fear. But it is a different kind of mental phenomenon from fear; for it is experienced as different because of the successful process of repression. Even the first thesis, that only human beings can experience anxiety, makes sense from our point of view. A dog, for example, may perhaps be said to be afraid of cars, but it cannot be said to be anxious. It cannot be anxious because it cannot repress its fears. And it cannot repress its fears because it cannot feel ashamed and guilty. In order for Anna to repress her fear, she must be able to feel that it would be wrong, shameful, disgraceful, nasty, etc. to act in a certain fashion. She must have a *moral sense*. If we can agree that animals do not have a moral sense, that they cannot distinguish between right and wrong, then we can also agree that they cannot repress anything and, hence, that they cannot experience anxiety. That anxiety is characteristic of the human condition is ultimately due to the fact that human beings, and only human beings, can distinguish between what is morally right and what is morally wrong.

Last but not least, there is Kierkegaard's claim that anxiety reveals to us the possibility of freedom. Through anxiety, we become aware of our freedom. The anxious person, as Sartre says, has "a vertigo of possibility" (J. P. Sartre, *The Transcendence of the Ego*, p. 100). If a person feels anxious, we would say, she has been confronted with her freedom to act. She has been confronted with the fact that she is capable of doing things which she never thought possible. Anna, for example, is confronted with the fact that she may make sexual advances to her father. This realization, the realization that she could act in such an unspeakable way, reveals to her how distant the horizon of her possibilities is. She may be saying to herself: "My God, if I could do a thing like that, then I am capable of doing anything!" Anna experiences a vertigo of possibility.

I have argued that anxiety is repressed fear. If my argument is sound, then it follows that Bollnow and the existentialists are mistaken when they hold that anxiety is a mood. But it also becomes understandable how they could make this mistake. For anxiety is experienced without a direction, without an object, just as a mood is.

In regard to the larger circle of our inquiry, we have seen that there is no such thing as the infallibility of "inner sense." Mistakes are possible, not only about the external world, but also about the contents and acts of our minds. Nor should this fact give us reason for despair. Fallibility, though part of the human condition, is not a part to be bemoaned. It is the price we have to pay for the thrill of discovering the truth. And the truth about ourselves, the truth about our desires, emotions, fears, and joys, is the truth that makes us free from neurosis.

Three

Mathematical Knowledge

PERCEPTION AGAIN

. . . for logic is concerned with the real world just as truly as zoology, though with its more abstract and general features.

—B. Russell, *Introduction to Mathematical Philosophy*

A. Historical Observations

ONE

Kant's Challenge

a) The Platonic Heritage

Plato's world consists of two realms, the realm of being and the realm of becoming. It consists of the realm of unchanging forms and the realm of changing individuals. There is the realm of atemporal forms and the realm of temporal things. But Plato's world threatens to split apart into these two realms, for the connection between them remains a mystery. In our world, no threat exists, no split is immanent. Our world is a fact, not a collection of properties to one side and a collection of individuals to the other. The world as a fact divides into further facts, and these contain, ultimately, both Plato's forms and his individuals. What binds properties to individual things is the undefinable nexus of exemplification. What is thus created is a simple fact. And this fact is part of the larger fact which is the world. Plato saw the distinction between properties (forms) and individuals. What he did not see is that these two kinds exist only as parts of a third kind, namely, as parts of facts. What he did not realize is that the fundamental category of ontology is the category of fact. The problem is not how properties and individuals can come together to form facts, but how facts can contain properties and individuals. Facts guarantee that all of the diverse categories in the end form just one world, for all of them are merely constituents of the one over-arching fact which is the world.

Corresponding to the two realms of Plato's world, there exist in his epistemology two "eyes": One eye sees the ever-changing individuals of the realm of becoming; the other eye is fixed on the eternal forms. The first eye can only see individuals; the second can only contemplate forms. How, then, is knowledge possible? Just as Plato's world is in danger of splitting into two unconnected parts, so is his knowledge in danger of breaking into two unconnected faculties: intuition of individual things and conception of properties. Intuition, the "eye" of the senses, acquaints us with the ever-changing realm of individuals. Conception, the "eye" of the mind, contemplates the atemporal forms. How, then, do we come to know that this individual has that property? Knowledge cannot be a matter of either intuition alone or of conception alone. This much the Tradition cannot help but admit. The two faculties must somehow combine. This combination is called "judgment." What is a judgment? This is the question to which the Platonic tradition has no reasonable answer. It is assumed that a judgment somehow results when the two "eyes" work together. But how, precisely, do they work together? How can they possibly work together if one of them is condemned to be fixed on the eternal forms, the other is doomed to be blind to everything but changing individuals? The important dogma of the Tradition, to enlarge our metaphor, is that there is no third "eye," that there is no further unique faculty in addition to intuition and conception. Just as the Platonic ontology lacks the uniting category of fact, so does its epistemology lack the unifying faculty of judgment. Obviously, these two fundamental shortcomings go hand in hand. Without facts, there is no need for judgments; and without judgments, there is no call for facts. But what holds the world together are facts. And what constitutes knowledge of the world are judgments.

However, the Platonic tradition does not only neglect the importance of judgments, it also embraces a most pernicious dogma, namely, the dogma that the senses can acquaint us with nothing but individuals. This dogma makes rationalism all but inevitable. For, if the senses acquaint us with nothing but individuals, then there must be another faculty that acquaints us with forms. Empiricism, as it turns out, has not just one but two strikes against it. Firstly, true knowledge cannot be concerned with the buzzing, booming confusion of the realm of becoming, but must be a matter of unchanging forms. Thus it cannot be acquired through the senses. Secondly, judgment, insofar as it plays a role in the Tradition, cannot involve the senses. Add to this that knowledge is contained only in judgments, and the conclusion is inevitable that the senses know nothing.

What chance does empiricism have against a view so heavily fortified with rationalistic premises? Very little. History shows that empiricism knows only one way out of its corner: It attacks the realm of being. Empiricism thus gets settled with nominalism. Quite obviously, if there is no realm of timeless entities, and if there is no special contemplation of the denizens of this realm, then knowledge, whatever it may turn out to be, can concern only the realm of temporal individuals. Two unholy alliances are formed: one, between empiricism and nominalism; the other, between rationalism and realism. But both combinations are doomed. Rationalism must fail, not because it embraces the realm of forms, but because it has no room for empirical knowledge. Empiricism must fail, not because it takes care of individuals, but because it rejects the realm of universals.

As far as the theory of knowledge is concerned, empiricists have one decisive argument: Rationalists never explain the mysterious faculty of conception; and, indeed, there is ample evidence that it does not exist. On the other hand, rationalists, too, can produce a powerful argument: Empiricists cannot explain the nature of mathematical knowledge.

The fight between rationalism and empiricism has an air of unreality about it because it takes place without regard for the existence of facts and judgments. Knowledge consists, as I mentioned earlier, neither in intuition nor in conception, but in judgment (assertion). And what judgment intends is neither a mere individual nor a property, but a state of affairs.

The two opponents, ironically, share a common dogma; a dogma that determines the traditional dialectic. According to this presupposition, the senses cannot acquaint us with anything but individuals. This dogma, in turn, rests on two unquestioned beliefs. Firstly, one takes for granted, as Kant succinctly puts it, that space and time are the forms of sensibility. Secondly, one assumes that properties (forms, universals), if there are such things, are not located in space and/or time. This assumption is almost a matter of terminology: what is not spatial and/or temporal is not called an "individual." It is the first of these two beliefs that is crucial to the dialectic. Let me formulate it differently: Perception ("the senses") cannot acquaint us with anything but individual things. Since I believe that this proposition is false, I believe that both rationalists and empiricists start out with a false premise. Perception acquaints us not only with individual things, but also with properties. It acquaints us not only with spatio-temporal entities, but also with non-spatial and atemporal things. The senses are a window through which we see not only the realm of becoming, but also the realm of being. The senses put us in touch not only with changing things, but also with timeless universals. No special faculty, no mysterious power of conception, contemplation, eidetic intuition, or what-have-you, is needed to explain how we are acquainted with universals.

The key to getting rid of the common dogma is the insight that perception is propositional. What we perceive are not individual things by themselves, but states of affairs. The eye of the senses sees states of affairs rather than isolated individuals. States of affairs, of course, have many kinds of ingredients. They contain individual things; but they also contain properties and relations. They even contain, as I shall argue, sets and numbers. Thus there really is only one eye, the eye of perception; and it acquaints us with temporal ("concrete") as well as atemporal ("abstract") things, for both are conjoined in states of affairs.

The Platonic tradition is partially correct: There do exist entities other than individual things; there do exist abstract entities. But the Platonist is mistaken when he thinks that knowledge consists in the contemplation of such abstract things. The empiricist is also partially correct: All of our knowledge (of the external world) comes ultimately through the senses. But he is mistaken when he goes on to deny the existence of the realm of being. One can be a realist and reject rationalism. One can be an empiricist and reject nominalism. This is the position I take: I am a realist when it comes to the existence of abstract entities, but I am an empiricist in regard to the nature of knowledge, for I hold that we perceive abstract things. I have chosen the "fourth way."

This position, I submit, opens up a new approach to the problem of mathematical knowledge. We can combine the view that numbers and sets are abstract entities with the contention that we perceive some numbers and sets. Not only do we perceive some numbers and sets, we also perceive some relations among them. Mathematical knowledge is therefore "empirical" knowledge, but "empirical" knowledge about structures of abstract entities.

b) Kant's Philosophical Situation

Kant's epistemological framework is on the whole Platonistic. But he adds an idealistic twist and makes some minor improvements. Temporal (and spatial) individuals are represented by (acts of) intuition; atemporal properties, by conception (concepts). Of equal importance is the fact that Kant subscribes to the Platonic dogma that the senses are confined to individual things. In other words, intuitions and only intuitions are sensible. This, as I said a moment ago, is the fatal dogma that makes a correct theory of knowledge impossible. According to the dogma, there are two basic faculties, intuition and conception, and each of these has its specific kind of object, intuitions (individuals) and concepts (properties). Kant's basic distinction between intuitions and concepts serves a dual purpose. It serves an ontological purpose, for it distinguishes between the ontological categories of individual and property. And it also serves an epistemological purpose, for it distinguishes between the two faculties of sensibility and conception.

But Kant also talks about judgments. Knowledge, he clearly sees, is neither a matter of blind intuition nor of empty conception. Knowledge only results when these two faculties work together harmoniously. Knowledge consists in seeing with both eyes simultaneously. But judgment, in Kant's opinion, does not constitute a third and equally unique faculty. It must be emphasized that Brentano's insight that judgments form a unique and indefinable kind of mental act eludes Kant. He defines judgment as a kind of presentation: "A judgment is the presentation of the unity of the consciousness of different presentations or the presentation of their relationship, insofar as they constitute a concept" (I. Kant, *Logik, Gesammelte Schriften*, Akademie Edition, 9:101). From our point of view, Kant's notion of judgment is doubly defective. He does not see, as Brentano later does, that judgments form an irreducible kind of mental act. Nor does he realize, as Bolzano later does, that their objects belong neither to the category of individual nor to the category of property, but belong to a third, irreducible, kind, namely, to state of affairs.

Knowledge resides in judgments. This much Kant clearly sees. What kinds of judgment are there? Kant's most important distinction, and a distinction he was very proud of, is between analytic and synthetic judgments. We shall have a close look at this distinction in a moment, but let us get clear, first, about the context. Leibniz had maintained that in all true judgments of the form *All F's are G's*, the predicate concept G is *contained* in the subject concept F. We need not go deeply into the reasons for Leibniz's view, for it is clear that he thought the only intelligible notion of predication is that of concepts being *contained* in concepts:

> We must consider, then, what it means to be truly attributed to a certain subject. Now it is certain that every true predication has some basis in the nature of things, and when a proposition is not an identity, that is to say, when the predicate is not expressly contained in the subject, it must be included in it virtually. This is what the philosophers call *in-esse*, when they say that the predicate is *in* the subject. So the subject term must always include the predicate term in such a way that anyone who understands perfectly the concept of the subject will also know that the predicate pertains to it.

> (G. W. Leibniz, *Discourse on Metaphysics*, pp. 471–72)

Leibniz speaks here of subject and predicate, but I think that we can substitute 'subject concept' and 'predicate concept' for these expressions. Of course, I would rather speak of properties: In all true judgments of the form *All F's are G's,* the property G is part of the property F. One of the most pernicious legacies of the Kantian school is the idealistic slant in thought and terminology that substitutes concepts for properties. Not even Bolzano and Frege were untouched by this curse.

Arnauld, in his correspondence with Leibniz, objects to Leibniz's view. The predicate concept, he maintains, is only contained in the subject concept if the judgment is not only *true,* but *necessary.* All necessary propositions, in other words, are of the "analytic" sort described by Leibniz. But there are also, contrary to Leibniz, true propositions in which the predicate concept is not part of the subject concept. Kant, viewed against the background of this controversy between Leibniz and Arnauld, sides neither with Leibniz nor with Arnauld, but claims that they are both mistaken. Leibniz is mistaken when he thinks that all true judgments are necessary; and Arnauld is mistaken when he holds that all necessary judgments are analytic as explained by Leibniz. There are, Kant objects, necessary judgments which are not analytic. It therefore becomes imperative to distinguish between *analytic* judgments and *a priori* judgments: The latter are necessary without being analytic. Looked at from another angle, it becomes imperative to distinguish between *two kinds of necessity:* the necessity of analytic judgments and the necessity of a certain kind of non-analytic judgement. *Kant discovers a new kind of necessity, a necessity which is not based on the fact that complex concepts contain other concepts,* and this discovery demands an answer to the question: Whence the necessity of non-analytic judgments?

Arithmetic (and mathematics as a whole) illustrates Kant's contention that neither Leibniz nor Arnauld grasped the philosophical situation. The judgment that $7 + 5 = 12$, Kant claims, is necessary. Yet it is not analytic: the concept 12 is not somehow composed of the concepts 7, 5, and plus. Thus Arnauld is mistaken. (But notice that this is not a categorial judgment like *All F's are G's.*) There is necessity without analyticity. Where does this necessity come from? To repeat, this is the crucial question with which Kant challenges all later philosophers. As we know, he gives a most original answer. Alas, his answer has so many problems that its popularity can only be explained by the fact that nobody proposed a better answer.

In order to clarify the context of Kant's answer, we must look at the nature of synthetic judgments. Knowledge can only be based on intuitions and concepts. This is a Kantian axiom. Well, if analytic judgments involve the analysis of concepts, then synthetic judgments must somehow be a matter of intuition. In a synthetic judgment of the form *All F's are G's,* where G is not a part of F, F and G must be connected in some other way:

> In all judgments in which the relation of a subject to a predicate is thought . . . this relation is possible in two different ways. Either the predicate B belongs to the subject A, as something which is (covertly) contained in this concept A; or B lies outside the concept A, although it does indeed stand in connexion with it. In the one case I call the judgment analytic, and the other synthetic.

> (I. Kant, *Critique of Pure Reason.* B 10)

Kant here formulates the problem but does not solve it: What, precisely, is the connection between A and B when B lies outside of A? One thing is clear, though, the connection must somehow be based on intuition. How else, a Kantian would ask, could it possibly be established?

I do not fully understand Kant's explanation of how intuition connects concepts with each other, but I shall bravely describe a view which, if not Kant's, is at least in the Kantian spirit. Consider the judgment that all men are mortal. This is a synthetic judgment: the concept mortal is not contained in, is not part of, the concept man. Yet, since it is a true judgment, the two concepts must somehow be connected with each other. Well, the concept man applies to certain intuitions; certain intuitions fall under the concept man. Also, the concept mortal applies to certain intuitions. The first concept applies, for example, to Plato and to Aristotle. Under the second fall not only Plato and Aristotle, but also my neighbor's dog Honey. Now, in every case in which an intuition falls under the concept of man, it also falls under the concept mortal (but not conversely). Plato is a man, and he is also mortal; Aristotle is a man, and he is also mortal; and so on. By *induction* from these individual cases, in each of which the respective concepts are *indirectly* connected by being *directly* attached to the same intuition, we establish a general connection between the two concepts; and we express this connection by means of the judgment *All men are mortal*. According to this interpretation, two things are essential to synthetic judgments. Firstly, there must be an intuition which connects the two concepts by virtue of the fact that both are attached to that intuition. You may think of F and G as being connected by the relation of being-jointly-exemplified. Secondly, there must occur induction in order to get from individual cases to the general judgment.

Synthetic judgments, to say it again, must be based on intuition. This follows from two Kantian axioms. According to the first, knowledge can only be based on intuitions and concepts; nothing else can be of importance for knowledge. According to the second, all conceptual knowledge is analytic; as long as nothing but concepts are involved, no synthetic judgment is possible. It follows that even in synthetic a priori judgments the connection between F and G must be established through intuitions. On the other hand, and here we touch upon a crucial point, such judgments cannot result from induction; for induction could never guarantee the necessity of a synthetic a priori judgment. The inductive leap precludes necessity. Somewhere, therefore, there must be an intuition which is such that (a) it serves to connect the respective concepts, and (b) by doing so in an individual case, it guarantees that the connection holds universally. This, I believe, is the mysterious *pure intuition* on which Kant's theory of the synthetic a priori rests.

c) An Explication of the Analytic-Synthetic Distinction

Kant's example of an analytic judgment is *All bodies are extended:* "I do not require to go beyond the concept which I connect with 'body' in order to find the extension as bound up with it. To meet with this predicate, I have merely to analyze the concept, that is, to become conscious to myself of the manifold which I always think in that concept." (Kant, 1965, B 10) There is much that is obscure in this passage. As has often been pointed out, it is not clear whether the analytic judgment is a result of a mental process of analysis, or whether analysis merely brings out the analyticity of a judgment (see, for example, Lewis White Beck, "Can Kant's Synthetic Judgments Be Made Analytic?"). This kind of ambiguity is the price one has to pay for an idealistic methodology. We can remove at least part of the ambiguity if we adopt the following interpretation. Whatever the psychological state of a person may be, the state of affairs before her mind, represented by the sentence 'All bodies are extended', either contains the simple property *body* or it does not. If it does, then the corresponding judgment cannot be analytic, for the simple property cannot contain any other property as a part. On the other hand, if *body* is not a simple property, then the property of being extended may or may not be a part of it. If *extended* is a part of the complex property *body*, then the corresponding judgment is analytic. In this case, 'body' is a mere abbreviation for a longer expression which, among other words, contains 'extended'. Assume, for example, that 'body' is merely short for 'extended individual thing'. The sentence 'All bodies are extended' is then merely short for 'All extended individual things are extended', and the judgment expressed by this sentence is analytic.

We have to distinguish between (1) (true) analytic sentences, (2) (true) analytic judgments, and analytic states of affairs (facts). The basic notion is that of an analytic state of affairs (which, *if it obtains*, is of course an analytic fact). So-called analytic judgments, it is clear, are judgments of the form *All things which are F, G, H, etc., are F*. In other words, what is judged is always a state of affairs of this form. A state of affairs of this form is an *instance* of the logical law: *All properties f, g, h, etc. are such that: if anything is f, g, h, etc., then it is f.* An analytic state of affairs, therefore, is an instance of this law of logic. An analytic judgment is a judgment that *intends* such an instance of the law. And an analytic sentence is a sentence that *represents* an instance of the logical law.

It follows from our explication that the notion of analyticity serves at best a minor function, and that in connection with sentences. It may be the case that a simple expression is used to represent a complex property. Then it is not obvious from the sentence that we are dealing with a logical truth. And then the expression 'analytic sentence' may be useful. An analytic sentence is a sentence which represents an instance of the logical law mentioned earlier, but which does not do so in an obvious way. We can make it perspicuous by replacing all abbreviations in it by their abbreviants. The analytic, therefore, plays a minor role in our philosophy, and we can easily do without it. It is "reduced," to speak for once in this misleading way, to the logical. An analytic sentence is simply a sentence that represents an instance of a certain logical law, that is, that represents a logical fact or logical truth. Is the judgment that all bodies are extended analytic? Well, what state of affairs is its intention? Equivalently, what state of affairs is represented by the "text" of the judgment, namely, the sentence 'All bodies are extended'? The answer to this question depends on the answer to another question: Is the word 'body' used as an abbreviation for a longer expression, an expression that represents a "conjunctive property" involving the property of being extended? What I wish to stress at this point is the fact that this last question may be difficult to answer, but that the difficulty is not of a philosophical nature. In order to answer the question, we may have to inquire into what a particular person had in mind, or into how a group of people commonly use certain words, or into whether or not anyone ever laid down an abbreviation proposal, and so on. But all of these inquiries are philosophically unproblematic, no matter how difficult they may be from a practical point of view.

There exists a well-known objection to the analytic-synthetic distinction which is based on such practical difficulties. Generally speaking, one tries to discredit the distinction by discrediting the linguistic notion of synonymity. But this seems to me to be the wrong approach. The notion of synonymity is perfectly clear, even though it may be hard if not impossible to decide in a given case whether or not two English expressions are synonymous. Our approach, by way of contrast, is to question specific claims about synonymity, for example, Hempel's assertion that '5 + 7' is synonymous with '12'. We understand the notion of synonymity perfectly well, and because we understand it, we are convinced that these two expressions are not synonymous.

Is 'bachelor' synonymous with 'unmarried male of marriageable age'? If the shorter expression is a mere abbreviation for the longer one, then the judgment that all bachelors are unmarried is analytic. We assume that the logical law mentioned earlier and its instances are (trivially) analytic, and then we ask whether or not the sentence 'Bachelors are unmarried' represents an analytic state of affairs. If I understand him correctly, Quine, in order to discredit the analytic-synthetic distinction, argues at this point that we cannot use without circularity the interchangeability of expressions *salva veritate* in all contexts as the criterion of synonymity. There is circularity because we must ask for "necessary" or "analytic" interchangeability, that is, the resulting expressions must be analytically equivalent. In our case, it is not enough that it is true that bachelors are unmarried if and only if unmarried males of marriageable age are unmarried. Rather, this equivalence must be analytic. But now we have to ask whether it, in turn, represents a logical law or an instance of one. And in order to answer this question, we must already know whether or not 'bachelor' is synonymous to 'unmarried male of marriageable age'. We are back to the original question and the circle is closed (W. V. Quine, "Two Dogmas of Empiricism"; and "Carnap and Logical Truth").

Quine's argument is pertinent as long as one thinks of synonymity in terms of substitutibility *salva veritate*. Unfortunately, this conception is so popular that I have little hope to change it. But I shall try. I contend that in our example the question is not whether or not 'bachelor' and 'unmarried male of marriageable age' are interchangeable *salva veritate*, but whether or not the first expression is an *abbreviation* for the second. The question is whether or not 'bachelor' is merely short for the longer expression. But this question is not a philosophical question. Nor is it one that raises philosophical problems. It is the question of whether or not certain people have agreed, explicitly or merely tacitly, to use 'bachelor' as an abbreviation for the longer phrase. It may well be that this question has no clear answer, even though it is a perfectly clear question. In that case, we shall not be able to decide whether or not the statement that all bachelors are unmarried is analytic. But this result does not imply that the notion of analyticity is vague, unclear, imprecise, etc. Let 'ground' be short for 'green and round'. Is the sentence 'All ground things are green' analytic? It is, for it is merely short for 'All green and round things are green', and this sentence represents an instance of the logical law mentioned earlier. There is nothing unclear about this notion of analyticity.

Of course, our notion presupposes that we have a firm understanding of logical laws. As long as we are content with Kant's narrow conception of logic, the problem of explicating what a logical law is, is not very pressing. We can just single out the law mentioned earlier and call it "the *logical* law." But if there are other logical laws, as we know there are, then the task of describing the nature of logic becomes urgent. Our generalized notion of analyticity then becomes:

(A) 'A sentence S is analytic' means (is merely short for) 'S represents an instance of a logical law after all abbreviations in S have been eliminated'.

As I said a moment ago, this explication is only as clear as the notion of logical law is. But it shows, and this is my main point, how unimportant, from a philosophical perspective, this notion of analyticity is. Does this meager notion suffice to tackle the urgent philosophical task before us? Does it suffice to answer the Kantian challenge? The history of philosophy of the last hundred years indicates that few if any philosophers agreed with us that the notion of analyticity is not equal to the task.

Our notion of analyticity was anticipated by Frege:

> The problem becomes, in fact, that of finding the proof of the proposition, and of following it up right back to the primitive truths. If, in carrying out this process, we come only on general logical laws and definitions, then the truth is an analytic one, bearing in mind that we must take account also of all propositions upon which the admissibility of any of the definitions depends
>
> (G. Frege, *The Foundations of Arithmetic,* p. 4).

But there is a difference between Frege's formulation and ours: he speaks of definitions, while I mention abbreviations. And thereby hangs a tale. No, not a tale, but a cluster of tales; for nothing less is at stake than the success or failure of logicism. In order to prove that arithmetic propositions are analytic, contrary to Kant's claim, Frege defines certain crucial terms. But these "definitions" turn out to be no mere linguistic conveniences, no mere abbreviations, no mere stipulations. Quite to the contrary, they turn out to be assertions among assertions. And since these propositions are not logical laws or instances of logical laws, the so-called "reduction" of arithmetic to logic fails. As a consequence, the "reduced" sentences of arithmetic do not deserve to be called "analytic." This, in a nutshell, is my objection to Frege's logicism.

d) One Kind of Necessity: Lawfulness

Necessity pervades the world on many layers. I shall argue that there is ontological necessity, logical necessity, set-theoretical necessity, arithmetic necessity, even biological and chemical necessity. What all of these necessities have in common is that they emanate from *lawfulness*. In this respect, too, Frege anticipated our view. He describes this kind of necessity in these words: "The apodictic judgment differs from the assertoric in that it suggests the existence of universal judgments from which the proposition can be inferred, while in the case of the assertoric one such a suggestion is lacking. By saying that a proposition is necessary I give a hint about the grounds for my judgment" (G. Frege, *Begriffsschrift*, in *Translations from the Philosophical Writings of Gottlob Frege*, p. 4). I would put the same idea as follows. The sentence 'It is necessary that P' is merely short for the sentence 'P follows (logically) from some (unspecified) laws'. Similarly, 'It is possible that P' is an abbreviation for 'P is consistent with some laws'. Laws themselves are supposed to be nonmodal and, of course, trivially necessary. Necessity, so conceived, may be said to be a "property" of facts, namely, the "property of following from laws." It is a "property" which pervades the world.

This kind of necessity is part of the furniture of the world, insofar as some facts do indeed follow from certain laws; insofar as they have this feature. To have this feature amounts, roughly speaking, to standing in the logical implication relation to laws. And this relation dissolves, in turn, into a general conditional. To say that P follows from L is to say that the fact *If L, then P* is an instance of a logical law. From an ontological point of view, therefore, this kind of necessity is doubly founded on lawfulness. There is, firstly, the lawfulness inherent in L; and there is, secondly, the lawfulness of logic. This kind of necessity is not an unanalyzable, not an irreducible, quality of facts. (It should be mentioned in passing that this kind of necessity can also be conceived of in terms of consistency between possible worlds. See my *The Categorial Structure of the World*, pp. 372–374, and J. M. Dunn, "A Truth Value Semantics for Modal Logic.")

It will be objected by some that our explication has things upside down: lawfulness must be explicated in terms of necessity, and not the other way around. Necessity, it may be claimed, is precisely that feature which distinguishes between laws and other (accidental) generalities. I must confess that I do not know how to resolve the issue, and to discuss it in detail would, at any rate, lead us too far astray. I shall therefore rest content with the confession that it is one of my basic assumptions in this book that necessity rests on lawfulness, and not the other way around.

It is a consequence of our analysis that there are many kinds of necessity (and of possibility), namely, as many as there are different fields of inquiry. For example, it is an *ontological* necessity that the pen before me on the desk is not exemplified by anything. This follows from the ontological law that no individual is exemplified by anything. It is also true that the pen is not both blue and also not blue (at the same time, all over). But this fact does not follow from any ontological law or laws. It is ontologically possible that the pen is both blue and not blue. However, there exists a law of logic from which it follows that the pen is not both blue and also not blue. This fact is therefore a logical necessity. Contradictions, in short, are ontologically possible, but logically impossible. The so-called formation rules for logical systems reflect not logical but ontological possibilities. What is ontologically possible may not be logically possibly. Similarly, what is logically possible may not be biologically possible. Certain states of affairs may not clash with the laws of logic, but may clash with biological laws. There exists, therefore, a hierarchy of necessities. On the very top are the necessities of ontology. On the next layer appear the necessities of logic, set-theory, and arithmetic. And on lower levels we find the necessities of science. However, this picture gets more complicated if we add that there also exist "bridge laws" which establish connections among some disciplines. As a result, the necessities of one field of inquiry spill over into the necessities of another. We shall return to this point later on.

I have called attention to the necessity which flows from lawfulness because it sheds some light on Kant's discovery of synthetic a priori truths. In Arnauld and Leibniz, as we have seen, the necessary is the analytic, and what is not necessary is synthetic. But consider the proposition that the sun will rise tomorrow. It is (a) not analytic and hence (b) synthetic; but it is also (c) necessary, for it follows from the laws of planetary motion. Thus there are synthetic propositions which are necessary, namely, all of those propositions which follow from laws other than the laws of logic, as understood by Arnauld and Leibniz. What happens to Kant's newly discovered kind of necessity? Arithmetic propositions, Kant claims, are synthetic and necessary. Is this kind of necessity lawfulness? Does Kant mean to assert that arithmetic propositions, even though they are not logical truths, follow from some other kind of law? I do not think so. Otherwise, he would have to hold that the statement about the sun's rising is just as synthetic a priori (necessary) as the propositions of arithmetic. No, Kant must have had some other kind of necessity in mind. And it is our task to hunt this sort of necessity down.

e) An Explication of the A Priori-A Posteriori Distinction

A priori knowledge, Kant tells us, is knowledge absolutely independent of all experience (Kant, 1965, B 3). This is the bone of contention between us. We wish to maintain that a certain kind of necessary knowledge, a priori knowledge, depends on experience. There are at least two ways in which we may proceed. We could either try to show directly, as it were, that examples of Kant's a priori knowledge do depend on experience, or else we could prove this indirectly by attacking Kant's axiom that a truth which is necessary and universal cannot be built on experience. As I see it, Kitcher adopts the first strategy (P. Kitcher, *The Nature of Mathematical Knowledge*). I shall adopt the second. I shall attack Kant's axiom by elucidating the twin notions of necessity and universality in such a way that it becomes clear that necessary and universal propositions rest on experience.

A priori knowledge is opposed to empirical knowledge, that is, to a posteriori knowledge. Kant states two criteria for a priori judgments:

Experience teaches us that a thing is so and so, but not that it cannot be otherwise. First, then, if we have a proposition which in being thought is thought as *necessary,* it is an *a priori* judgment; and if, besides, it is not derived from any proposition except one which also has the validity of a necessary judgment, it is an absolutely *a priori* judgment. Secondly, experience never confers on its judgments true or strict, but only assumed and comparative *universality,* through induction . . . If, then, a judgment is thought with strict universality, that is, in such a manner that no exception is allowed as possible, it is not derived from experience, but is valid absolutely *a priori.*

(Kant, 1965, B3–B4)

Necessity and universality are the characteristics of a priori judgments. A posteriori judgments are neither necessary nor universal. But what is this necessity and this universality that defines the a priori? We cannot possibly take a journey through the jungle of Kantian scholarship and Kant interpretations. But our goal is not to vindicate or condemn Kant, but to understand the true nature of our knowledge of arithmetic; and for this purpose, a concise nonhistorical discussion must suffice.

Let us look at the alleged necessity and universality of the judgment that $5 + 7 = 12$. The first thing to notice is that this is not, as it stands, a general truth. It resembles the proposition that point B is between points A and C more than it resembles the paradigm that all bodies are extended. But we can supplant this arithmetic proposition by the general truth that five things plus seven things are twelve things. Kant, I shall assume, claims that this general judgment is not gotten by induction. To put it differently, Kant holds that this is a *universal* judgment, not just a *general* judgment. This judgment is not arrived at by induction from such individual instances as that these five oranges plus those seven oranges are twelve oranges, and that these five pencils plus those seven pencils are twelve pencils, etc., etc. Since it is not arrived at by induction, so Kant seems to argue, and since it is nevertheless "general," it is universal.

Well, is it or is it not arrived at by induction? Consider the truth that all midnight blue things are darker (in color) than all lemon yellow things. Is this true generalization arrived at by induction? It seems to be quite obvious that it is not. It would not occur to us to confirm this law by looking at more and more midnight blue and lemon yellow objects. What we see is that midnight blue, this color shade, is darker than lemon yellow, that color shade. What we recognize is that the first shade stands in the relation of being darker-than to the second. There exists a relation between color shades, and this relation holds between midnight blue and lemon yellow. Since this relation holds between the two properties, it *follows logically* that anything which has the first property has a property which stands in this relation to the property which anything has that has the second property. More elegantly expressed, it follows from the fact that P stands to Q in the relation R, that anything which has P and anything which has Q are such that the properties they have stand in the relation R. Thus the truth of the general judgment is *implied* by the truth of the relational proposition. No induction is necessary or even possible. Yet, the truth of the general law rests on experience; for it rests on the truth of the relational judgment, and that proposition is known by experience: we see, with our very eyes, that midnight blue is darker than lemon yellow.

Now if we think of the arithmetic general truth in analogy to this color shade example, then we see immediately why the arithmetic law is universal and not just general. We understand why it holds for all things, even though it is not arrived at by means of induction from individual instances. Here, too, we have a relation among things: the sum relation among numbers. In this case, the relation holds not between properties, but between entities of a different category. But the principle is the same: Since this relation holds between these entities, it is true that all things are such that the relation holds between the numbers of these things. The proposition that five things and seven things are twelve things *follows* from the proposition that five plus seven is twelve. The general proposition is thus universal and not merely general. But, as in the first case, its truth derives from the truth of the proposition that five plus seven is twelve and is not arrived at by induction.

There is a difference between the color case and the number case. That midnight blue things are darker in color than lemon yellow things follows *logically* from the fact that midnight blue is darker than lemon yellow, for the following is a law of logic (of the general theory of properties and relations, of the "functional calculus"):

All properties of properties, all properties of individuals, and all relations between properties are such that: If a relation r^2 holds between two properties f^1 and g^1 which share a property h^2, then all individuals x^0 and y^0 are such that if x^0 is f^1 and y^0 is g^1, then there exist two properties i^1 and j^1 such that x^0 is i^1 and i^1 is h^2, and y^0 is j^1 and j^1 is h^2, and r^2 holds between i^1 and j^1.

There exists, to be precise, no such *logical* law for the number case, because numbers, as I shall argue, are not properties (or relations). But there exists a law that corresponds to this logical law:

All numbers and relations among numbers are such that: If a relation r holds between the numbers n_1, n_2, and n_3, then all things, e_1, e_2, and e_3 are such that if n_1 is the number of e_1, n_2 is the number of e_2, and n_3 is the number of e_3, then there exist the numbers m_1, m_2, and m_3, such that r holds between m_1, m_2, and m_3, and m_1 is the number of e_1, m_2 is the number of e_2, and m_3 is the number of e_3.

We see why a well-known argument for the analyticity of the arithmetic proposition fails. According to this argument, the proposition must be analytic because it is not an empirical generalization. It is not an empirical generalization because there can be no disconfirming instances (see, for example, Carl G. Hempel, "On the Nature of Mathematical Truth," pp. 367–68). Of course, there can be no disconfirming instances. Nobody in his right mind would try to disprove the law that midnight blue things are darker in color than lemon yellow things by trying to find a midnight blue thing and a lemon yellow thing such that the first is not darker in color than the second. But it is also true that nobody would try to confirm this law by citing more and more instances of midnight blue and lemon yellow individuals. No, this law is neither established nor can it be discredited by individual cases. In this regard, it is indeed fundamentally different from "ordinary, inductive" laws.

This law follows logically from a nongeneral fact, namely, from the fact that a certain relation holds between the two colors midnight blue and lemon yellow. And the same is true for the arithmetic law under discussion. It, too, follows from a nongeneral relational fact about the numbers five, seven, and twelve. Hempel makes the simple mistake, a mistake quite common among logical positivists, of assuming that a law which is not established by induction (and therefore cannot be discredited by a counter instance) must be analytic.

We now face the crucial question: Is the arithmetic proposition that five plus seven is twelve based on experience? I shall argue that it is, thus extending the analogy between the color case and the number case. But let us first return to Kant. We have just seen that the arithmetic law, just as the law about colored objects, is indeed universal. Kant is quite correct in his claim that there are general propositions which are not arrived at by induction. But we have also seen that universality can be based on experience. Kant is mistaken about the source of this universality. Since he did not realize that relational facts can yield the universality of general propositions, he searched for a different source for universality. He found it, as we know, in the pure intuitions of space and time. Since this is such a crucial turning point of Kant's philosophy, let me diagnose the situation once again. From my point of view, Kant saw correctly that certain judgments are universal; that, though general, they are not based on induction. They have a "necessity" about them which induction cannot provide. What Kant did not see was that there are relations among properties and other kinds of nonindividuals, and that these relations account for the universality of those judgments. Put in a more Kantian terminology, his greatest mistake was that he did not realize that there exist relations (other than partial identity) among concepts. Had he realized this fact, there would have been no "Transcendental Turn."

We have discovered the source of the universality of a priori judgments; what about their necessity? Of course, our arithmetic law is trivially necessary in the sense which we have explicated in the last section. But this is not the necessity which Kant is trying to explain. In his sense, the arithmetic statement is necessary, but a biological law is not. I think that this kind of necessity is a matter of *imaginability*. We cannot imagine five things and seven things not being twelve things, and that is why we hold it to be necessary that five things and seven things are twelve things. And we cannot imagine midnight blue not being darker than lemon yellow, and that is why we also say that it is necessary that blue things are darker than lemon yellow things. On the other hand, since we can imagine that a horse has a horn, we do not believe it to be necessary that horses are without horns. Imaginability is the second important source of necessity, in addition to lawfulness. If I am correct, then the a priori is characterized by a universality that flows from certain relations among abstract entities, and by a necessity that derives from unimaginability. This is my alternative to Kant's transcendental idealism.

Synthetic a priori judgments, according to Kant, must be based on intuitions rather than concepts. The connection between the subject concept and the predicate concept must somehow be established through intuitions, that is, through individuals. But the universality of such judgments precludes the possibility that this connection is established by means of induction from a number of individual cases. How, then, can the universality and necessity of this connection be explained? This is Kant's most pressing problem. His solution is infamous. He postulates a mysterious kind of intuition, pure intuition, which (a) establishes a connection between the respective concepts, and (b) guarantees that this connection holds universally (without induction) and is necessary. This is obviously one of the weakest spots of Kant's philosophy. It is not surprising that Kant's great critic Bolzano attacked the notion of pure intuition, as we shall see later on.

f) Kant and the Concept of Number

Arithmetic is about numbers. What are numbers and how are we acquainted with them? Let us start with simple things, the positive integers (natural numbers). What kind of thing is the number two and how do I know it? Kant is primarily interested in the epistemological question. He does not say much about the ontological problem. However, his explanation of how we know numbers is notoriously obscure. Somehow, pure intuition is involved, and so is time. We have already ventured a guess as to why Kant invents pure intuition. He may have reasoned like this. Arithmetic truths are synthetic a priori. Since they are synthetic, they cannot be conceptual truths; for all such truths are analytic. Thus they must rest on intuition. But they cannot be based on ordinary intuition, for such intuition can only yield a posteriori knowledge. Hence there must be an intuition which is unique in that it can deliver universality and necessity. This is pure intuition.

Intuition, as I pointed out, plays a double role in Kant's philosophy. It is both an epistemological as well as an ontological notion. It is both a kind of mental act, sensibility, and a kind of object (individuals). The riddle of pure intuition, therefore, has two sides to it. What is this special kind of mental act; how is it distinguished from ordinary intuition? And what is this special kind of object; how is it distinguished from ordinary individuals? What, for example, is the object of pure intuition in geometry? I find no plausible answer to this urgent question in Kant. Nor do I find one for the case of arithmetic. Kant's penchant for symmetry dictates that time must play a role in arithmetic, for does not geometry deal with space? But what kind of temporal object could possibly play a role in the theory of numbers?

What does Kant say about numbers? Here is a famous passage:

> We might, indeed, at first suppose that the proposition $7 + 5 = 12$ is a merely analytic proposition, and follows by the principle of contradiction from the concept of a sum of 7 and 5. But if we look more closely we find that the concept of the sum of 7 and 5 contains nothing save the union of the two numbers into one, and in this no thought is being taken as to what this single number may be which combines both. The concept of 12 is by no means already thought in merely thinking this union of 7 and 5; and I may analyze my concept of such a possible sum as long as I please, still I shall never find the 12 in it. We have to go outside these concepts, and call in the aid of the intuition which

corresponds to one of them, our five fingers, for instance, or, as Segner does in his Arithmetic, five points, adding to the concept of 7, unit by unit, the five given in intuition. For starting with the number 7, and for the concept of 5 calling in the aid of the fingers of my hand as intuition, I now add one by one to the number 7 the units which I previously took together to form the number 5, and with the aid of that figure see the number 12 emerge [Kemp Smith has: "come into being"]. That 5 should be added to 7, I have indeed already thought in the concept of a sum = 7 + 5, but not that this sum is equal [Kemp Smith: "is equivalent to"] to the number 12.

(Kant, 1965, B15–B16)

Kant speaks here of the *concept* of the sum of 7 and 5. With our realistic bias, 'concept' translates into 'property': There is a property, in other words, of being the sum of 7 and 5, and a certain number has this property. More accurately, from our point of view, there is a *description* (to be distinguished from a description *expression*): *The number which is the sum of 7 and 5*. This is a *relational* description: A number is described as the number which stands in the sum relation to the two numbers 7 and 5. We may write this perspicuously as: The n such that: Sum (n, 7, 5). Assume that there are a number of peas lined up on a table, and let us call the peas "a," "b," "c," etc. We can now describe one of the peas, say b, as the pea which lies between the peas a and c: The x such that: Between (x, a, c).

Kant argues that the concept of the sum of 7 and 5 does not contain the concept of 12. Notice that he seems to think of the number 12 as a concept. Extrapolating in our usual uninhibited way, we conclude that for Kant numbers are concepts. (What else could they be in an ontology as poverty stricken as Kant's? Individuals, located in space and/or time? Judgments?) Removing the idealistic bias: Numbers are properties. But if they are properties, then we must immediately ask with Frege: What are they properties of? We know from Frege's brilliant analysis that this question is hard to answer. But let us not get ahead of ourselves. Kant maintains, at any rate, that the property of being twelve is not contained in the property of being the sum of seven and five. At this point, our terminological adjustments become crucial. The number twelve, I hold, is not a property. Therefore, it cannot be contained as a part in another property. But we can reformulate Kant's point within our framework: Does the description *the number which is the sum of 7 and 5* describe something in terms of the number 12? Obviously not. Compare this case with the question of whether the description *the unmarried cousin of mine* describes somebody in terms of the property of being unmarried. In this case, the answer is obviously affirmative. We think therefore of the statement that the unmarried cousin of mine is unmarried as analytic. (Never mind, for the moment, that this statement has "existential import.")

Is the following statement analytic: The number which is the sum of 7 and 5 is the same as 12? We have here a description of a number in terms of the sum relation which this number has to two other numbers, and we have also a name for this number. This case is precisely like our pea example: Is the statement that pea b lies between peas a and c analytic? Of course, not! Why, then, would anyone think that the arithmetic truth is analytic?

Kant appeals to intuition in order to establish a connection between the concept of the sum and the concept of 12. The reasoning behind this move is clear: Since we cannot establish a connection between these two concepts directly, we have to connect them indirectly by means of a common individual. But even though the principle of the philosophical move is clear, its actualization is shrouded in mystery. Why do we need an intuition for the number 5 (the five fingers or points), but not for the number 7? Or do we also have to look, first, at seven fingers? And how, precisely, is the addition of units to be understood? Do we move fingers over? Or do we open them up, one by one? And how does the number 12 emerge? Do we have to look at twelve fingers? Do we need someone else for this intuition, someone who lends us two fingers? Or can we use two of our toes? But let us give Kant a run for his money and try to give an account which, at least, is in the spirit of Kant's analysis. Take the simple case of the sum of 2 and 1. In order to realize that 3 is the sum of 2 and 1, we must use intuition, since the concepts are not contained in each other. We turn to two of our fingers. These two fingers, we assume, form some kind of individual which falls under the concept 2 (which has the property 2). Now we add one finger, that is, an individual thing which falls under the concept 1. What results is a third individual, namely, the three fingers in close proximity. And now we notice that this individual thing falls under the concept 3 (that is, has the property 3). Thus we learn that 2 plus 1 is 3. We learn that the three concepts are connected with each other in this fashion.

Even this account has many flaws. Firstly, there is again the Fregean question of what, precisely, falls under the concepts 2 and 3, respectively. Secondly, there is the problem of what the addition of fingers could possibly be. Thirdly, there is the Kantian objection that in this way we can learn, at best, that these two fingers and that one finger are these three fingers, but not that two plus one is three. We have not even learned that any two fingers plus one finger are three fingers. To arrive at this conclusion, we obviously need induction. But arithmetic, according to Kant, is not a matter of induction. The problem is, of course, that in our example we have used "empirical" intuition. Kant knows that this will not do. Our story provides, at best, an "empirical" account of arithmetic, and not the "transcendental account" defended by Kant. To get a transcendental view, pure intuition and time must enter into the picture. But the quotation from Kant gives us no clue whatsoever how they enter.

g) A Preview

According to Kant, arithmetic truths are not analytic and yet necessary. If arithmetic truths were analytic, then their necessity would be explained: their necessity would then be the necessity of logic. But they are not analytic. From where, then, do they get their necessity? What kind of necessity is the necessity of arithmetic? This is the dialectic that has confronted philosophers since Kant.

The most obvious response to Kant, a response made famous by Frege, is to deny Kant's claim that the necessity of arithmetic is not the necessity of logic. Frege maintains that, contrary to Kant's view, arithmetic is analytic. Kant thought otherwise, so the objection goes, because of his limited understanding of logic. If one has a firm grasp of the variety of logical truths, then one can show that arithmetic can be "reduced" to logic. Arithmetic, one can show, is merely logic in verbal disguise. But this response fails, I shall argue, because it rests on a tainted notion of definition. The so-called definitions of the reduction are not mere abbreviational conveniences, but bridge laws disguised as conventions.

In addition to the logicist's response to Kant's thesis, there is what I shall call the "semantic" theory. The necessity of arithmetic, according to this view, is indeed not based on logic, but is a matter of meaning. Meaning is the source of a special kind of necessity: some statements are necessarily true by virtue of the meaning of their terms. What Kant did not realize, it is said, is that in addition to empirical truths and purely logical truths, there exist also semantic truths. These truths rest not on inclusions among concepts or on pure intuitions, but on relations among meanings. That midnight blue is a color is not analytic, because the concept of color is not a part of the concept of midnight blue, but it is not an empirical truth either. Rather, it belongs to a third and peculiar kind of truth, namely, semantic truths, that is, truths that rest on certain meaning relations among concepts. Actually, there are two versions of this semantic theory. According to an ontological version, meanings are entities dwelling in Plato's realm of being. This is Husserl's view. According to a linguistic version, meanings are linguistic practices; they are rules of use. This, of course, is the Wittgensteinian position.

Last, but by no means least in popularity, is the view that the necessity of arithmetic derives from convention. According to the conventionalist theory, truths divide into two large groups, empirical truths and conventional truths. Conventional truths play then the role of analytic truths in other philosophies. The verbal bridge that leads from necessity to conventionality is easy to spot: What is true by convention could not possibly be false; it is true, irrespective of what the world is like. But what could not possibly be false, no matter what the world is like, is necessary. This view has been adopted by many Logical Positivists in the face of the Kantian challenge. When one reads the literature of the Vienna Circle, one finds a curious shift back and forth between some kind of semanticist view and some version of the conventionalist position, and one gets the impression that these philosophers were not really happy with either view, but could find no better response to Kant's challenge.

These three alternatives to Kant's explication of arithmetic necessity agree with the traditional wisdom that arithmetic is necessary. While Kant grounds this alleged necessity in pure intuition, they try to ground it in logic, semantics, or convention, respectively. In addition to these alternatives, however, there are two more radical objections to Kant's analysis.

Firstly, there is the empiricist denial that arithmetic is a priori and hence universal and necessary. Arithmetic truths, according to this view, are not different from other "empirical laws." They are not, in essence, different from the laws of physics or from the laws of biology. They are justified, like the laws of science, by observation and induction. This is Mill's answer to the Kantian challenge. Contrary to received opinion, there is much to be said for Mill's empiricism. The laws of arithmetic (even the laws of logic) are indeed in some sense empirical. But Mill is mistaken, I shall argue, when he puts them side by side with the laws of science. Knowledge of arithmetic, as all knowledge, is a matter of perception and introspection, but not all perceptions are perceptions of individual things and their properties.

Secondly, there is a radical response to Kant associated with Wittgenstein's early philosophy. According to this view, logical truths are "empty tautologies." They say nothing about the world. They are necessary in the perverse sense that they are vacuous. To some philosophers, this conception of logic seemed to offer a way out of the problem posed by Kant: if logic is necessary because it is vacuous, perhaps arithmetic is necessary for the same reason. I shall let Carnap describe this line of reasoning:

> Wittgenstein formulated this view in the more radical form that all logical truths are tautological, that is, that they hold necessarily in every possible case, therefore do not exclude any case, and do not say anything about the facts of the world.
>
> . . . he did not count the theorems of arithmetic, algebra, etc., among the tautologies. But to the members of the Circle there did not seem to be a fundamental difference between elementary logic and higher logic, including mathematics. Thus we arrived at the conception that all valid statements of mathematics are analytic in the specific sense that they hold in all possible cases and therefore do not have any factual content.
>
> What was important in this conception from our point of view was the fact that it became possible for the first time to combine the basic tenet of empiricism with a satisfactory explanation of the nature of logic and mathematics.
>
> (R. Carnap, "Carnap's Intellectual Autobiography," in
The Philosophy of Rudolf Carnap, pp. 46–47)

To us, this is a funny kind of empiricism indeed. The laws of science, upon this view, are empirical. But the statements of logic, arithmetic, etc. are turned into nonstatements, so that the question of how we know these truths simply cannot arise. This is the reason why I called this response to Kant's challenge "radical." It solves Kant's problem by denying that there is a problem; and there is no problem, because there are no *statements* of arithmetic. Since there are no such statements, no such truths, the question of whether they are a priori or a posteriori cannot arise.

This preview of some of the recent and contemporary attempts to answer Kant reminds us of the fact that his account of arithmetic takes for granted that the necessity peculiar to logic poses no philosophical problem. We now know better, and so do most contemporary philosophers. Our inquiry into the nature of the necessity of arithmetic leads inevitably to an even deeper inquiry into the necessity of logic. It is not simply a question of how we come to know the truths of arithmetic, but we must also answer the question of how we come to know the truths of logic. Rationalism must be overcome, not only in regard to arithmetic, but also in regard to logic. We shall therefore turn next to one of the most astute philosophers of logic and one of the greatest critics of Kant: Bernard Bolzano.

Bolzano's Response

The Ontological Turn

a) The Rejection of Pure Intuition

Earlier, I spoke of escaping from Plato's cave and compared Reid's philosophy to a bright spring morning. A similar experience awaits us if we turn from the jungle of Kant's system to the clear world of Bolzano's philosophy. To my mind, Bolzano is one of the greatest philosophers of the 19th century. A contemporary of Hegel, Schelling, and Kierkegaard, he was at once one of the greatest mathematicians and one of the most profound metaphysicians of his day.

Bolzano saw clearly that Kant's explanation of the synthetic a priori character of arithmetic in terms of pure intuition is unacceptable. In a remarkable paper of 1817, he gives a demonstration of how intuition, empirical or pure, can be eliminated from a mathematical proof (B. Bolzano, *Rein analytischer Beweis* . . .). Bolzano considers the problem of how we know that a continuous function, taking values both below and above zero, must take a zero value in between. The problem is to be solved by appealing only to basic assumptions concerning numbers and functions. In the process of solving the problem, Bolzano gives the first clear explanation, as far as I know, of the epsilon-delta description of continuity. In response to Kant, he raises the same objection we made earlier:

> Kant poses the question, "What justifies our understanding in assigning to a subject a predicate which is not contained in the concept (or explanation) of the former?"—And he thought he had discovered that this justification could only be an intuition that we link with the concept of the subject and which also contains the predicate. Thus, for all concepts from which we can construct synthetic judgments there must be corresponding intuitions. If these intuitions were always merely empirical the judgments which they mediate should also be empirical. Since nonetheless there are synthetic a priori judgments (as those undeniably contained in mathematics and pure natural science) there must also be a priori intuitions, however odd this might sound. And once one has decided that there can be such, one will also convince oneself easily that for the purposes of mathematics and pure natural science that time and space are these intuitions.
>
> (Quoted from J. A. Coffa, "To the Vienna Station,"
> unpublished manuscript, chap. II)

Bolzano's opposition to Kant's doctrine started very early. Here is how he describes it, speaking of himself in the third person:

> From very early on he dared to contradict him directly on the theory of time and space, for he did not comprehend or grant that our synthetic a priori judgments must be mediated by intuition and, in particular, he did not believe that the intuition of time lies at the ground of the synthetic judgments of arithmetic, or that in the theorems of geometry it is allowable to rest so much on the mere claim of the visual appearance, as in the Euclidian fashion.

(Quoted from Coffa, chap. II)

In paragraph 305 of his *Wissenschaftslehre,* Bolzano gives a detailed criticism of Kant's mysterious notion of pure intuition (B. Bolzano, *Wissenschaftslehre*). Let us follow him step by step. (1) Bolzano points out that the distinction between two kinds of intuition, empirical and pure intuition, does not by itself explain how pure intuition gives rise to synthetic a priori judgments. And he complains that not a single passage in all of Kant's work makes this point clear. (2) However, from some passages it is obvious that Kant believes he has discovered an important difference between an intuition which results from the actual drawing of, say, a triangle, on the one hand, and the intuition which occurs in mere imagination (Einbildungskraft), on the other. Bolzano thinks that this distinction is rather unimportant. The only difference between the two is that the former is more vivid and can more easily be fixed and reproduced. (3) Kant himself seems to have noticed this and therefore claims sometimes that it is not just imagination, but pure imagination which plays a role. Bolzano comments that this amounts to playing hide and seek with an obscure term. We must ask: What is pure imagination and how does it differ from empirical imagination? (4) Kant answers that empirical imagination merely produces pictures, while pure imagination produces schemata, and that schemata are not pictures, but rather ideas of methods or rules for the creation of a picture for a given concept. But how, asks Bolzano, can the idea of a method be called an intuition? How, moreover, does the idea of a method to provide a picture for a given concept differ from a so-called *genetic definition* of the concept? For example, if the schema of a circle is merely the idea of how one provides an object for the concept of a circle, then the schema is nothing else but the idea of how a circle is generated, that is, nothing else but the familiar description of a circle as a line which a point travels if it moves in a plane in such a way that it remains at a constant distance from another point. Bolzano concludes with these words: "If one therefore recognizes the truth of a synthetic judgment from a consideration of the schema of its subject concept, then one recognizes its truth from a consideration of a mere concept." Never before and never since, I think, has this point been made so concisely and decisively.

b) Bolzano's Notion of Number and the Beginnings of Logicism

From geometry, Bolzano turns next to arithmetic. He explains what numbers are and claims that arithmetic is analytic rather than synthetic.

According to Kant, we add the units of the number five to the number seven step by step, and this shows that the addition must be based on an intuition of time. Bolzano exlaims: "What an inference! One may as well reason that every sorites is based on the intuition of time, since we arrive at the conclusion only in the course of time." But more important than Bolzano's scorn is his attempt to prove that the addition in question is an analytic truth. His discussion contains the program of logicism in a nutshell. Bolzano claims, firstly, that the equation:

$$a + (b + c) = (a + b) + c$$

is analytic and follows from the explanation (Erklaerung) of a sum: "By a sum we think of a totality (Inbegriff) such that the order of its parts are not attended to, and the parts of the parts are considered to be parts of the whole" (cf. G. Frege's *The Foundations of Arithmetic,* p. 8, where Frege discusses a similar ploy by Grassmann). Secondly, he maintains that from this analytic equation and the explanation that $7 + 1 = 8$, $8 + 1 = 9$, etc., the proposition that $7 + 5 = 12$ emerges as a purely analytic truth. I think we may put it this way: From the *definition* of a sum and the *definitions* of the numbers as sums, it follows logically that $7 + 5 = 12$.

As always when we consider a version of logicism, the crucial notion is that of a definition. It is clear that if Bolzano's alleged definitions (Erklaerungen) are anything other than either logical truths or mere linguistic conventions, then the result of employing them cannot be an analytic truth.

Bolzano's sums are wholes of a certain sort. They are not sets, for the members of the members of a set are not members of the set, as Bolzano stipulates for sums. In order to remove all temptation to think of these wholes as arithmetic sums in the ordinary, pre-philosophical, sense of the term, let me call this kind of whole, the kind for which the associative law is stipulated to hold for its "generating relation," an "aggregate." Are there such aggregates? I think that spatial wholes are aggregates if, and this is an important if, we take as the crucial relation the relation of spatially-consisting-of. Consider the patterns of a chessboard. The squares that form the rows of the board are parts of the rows, and since the rows are parts of the board, the squares are also parts of the board. Notice that the squares are not members of the set consisting of rows, even though they are members of the sets consisting of squares from rows. (Nelson Goodman would therefore embrace Bolzano's aggregates, even though he abhors sets.)

Bolzano's claim that arithmetic is analytic rests, as we have just seen, on the following assumptions:

(1) There are wholes of a certain sort, namely, aggregates.

(2) Numbers, with the exception of the number one, are such aggregates.

(3) Certain truths about aggregates are analytic.

In the manuscript *Reine Zahlenlehre (Pure Science of Number),* Bolzano explains his view further:

> If we form a series such that its first member is a unit of an arbitrary kind A, every other member, however, is a sum which appears if we connect an object which is equal to the preceding member with a new unit of kind A, then I call every member of this series insofar a number, as I conceive of this member by means of an idea which shows its

manner of originating. In order to distinguish [this series] from other series which appear if one takes instead of things of kind A things of another kind as units, I call the members of the series we considered earlier *numbers of kind A* or numbers which are *based on the unit A*. The property through which every one of these members becomes a number (which it therefore retains however one may change the things themselves which one takes as units), I call a *number in the abstract meaning of this term,* or an *abstract number;* and in contrast to such abstract numbers (that is, the mere properties), I call the members themselves *concrete* numbers in the *concrete* meaning of the term.

(My translation, quoted from the German in J. Berg, *Bolzano's Logic,* pp. 165–66)

Consider the kind *pea,* corresponding to kind A in Bolzano's explanation, and take a particular pea P_1. P_1 is the first member of the following series. We take another object of the sort pea, equal to P_1, call it "P_2," and connect it with another pea, say, P_3. This gives us the aggregate consisting of P_2 and P_3. This aggregate is the second member of our series. In order to form the third member, we take an aggregate equal to the previous one, say the aggregate consisting of the two peas P_4 and P_5, and add another pea, so that we get the aggregate consisting of P_4, P_5, and P_6, and so on. Next, we consider the properties which the respective members of different series have in common, namely, such properties as being an aggregate consisting of a member which is equal to the first member of a series and of another member. This property, for example, is the abstract number two.

It is important to realize that we can start with any property in order to form a series of that sort. The things which are A need not even be individual things; they could be properties themselves. Nor, of course, do they have to be spatio-temporal. For example, Bolzano holds that his *Saetze an sich* (propositions) are not "real," are not spatio-temporal. Yet they can be numbered. Aggregates, therefore, are not spatio-temporal heaps. The crucial relation, characteristic of aggregates, cannot be the relation of spatially-consisting-of. We must not be misled by Bolzano's talk about "concrete" numbers. A certain aggregate may consist of three propositions. But aggregates are not sets either, as we noted earlier. This is an important difference between Bolzano's conception of number and many later ones, especially Cantor's. Cantor explains his notion of cardinal number in this way: "I call 'cardinal number [Maechtigkeit] of a multitude [Inbegriff] or set of elements' (where the latter may be homogenous or not, simple or complex) that general concept [Allgemeinbegriff] under which all and only those sets fall which are similar to the given one" (G. Cantor, *Gesammelte Abhandlungen,* p. 441). According to this explanation, the number three, for example, is a property (or concept) which all sets share which are similar to a set of three peas.

Aggregates, then, are neither spatio-temporal wholes nor are they sets. What are they? What amounts to the same: What is the characteristic relation of an aggregate?

At this point, we can adopt either one of two attitudes, depending on whether we take seriously Bolzano's talk of a sum or else his story about what constitutes a concrete number. Let us adopt the latter first. From this point of view, concrete numbers are a certain kind of whole, and the puzzle is what *kind* they are. They cannot be spatial wholes, nor can they be sets. We are merely told that the "internal arrangement" of their parts does not matter and that the "consists of" relation is transitive. I cannot think of a kind of whole that fulfills these two conditions (and that consists of peas or of propositions). I do not think, therefore, that there are such wholes. I do not think that there are aggregates of the sort required by Bolzano's theory of number.

I know the familiar objection to my conclusion. It will be said that an aggregate is simply anything that fulfills the two conditions just mentioned, so that a spatial whole, for example, is an aggregate. But this will not do. My point is not that the alleged aggregate consisting of three propositions is not a spatial whole, but rather that there is no such aggregate at all. To see this, we merely have to ask what kind of whole these three propositions are supposed to form. I can think of no reasonable answer to this question. Nor will it do to "postulate" aggregates for the cases where there are none. Whether or not three propositions form a certain sort of whole is not up to us; it is not a matter of fiat.

On the other hand, our emphasis may be placed on Bolzano's talk about sums. From this perspective, aggregates are simply sums understood in the familiar arithmetic way. So conceived of, a spatial whole is not a sum of its spatial parts. But then the only sums there are, are numbers. There are no sums of peas or sums of propositions. Consider the assertion that the sum of two peas and one pea is three peas (or that two peas plus one pea are three peas). Now this, as I said earlier, is a true statement. Furthermore, its truth follows from the fact that two plus one is three (that the sum of two and one is three). The sum relation, according to my analysis, holds between these three numbers, not between "aggregates" consisting of peas. To say that the sum of two peas and one pea is three peas, is to say, more perspicuously, that the number of peas which is the sum of the number of two peas and the number of one pea is three. Compare this once again to the color example. To say that midnight blue sweaters are darker than lemon yellow blouses is to say, not that the relation of darker than holds between sweaters and blouses, but rather that midnight blue sweaters have a color that is darker than the color of lemon yellow blouses. Bolzano's view, transferred to the color example, would come to this: There are certain wholes, for example, blue sweaters, yellow blouses, green apples, red flags, etc., and the relation of darker than holds between these wholes. These wholes are the "concrete colors." When we abstract from the particular objects that form these wholes, that is, sweaters, blouses, apples, flags, etc., we get "the abstract colors." Our analysis precisely reverses this process.

That there is something wrong with Bolzano's notion of a concrete number can be seen when we return to his description of how a series of such numbers is formed. Starting with one pea, the next member of the series consists of an object which is "equal" (gleich) to this one pea and of another pea. What does the word 'equal' here mean? It does not mean identical or same. If it did, then Bolzano could have said that the next member of the series consists of the first member (the first pea) and another pea, but he does not. The most plausible interpretation is that 'equal' means equal in number. We take an object that is equal in number to the previous object—in our case, one other pea—and add one more thing of the same sort, namely, another pea. But upon this interpretation, we are obviously using the concept of number in order to explain what a number is. There is one other possibility that I can see. 'Equal' could mean isomorphic to. We are then instructed to take an object which is isomorphic to the previous object of the series and add one more object of the same sort. We are instructed, in other words, to pick an object whose parts can be coordinated one to one to the parts of the previous object of the series. Put still differently, we are invited to consider a *set* of things isomorphic to the previous set. Upon this interpretation, Bolzano's aggregates are really sets ("the order of its parts are not attended to"), and we must disregard his assertion that "the parts of the parts are considered to be parts of the whole."

Abstract numbers are presumably formed when we abstract from the particular properties (being a pea, being a proposition, etc.) which characterize the parts of the aggregates of the various series, and pay attention only to how these series are created. Consider an aggregate of two peas and an aggregate of two propositions. What do these two aggregates have in common? Well, they both consist of the first member of a series plus one other member. And they share this property with all other two-part aggregates: they all share the property of consisting of one of a kind and one other thing of the same kind. This property, it seems, is the number two. In short, the number two, according to Bolzano, is the property of consisting (of being the sum) of one and one. The number three is the property of consisting of two and one. And so on. It is clear that this conception rests on two notions, namely, on the notion of the (abstract) number one (the "unit" of kind A) and the conception of a consisting-of relation (the sum relation) among numbers. In the end, then, Bolzano's analysis may perhaps be summarized as follows. Numbers, with the exception of the number one, are properties of certain wholes. The number one is a property of a unit of any sort. The other numbers are sums of numbers. For example, the number two is the sum of the unit and one other thing.

c) Analyticity and Form

Bolzano's notion of analyticity is at once brilliant and idiosyncratic. I shall concentrate on those parts of it which have endured. Just as Bolzano's concept of number was to become the first in a line of modern attempts to give an ontology of arithmetic, so has his notion of analyticity turned out to be the forerunner of several contemporary explications of analyticity in terms of form.

Consider the proposition:

The man Caius is mortal,

and think of the idea *Caius* as being arbitrarily changeable, so that in its place other ideas occur; for example, the ideas *Sempronius, Titus, rose, triangle,* etc. The resulting propositions are true as long as their subject ideas have objects. The proposition *The man Titus is mortal* is true, and so is the proposition *The man Frege is mortal.* On the other hand, *The man rose is mortal* is not even a proposition, since its subject idea, *the man rose,* has no object. And the same holds for expressions like 'The man plus is mortal', 'The man neither is mortal', 'The man Paris is mortal', etc. In short, all the propositions derived from the given one which substitute for the idea of Caius a "proper" idea are true. Next, consider the proposition:

The man Caius is omniscient.

You can easily see that all of the propositions derived from this one by "proper" substitution are false. The proposition itself is false, and so are such propositions as *The man Titus is omniscient* and (even) *The man Frege is omniscient.* Finally, consider the proposition:

The being Caius is mortal.

If we substitute for the idea *Caius* the idea *Titus,* we get a true proposition, but if we substitute for it the idea *God,* we get a false proposition.

Here is another of Bolzano's examples. He claims that the proposition:

This triangle has three sides

yields only true propositions as long as we treat only the idea *this* as a variable. What he has in mind, I think, is that a proposition like *That triangle has three sides* is true, while something like *Caius triangle has three sides* has a subject idea which lacks an object. I shall assume that this last string of words does not really represent a proposition at all. Given this assumption, we can describe Bolzano's view as follows: If we think of an idea in a proposition as variable and replaced by other ideas, but in such a way that the result is a proposition and not nonsense, then there are three possible cases: (1) All the resulting propositions are true, (2) all of them are false, and (3) some are true and some are false. It is clear that there is no proposition such that we can change all of its ideas arbitrarily and get only true or only false propositions; for, as Bolzano remarks, if we can change all of the ideas, then we can turn any proposition into any other proposition and hence get some true propositions and some false propositions (Bolzano, 1981, par. 148).

We come now to Bolzano's notion of analyticity:

> But if there is even a *single* idea in a proposition which can be varied arbitrarily without destroying its truth or falsety . . ., then this characteristic of the proposition is peculiar enough to distinguish it from all of those [propositions] for which this is not the case. I allow myself, therefore, to call propositions of this sort, with an expression borrowed from Kant, *analytic,* all others, however, . . . synthetic.

> (Bolzano, 1981, par. 148)

Bolzano then gives the following two examples of analytic propositions:

A morally evil person does not deserve respect,

and

A morally evil person may still enjoy continued happiness.

These two propositions are analytic, because they contain the idea *person* (Mensch) which, if varied, yields nothing but true propositions in the first instance and nothing but false propositions in the second. In effect, these two propositions are analytic because they are of the *forms:*

A morally evil X does not deserve respect,

and

A morally evil X may still enjoy continued happiness.

Bolzano later on gives the following examples of true *logically* analytic propositions:

(1) *A is A,*

(2) *A, which is B, is A,*

(3) *A, which is B, is B,*

(4) *Every object is either B or not B.*

And then he adds:

> These examples of analytic propositions which I have just mentioned differ from those in number 1 [about the evil person] in that a judgment concerning their analytic nature necessitates no other but logical knowledge, since the concepts which form the invariable part of these propositions all belong to logic . . .
>
> This difference, however, is not strict, since the domain of concepts which belong to logic is not so sharply delimited that one could never raise a controversy.
>
> (Bolzano, 1981, par. 148)

Let us set aside this reservation and try to fully understand Bolzano's notion of logical analyticity. As our example we shall take the proposition: *Males, which are unmarried, are unmarried.* This proposition is logically analytic, as I understand Bolzano, because it is of a certain *form,* namely, of the form: *F's, which are G's, are G's.* This form is such that however we vary F and G, the result is always a true proposition. Furthermore, F and G are the only nonlogical ideas which can occur in propositions of this form. In a nutshell, our example is a logical analytic truth *in virtue of its form.*

In paragraph 186 of the *Wissenschaftslehre,* Bolzano discusses the quite different view that logic is a matter of form, not of content. He is especially critical of the view that all of the ideas which occur in a judgment belong to the content of the judgment. This view implies that "logical" words like 'and', 'or', 'if', 'then', etc. do not stand for ideas. Bolzano objects that one can only describe the form of a judgment by specifying that certain ideas are connected in this and no other way, precisely because a certain concept, the concept *and,* for example, connects them. So-called logical terms, he insists, represent concepts just as much as "ordinary" expressions. Logic, therefore, could not possibly be characterized by distinguishing between "descriptive" expressions which represent something and "logical" expressions which do not. Bolzano, I submit, has a decisive argument against such a conception of the nature of logic. If 'and' and 'or' have no "meaning" (if they do not represent relations, if they do not express ideas, or however you may wish to put it), then why can we not interchange these words willy-nilly in sentences? Surely, these words contribute just as much to the "meaning" of a sentence as other words do. It is therefore simply false to claim, as Quine does at one place, that logical truths are characterized by the fact that they are "invariant under lexical substitutions" (W. V. O. Quine, *Philosophy of Logic,* p. 102).

Bolzano concedes that there is a sense in which logic may be said to be a matter of form. In logic, he maintains, we are interested not in individual propositions, but in kinds of proposition. We divide propositions into groups, according to certain properties: "If one permits oneself to call such properties the common forms of these propositions, that is, their configuration (Gestalt), then one can rightly assert that all the divisions of propositions occurring in logic concern only their form, that is, concern only that which several, even infinitely many, propositions have in common" (Quine, 1970, p. 102). I do not think that propositions of the same form share a common property. In order to fully understand the fashionable view that logic is a matter of form, we must be clear about the ontological status of form. After we have cleared up this matter, we shall return to our main argument and explain in what sense logic is and in what sense it is not a matter of form.

d) The Ontological Status of Form

Let us return to our example: *Males, which are unmarried, are unmarried.* This proposition, I said, is of the form: *F's, which are G's, are G's.* What, precisely, does it mean to say that a proposition is of a certain form? What is a form? What are those F's and G's in the form? In the world, there are no F's and G's; Bolzano would say that there are no ideas corresponding to 'F's' and to 'G's'. There are only the expressions. Let us therefore shift from the form to the expression for the form: 'F's, which are G's, are G's'. What does this expression represent? The short answer is: Nothing! There is no entity, the form of a proposition, which is represented by this expression. It represents neither a property nor, in Bolzano's terminology, an idea. However, there do exist a number of propositions (states of affairs, facts, circumstances) which are *partially identical* with the proposition of our example. There are propositions *of this form.* If we wish to talk about propositions which are partially identical with the given proposition, then we may use "schematic letters" like 'F' and 'G'—or any equivalent device—in order to indicate what propositions we have in mind. For example, if we wish to talk about all of the propositions that start with a plural property idea, followed by the logical idea(s) *which are,* followed by another property idea, and so forth, we can do so more conveniently by mentioning the form: *F's, which are G's, are G's.* Expressions for forms allow us to abbreviate talk about groups of complex things which are partially identical. It is important to notice that things of the same form do not, precisely speaking, share a common property, as white billiard balls share a common color. Rather, what they have in common is that they are partially identical. This partial identity can only be described in the cumbersome way of which we gave an example.

Expressions for forms contain "schematic letters." Schematic letters are not "free variables." They acquire their significance in the manner just explained: They serve to depict a partial identity among complex things. So-called free variables are either not variables at all, for example, when one mistakenly calls schematic letters "free variables," or else they are bound variables in expressions that have been amputated. If we start out with the expression:

'All f's and all g's and all x's are such that: If x is f and x is g, then x is g' and then drop the part before the 'If', we get an expression in which 'x', 'f', and 'g' occur "free," that is, without a quantifier. But I insist that we can only make sense of such expressions by reminding ourselves of the sense which the original expressions have.

I said earlier that expressions for forms represent nothing. This sounds like a contradiction, but I think that you can now see what is meant. Such an expression does not represent an entity, but we can use it in order to make a long story short, namely, a story about complex things which are partially identical. In particular, we must realize that such expressions do not represent properties or functions (relations). To certain philosophers, the conviction comes naturally that an expression like 'F's, which are G's, are G's' represents a function which yields true propositions as values for ideas (or concepts, or properties) as arguments. Russell even presents an argument to the effect that form expressions are needed in order to represent functions. Compare the expression just mentioned with the following expression: 'A's, which are B's, are C's'. If we hold that these two expressions do not represent functions, so Russell argues, but that the function is instead represented by something like 'which are, are', then we cannot distinguish between the first function and the quite different second one. Hence we are forced to hold that those form expressions represent functions (B. Russell, *Principles of Mathematics,* pp, 84–85, 508–509). Russell's argument presupposes that we are confronted here with two different functions. But this is a mistake. The two expressions deal with the same function, namely, the function represented by 'which are, are.' We have here, not two different functions, but two *different forms,* forms which contain the same function. The fact that two propositions are not of the same form does not imply, as Russell assumes, that they must contain different functions. Another example may help to make this clear. Consider the two descriptions: *The sum of 2 and 3* and *the sum of 2 and 2.* The first is of the form *The sum of X and Y,* while the second is of the form *the sum of X and X.* But though the forms are different, the function (relation) contained in the two descriptions is the same, namely, the sum function (relation).

Since we are talking about Russell, we may take this opportunity to say a few words about Russell's version of the popular view that logic (and pure mathematics) is "purely formal" (see B. Russell, *Introduction to Mathematical Philosophy,* pp. 194–201). Russell asks: "What is this subject, which may be called indifferently either mathematics or logic?" The question, of course, makes an assumption which I consider to be most certainly false, namely, that logic and mathematics are the same. But never mind, what is, according to Russell, the nature of logic? He points out the familiar fact that the validity of arguments depends only on their form, and then he wrestles with the problem of the nature of form. He considers the form $x R y$ which may be read: "x has the relation R to y." Here I must interrupt our inspection of Russell's view for a moment and amend something I said earlier. To talk about propositions of a certain form, I said then, is to talk about propositions which are partially identical. This was correct within the context, but must be changed for the general case, as Russell's example shows. Propositions of Russell's form may have no *part* in common. Rather, what they have in common is that they consist of two individuals and a relation in a certain order (or of ideas of a certain sort in a certain order). Still, my main contention stands: There is no such entity as the form of a proposition. In particular, the form of a proposition is not a property of the proposition.

Russell, in distinction from us, thinks of forms as things of a certain sort:

> Given a proposition, such as "Socrates is before Aristotle," we have certain constituents and also a certain form. But the form is not itself a new constituent; if it were, we should need a new form to embrace both it and the other constituents. We can, in fact, turn *all* the constituents of a proposition into variables, while keeping the form unchanged. This is what we do when we use such a schema as "x R y," which stands for any one of a certain class of propositions, namely those asserting relations between two terms. We can proceed to general assertions, such as "x R y is sometimes true"—i.e. there are cases where dual relations hold. This assertion will belong to logic (or mathematics) in the sense in which we are using the word. But in this assertion we do not mention any particular things or particular relations; no particular things or relations can ever enter into a proposition of pure logic. We are left with pure forms as the only possible constituents of logical propositions.

> (Russell, 1956a, pp. 198–99)

This paragraph clearly shows Russell's confusion. From a proof that forms *cannot* be constituents of the propositions whose forms they are, he arrives at the conclusion that "forms *are* the only possible constituents of logical propositions." The proof is relatively clear. If the form *x R y* were a constituent of the proposition *Socrates is before Aristotle,* then the proposition could not be of the form *x R y,* for this form does not show the form as a constituent of the proposition. Rather, the form would then have to be something like *f-x R y,* where the 'f' indicates the form. But now we can repeat the reasoning and argue that if this form is a constituent of the original proposition about Socrates and Aristotle, then the form of this proposition cannot be *f-x R y* either. Russell concludes, reasonably it seems to me, that the original proposition does not contain its form as a constituent. For us, the problem does not arise: since there are no such things as forms, they cannot be parts of propositions.

Next, Russell claims that we can turn *all* the parts of a proposition into variables: *x R y.* This shows, I take it, that the form was not part of the proposition to begin with; otherwise, there would occur a variable for it in the form (our 'f' above). But note that Russell speaks here of "variables." This is a second mistake. The form is depicted, in our view, not by '*x R y*', but by an expression with schematic letters, say, by '*X R Y*'. When we consider the expression with variables, we can only make sense of it, as I claimed earlier, as a part of a "closed" expression; for example as a part of the sentence: 'There is an individual thing x, and there is an individual thing y, and there is a relation R such that: x R y (that is, x stands in R to y)'. For a moment, Russell seems to take a step toward our view when he says, not, as we would expect, that '$x R y$' stands for the form but that it stands "for any one of a certain class of propositions." At this moment, he takes his talk about variables seriously. But the impulse is immediately repressed: the logical proposition that emerges is not our quantified proposition, but the rather strange "x R y is sometimes true." And then Russell concludes from this example that the *pure form x R y* is a part of the logical proposition. Whatever happened, we may want to ask, to the claim that '$x R y$' stands for any one of a class of propositions? It is clear that Russell is torn between treating the expression '$x R y$' as a variable "ranging over certain propositions," on the one hand, and as a name for a certain kind of entity, namely, a form, on the other.

How uncomfortable Russell feels can be seen from the next paragraph. He says, first, that he does "not wish to assert positively that pure forms—e. g. the form "x R y"—do actually enter into propositions of the kind we are considering." But then he concludes two sentences later that "we may accept, as a first approximation, the view that *forms* are what enter into logical propositions as their constituents." I have so far argued that we may not accept this view. Logic is not about a certain kind of entity called "form."

e) Form and Logical Laws

Logic is not about forms. What is it about? Bolzano, as we see from his examples, thinks of identity statements of the form "A is A" as belonging to logic. I do not. Of course, it is in part "merely a terminological matter" whether we call the identity relation a "logical relation." But our terminology should be guided by a desire to make philosophically illuminating distinctions. In this spirit, I think of identity statements as ontological statements rather than logical ones. I hold that there exists an ontological *law of identity* (or of self-identity): *Every entity e is such that: $e = e$.* This law holds for any entity whatsoever. It holds for properties as well as for individual things; it holds for numbers as well as relations; it holds for simple things and for complex things; it even holds for identity itself. In brief, it holds for all categories. But though it holds for everything, it does not hold for non-existents. Entities and only entities are self-identical. I do not believe, as some philosophers do, that Pegasus and Hamlet are self-identical. Hamlet can no more stand in the relation of identity than he can stand in the relation of being-a-son-of. What is true is, rather, that he is depicted as the son of the king of Denmark; and it goes without saying that he is thought of as being self-identical. This is a long story which I cannot here pursue (see my "Nonexistent Objects Versus Definite Descriptions," pp. 363–77). What I wish to emphasize is that in my view the law of self-identity is an ontological law, and that an instance of this law is an ontological fact. The same is true, by the way, for the so-called axiom of infinity: it, too, if it is a fact, is an ontological rather than logical fact. That there are infinitely many things (as distinguished from that there are infinitely many numbers), if a fact, is a fact of ontology. The axiom of choice, on the other hand, seems to me to be a purely set-theoretical fact. That it is a fact, I have no doubt.

Since an instance of the law of self-identity is not an instance of a logical law, it is not, in our specific sense, an analytic truth. And neither are the axioms of infinity and of choice. However, this does not mean that these truths, if they are truths, are not necessary. Necessity, we must constantly emphasize, does not coincide with analyticity.

Returning to Bolzano, he also mentions as an example of a logically analytic statement: Every object is either B or not B. I take this to mean: Every entity either has the property F or does not have the property F. A fact of this form is an instance of the law: All properties f are such that: all entities e are such that: e is f or e is not f. (This is rather awkward and abominable English, but it has the advantage that I can fit different English sentences into the same mold.) This is a law of logic. I call it a "logical law," because it says something about all *properties*. It tells us that all *properties* behave in a certain fashion. It is clearly different from the law of self-identity which tells us something not only about all properties, but about all entities whatsoever. An instance of this law of logic is thus a proposition of logic and therefore an analytic truth.

Ontological laws are about entities in general; (some) logical laws are about properties in general. According to this criterion, the second and third examples of Bolzano's list of logically analytic truths belong to logic. And so do all of the laws of what is known as "the singulary functional calculus of higher order" or "the monadic predicate calculus of higher order" (see, for example, A. Church, *Introduction to Mathematical Logic*). However, logic as commonly understood is not restricted to a general theory of properties. There is also a general theory of relations. These two theories are usually combined into one. What we get then is "the higher functional calculus." Finally, there exists also a quite different theory about states of affairs (propositions) in general. This theory is sometimes called "the propositional calculus" and counted as a part of logic. In short, what is commonly called "logic" consists in my opinion of three distinct theories, namely, (1) a theory about properties in general, (2) a theory about relations in general, and (3) a theory about states of affairs in general. The first theory describes under what general conditions properties are *exemplified;* the second states under what general conditions relations *hold;* and the third describes under what general conditions states of affairs *obtain.* I hope that it will become clear as our investigation proceeds how profoundly this conception of logic differs from almost all of the views about logic which have been proposed during the last hundred years.

Earlier, I explained Bolzano's notion of *logical* analyticity in terms of the form of propositions. For example, I said that propositions of the form: *F's, which are G's, are G's* are logical analytic truths. It must be emphasized, though, that I could have talked instead about instances of a certain law. From my point of view of logic, this would indeed have been the more perspicuous approach. Consider the logical law:

All properties f and g are such that: All entities e are such that: If e is f and e is g, then e is g.

Every instance of this law is a logical truth. It is also obvious that all of its instances share the same form and that all propositions of this form are instances of the law.

If one seeks an explication of logic which is centered around the notion of form rather than the notion of law, one may easily make the following mistake. It is obvious that there are many quite different forms which yield logical truths. *F's, which are G's, are G's* is one such form. But so are *P or not P*, and also *If P, then (if Q, then P)*. One is forced to ask what all of these diverse forms have in common that accounts for their logical nature. Well, it is obvious that what they have in common is a stock list of shared concepts, namely, the concepts *or, and, if-then, all, some, not*, etc. While all the other words are replaced by "variables" (actually schematic letters), words for these concepts remain "constant." And this suggests to some philosophers that the forms under study are logical in nature because they contain these "logical concepts." Thus logic is characterized by the fact that is is about (that it involves, that it is based on) a peculiar set of logical concepts (logical constants, logical terms).

But this conclusion is wrongheaded. What is essential to logic is not that it involves words like 'not', 'all', and 'or', but that it is about properties, relations, and states of affairs. The relation *or* is no more a logical relation than it is a biological relation; the quantifier *all* is no more a logical entity than it is a chemical thing. The relation *or* and the quantifier *all* are parts of all kinds of laws, not just of the laws of logic. They occur in laws of chemistry and geometry just as much as in the laws of logic. They are the stuff facts are made of. What describes a field of inquiry is its laws. And what distinguishes laws from each other is what they are about, that is, what the variables of the laws range over. In the so-called "propositional calculus," the variables range over states of affairs (propositions). This is why it is a theory of states of affairs, not a theory of chemistry or biology. In the so-called functional calculus, the variables range over entities and properties and relations (let us agree to say that they range over entities and *attributes*). This is why it is a theory of attributes, not of geology or of geometry. Nor is it the same as set theory. In set theory, the same quantifiers and connectives occur as in "attribute theory," but the variables of set theory range over sets, while the variables of attribute theory range over attributes. While set theory is about sets, logic (the "functional calculus") is about attributes. From our point of view, it is absurd to hold that there is such a thing as propositional logic, but that there are no propositions (states of affairs, circumstances, etc.). From our point of view, it is absurd to teach that there is such a thing as the functional calculus, but that there are no attributes. This is just as absurd as to believe that there is chemistry without chemical elements, zoology without animals, and set theory without sets.

My main objection to the view that logic is a matter of form and that form is characterized by logical concepts (or logical terms) is not that it is impossible to draw a line between logical and nonlogical concepts. If challenged, we could simply enumerate the so-called logical concepts or terms. Rather our objection is that there are, precisely speaking, no logical concepts or terms. The concepts which are usually singled out as logical concepts are no more characteristic of logic than they are of chemistry. I share, therefore, Bolzano's skepticism about how fruitful the notion of form is for an elucidation of the nature of logic. And in another respect, too, our views are related.

The view that logic is a matter of form, not of content, may give rise to the conviction that logic is not concerned with facts. This, in my opinion, is its most insidious corollary. The proposition:

Males, which are unmarried, are unmarried

is a *logical* truth. It is a logical truth because it is an instance of the *logical* law:

All properties f and g are such that: If an entity e is f and is g, then it is g,

and this is a *logical* law, because it says something about *properties* in general. *Two* facts are involved: a fact about males and a fact about properties. The fact about males is true because it is an instance of the law, but the law itself is also a fact. The law, to emphasize, is just as much a fact as any law of biology, any law of set theory, any law of arithmetic. There are facts about properties in general just as there are facts about whales in general, or about certain sets in general, or about natural numbers in general. Just as the logical law is a law about properties in general, so is the law that all whales are mammals a law about whales in general. Assume that there exists a certain whale called "Moby." It is a fact that Moby is a mammal. This is a fact because Moby is a whale and because of the law about whales. But we could also say that *Moby is a mammal* is true by virtue of its form, for any proposition of the form *X is a mammal* is true, assuming, of course, that *X* is a whale. However, would it not be absurd to conclude that it is not a fact that Moby is a mammal, or that zoology is not a matter of facts? Bolzano's somewhat idiosyncratic conception of analyticity has the priceless virtue of showing that propositions which are obviously empirical can be said to be true in virtue of their form!

Of course, there is a difference between the law of logic and the law about whales. As a matter of fact, there are at least three important differences. Firstly, while the law of logic is about properties, the second law is about whales: there is a difference in subject matter. Secondly, while the law about logic may be said to be necessary in the sense that we cannot imagine exceptions to it, the law about whales is not necessary in this sense. Thirdly, and this is the difference I wish to dwell on, while the logical law is very general—it concerns all properties whatsoever—the second law is specifically about whales. There is thus a great difference in the *degree of generality*. This difference is partially hidden by the fact that we formulated the logical law, as is common, in terms of property variables. To emphasize its full generality, we should however give the following version of it:

All entities e_1, e_2, and e_3 are such that: If e_1 and e_2 are properties, and if e_3 exemplifies both e_1 and e_2, then e_3 exemplifies e_2.

It is this amazing generality of logical laws which accounts, at least in part, for our reluctance to give them up in the face of contrary evidence. Surely, to scrap a law about all properties will involve revisions a philosopher seldom dreams of.

f) Logic and Empiricism

If the logical law, in either form, is a fact, then we cannot avoid the Kantian question of how we know this fact. Before we turn to this important question, let us note another point about analyticity. Recall our paradigm of Bolzano's logically analytic truth: A, which is B, is B, or: Males, which are unmarried, are unmarried. But what about the background law; is it an analytic truth? Bolzano's answer can be glimpsed from the following, somewhat different, case:

> The proposition: If all humans are mortal, and Caius is a human being, then Caius, too, is mortal, may perhaps (allenfalls) be called analytic in the wider meaning given in paragraph 148; however, the rule itself that from two propositions of the form A is B and B is C a third one follows of the form A is C, is a synthetic truth.
>
> (Bolzano, 1981, par. 315, 2)

From this quotation it appears that Bolzano would say that our law of logic is a *synthetic* truth. Generally, the laws of the theory of attributes are *synthetic*. And so they are! With the Kantian notion of analyticity in mind, it is obvious that the concept of a property does not consist (in part) of "the concept that if something has two properties f and g, then it has the property g." (I hardly know how to put this intelligibly.) This latter "concept" is no more contained in the concept of a property than it is contained in the concept of a whale that it is a mammal. Of course, it is true that properties behave in this way, just as it is true that whales are mammals. But the respective concepts of a property and of a whale, to speak Kant's language, do not contain as parts those other concepts.

From our un-Kantian point of view, it is equally clear that the laws of logic are not analytic. This follows from our very explication of the term. A sentence is analytic, we said, if and only if, in its unabbreviated form, it represents an *instance* of a logical law. The laws of logic, though they follow from each other, are not instances of each other, except in that pickwickian sense in which every logical law is an instance of itself. And this shows once again how unimportant this notion of analyticity is for the philosophy of logic and mathematics.

How do we come to know logical laws? Bolzano, I think, gives the correct answer. He readily concedes that logic and mathematics are more reliable than other fields of inquiry, but he rejects Kant's explanation of this fact:

> And here, I believe, we have no reason to forsake an explanation which was given long before Kant. One has always said that these sciences [logic, arithmetic, geometry, and pure physics] enjoy such a high degree of certainty, only because they have the advantage that their most important theses can be tested easily and variously by experience, and have been so tested; and, furthermore, because those theses which cannot be tested directly, can be deduced by means of arguments which one has tested innumerable times and always found to be correct; and, finally, because the results, which one obtains from these sciences, do not affect the human passions, so that investigations can almost always be started and finished without bias, and with the proper leisure and calmness. The only reason why we are so certain that the rules Barbara, Celarent, etc. are correct is that they are confirmed by thousands of arguments to which we have applied them. This is also the true reason why we assert so confidently in mathematics that factors in a different order give the same product, or that the total angles in a triangle are equal to two right angles, or that the forces on a lever are in equilibrium when they stand in the inverse relation of their distances from the fulcrum,

etc. But that the square root of 2 equals 1.414 . . . , that the content of a sphere is exactly two-thirds of the circumscribed cylinder, that in each body there are three free axes of revolution, etc. we assert with such confidence because they follow from propositions of the first kind by arguments which others, too, have used a hundred times and found to be correct; . . . .

(Bolzano, 1981, par. 315, 4; similar remarks, by the way, can be found in Russell)

The case for empiricism could hardly be stated any better. Bolzano clearly distinguishes between certain basic propositions of logic and arithmetic, on the one hand, and more complicated theorems, on the other. An example of the first kind from logic is the form *Barbara;* from arithmetic, the law that the order of the factors of a product does not matter. Why are we so *certain* that an argument of the form *Barbara* is valid? We are so certain, because we and many others have tested it innumerable times and found that it always leads from true premises to a true conclusion. Recall our earlier example of a logical law. We can easily verify—and it has been verified millions of times—that if a thing has the properties F and G, it has at least the property G. If you doubt this law, give me an example of a property, G, which does not behave in this fashion. Or show me that the negation of this law follows from some alleged truths. Or, finally, put forward an argument to the effect that the law in conjunction with some other true propositions yields a falsehood. No matter what you try, I am sure that you will fail. But though I am sure that you will not succeed, I am willing to consider this *kind* of refutation of the putative law. I admit that the putative law could be shown to be false in this manner.

It is at this point that empiricists like me part ways with many other philosophers. Ernest Nagel, for example, has argued that any suggestion that, say, *modus ponens* is not a valid rule of inference would be "dismissed as grotesque and as resting upon some misunderstanding" (Ernest Nagel, "Logic without Ontology", p. 310). Of course, it would. Of course, we would suspect that one of the premises of the supposed exception to the rule must be false after all. Or else we may insist that the conclusion cannot but be true. But Nagel and I disagree about the reason for our stubbornness. I resist any suggestion that the rule is mistaken (that the underlying law is false) because of the fact that it has been confirmed a million times. Nagel, on the other hand, believes that "statements of the form: 'If A and (if A then B) then B' are necessarily true, since not to acknowledge them as such is to run counter to the established usage of the expressions 'and' and 'if . . . then' " (Nagel, p. 310). According to him, "the laws which are regarded as necessary in a given language may be viewed as implicit definitions of the ways in which certain recurrent expressions are to be used or as consequence of other postulates for such usages" (Nagel, p. 319). We shall later discuss implicit definitions in some detail. For the moment, I wish to point out that what matters for the truth of statements of the form *modus ponens* is not just the "established usage of the expressions 'and', and 'if . . . , then,' " but also the usage of the word 'proposition' ('state of affairs', 'statement'). What is true is the statement: All *propositions* p and q are such that: If p and (if p, then q), then q. If it were not for the truth of this law, statements of form *modus ponens* would not be true. As soon as we realize that what we mean by 'proposition' ('state of affairs', 'statement', etc.) is as important for laws of (propositional) logic as what we mean by 'and', 'or', etc., we realize the futility of trying to base the certainty of logic on "established usage." If we meant by 'proposition' something other than what we do mean by it, the logical law which justifies *modus ponens* might not be true. But by the same token, if we meant by 'whale' something different from what we do mean by it, the sentence 'All whales are mammals' might not be true.

Empiricists are sometimes challenged to name just one instance in which a logical law was abandoned for the reasons given above (see, for example, Nagel, p. 310). I shall take up the challenge. Consider the proposition that every property (which is exemplified) determines a set. Now, this is not strictly speaking a law of logic, although Frege thought of it as one, but I think that it is not any less evident to "informed common sense" than the laws of logic are. Surely, that a given property determines a certain set is confirmed millions of times: To the property of being a pen on my desk, there corresponds the set of all pens on my desk; to the property of being a citizen of the United States on a given date, there corresponds a set of persons; to the property of being a natural number, there corresponds the set of natural numbers; etc., etc., etc. Yet, the proposition is false: There are properties which do not determine sets! It took logicians and mathematicians many years to give up this law. They were so certain of it that they searched in a hundred different directions for a way of preserving it. How did we find out that the alleged law was false? In precisely the same way in which we on other occasions find out that an alleged law is not really a law: We found an exception! The property of being a set, it turns out, does not determine a set. Thus it is not true that all properties determine sets; only some properties do. Our strongest intuition, confirmed by millions of examples, turned out in the end to be mistaken.

The laws of logic and arithmetic, just like the laws of biology and chemistry, are "about the world." They, too, have a specific "subject matter." Part of logic is about propositions (states of affairs); another part is about attributes (properties and relations). Arithmetic, of course, is about numbers. The laws of logic and arithmetic, just like the laws of biology and chemistry, are established "empirically." We are more or less certain that they hold, as long as we have found no exceptions. Does this mean that the vaunted necessity of logic and arithmetic is but a chimera? We shall have to discuss this question in the next chapter. One thing, though, is already clear. Whatever distinguishes between logic, arithmetic, and set theory, on the one hand, and the "empirical sciences," on the other, cannot be a fundamental difference between their respective statements. On both sides, there are laws and instances of laws. In both cases, the laws necessitate their instances. In both fields, instances suggest (confirm) the laws. And on either side of the division, alleged laws are vulnerable to exceptions.

g) Propositions and the Murky Realm of Meaning

Bolzano breaks with the two-thousand-year-old tradition of Western philosophy and makes the category of proposition the center of his ontology. However, this revolution, like most revolutions, turns out to be a mixed blessing. On the positive side, there is the valuable insight that it is judgments and their contents which constitute knowledge. Bolzano holds that in addition to mental acts of judgment and linguistic expressions (sentences), there exists a third kind of thing which is neither mental nor linguistic. This kind is comprised of his so-called *Saetze an sich,* what I have in this chapter called "propositions." Bolzano clearly sees that these propositions are "abstract" entities, that is, that they are not spatio-temporal. In addition to these major discoveries, Bolzano's ontology contains numerous innovations that I cannot mention in this context.

On the negative side, Bolzano's propositions turn out to be denizens of a murky realm of meanings, not the robust facts around us. The proposition *Socrates is mortal,* for example, is not the same as what I call the *fact* that *Socrates is mortal.* This fact contains Socrates as a constituent. It consists of Socrates, the property of being mortal, and the nexus of exemplification. Bolzano's proposition, on the other hand, contains not Socrates, but the "objective idea" of Socrates. What, precisely, is this "objective idea"?

Bolzano distinguishes between subjective and objective ideas. A subjective idea, as one would expect, is a mental occurrence in an individual mind. When I think of Socrates, there occurs in my mind a certain subjective idea; and when you think of Socrates, there occurs in your mind a different subjective idea. If there were no minds, no such ideas would exist. But, according to Bolzano, there are also, corresponding to subjective ideas, certain objective ideas. These things are not mental and they are not confined to individual minds. Nor are they "concrete" like subjective ideas. They are abstract things, that is, they are not spatio-temporal. Propositions consist of these objective ideas. Bolzano holds that what the sentence 'Socrates is mortal' represents, the proposition, is of the form: *Socrates has mortality.* And this proposition consists of the three objective ideas: Socrates, the idea of having, and the idea mortality.

Every objective idea has an "extension," that is, a certain set of objects (see, for example, Bolzano, 1981, par. 126, 127, and 131). This set may be empty, or it may consist of just one thing. The extension of the objective idea *round square,* for example, is empty. The objective idea *Socrates,* on the other hand, has just one object. The idea *mortal,* finally, has an extension with many objects. In order to get some understanding of what an objective idea is, we should ask: What, precisely, is the relationship between an objective idea and its extension? This seems to me to be the most important question about Bolzano's ontology.

I think that there are two possible interpretations of Bolzano's view. According to the first, the relation between an objective idea and its object is the intentional nexus. It is the relationship between an idea, in the ordinary sense of the word, and what the idea is an idea of, its object. The second possibility is that the relation is roughly the relationship between a property and the set it determines. I have the impression that Bolzano thinks of the connection between objective idea and extension in both ways simultaneously, and that this is one of the most important flaws of his theory. But be that as it may, the fact remains that Bolzano distinguishes between the objective idea Socrates, which is a constituent of the proposition, and the person Socrates. The objective idea (of) Socrates thus is placed somewhere in the middle between the subjective idea in the mind and the real person Socrates in the world. Some philosophers may be tempted to think of the objective idea Socrates as the "meaning" of the name 'Socrates', where the meaning must be distinguished from both the idea in the mind and the person in the world.

I do not think that there are propositions, as conceived of by Bolzano, because I do not think that there are "meanings" in this sense of the word. I do not deny that there is meaning. I believe that there is both meaning expressed and meaning represented by language. For example, the sentence 'Socrates is mortal' *expresses,* on a certain occasion, a judgment (or a belief, or an assertion, or a doubt, etc.), and it *represents* on that occasion the fact that Socrates is mortal. Thus we may say that it means the judgment and that it means the fact or, better, that its meaning is the judgment and that its meaning is the fact. (Of course, there are many other meanings of 'meaning', but they are not relevant to our discussion.) To say it again: I have no quarrel with meaning. But I do not believe that in addition to the judgment and the fact, there exists a third, Bolzano's proposition.

Bolzano's distinction between the subjective judgment, on the one hand, and its objective content, on the other, is not only correct, but essential for a rejection of Kant's idealism. But Bolzano does not get the objective side right. What corresponds in the nonmental world to the subjective idea of Socrates is not an objective idea, but Socrates himself. What corresponds to the subjective idea mortality, is not an objective idea, but the property of being mortal. And what corresponds to the judgment that Socrates is mortal is not the proposition, but the fact. Bolzano overcomes Kant's idealism, but the idealistic terminology lingers on, and with it, a tendency to subjectify the external world. To the realist, who has a firm grasp of the nature of the external world, this subjectified world must appear as a superfluous third, a "Mittelding," neither fish nor fowl. Bolzano speaks of "Vorstellungen an sich" (what I have called "objective ideas"). These "Vorstellungen an sich" are divided into "Anschauungen" and "Begriffe." These are all terms taken from the mental vocabulary. Yet they are supposed to represent nonmental things. What corresponds in the world to a mental "Anschauung" should not be called an "Anschauung an sich"; it is an individual thing. What corresponds in the world to a mental "Begriff" should not be called a "Begriff an sich"; it is a property. And what corresponds in the world to a mental judgment should not be called a "Satz an sich"; it is a state of affairs (or a fact). Bolzano escapes from Kant's idealism by projecting Kant's mental categories into the outside world. In doing so, he creates a world which is neither mental nor the world of facts, things, and properties. He invents a world that is a mirror image of the mental world, a world of meanings.

The curse of the Kantian terminology haunts not only Bolzano's philosophy, but Frege's as well. Just think of Frege's use of 'concept' ('Begriff'). A concept turns out to be a property, something that has nothing at all to do with the mind (G. Frege, *Translations from the Philosophical Writings of Gottlob Frege,* p. 51). But the height of terminological confusion is reached with Frege's use of 'thought' ('Gedanke'). Surely, if anything is mental, it is a thought. Yet thoughts are supposed to be nonmental things. Roughly speaking, they correspond to Bolzano's propositions ("Saetze an sich"). The sentence 'Socrates is mortal', according to Frege, expresses a thought and represents the truth-value true. The thought consists of the sense of 'Socrates' and of the "unsaturated" sense of 'mortal'. What I wish to point out is that the person Socrates is not a part of the sense of the sentence. Senses, like propositions, are therefore not facts. Since truth-values are obviously not facts either, Frege's ontology, like Bolzano's, leaves out one of the most important categories, the category of fact.

THREE

▬▬▬▬▬

Mill's Response

Empiricism's Last Stand

a) Another Kind of Necessity: Unimaginability

Let us return to Kant, and let me remind you of our explication of his claim that arithmetic truths are a priori. I have assumed that Kant thinks of the particular arithmetic truth under discussion as being general, that is, as being of the sort: Seven things plus five things are twelve things. Kant observes that this generality is not established by induction. It is therefore not merely a general truth, but is universal. Since it is a dogma of Kant's philosophy that concepts and judgments which contain necessity and universality do not come from experience, he concludes that this arithmetic truth cannot be derived from experience. And then we are invited to a forced march through the jungle of the transcendental aesthetic. According to our view, the universality of the arithmetic generality is due to the fact that it follows from the truth that the sum relation holds between seven, five, and twelve. Kant simply did not realize that a generality may be justified in this way. But this realization proves Kant's dogma wrong. *A judgment with universality can be based on experience.* In our example, it is based on experience, because it follows logically from a proposition that is based on experience, namely, on the relational truth about seven, five, and twelve. Just as we *see* that midnight blue is darker than lemon yellow, so do we *see,* I claim, that two plus one is three. And just as we could not see that midnight blue is darker than lemon yellow unless we saw the two colors, so we could not see that two plus one is three unless we saw the three numbers. My view thus implies that we are acquainted with (small) numbers. What stands in its way is the common prejudice that one cannot perceive numbers.

So much about the universality of the arithmetic statement. What about its alleged necessity? As I mentioned before, I trace this kind of necessity to the fact that we cannot *imagine* the statement to be false. While we can imagine that a horse has wings, we cannot imagine that midnight blue is lighter than lemon yellow. We know that horses do not have wings, but we believe that it is not necessary that horses have no wings. And this same sort of necessity attaches to arithmetic propositions of the kind under consideration. We simply cannot imagine that two things plus one thing is anything but three things, and therefore believe, not only that it is true that two things plus one thing is three things, but also that it is necessary.

This sort of necessity plays an important role in Mill's philosophy. He says:

> It is strange that almost all the opponents of the Association psychology should found their main or sole argument in refutation of it upon the feeling of necessity; for if there be any one feeling in our nature which the laws of association are obviously equal to producing, one would say it is that. Necessary, according to Kant's definition, and there is none better, is that of which the negation is impossible. If we find it impossible, by any trial, to separate two ideas, we shall have all the feeling of necessity which the mind is capable of.

(J. S. Mill, *An Examination of Sir William Hamilton's Philosophy,* pp. 260–61)

Mill defends here the "Law of Inseparable Association." This law explains, for example, why "it is not in our power to think of colour, without thinking of extension" (James Mill, as quoted by John Stuart, 1979a, p. 253). It explains why we cannot imagine an unextended color, or a surface which is both red and green all over at the same time, or "two and two not making four" (Mill, 1979a, p. 263). Mill thinks that he has located the psychological reason for our inability to imagine certain situations. Since he believes, as we do, that this inability is the source of Kant's necessity of the a priori, he concludes that he has found the psychological basis for the kind of necessity which is supposed to prove "an *a priori* mental connexion between ideas" (Mill, 1979a, p. 261).

At first glance, Mill's defense of this piece of association psychology seems to be an instance of love's labor lost. If the uniform and intimate association between the idea of extension and the idea of color is to account for a feeling of mental necessity to the effect that color must be together with extension, then we should expect the same kind of necessity in many other instances in which, as a matter of fact, it does not occur. For example, we have never seen a stone float on water, yet we have no difficulty imagining such a situation. Here is Mill's response to this example:

> But, in the first place, we have not seen stones sinking in water from the first dawns of consciousness, and in nearly every subsequent moment of our lives, as we have been seeing two and two making four, intersecting straight lines diverging instead of enclosing a space, causes followed by effects and effect preceded by causes. But there is still a more radical distinction than this. No frequency of conjunction between two phenomena will create an inseparable association, if counter-associations are being created all the while. If we sometimes saw stones floating as well as sinking, however often we might have seen them sink, nobody supposes that we should have formed an inseparable association between them and sinking. We have not seen a stone float, but we are in the constant habit of seeing either stones or other things which have the same tendency to sink, remaining in a position which they would otherwise quit, being maintained in it by an unseen force.

(Mill, 1979a, pp. 263–64)

Given these and other refinements of the law of inseparable association, I think that, in the end, it may merely restate the important fact that we cannot imagine certain situations. In connection with the arithmetic example, for example, Mill says at another place that "The experience must not only be constant and uniform, but the juxtaposition of the facts in experience must be immediate and close, as well as early, familiar, and so free from even the semblance of an exception that no counter association can possibly arise" (Mill, 1979a, p. 270).

The fact remains that we cannot imagine certain circumstances, and I maintain that this fact explains the kind of necessity attached to so-called synthetic a priori truths. In order to strengthen our thesis, we must draw a sharp distinction between *imagination,* on the one hand, and *conception,* on the other.

Mill does not make this distinction, but talks about different kinds of *inconceivability.* He gives examples of things the mind "cannot put together in a single image":

> We cannot present anything to ourselves as at once being something, and not being it; as at once having, and not having, a given attribute . . . We cannot represent to ourselves time or space as having an end. We cannot represent to ourselves two and two as making five; not two straight lines as enclosing a space. We cannot represent to ourselves a round square; nor a body all black, and at the same time all white.

> (Mill, 1979a, p. 70)

He speaks here of the mind's putting together images, but he also claims that these things are *inconceivable,* "our minds and our experience being what they are" (Mill, 1979a, p. 70). In my view, his examples are unimaginable, but not at all inconceivable. I agree that we cannot imagine that something has the property F and also, at the same time, does not have the property F; and we cannot imagine that two plus two are five; and we cannot imagine that something is both round and square at the same time. But I also insist that we can conceive of these three circumstances.

b) Imagination Distinguished from Conception

Mill holds that all cases of inconceivability reduce to two kinds: There is the inconceivability of contradictions, and there is the inconceivability of inseparable association. Let us consider the round square. Mill points out that, strictly speaking, a round square is not a contradictory thing. But he claims that in our experience "at the instant when a thing begins to be round it ceases to be square, so that the beginning of the one impression is inseparably associated with the departure or cessation of the other. Thus our inability to form a conception always arises from our being compelled to form another contradictory to it" (Mill, 1979a, pp. 70–71). The law of inseparable association leads us to associate the idea of not-square with the idea of round; and the inconceivability of contradictions does the rest. The inconceivability of contradictions, therefore, is not a matter of inseparable association. This bears directly on my contention that we can conceive of many situations which we cannot imagine, and, in particular, that we can conceive of contradictory circumstances.

What prevents a clear understanding of the important difference between imagination and conception is a philosophical muddle that reaches from Mill to the present. Mill, like many recent and contemporary philosophers, thinks that con- tradictions are "unmeaning": "That the same thing is and is not—that it did and did not rain at the same time and place, that a man is both alive and not alive, are forms of words which carry no significance to my mind" (Mill, 1979a, p. 78). And then he continues: "Whatever may be meant by a man, and whatever may be meant by alive, the statement that a man can be alive and not alive is equally without meaning to me" (Mill, 1979a, p. 78). Contradictions, in short, are said to be *meaningless*. Since they are meaningless, they are inconceivable. Not only can they not be imagined, as I have granted, but they cannot even be thought; for there is no thought connected with them.

I wish to defend the view that contradictions are perfectly meaningful, intelli- gible, and conceivable. But I also insist, on the other hand, that they are not imaginable. There are mental acts, other than acts of imagination, which can intend contradictory states of affairs. We can and do *deny* that it is the case that it is both raining and also not raining at a certain moment at a certain place. We can and do *assume* that if it were the case, then it would also be the case that: If P, then not-P, and if not-P, then P, where P is the circumstance that it is raining at a certain place at a certain moment. That a contradiction is not meaningless and hence that it can be conceived, is proven by the fact that we draw legitimate inferences from it. There is no difficulty in conceiving what the state of affairs *P and not-P* "would be like": P would be the case, and not-P would also be the case. Of course, I cannot imagine what that would "look like," but I can conceive of it. I know that a contradictory state of affairs cannot obtain. How can I know this, I ask Mill, if I cannot conceive of such a state of affairs?

The case of contradictions illuminates the distinction between what is un- imaginable and what is inconceivable. What we cannot imagine is a matter of our perceptual constitution; what we cannot conceive is a matter of our conceptual constitution. Generally speaking, if we can imagine P, then we may or may not be able to imagine not-P, but if we can conceive of P, then we can also conceive of not-P. And this means that we can conceive the negation of any law. For example, we can conceive that bodies move with a speed greater than the speed of light. Much of science fiction would otherwise be unintelligible. We can even conceive of the negations of the laws of arithmetic, set theory, and logic. I can conceive of two plus two being five rather than four. Of course, I cannot imagine a situation in which this would be the case. But I do know what is meant by 'two plus two is five.' What is meant is that two plus two is five or, put more pedantically, that the sum relation holds between five, two, and two.

Conceivability extends even beyond the boundaries of arithmetical, set theoret- ical, and logical falsehoods: It reaches the laws of ontology! For example, it is a law of ontology that the relation of conjunction holds between states of affairs and only between states of affairs. (I assume that there are no "conjunctive properties.") Yet, I understand perfectly well what the expression 'P and 7' purports to represent: It purports to represent a conjunction of the state of affairs P and the number 7. Of course, I know that there is no such fact; for I know the ontological law just mentioned. And I cannot imagine what such a conjunction would be like. To give another example, it is a law of ontology that individual things, though they exemplify properties, are not exemplified by anything. Yet, I can easily conceive of, say, a certain shade of blue exemplifying the pen before me on my desk. According to my assumption, the exemplification relation holds, not between the pen and the color—as it does—but conversely between the color and the pen. Needless to say, I cannot imagine what this situation "looks like." I cannot paint it, for example, as I can paint a blue pen.

It has been quite the fashion in our century to claim that this or that sentence is meaningless or that this or that expression is unintelligible. Russell's theory of types is a case in point. That the color midnight blue is not midnight blue seems to me to be, not only a perfectly intelligible proposition, but a true proposition to boot. Nor do I find the negation of this assertion to be nonsense. Not only specific philosophical theories, but conceptions of the very nature of philosophy have been based on exaggerated claims about what is and what is not meaningful. Surely, it takes more than just ordinary philosophical gullibility to agree with Wittgenstein that his pronouncements about the nature of logic and the structure of the world are nonsense. False they may be, but nonsense they are not. Nor would it occur to anyone but the most fanatic philosopher that the philosophical statements of Aristotle, Descartes, and Frege are one and all meaningless.

One cannot but be amazed that so many philosophers have tried to do what, according to their own view, cannot be done, namely, give genuine examples of nonsense. That procrastination eats Wheaties for breakfast may be an outrageous or hilarious statement, but it is hardly nonsensical. Or consider Mill's example: Humpty Dumpty is an Abracadabra. Mill says that he does not know what this proposition states since he does not know what is meant by 'Humpty Dumpty' and by 'Abracadabra' (Mill, 1979a, p. 78). Well, the same could possibly be said by Mill about any sentence in Albanian. The question is not whether expressions in an unknown language mean something to us, but whether an expression means something *in a language*. It is surprising that Mill claims not to know what those two expressions mean. 'Humpty Dumpty' is a certain creature in a nursery rhyme who fell off a wall, broke into many pieces, and could not be put together afterwards. An abracadabra is a spell; something that wards off sickness and, perhaps, evil spirits. Humpty Dumpty is not such a spell, for spells do not fall off walls and break into pieces. Thus the sentence 'Humpty Dumpty is an abracadabra' is not only quite meaningful, but obviously false. Of course, there are other interpretations of the sentence. 'Abracadabra' is often used to signify a meaningless jumble of words, an incantation without meaning. We have here the curious situation that a meaningless string of letters becomes meaningful by being used to represent gibberish. But this makes the sentence meaningful: It states under this interpretation that Humpty Dumpty is a meaningless jumble of letters, and that, again, is simply false.

I have claimed that we can conceive of contradictions. The expression 'P and not P', as one says in certain contexts, is *well-formed*. The expression 'P and not', by contrast, is not well-formed. We can also put it this way: While the first sentence represents a state of affairs, the second does not. The so-called formation rules of an artificial language (the rules for well-formedness) prescribe (among other things) what expressions represent propositions (states of affairs). Logic then tells us which of these propositions are tautologies, which are contradictions, and which are neither. This conception, too, contradicts the claim that contradictions are meaningless. But I wish to make another point. The formation rules of a language, it may be noted, reflect the *ontological* laws of the world. They prescribe what is ontologically possible. For example, the proposition *P and not-P* is ontologically possible, but · logically impossible. The combination *P and not*, on the other hand, is not even ontologically possible, for it is a law of ontology that the conjunction relation always holds between states of affairs (propositions). The combination *P and not* is not a proposition. But notice that I speak nevertheless of the "combination" *P and not*. I do understand this combination: a proposition P is related by conjunction to negation. Thus we must distinguish between a narrower and a wider sense of 'proposition'. According to the rules of well-formedness, which delineate the narrower notion, the expression 'P and not' does not represent a proposition. We may say, with this notion in mind, that it is gibberish. But according to the wider notion of a proposition, the sentence represents a proposition (state of affairs), namely, the proposition that *P stands in the conjunction relation to not*. Anything of the form *X R Y* is then a proposition, where R is a relation, and X and Y are any two entities whatsoever.

I shall again look ahead. The distinction we have just made has an important bearing on one of Wittgenstein's views to the effect that an expression like 'P and not' has no meaning, since it gets its meaning from use, and it is not used. In a lecture at Cambridge, Wittgenstein reportedly talked about applying negation to an individual thing, an apple, rather than to a proposition. And then he claimed that we are wavering between two different views. On the one hand, we think that to 'apple' and 'not' there correspond definite things or ideas, and that these things or ideas may or may not fit (as a certain shape may or may not fit another shape). On the other hand, we think that these words are characterized by their use, and that negation is not completed until its use with 'apple' is completed. We cannot ask whether the uses of these two words fit, for their use is given only when the use of the whole expression 'not apple' is given (Wittgenstein, as cited by Coffa, in J. A. Coffa, *To the Vienna Station,* chap. XIV).

As usual, Wittgenstein does not spell out the details of his argument for the last sentence. But it is not hard, I think, to guess how it would proceed. The question before us is: Does the meaning of 'not' fit together with the meaning of 'apple'? We assume that the meanings of these two words are their uses. So the question becomes: Does the use of 'not' fit the use of 'apple'? But the use of 'not' is determined, among other things, by whether or not there is a use for 'not apple'. And this shows that we must already know whether or not the meaning of 'not' fits together with the meaning of 'apple' before we can answer the question of whether or not they fit. In other words, if we assume that the meanings of words are their uses in connection with other words, then the question of whether or not a given word fits another word cannot be answered. The question "makes no sense." I suppose that Wittgenstein's later philosophy rests on the conviction that considerations of this sort show that the meanings of words are their uses. But there is obviously a different possibility. What the argument proves, one may hold, is that the meaning of a word, *in the sense relevant for the argument,* cannot be its use, *as understood for the argument.* And this is, indeed, the conclusion which we draw. The expression 'not apple' does not represent an ontologically possible entity, because negation, according to a law of ontology, does not attach to properties. This is the reason why 'not' and 'apple' do not "fit."

I have argued that our ability to conceive of things and situations is much greater than most philosophers assume. We can conceive not only of contradictory states of affairs, but even of ontologically impossible situations. But we cannot imagine such states of affairs. We cannot imagine logical laws other than ours; we cannot imagine arithmetic laws other than ours; we cannot imagine set theoretic laws other than ours; we cannot even imagine geometric laws other than ours. We cannot imagine non-Euclidian space. But this fact brings another important point to our attention. What we can and cannot imagine is one thing, what is and is not the case, is quite another. From the fact that we cannot imagine non-Euclidian space, it does not follow that the universe has to be Euclidian. The world does not have to conform to our quite limited ability to imagine things. And this means that what we cannot imagine to be otherwise, may nevertheless not be the case. And this implies that what we think to be necessary (in this sense of 'necessary'), may nevertheless be false. It would never have occurred to Kant, but: *Necessity does not imply truth!*

c) The Synthetic A Priori and Our Sense Dimensions

Using the word 'part' loosely, one can distinguish between separable and inseparable parts of things. The color of a horse is an inseparable part of it, while its head is a separable part. From Berkeley on, some philosophers have stressed this distinction and built ontologies around it (see, for example, B. Smith, ed., *Parts and Moments, Studies in Logic and Formal Ontology*). One of the most thorough discussions of it occurs in Husserl's *Logical Investigations.* In this context, Husserl makes a profound remark that bears directly on our investigation: "It is now immediately plain that all the laws or necessities governing different sorts of non-independent items fall into the spheres of the synthetic a priori: one grasps completely what divides them from merely formal contentless items" (E. Husserl, *Logical Investigations,* vol. 2, p. 456). He then goes on to say that laws governing the non-independence (read: inseparability) of qualities, intensities, extensions, boundaries, relational forms, etc., must be distinguished from purely "analytic" generalizations. Taking a cue from Husserl, I shall maintain that the most noteworthy area of synthetic a priori truths can be found within the boundaries of our sense dimensions. Synthetic a priori truths rule the structures which are formed by sensible properties and relations.

Bergmann lists six kinds of such truths and then describes the principles of his classification:

(A) Round is a shape. Green is a color. e is a pitch. Of two pitches, one is higher than the other; only a pitch is higher than anything else.

(B) e is higher than c. (This shade of) brown is darker than (that shade of) yellow.

(C) If the first of three pitches is higher than the second and the second is higher than the third, then the first is higher than the third.

(D₁) What has pitch has loudness and conversely. What has shape has color and conversely.

(D₂) Nothing (no tone) has two pitches. Nothing (no area) has two shapes.

(E) If the first of three things (areas) is a part of the second, and the second is a part of the third, then the first is a part of the third.

The truths of (A) are those and only those constituting the several dimensions. Some of them are atomic; some are general. A simple relation obtaining between two (or more) members of a dimension is an atomic fact. (B) is the class of all such facts. The truths of (C) are all general. They are all those and only those which connect the properties of a single dimension with the simple relations between them. The truths of (D₁) are the general truths by which the members of two dimensions depend₂ on each other. The truths of (D₂) are those and only those by which the members of one or two dimensions exclude each other. The last two classes are labeled with the same letter because they have long provided the most popular examples of *a priori* truths. The class (E) corresponds to (C). The reason for setting it apart is that the spatial relations "in" the facts of E are the only relations of the first type that are mentioned in the list.

(G. Bergmann, "Synthetic A Priori", pp. 295–96)

It is clear that to (E) also belong certain truths about temporal relations.

Here then we have a list of all kinds of a priori truth about such perceptual properties as colors, shapes, pitches, etc., and such perceptual relations as being higher (in pitch), being darker (between colors), etc., and spatial and temporal relations. All of these truths either are "universal" and "necessary," or else logically imply "universal" (and "necessary") truths in the way described earlier. The peculiar necessity Kant discovered and which he describes in the *Transcendental Aesthetic* reduces to our inability to imagine certain states of affairs. This inability, certainly, is a function of our sensibility. Thus Kant is correct when he claims that the necessity of certain laws is grounded in our constitution. If we had different sense organs, so that we could perceive properties and relations different from the ones we do perceive, then our imagination would also be quite different and, hence, quite different states of affairs would appear to us to be necessary. But Kant is mistaken when he draws from this fact the idealistic conclusion that the world must *conform* to our imagination. What we can and cannot imagine to be the case, as I said before, does not determine what is the case. The most important lesson to be learned from Kant's "Irrweg" is that what we cannot imagine to be otherwise may yet prove to be false. We can prove it to be false, because conception, in distinction to imagination, reaches to the limits of the world. We may not be able to imagine the physical structure of space and time, but we can discover it, because we can conceive of it. We cannot imagine the properties of and relations among elementary particles, but we can discover them, because we can conceive of them. We cannot imagine that a property has no extension (set), but we can prove that there is such a property. The Kantian idealist is not only mistaken when he claims that the structure of the world must with necessity conform to our sensibility, he makes an even more fundamental mistake since he believes that what is necessary must be true!

One more word about necessity before we return to Mill's philosophy of arithmetic. The kind of necessity we have studied attaches to propositions (states of affairs, circumstances). A state of affairs is necessary if and only if we cannot imagine what it would be like for the state of affairs not to obtain; in other words, if and only if we cannot imagine its negation. A possible state of affairs, on the other hand, is a state of affairs which we can imagine to obtain. We may therefore think of being imaginable as a property of certain states of affairs. If we do, then we can distinguish between four kinds of state of affairs:

(1) Imaginable states of affairs,

(2) states of affairs that cannot be imagined,

(3) states of affairs for which we can imagine their negation,

(4) states of affairs for which we cannot imagine their negation.

We may then speak of:

(1') *Possible* states of affairs,

(2') *impossible* states of affairs,

(3') *contingent* states of affairs, and

(4') *necessary* states of affairs.

It follows that a state of affairs is possible if and only if it is not the case that its negation is necessary:

(I) P is possible if and only if it is not the case that not-P is necessary. We may also say that a state of affairs *entails* another state of affairs if and only if we cannot imagine that it is not the case that, if the one state of affairs obtains, the other also obtains:

(II) P entails Q if and only if it is necessary that, if P obtains, then Q obtains.

Furthermore, whether or not a state of affairs is imaginable does not depend on whether or not it obtains. This means that the truth of 'P is possible' is not a truth function of 'P'. And this means that none of the following equivalences holds:

P is possible if and only if P,

P is possible if and only if not-P,

P is possible if and only if (P or not-P), and

P is possible if and only if (P and not-P).

Proceeding in the Kantian vein, we may add:

(III) If P obtains, then P is possible.

Next, if we are interested in formulating an axiomatic system that catches these and other "necessary" truths about the possible and the necessary, we shall also have to assume that any theorem of our system is itself necessary:

(IV) If P is a theorem, so is necessarily-P.

Finally, we may believe that whatever follows from a necessary state of affairs is itself necessary and adopt the following equivalent principle:

(V) If it is necessary that if P obtains, Q obtains, then if it is necessary that P obtains, it is necessary that Q obtains.

If we accept the five statements (I) to (V), and add the obvious truths of the so-called propositional calculus, we get a well-known system of "modal logic," namely, the system T (see G. E. Hughes and M. J. Cresswell, *An Introduction to Modal Logic*). From my point of view, this is an axiomatization of the Kantian notion of the necessity (and possibility) that attaches to the synthetic a priori. Hence we are dealing, not with a system of *logic*, but rather with a theory of what is *imaginable*.

d) Arithmetic and "Physical Facts"

There are two basic kinds of arithmetic propositions: (1) propositions that state arithmetic relations among numbers, and (2) laws about numbers. Frege, in his scathing criticism of Mill's conception of arithmetic, starts with Leibniz's proof that $2 + 2 = 4$ (G. Frege, *The Foundations of Arithmetic*, pp. 7–14). This proof starts with the following "definitions":

(D) 2 is 1 and 1,
  3 is 2 and 1,
  4 is 3 and 1.

This is the way Leibniz puts it and Frege cites it. But I shall take for granted that the 'and' here can be replaced by 'plus'. Frege points out that Leibniz's proof rests on the association law:

(L) All natural numbers are such that: $n_1 + (n_2 + n_3) = (n_1 + n_2) + n_3$.

We are asking: What kinds of proposition are (D) and (L)? In particular, are they analytic or synthetic? And also: How do we discover these propositions (facts)?

Take for example: (a) $2 = 1 + 1$. Leibniz calls this statement a definition, and Frege agrees with him. Mill, on the other hand, observes that this is not a definition in the logical sense. It does not merely fix the meaning of an expression, but asserts an observed matter of fact. He holds that (a) is not just a (consequence of a) stipulation of the sort: Let us agree to let the arbitrary expression '2' stand for whatever '1 + 1' represents. It does not introduce an arbitrary sign, say, '#', as an abbreviation for '1 + 1' (J. S. Mill, *A System of Logic, Collected Works*, vol. 7, pp. 253–54). At this point, we must be very picky. I take it that '1 + 1' is merely short for (just another expression for) something like 'the sum of 1 and 1', that is, for a *description expression*. Things are rather complicated at this point because description expressions, as Frege was the first philosopher to notice, are "connected" with *descriptions* as well as with *what these descriptions describe*. In our case, we must distinguish between what the expression *represents*, namely, the description *the sum of 1 and 1*, and what it *describes*, namely, *the number 2*. Because of this peculiarity of description expressions, the numeral '2' may be introduced in two quite different ways. It may be a mere abbreviation for the description expression. In this case, it represents, not the number 2, but the description. Given that we mean by '2' the number and not the description, this would be a perverse way of using the numeral. Or else it may be introduced as a name for whatever it is that the description represented by the expression describes: Let us call what is described by the expression: '2'. We must note that in this second case, '2' is not really an *abbreviation* of anything. What happens is, rather, that we give a name to something that has so far only been described.

With this essential refinement in mind, the dispute between Mill and Frege (and Leibniz) comes down to this: Frege claims that in this context '2' is an arbitrary sign, with no prior referent, which is introduced as a name for whatever the description describes, while Mill holds that it is the name of a number, so that we have an assertion to the effect that the number 2 is what the description describes. I think that Mill is correct and Frege mistaken. But if Mill is correct, then the question arises whether the equation '2 = 1 + 1' is analytic or synthetic; the question arises whether the assertion that the number 2 is the same as the sum of 1 and 1 is analytic or synthetic. And according to our explication of analyticity, this question is the same as whether or not it is a logical truth. By calling (a) a definition, Frege and his followers simply try to avoid this unavoidable question.

Why do I think that Mill is correct and Frege mistaken? Compare (a) with the following assertion: (b) 2359 = 2358 + 1. I think that (b) is indeed a "definition" in the relevant sense. I am not *acquainted* with the number 2359, I only "know it" as the sum of 2358 and 1 (or, better, as the immediate successor of 2358). Most numbers are indeed presented to us merely through descriptions. We only *know* them, as Russell might say, by description. That we are not acquainted with them is due to the special constitution of our mind. Very small numbers, on the other hand, are known "by acquaintance." The number 2, for example, is presented to us in perception; we see it, when we see, for example, two apples. We use the numeral '2' to represent this number with which we are acquainted. The assertion (a), therefore, states that this number is the same number as the number which is the sum of 1 and 1 (or as the number which is the successor of 1). (a) can be used to assert that this number is the same number as the one that stands in a certain relation to 1 and 1 (or to 1).

For numbers the familiar distinction holds between two quite different assertions:

(c) Tom, of course, is the only brother of Dick, because we have agreed among ourselves to call his only brother "Tom," and

(d) Tom, with whom we are acquainted, is the only brother of Dick, as it turns out to our surprise.

I believe that we are acquainted with certain (small) numbers, just as we are acquainted with certain people. Larger numbers, on the other hand, we only know through the relations which they have to other numbers. Roughly, most numbers are known to us as the successors of the successors of the successors, and so on, of the small numbers with which we are acquainted. What distinguishes our view from the view of Leibniz and Frege is that we hold that some, though not all, of the statements of kind (a) are not the consequences of mere stipulations.

If (a) is not the result of a convention, then we can ask whether or not it is analytic. I think that the answer is obvious: It is not analytic, since it is not a truth of logic. But if it is not a truth of logic, what kind of truth is it? It is in answer to this question that Mill errs and Frege scores his most telling points against him. According to Mill, the proposition 2 + 1 = 3 states an "observed matter of fact."

He even call it a "physical fact" (Mill, 1979b, vol. 7, p. 257). What is this "observed fact"? Mill answers:

> And thus we may call "Three is two and one" a definition of three; but the calculations which depend on this proposition do not follow from the definition itself, but from an arithmetical theorem presupposed in it, namely, that collections of objects exist, which while they impress the senses thus, $^Oo^O$, may be separated into two parts, thus, oo o. This proposition being granted, we term all such parcels Threes, after which the enunciation of the above mentioned physical fact will serve also for a definition of the word Three.
>
> (Mill, 1979b, p. 257)

To this, Frege replies: "What a mercy, then, that not everything in the world is nailed down; for if it were, we should not be able to bring off this separation, and 2 + 1 would not be 3!" (Frege, 1974, p. 9). Later on, Frege zeroes in on Mill's expression "physical fact" and points out that if the arithmetic statement were a statement of *physical* fact, then it would be incorrect to speak of three sensations or of three solutions of an equation. Frege is surely right when he objects that the statement does not assert a "physical" fact about the spatial arrangement of three perceptual objects. But this is not exactly what Mill wishes to say, as it turns out. It would be premature at this point to dismiss Mill's view out of hand.

Mill maintains that 2 + 1 = 3 is a generalization from experience. What this expression really represents is a general fact:

(G) All things are such that: 2 things + 1 thing = 3 things.

In one of the most interesting and revealing passages of his book, Mill says:

> All numbers must be numbers of something: there are no such things as numbers in the abstract. *Ten* must mean ten bodies, or ten sounds, or ten beatings of the pulse. But though numbers must be numbers of something, they may be numbers of anything. Propositions, therefore, concerning numbers, have the remarkable peculiarity that they are propositions concerning all things whatever; all objects; all existences of every kind known to our experience . . . That half of four is two, must be true whatever the word four represents, whether four hours, four miles, or four pounds weight.
>
> (Mill, 1979b, pp. 254–255)

We see that Frege's criticism concerning the three sensations or three solutions to an equation is not justified. Or, at least, it is not justified if we interpret the phrase 'known to our experience' sufficiently widely.

Let us take a look at the first two sentences of this quotation from Mill. I agree, of course, that numbers are always numbers of something, just as colors are always colors of something. Numbers, like colors, do not float around by themselves. They are firmly anchored in reality. *They quantify kinds of things.* But Mill says next: "*Ten* must mean ten bodies, or ten sounds, . . ."; and this seems to me to be false. 'Ten' means the number ten; it represents this number and nothing else. In particular, it does not represent what 'ten bodies' represents. Contrary to Mill, I hold that there are "numbers in the abstract" in the sense that they form a kind of entity distinguishable from the properties which they quantify. The expression 'ten bodies' clearly mentions two things: It mentions the number ten and it mentions bodies. This is obvious from the fact that we can vary the two words involved and also speak of ten sounds and four bodies. This emphasis on the independence of numbers from the things they number is necessary, because we wish to hold that the sum relation, for example, is a unique relation among numbers, and not some kind of "physical" relation among heaps of things or aggregates of things.

Mill seems to think of the numeral '3' as some kind of *common name* for such aggregates (complexes, wholes, or what have you) as are presumably formed by three bodies, three sounds, three beatings of the heart, etc. The common name 'number', then, is thought to name (commonly, indifferently) all such *kinds* of aggregates (Mill, 1979b, vol. 7, p. 55). From Mill's point of view, what (G) says is that all 3-aggregates consist of 2-aggregates and 1-aggregates or, for short: All 3's consist of 2's and 1's. But what is here the meaning of "consists of"? Since many aggregates are not spatial "heaps," this relation cannot be the spatial whole-part relation. What then is it? In what reasonable sense can three solutions of an equation be said to *consist* of two solutions and one solution? I do not think that there is a plausible answer to my rhetorical question.

Mill points out that our familiar way of depicting that 2 plus 1 is 3 as an equation makes it appear as if we are dealing with an "identical proposition" (Mill, 1979b, vol. 7, p. 256). It makes it look as if we were dealing with the result of a stipulation. Mill wants to dispel this impression. On this point, as I said earlier, we fully agree with him. '3' is not a purely conventional sign for the number which is the sum of 2 and 1. It would be much less misleading, as we see things, to write instead: '+(3, 2, 1)'. How does Mill back up his view that this is not a definition? He says that the expression 'two pebbles and one pebble' and the expression 'three pebbles' "stand indeed for the same aggregation of objects, but they do by no means stand for the same physical fact" (Mill, 1979b, vol. 7, p. 256). He continues: "They are names of the same objects, but of those objects in two different states: though they *de*note the same things, their *con*notation is different" (Mill, 1979b, vol. 7, p. 256). What are these different "states"? Three pebbles are three pebbles, as Frege points out, no matter how they are arranged or where they are located. Mill retreats at this point to the different impressions which different arrangements of the pebbles make on our senses. We are reminded of the difference between $^{o}o^{o}$ and oo o. The arithmetic statement is not a mere definition, according to Mill, because it asserts that the same three things can be arranged in different ways. It states that any aggregate of three things can appear as arranged in one way or in another. And this statement, Mill would insist, is clearly based on experience. But what could possibly be meant here by "arranged"? Of course, pebbles allow for different spatial arrangements. But can we conclude that the statement that two pebbles and one pebble are three pebbles says that three pebbles can be arranged in certain ways? Certainly not; for, as Frege points out, two pebbles and one pebble would be three pebbles if pebbles could not be arranged in any other way at all. Moreover, what kind of arrangement do we have to envisage for three colors, three sensations, or three solutions of an equation? Mill's view, in a nutshell, clashes with the true nature of the sum relation.

But do we not use pebbles or fingers when we teach children that two plus one is three? Of course, we do. Mill appeals to this undeniable fact in order to defend his view:

> The fundamental truths of that science [the science of Number] all rest on the evidence of sense; they are proved by showing to our eyes and fingers that any given number of objects, ten balls for example, may by separation and re-arrangement exhibit to our senses all the different sets of numbers the sum of which is equal to ten. All the improved methods of teaching arithmetic to children proceed on a knowledge of this fact. All who wish to carry the child's *mind* along with them in learning arithmetic; all who wish to teach numbers, and not mere ciphers—now teach it through the evidence of the senses in the manner we have described.
>
> (Mill, 1979b, vol. 7, pp. 256–257)

In order to teach a child that two plus one is three, we may indeed arrange three pebbles first like this: o oo, and then like this: ooo. But does learning that two plus one is three consist in learning that three pebbles can form these two different spatial patterns? Has the child learned the *arithmetic* truth when he has grasped the *geometric* truth? Obviously not! Knowledge that three pebbles can be spatially arranged in countless ways is not knowledge that two plus one is three. We must distinguish between *how* we teach the child and *what* we teach it. What the child of our example is supposed to grasp when we rearrange the pebbles is some "abstract" relationship among numbers, not something about what happens when pebbles are arranged in different spatial patterns. The arrangement of the pebbles is merely the "occasion" for seeing that "abstract" relationship. It is a visual aid. We use pebbles, or peas, or oranges, because we can see and feel these things. But the truths we teach on these occasions are not about pebbles, or about peas, or about oranges. They are truths about numbers. We know that the child has understood the relationship between three, two, and one, when he no longer cares either about the particular things numbered or about the particular arrangements of these things.

The situation is quite similar when we teach a child that midnight blue is darker than lemon yellow. We may show her a blue sweater and a yellow ball, and we may show these two items first separately and then together side by side. But we are not trying to teach anything about spatial arrangements. Nor are we interested in the fact that the sweater is made from cotton, manufactured in Hong Kong, and bought as a birthday present, while the ball is made from rubber, manufactured in Indianapolis, and was found in the street. These things are true but unimportant. And in this situation, too, we know that the child has grasped the relationship between the two colors when she no longer cares what particular objects we show her, how these objects are spatially arranged, where they have been made, etc. All that matters is the relationship between the colors of the objects, just as all that matters in the previous case is the relationship among the numbers.

The temptation to think of arithmetic as somehow concerned with operations on perceptual objects lingers on. Hilbert, for example, gives the following account of the equation $2 + 3 = 3 + 2$:

2 + 3 = 3 + 2 is intended to communicate the fact that 2 + 3 and 3 + 2, when abbreviations are taken into account, are the self-same numerical symbol ı ı ı ı ı. Similarly, 3 > 2 serves to communicate the fact that the symbol 3, i.e., ı ı ı, is longer than the symbol 2, i.e., ı ı; or, in other words, that the latter symbol is a proper part of the former.

(D. Hilbert, "On the Infinite," p. 143)

In Hilbert's philosophy of arithmetic, Mill's pebbles have been replaced by numerals; the arrangements of pebbles, by arrangements of numerals.

More recently, Kitcher has proposed a conception of arithmetic that harks back to Mill's emphasis on how we can arrange and rearrange pebbles:

Children come to learn the meaning of 'set', 'number', 'addition' and to accept basic truths of arithmetic by engaging in *activities* of collecting and segregating. Rather than interpreting these activities as an avenue to knowledge of abstract objects, we can think of the rudimentary arithmetical truths as true in virtue of the operations themselves. By having experiences like that described in the last paragraph, we learn that particular types of collective operations have particular properties: we recognize, for example, that if one performs the collective operation called 'making two', then performs on different objects the collective operation called 'making three', then performs the collective operation of combining, the total operation is an operation of making five.

(Philip Kitcher, *The Nature of Mathematical Knowledge,* pp. 107–108)

Kitcher, if I understand him correctly, goes Mill one better: Arithmetic, according to him, is not about the different *arrangements* of pebbles, but is about the *operations* of arranging the pebbles. Here are some further quotations that seem to confirm this interpretation:

Knowledge of such properties of such operations is relevant to arithmetic because arithmetic is concerned with collective operations.

(Kitcher, p. 108)

One central idea of my proposal is to replace the notions of abstract mathematical objects, notions like that of collec*tion,* with the notion of a kind of mathematical activity, collec*ting.*

(Kitcher, p. 110)

I propose that the view that mathematics describes the structure of reality should be articulated as the claim that mathematics describes the operational activity of an ideal subject.

(Kitcher, p. 111)

In the same vein, I suppose, one may argue that the statement that midnight blue is darker than lemon yellow is not about colors, but about the operation of comparing certain blue and yellow objects. It seems to me, however, that the statement is not about this operation, but about what we recognize (see) as a consequence of it.

Would two plus three be five if nobody performed any "collective operations"? Since I believe that it would, just as midnight blue would be darker than lemon yellow if nobody compared the two colors, I cannot agree with Kitcher's conception of the nature of arithmetic. If arithmetic were about operations, then there would be no arithmetic, if nobody performed any operations. However, I am convinced that the truths of arithmetic do not depend on there being human beings or other "operators," just as they do not depend on there being different arrangements of the same pebbles.

On a less global scale, I find fault with Kitcher's view because I can make little sense, for example, of an addition of operations. Kitcher states that "When we combine the objects collected in two segregative operations on distinct objects we perform an addition on those operations" (Kitcher, p. 112). So you take two peas away from a group of peas, and you take three lentils away from a little heap of lentils, and you put them together in one small pile. It seems to me that you have performed three operations: (1) You have taken the two peas away and put them down, (2) You have taken three lentils away and put them down, and (3) you have combined the peas and lentils into one pile. So far, so good. But is this third operation, the putting together of the peas and the lentils, an "addition on operations," as Kitcher claims? Surely not. It is clearly not an operation on operations, but an operation with peas and lentils, on a par with the operations of taking away two peas and taking away three lentils. In my view, addition is just as little an operation on the activities of separating peas from peas and lentils from lentils, as it is an operation on the peas and lentils themselves.

e) Arithmetic and Induction

We turn now to the second kind of arithmetic statement, namely, to arithmetic laws. Our example is the so-called law of association (L). I believe that Mill thinks of this law as an expression of the general principle that whatever is made up of parts, is made up of the parts of those parts (Mill, 1979b, vol. 7, p. 613). This reminds us of Bolzano's thesis that the associative law follows from the explanation of the notion of a sum. But there is also a big difference between Mill and Bolzano. While Mill thinks of that principle as a law of nature, Bolzano introduces it as part of a definition, so that he can claim that the associative law is analytic. Mill, I think, would correctly argue that Bolzano's explanation does not imply the associative law, for the law presupposes that there are things of the explained sort, that is, that there are so-called sums. Assume that we "define" 'mermaid' as something that has a fishtail, a female torso, long blond hair, etc. Does it follow from this explanation that there is a law to the effect that mermaids have fishtails? Obviously not. What follows is merely that *if there were* mermaids, *then they would have* fishtails. Bolzano's "definition," therefore, merely implies that if there are sums, they obey the associative law. That there are sums, however, is not an analytic truth.

Mill thinks of the associative law as a law about wholes and the parts of their parts. This law, he says, "is obvious to the senses in all cases which can be fairly referred to their decision, and so general as to be coextensive with nature itself, being true of all sorts of phenomena (for all admit of being numbered,) must be considered an *inductive truth, or law of nature,* of the highest order" (Mill, 1979b, vol. 7, p. 613, my italics). I think that Mill is correct: The associative law is a general truth that can only be justified by induction. Unlike Mill, I would not call it a "law of nature." Nor would I tie it to the observation of "physical phenomena." The associative law is a law of arithmetic. It is not a law of nature, if we mean by this expression a law about physical or mental phenomena. Numbers are neither "physical" nor "mental" things. Mill once again builds his empiricism on too narrow a notion of "sense experience." When I notice that the squares of a chess board, which are parts of the rows of the board, are parts of the chess board, I have not observed an instance of the associative law of arithmetic, as Mill seems to think. What I have noticed is an instance of the law that spatial parts of spatial parts of wholes are spatial parts of those wholes. This law holds for the spatial part-whole relation. It does not hold for every part-whole relation. For example, it does not hold for the membership relation (for sets). It happens to hold also for the sum relation. But, and this is the important point, the sum relation is not the spatial part-whole relation, and to observe an instance of the latter is not to notice an instance of the former.

But this objection does not affect what I consider to be Mill's main point, namely, that (G) is a general truth which, if it can be justified at all, can only be justified through its instances, that is, as the saying goes, by induction. We observed earlier that this is also Bolzano's view in regard to the basic laws of logic, mathematics, geometry, and physics (see, for example, B. Bolzano, *Wissenschaftslehre,* par. 315, 4). In regard to the specific law (G), though, they differ: While Mill treats it as a generality, Bolzano thinks of it as the consequence of a stipulation (definition).

f) A Word about So-called "Recursive Definitions"

I imagine that some readers may have been chafing at the bit for some time now, because they learned a long time ago and as a matter of course that one can *prove* the associative law from (1) the recursive definition of addition, and (2) the axiom of mathematical induction. Hence (G), they believe, is not a primitive law of arithmetic, and it can be justified by deduction rather than induction. This is perfectly true but does not change the philosophical thrust of our discussion. We merely have to switch from the associative law to the principle of mathematical induction:

(MI) All natural numbers are such that: If 0 has a certain property P, and if the successor of a number N has P if N has P, then all N have the property P.

What I claimed earlier for the associative law, I now claim for (MI): It is not analytic (but synthetic), it is a true generality, and it can only be justified, if it can be justified at all, by induction. (MI) is not analytic, for it is not a logical truth. It is neither a mere reformulation of a logical truth nor is it an instance of a logical law. It is a true generality. This distinguishes it, in my view, from any particular truth about addition. Finally, since it is a generality, it can only be justified in one of two ways, either by being deduced from other laws, or else by induction. (I take for granted that it cannot be deduced from a relational statement like the truth can that seven things and five things are twelve things.) Since we have assumed that (MI) is an axiom, it cannot be deduced from other laws. Hence it can only be justified, if it can be justified at all, by means of induction from individual cases. I see no other possibility. It is obvious why a logicist must argue that (MI) is analytic, even though it is apparently not analytic. For, only if he can make a case that it is analytic, can he hope to convince us that the associative law (and other such laws) are also analytic.

But even if the impossible were possible, even if a law of arithmetic were a law of logic, this would not suffice to show that the associative law is analytic. This law follows from the principle of mathematical induction plus the so-called *recursive definition of addition*. This so-called definition, however, turns out to be not an innocent stipulation, not a mere linguistic convention, but another law of arithmetic. We shall have to look into this matter a little more deeply, leaving Mill for the time being, because it touches on many other things and it will pay to clear up, once and for all, some of the technical issues.

The great Dedekind proves in his famous essay *Was sind und was sollen die Zahlen?* that there is one and only one function R such that the following holds for all natural numbers m and n:

(1) R (m, 1) = the successor of m,

(2) R (m, the successor of n) = the successor of R (m, n).

(The theorem of section 126 of Dedekind's work is actually more general, but I shall omit what is not essential to our discussion.) The function R is of course our intuitively given sum relation. Looked at from our epistemological point of view, Dedekind merely confirms what we already know from *observation*, namely, that there exists a certain relation among natural numbers. It is as if someone proved that there exists a certain relation among color shades, namely, the relation of being-darker-than. Dedekind, however, pursues mathematical interests. He introduces the expression 'sum of the numbers m and n' for the expression 'function which fulfills conditions (1) and (2)'. It is clear that he does not pick the term 'sum' out of thin air. This word has a well-established meaning. But Dedekind pretends that he does. He acts as if calling his function 'sum' is as arbitrary as if he had called it 'humpty.' There is no argument; we could have chosen 'humpty' instead. Nor is there an argument against pretending—for the sake of making a point—that the word 'sum' has no previous meaning. But it is also true that this pretense will not "reduce" the sum relation to anything else, and that it will not transform the assertion that there is such a relation into an analytic truth.

I have just spoken both of functions and of relations. Mathematicians usually speak of the former. I shall from now on use the term 'relation(s)', because in my ontology so-called functions are relations. What Dedekind shows, in these terms, is that there is precisely one relation which fulfills the two conditions (1) and (2); and we know, of course, what this relation is, namely, the sum relation.

So-called *recursive definitions of functions*, as you can now see, are really *recursive descriptions of relations*. Therefore, the relations so described are as little "reduced" to something else as Scott is when we describe him as the author of

Waverley. But recursive descriptions are peculiar; they are different from "ordinary descriptions." And it is this peculiarity, one may assume, that has led mathematicians and philosophers to attribute magical ontological powers to them.

Consider the first condition of the recursive description:

(1) + (m, 1) = the successor of m.

(1) states that the number which is the sum of m and 1 is the same number as the number which is the successor of m; (that the number which is the sum of m and 1 is *identical* with the number which is the successor of m). One and the same number is described in two different ways, once as a sum, once as a successor. Furthermore, this is a general identity statement which holds for all natural numbers m. Any description expression of the form 'the sum of M and 1' describes the same number as any description expression of the form 'the successor of M', where M is a specific natural number. But this means that any description expression of the first kind "can be replaced" by a description expression of the second kind. Any description expression that mentions the sum relation "can be replaced" by an expression that no longer mentions this relation, but mentions the successor relation instead. Condition (2), similarly, makes it possible "to replace" any description expression of the form 'the sum of M and the successor of N' by an expression of the form 'the successor of the sum of M and N'. And this possibility, combined with the first condition, allows us "to replace" any description expression of a natural number as the sum of two numbers by an expression which no longer mentions the sum relation, but mentions the successor relation instead. For every description of a natural number as a sum there is a description of it as a successor.

Notice that I always put 'can be replaced' in quotation marks. We have two different descriptions of the same thing. *We do not have two description expressions for the same description.* Only if we confuse the descriptions with what they describe can we conclude that the "recursive definition" does away with the sum relation in favor of the successor relation. Only then can we claim that we have here two expressions for the very same thing. As soon as we distinguish, as we must, between a description and what it describes, we realize that although the two descriptions describe the same number, the descriptions themselves are clearly different. How could they possibly be the same, we may ask in wonder, if the first describes the number in terms of the sum relation and the second describes it in terms of the successor relation? Assume that Mary is the mother of John and the spouse of Tom. We can describe Mary either as the mother of John or as the spouse of Tom. We have two descriptions of the same person; but the descriptions are not the same. It is as mistaken to claim that there is no sum relation but only the successor relation, as it is to maintain that there is no mother relation but only a spouse relation. (We assume, for the sake of the analogy, that every woman is a spouse of one man and the mother of one child.)

The mistaken dogma that "recursive definitions" have ontological significance is probably reinforced by the pernicious practice of calling description expressions "singular terms." According to this mind set, a prejudice so firm that nothing can apparently shake it, our arithmetic example involves two singular terms for the same number, just as Tully and Cicero are two singular terms for the same person.

The distinction between descriptions (not description expressions) and what they describe thus gets lost, and with it the insight that one and the same thing may be described in terms of two equally real and important relations.

Condition (1) is a general truth. Properly stated, it says that *all natural numbers are such that: the sum of a natural number and one is the same number as the successor of the natural number,* This general truth is neither a law of logic nor an instance of a law of logic. Therefore, it is not analytic. Hence it is synthetic. Furthermore, it is not deduced from other laws of arithmetic. Therefore, if it can be justified at all, it can only be justified inductively. We believe that the sum of 1 and any natural number is the same as the next number after the natural number, as Mill probably would say, because we have verified millions of times that the sum of 1 and 1 is the number after 1, that the sum of 2 and 1 is the number after 2, etc., etc., and we have no reason to believe that the same would not be true for big numbers as well. Mill would probably also claim, and this is where I part company with him, that we have arrived at these individual instances by induction from observing certain "physical phenomena." However, I agree with him that the general truth under discussion is synthetic, and that it can only be justified by induction.

g) Mill's Conception of Numbers

We have already touched upon Mill's conception of numbers, but shall now take a closer look at it. Mill distinguishes between the denotation and the connotation of numerals and says:

> Each of the numbers two, three, four, etc., denotes physical phenomena, and connotes a physical property of those phenomena. Two, for instance, denotes all pairs of things, and twelve all dozens of things, connoting what makes them pairs, or dozens; and that which makes them so is something physical; since it cannot be denied that two apples are physically distinguishable from three apples, two horses from one horse, and so forth: that they are a different visible and tangible phenomenon.

> (Mill, 1979b, vol. 7, p. 610)

I shall assume that Mill means to say that the numeral 'two', not the number two, denotes all pairs of things. It may look at first as if Mill holds that 'two' is a name of the set of all pairs, and that he thus anticipates Russell's conception of numbers. But this impression must be mistaken. Firstly, it is fairly clear that Mill believes that 'two' denotes, not the set of pairs, but each pair individually. Thus 'two' denotes the shoes I am wearing at this moment. 'Two' is therefore a "general name" (or "common name") of all couples rather than a proper name of a certain set. Secondly, there is Mill's insistence on the physical nature of the couples, triples, etc. A set, it is generally agreed, is not a "physical thing."

Perhaps Mill's use of 'physical' should not be taken too narrowly. Two apples, he says, are physically distinguishable from three apples; they are different visible and tangible phenomena. Two tones, we may add, are different from three tones as auditory phenomena. Finally, two pains are distinguishable from three pains, not by means of the senses, but by means of "inner experience." Perhaps Mill's claim is merely that we can distinguish, either by outer or by inner sense, between two things and three things. Perhaps Mill is merely saying that, in the case of apples, we know how many apples there are before us *by means of perception*. His view, in short, may amount to nothing more than a rejection of the Platonic dogma.

We must distinguish between the claim that numerical difference can be known through perception and the question in what this observed difference consists. It is in regard to this latter question that Mill, in my opinion, clearly goes wrong. What is connoted by the name of a number, he tells us, is "some property belonging to the agglomeration of things which we call by the name; and that property is, the characteristic manner in which the agglomeration is made up of, and may be separated into, parts" (Mill, 1979b, vol. 7, p. 611). And a few lines later he says:

> What the name of number connotes is, the manner in which single objects of the given kind must be put together, in order to produce that particular aggregate. If the aggregate be of pebbles, and we call it *two*, the name implies that, to compose the aggregate, one pebble must be joined to one pebble.

> (Mill, 1979b, vol. 7, p. 611)

An aggregate of pebbles, so it seems from this passage, is formed by "bringing together" one pebble and another pebble, by putting them side by side. Only in this fashion is formed the whole which is presumably denoted by the word 'two'. An aggregate of two tones, we may surmise, is formed by playing them together, one after the other. Thus it seems to be an essential part of Mill's view that certain wholes are the denotations of numerals. What kind of whole is formed depends in a particular case on the nature of the parts. Pebbles, for example, form spatial wholes, while tones form temporal wholes. In the former case, the essential relation among the parts of the whole is spatial; in the latter, it is temporal. Mill's aggregates clearly are not sets, but are structures of several sorts.

By contrasting sets with structures of these sorts, we can illustrate Mill's mistake. Frege, we remember, asks Mill rhetorically: "Besides, need the straws form any sort of bundle at all in order to be numbered: Must we literally hold a rally of all the blind in Germany before we can attach any sense to the expression 'the number of blind in Germany'?" (Frege, 1974, p. 30). We can put it this way: Does not a set of straws have a number (of members), even if the straws do not form a bundle? And does not a set of blind people have a number (of elements), even if these people do not hold a rally?

What happens in Mill's view to the sum relation? As I understand Mill, the word 'two' denotes the spatial structure consisting of two pebbles, and it also denotes the temporal structure consisting of two tones. It is a common name of these two agglomerations as well as of many others. It names "indifferently" any one of these quite diverse wholes. I think that this view is false: 'two' represents one and only one thing, namely, the number two. But 'two' does not only denote indifferently different things, according to Mill's view, it also connotes indifferently many different "properties," many different characteristic ways in which those structures are formed. Thus 'two' connotes the way in which the pebbles are connected to form a spatial "heap," but it also connotes the way in which the two tones are conjoined in order to form the temporal whole. I think that this view as well is mistaken. 'Two' does not connote anything. How would one "add" one pebble to the two pebbles? I am not sure what Mill would say, but it seems to me that the only thing he could say is: By forming a new structure consisting of three pebbles; by creating a new "heap." But this answer implies that the "operation" of addition consists in this case of bringing another pebble into spatial contiguity with the already existing heap of two pebbles. Of course, such "addition" is not possible in the case of tones. Here, I assume, addition would consist in playing a third tone after the other two. Thus addition of tones would involve an operation quite different from the one appropriate for pebbles. And similarly for other kinds of structure. In short, addition, too, would mean quite different things for different agglomerations. And again, I think this view is false: addition, the sum relation, is one thing and not many.

This is Mill's predicament: His empiricism demands that numbers be "sensible" things. We must be acquainted with them through the senses. No mysterious "Platonic" faculty of contemplation or "Husserlian" power of eidetic intuition exists. Mill must therefore look for something that (a) is sensible and (b) can reasonably be called a number. What he comes up with are his so-called "aggregates," that is, structures of certain sorts: spatial structures, temporal structures, etc. These wholes are "sensible"; we can perceive them. But these structures are not numbers, and their characteristic relations are not the sum relation. What leads Mill astray is the powerful dogma that has ruled the minds of almost all philosophers, that the only things that can be perceived are things in space and time, that is, "physical phenomena." Frege, as we shall see in the next section, concludes from Mill's failure that numbers cannot be sensible and therefore abandons empiricism. As Mill and Frege both see it, numbers either can be perceived or they cannot. If they can be perceived, then they must be spatio-temporal things of the sort Mill talks about. If they cannot be perceived, then there must be some other "rational" faculty which acquaints us with them. Mill cannot bring himself to abandon empiricism. He therefore embraces the first horn of the dilemma. Frege, on the other hand, clearly sees that Mill's view of numbers is untenable. He concludes that numbers cannot be spatio-temporal structures. But since he subscribes to the same dogma as Mill concerning the objects of perception, he cannot but reject empiricism. It is a measure of Frege's genius that he came very close to finding a way out of the dilemma.

Before we leave Mill, let us cast a quick glance at a recent attempt to improve on Mill's conception of number. Kessler has proposed the following view:

> On the model I am suggesting, a number is to be understood as a special sort of relation which holds between aggregates and properties that pick out parts of those aggregates. For example, in claiming that a certain aggregate x contains 52 cards we are claiming that the numerical relation 52 obtains between the aggregate x and the property of *being a card*.

> (G. Kessler, "Frege, Mill, and the Foundations of Arithmetic," p. 69)

There is a problem with this account concerning what spatial structures, for example, are to be counted as "one-square" aggregates or as "two-square" aggregates, and so on (see P. M. Simons, "Against the Aggregate Theory of Number"). But I wish to voice a different kind of criticism. Consider any structure S consisting of n parts. According to Kessler, n is a relation between S and a property P, namely, the property that individuates the parts of S. For example, the deck of cards consists of 52 cards, the series of natural numbers from 1 to 10 consists of 10 numbers, and so on. Kessler considers any kind of structure, S, and any kind of consists-of relation, so that the general schema is: S consists of n P's. And then he simply re-writes 'S consists of n P's' as 'n (S, P)'. But surely the relation between the deck of cards and the property of being a card is not identical with the number 52. Rather, this relation is the relation of "consisting of 52 things which have that property." And here 52 is not a relation, but only part of a relation. Here 52 is not a relation, but something that quantifies *things which are*. The situation is analogous to the following. Someone (Cantor, for example) may hold that the property of being a card of the deck has the property 52, so that numbers turn out to be properties of properties. But what is true is not that P has the property 52, that is, 52 (P), but rather that the property of being a card of the deck has the property *of having* 52 *things exemplify it*. Here the number appears as a part of the relevant property, just as in Kessler's example it occurs as part of the relevant relation. Here, the "property" which the property of being a card of the deck may be said to have is not 52, but the property *of being exemplified by* 52 *things*. There, the relation which the deck may be said to have to the property of being a card of the deck is not 52, but the relation *of consisting of* 52 *things with that property*.

FOUR

Frege's Response

The Zenith of Logicism

a) The Category of Number

To what category do the natural numbers belong? So far, we have met with three quite different answers. According to Kant, numbers are concepts. Kant, of course, does not have much of a choice: a number can only be either an intuition or a concept. If it were an intuition, then it would be an individual thing, that is, spatio-temporal. If it were an individual thing, then one could ask where it is located and how long it has existed. Since there are no reasonable answers to these questions, it seems clear that numbers cannot be intuitions. But if not intuitions, then they must be concepts.

Kant is not the only philosopher whose choice is severely limited. Within the Platonic framework, numbers must be either temporal individuals or eternal forms. Since they cannot be the former, as I just argued, they must be the latter. Within the Aristotelian ontology, numbers must be either parts of substances or accidents. If the former, then they must be either prime matter or essences. They could not possibly belong to the category of prime matter, for prime matter by itself is not separated into particular entities as the individual numbers are. Thus numbers can only be either essential properties or accidental properties.

Even Bolzano is confined in his categorization by the tradition. We saw that he holds that (abstract) numbers are properties of peculiar sorts of wholes, namely, of what he calls sums. Mill, on the other hand, argues that they are perceptual structures. Thus while Bolzano thinks of them as "abstract things," Mill conceives of them as being concrete. Very roughly, while Bolzano assigns numbers to Plato's realm of being, Mill locates them in the realm of becoming. However, in either ontology, numbers somehow arise from wholes; in Bolzano's ontology, from abstract wholes, in Mill's from concrete wholes. The reasons for this affinity is clear: Numbers are "multiplicities" of some sort or other, and wholes have a "multiplicity" of parts.

Bolzano and Mill cannot bring themselves to claim that numbers are properties of ordinary individual things. They are forced to break out of the ontological straightjacket of the tradition. Bolzano introduces the category of sum, Mill makes use of the category of structure. Bolzano, as we would expect, is the more radical of the two. His sums are really unique "arithmetic" entities. Mill's structures are ordinary wholes, formed by ordinary relations; for example, by spatial relations or relations among color shades. I have argued that both of these views are false.

It is important to realize that neither Bolzano's sums nor Mill's structures are sets. A number of possibilities opens up as soon as one breaks out of the ontological circle of the tradition and acknowledges the category of set. We shall now look at some of these possibilities.

I) NUMBERS AS MULTITUDES: HUSSERL

At the beginning of Book IV of the *Elements,* Euclid gives the following explanation of number: A unit is that by virtue of which each of the things that exist is called one. A number is a multitude composed of concepts.

A number is a multitude. But what is a multitude? If multitudes are sets, then Euclid holds that a number is a set of units. I believe that this is very close to what Husserl maintains in his *Philosophie der Arithmetik.* Consider the number three. According to Husserl, there are concrete multitudes (Vielheiten). The color red, the moon, and Napoleon form such a multitude of three things. Another such multitude consists of a certain pain, an angel, and Italy. By *abstracting* from the particular things contained in the multitudes, we are supposed to arrive at the notion of a *multitude of this sort* by reflecting on the characteristic relation that obtains in each case between the parts of the multitude. In other words, we discover what kind of whole a concrete multitude is by paying attention to the peculiar relation which is characteristic of multitudes. In this fashion, we find out that multitudes are formed by the relation of *collective connection* (kollektive Verbindung). A multitude is a whole whose parts are collectively connected. Here is how Husserl describes the process by means of which we get from concrete multitudes to multitudes in general and, hence, to "sets":

> Somehow, determinate single contents [read: particular things] are given as collectively connected; by proceeding through abstraction to the general concept, we do not pay attention to them as such and such determinate contents; the main interest is concentrated, rather, on their collective connection, while they themselves are merely viewed as some contents or other, each one of them, as *something,* as *some one thing.* We shall take advantage of this result by relating it to an earlier remark, according to which the collective connection can be linguistically indicated in a completely clear and intelligible way by means of the conjunction *and.* Multitude in general, as we can now express it simply and straightforwardly, is nothing else but: something and something and something, etc.; or any one and any one and any one, etc.; or, for short: one and one and one, etc.

> (Husserl, 1970b, pp. 79–80)

Before we take a closer look at Husserl's conception of the number three, let me call your attention to the fact that this conception plays an essential part in mathematical intuitionism. Compare Husserl's words with the following quotation from Heyting:

> INT. We start with the notion of the natural numbers 1, 2, 3, etc. They are so familiar to us, that it is difficult to reduce this notion to simpler ones. Yet I shall try to describe their

sense in plain words. In the perception of an object we conceive the notion of an entity by a process of abstracting from the particular qualities of the object. We also recognize the possibility of an indefinite repetition of the conception of entities. In these notions lies the source of the concept of natural numbers.

(A. Heyting, *Intuitionism, An Introduction,* p. 13)

Mathematical intuitionism, we may say tongue in cheek, is Husserl's philosophy of arithmetic taken seriously by brilliant mathematicians.

The multitude one and one and one, according to Husserl, is the number three, Similarly, other natural numbers are multitudes with different numbers of ones. We arrive at the notion of number in general, according to his view, by a second act of abstraction: we simply abstract from the particular number of times that the one, the unit, occurs in the multitude.

Husserl's analysis contains two essential steps. Firstly, he claims that abstraction leads from the notion of the concrete multitude to the notion of *something and something and something.* Secondly, he identifies this notion with the notion of *one plus one plus one.* This identification has two parts: the notion of *something* is identified with the notion of *one,* and the concept of *and* is identified with the concept of *plus.* I think that all three steps are mistaken.

As Frege explains in great detail, abstraction will not yield the notion of a multitude in general (see G. Frege, *The Foundations of Arithmetic,* pp. 45–51). If we abstract from every characteristic, property, or feature that distinguishes the color red from both the moon and from Napoleon, we do indeed get the notion of a mere something or other. But if we do the same for the moon and for Napoleon, then we get again in either case the mere concept of something or other. By abstraction, we arrive three times at the *same* notion (of a mere something). We do not get the notion of *something and something and something,* that is, of some sort of triple. On the other hand, if we do not press the process of abstraction to its limit, so that we still have three different notions of three different things, then we arrive at the concept, not of *something and something and something,* but of the concept of *something and something else and something else again.* And from this notion we cannot jump to the notion of a multitude consisting of three *units;* for one unit is supposed to be the same as any other unit. In short, abstraction does not yield the notion of *something and something and something.*

Next, we must take a look at the "collective connection" which, according to Husserl, characterizes concrete multitudes. It seems to me that these multitudes are sets all but in name, because the collective connection is a mere wisp of a relation:

A multitude comes about when a uniform interest, and in and with it simultaneously a uniform awareness, sets off and comprehends different contents. . . .

The fullest confirmation for our conception comes again from inner experience. If we ask in what the connection consists when we, for example, think a multitude of such dissimilar things as redness, the moon, and Napoleon, we receive the answer that it merely consists in that we think these contents together, think them in one act.

(Husserl, 1970b, p. 74)

Compare this way of "collecting" things with the following quotation from Kitcher:

> One way of collecting all the red objects on a table is to segregate them from the rest of the objects, and to assign them a special place. We learn to collect by engaging in this type of activity. However, our collecting does not stop there. Later we can collect the objects in thought without moving them about. We become accustomed to collecting objects by running through a list of their names, or by producing predicates which apply to them.
>
> (P. Kitcher, *The Nature of Mathematical Knowledge*, pp. 110–11)

It seems to me that Kitcher describes here two quite different "operations," and that the second one does not at all deserve to be called a "collecting." To arrange things in spatial patterns is one thing, to think of their names or to think of "predicates which apply to them," it seems to me, is quite a different thing. In the first instance, we do produce a certain spatial structure with definite spatial relations among its parts. In the second case, no such structure or whole is produced. Notice that we are not even supposed to run through a list of the objects themselves in order to "collect" them, but merely through a list of their names. By thinking of a list of names, we are said to "collect" the objects so named. If Husserl's "collective connection" is a mere wisp of a relation, then Kitcher's relation is hardly there at all: it consists of nothing else but that the names of the objects to be collected are thought together.

But it is obvious, I think, that the alleged relation created by thinking of things together is not the sum relation of arithmetic. To think of things in one mental act is not the same as to add two numbers. By thinking of redness, the moon, and Napoleon as a group of things, I do not sum them up. I do not think of a sum at all. At best, I think of a *set* of things. What else could it mean to think of these things *together*, to think of them in *one* mental act?

Perhaps we are supposed to think of the constituents of the multitude *as its constituents*. Perhaps we are supposed to think of a list of its constituents. Perhaps we are supposed to think that this particular multitude consists of the color red *and* the moon *and* Napoleon. But the *and* of which we are then thinking is not the sum relation either. (Nor is it a relation among the members of the set.) It is the familiar conjunction. We are thinking (asserting, judging) that this multitude consists of the color red *and* that it consists of the moon *and* that it also consists of Napoleon. This relation holds between states of affairs and only between states of affairs, while the sum relation holds between numbers and only between numbers. Furthermore, while the conjunction is a two-term relation, the sum relation is a three-term relation. Husserl's analysis fails, because the collective connection is not the sum relation of arithmetic.

But it also fails, I submit, because the notion *something* is not the same as the notion *one*. More succinctly, *something* is not the same thing as *one*. One, of course, is the familiar number. Something, on the other hand, is a complex entity, consisting of the quantifier *some* (to be contrasted with such different quantifiers as *all, no, almost all, quite a few,* etc.) and of the variable *thing* (either in the sense of *entity,* or else in the sense of *object* of the mind). *Something* is of the same sort as *one thing.* (It is merely an accident of language that we do not write 'onething'.) In the latter expression, too, we can distinguish between the quantifier, *one,* and the variable *thing.* I should mention that the very nature of the topic forces me to diverge from customary terminology. For example, I call the entity *some,* not the word 'some', a quantifier. Furthermore, I do not think of the complex phrase 'something' ('some thing') as a quantifier. And, finally, I think of the entity *thing (object, entity)* as the variable; the expression 'thing', I call "the expression representing the variable." Thus I sharply distinguish for "quantifiers" and "variables," as well as for other expressions, between the expressions and what they represent.

Back to Husserl. He seems to have some misgivings about his cavalier identification of *something* with *one.* He admits that the two expressions do not mean the same thing (Husserl, 1970b, p. 84). But this difference is due, he claims, to our paying attention to different aspects of one and the same thing. We call something "one," he says, when we conceive of it as a part of a multitude; and we call it "something" when we do not relate it to a multitude. It seems to me that there may be a smidgen of truth to this claim. The number one is indeed a constituent of the structure formed by the natural numbers, while this is not the case for the thing *something.* But this is hardly what Husserl had in mind.

To summarize our discussion of Husserl's notion of number: Husserl comes very close to saying that the number three is a *set* consisting of units. But such a set, as Frege points out, collapses into a set with just one member, namely, the unit. In other words, a set consisting of "three ones" contracts into a set which consists just of the number one. On the other hand, if we assume that the members of the set are different from each other, that they are not all identical with the number one (or the thing *something*), then we do not have a set of units or of number ones.

2) NUMBERS AS PROPERTIES OF INDIVIDUAL THINGS

Frege as we know, gives a series of arguments against the view that numbers are properties of individual things. He argues, for example, that the number one cannot be a property (in *Frege,* 1974, p. 40). If it were a property, then everything would have to exemplify it. Frege then wonders: "It is not easy to imagine how language could have come to invent a word for a property which could not be of the slightest use for adding to the description of any object whatsover." I do not find this consideration very convincing. Even though a word does not add to "the description of an object," it may still be extremely useful. The term 'entity' ('thing', 'being'), for example, is extremely useful, even though it is true that everything is an entity. [But not every object (of thought, imagination, etc.) is an entity, since some objects do not exist.] We may have to talk about entities of very different kinds. However, the analogy between the case for 'one' and my case for 'entity' is not perfect. We are supposed to contemplate the possibility that 'one' is the name of a property, while I hold that 'entity' is not the name of a property, but is the name of a unique and altogether extraordinary entity, namely, of existence (see my *The Categorial Structure of the World*, pp. 387–416 and also *Phenomenology and Existentialism*, pp. 178–95). For this reason, the analogy with identity may be more appropriate. Being self-identical is a characteristic of everything (of every entity, though not of every object of the mind). Yet to say of something that it is self-identical does not add to the description of that thing. Would Frege therefore also hold that 'identity' is not the name of a relation, since this relation "could not be of the slightest use for adding to the description of any object whatsoever"? (Frege, we should gleefully remember in this context, argues at one point that existence is nothing but self-identity, because to say of something that it exists, does not add to the description of that thing! See his *Dialogue with Puenjer on Existence*.)

Be that as it may, I find Frege's second argument against the view that the number one is a property more convincing. If 'one' were a property, he says, then we should be able to use 'one' as a grammatical predicate. (G. Frege, 1974, pp. 40–41). I would prefer to put it somewhat differently: If 'one' were a property, then it would be exemplified; but it is not exemplified. If it were a property, according to Frege, then 'Solon is one' should make just as much sense as 'Solon is wise', but it does not. Of course, there are contexts in which 'Solon is one' makes sense, but then 'one' does not occur as a predicate. What 'one' means then is that Solon is one person. In such contexts, what we predicate of Solon is, not the number one, but the "property" of being one person, one thing. The number one is then only a part of this property. But here, too, we must be cautious. We cannot assume without further ado that there is such a property as the property of being one person. That is why I put 'property' in quotation marks. Rather, we must ask: What kind of entity is *one person, one individual, one entity?* How, precisely, does *Solon is wise* differ from *Solon is one person? The* question after the nature of number is, in part, a question about the structure of such facts.

Frege also points out that properties behave differently from the number one in regard to plural expressions. While it is true that Solon and Thales are wise, it is not true that Solon and Thales are one. They are two persons and not one. Solon is one person, and Thales is one person; and one person plus one person are two persons. This shows that the 'and' in 'Solon and Thales are two persons', unlike the 'and' in 'Solon and Thales are wise', represents the arithmetic plus.

Now, if it is true, as I have contended, that the number one is not a property because it is not exemplified, then it stands to reason that no natural number is a property; for we may assume that what holds for 'one', holds for the rest of the natural numbers. But let us look at some further possibilities.

Frege considers the possibility that numbers, in general, are properties of individual things. His example is an individual tree, and he assumes that this tree, at a certain moment, has precisely one thousand leaves (G. Frege, 1974, p. 28). He asks: What is the individual thing in this situation that has the property one-thousand? There simply is no plausible answer to this question. It is clear that any particular leaf does not have this propertyy, for it is one leaf and not a thousand. Nor can the foliage of the tree—a certain spatio-temporal structure—be said to have this property, for it, too, is one and not a thousand: the tree has one such foliage. But there is no other individual which could reasonably qualify for the alleged property one-thousand. Hence we are forced to conclude that this number is not a property at all.

Frege's second example concerns a deck of (German) playing cards. If we hand someone this deck of cards and ask her how many things she holds in her hand, she may be baffled by our question. To make our question clear, we must tell her what kind of thing she is supposed to count: decks, suits, or individual cards. If numbers were properties of individual things, so Frege seems to reason, then one and the same individual thing, the deck of cards, would have to exemplify different numbers. It would have to be one, four, and thirty-two. But it can only have one number.

It has been said in response to Frege's argument that the deck of cards may well have all three numerical properties (see D. Armstrong, *Universals and Scientific Realism*, vol. 2, pp. 71–74). The deck is simultaneously one-parted, since it is one deck, four-parted, since it consists of four suits, and thirty-two-parted, since it consists of thirty-two cards. In general, Armstrong claims, a complex entity has as many numerical properties as it has parts. But this reply to Frege overlooks the distinction which we have drawn between the number four, on the one hand, and four suits, on the other. It is granted that the one deck has four suits as parts and also has thirty-two cards as parts. But these two features are not the same as the numbers four and thirty-two. The feature of having four suits as parts is not the number four. The deck also has the feature of having four aces as parts. Now, if the first feature were the number four, then there would be no reason to deny that the second feature also is the number four. Then the first feature would be identical with the second feature. But it is not.

Numbers are not properties of individual things. Are they properties of things from a different category? Although Frege holds that numbers are what he calls "objects" rather than "functions," there are passages in the *Foundations* which point to a different view. He speaks repeatedly of *assigning* numbers to concepts and of numbers as *belonging* to concepts (G. Frege, 1974, pp. 59, 63, 64, and 66). He even writes in a footnote (p. 80) that instead of saying that the number of F's is the *extension* of the concept *similar to F,* he could have said that it is the *concept similar to F*. This suggests the view that the number of F's is the relational property of being similar to F. Numbers, according to this view, are relational properties of properties. The number two, for example, is the relational property of being similar to the property of being a shoe which I am now wearing. This relational property is of course shared by all and only those properties which are exemplified by precisely two things. In other words, all of these properties have something in common, namely, the property of being similar to the property of being a shoe which I am now wearing. A moment's reflection shows, though, that this view will not do. Consider the property of being similar to the property of being a thumb of mine. This property as well is exemplified by those and only those properties which are exemplified by precisely two things. We should conclude, therefore, that this property, too, is the number two. But how could it be, since the two relational properties are obviously not the same? Or else we shall have to conclude that there is not just one number two, but many two's. And this conclusion, it seems to me, is quite obviously false.

3) NUMBERS AS PROPERTIES OF PROPERTIES: CANTOR

Another treatment of numbers as properties of properties can be found in Hilbert and Ackermann's *Principles of Mathematical Logic*. They agree that numbers are not properties of individual things: "For example, the fact that the number of continents is five cannot be expressed by saying that each continent has the number five as a property; but it is a property of the predicate "to be a continent" that it holds for exactly five individuals" (D. Hilbert and W. Ackermann, *Principles of Mathematical Logic*, p. 136). And then they conclude: "Number thus appears as the properties of predicates, and in our calculus *every number is represented as a predicate constant of second level*" (Hilbert and Ackermann, p. 136).

As you can see, I have taken liberties in describing Hilbert's and Ackermann's view. When I spoke of properties, they speak of predicates. But their characterization of numbers is at any rate merely a preliminary to the real task at hand which consists of providing "expressions for the numbers 0, 1, and 2, i.e., for the second level predicates 0 (F), 1 (F), 2 (F)." I shall give these expressions here in words rather than in symbols:

> 0 (F): There is no x for which F is true,
> 1 (F): There is an x for which F holds, and any y for which Fy holds is identical with x,
> 2 (F): There are two different x and y for which F is true, and any z for which Fz holds is identical with x or with y.

(Hilbert and Ackermann, pp. 136–37)

Contrary to what Hilbert and Ackermann say, they do not give expressions for 0, 1, and 2. Rather, they give so-called contextual definitions. At this point, two issues arise which we must keep apart. Firstly, there is the question of the ontological efficacy of "contextual definitions." I have argued elsewhere at some length that such "definitions" have no reductive power (see my *Ontological Reduction*, pp. 109–16, and *The Categorial Structure of the World*, pp. 302–304). My argument comes down to this. If '0 (F)', for example, is an arbitrary expression which has no prior meaning, then the "contextual definition" turns out to be a mere abbreviation proposal to the effect that '0 (F)' shall be nothing but a shortened version of the expression 'There is no x for which F is true'. In this case, of course, '0 (F)' says nothing about the number zero. The occurrence of '0' in this expression is totally gratuitous. On the other hand, if '0' is supposed to represent the number zero, and if 'F' is taken to stand for a property, and if concatenation is meant to represent exemplification, then the so-called contextual definition turns out to be an equivalence statement to the effect that a property F has the property zero *if and only if* there is nothing which has the property. In this case, it is always legitimate to ask whether or not the so-called contextual definition is true. In this case, it is clear, no ontological reduction of something to something else takes place.

The second issue is the more specific question of whether or not a property F can truly be said to exemplify the property zero. Is zero a property of properties? I shall try to answer this question in connection with Cantor's conception of the category of number.

Cantor states in his review of Frege's *Foundations:* "I call 'Cardinal Number [Maechtigkeit] of a multitude [Inbegriff] or set of elements' (where the latter may be homogeneous or not, simple or complex) that general concept [Allgemeinbegriff] under which all and only those sets fall which are similar to the given one" (G. Cantor, *Gesammelte Abhandlungen,* p. 441). If we make allowance for the Kantian terminology ("concept" instead of "property"), then what Cantor maintains is that the number of a set is a property exemplified by all and only those sets which are similar to the given one.

I believe that this is an extremely plausible view. It answers Frege's question to what we attribute the number one-thousand when we say that the tree has one-thousand leaves. It is attributed, not to the tree or the foliage, but to the set of leaves. (Alternatively, it may be said to be attributed to the property of being a leaf of this tree.) It also explains how different numbers can be attributed to Frege's deck of cards. The number one, for example, is a property of the set whose only member is the deck of cards. The number four, on the other hand, is a property of the set of suits contained in the deck. However, in spite of these and other advantages, Cantor's view seems to me to be mistaken: Numbers are not properties of sets (or properties of properties). And this for at least two reasons.

Firstly, as Frege points out, we cannot form plurals for number words as we can for property words. To put it less linguistically:

> The fact that 1/2 is neither spatial nor real notwithstanding, it is not a concept in the sense that objects could fall under it. One cannot say: "this is a 1/2", as one can say: "this is a right angle," nor are expressions like "all 1/2", "some 1/2" admissible; rather, 1/2 is treated as a determinate single object. . . .
>
> (G. Frege, "On Formal Theories of Arithmetic," in *Collected Papers on Mathematics, Logic, and Philosophy,* p. 120)

I think that what these facts show is that numbers cannot be properties because they are not *exemplified* by something. I take it to be one of the fundamental laws of ontology that all and only properties are exemplified, so that an entity cannot possibly be a property unless it is exemplified by something. (Using one of our two important notions of necessity, we could say: It is necessary that entities which are not exemplified are not properties!) When we talk about elephants in the plural, we are talking about things which *are* elephants; we are talking about things which exemplify the property of being an elephant. An elephant is a thing which *is* an elephant. If the number three were a property, then there would have to exist things which *are* three in the very same sense in which there are things which *are* elephants. But there are no things which are three in this sense.

It may be replied, in defense of Cantor's view, that our example is unfair. What correspond to elephants are certain sets (or properties), not individual things. But this reply brings us to the second reason why, in my opinion, Cantor's view is false. Consider a set of three things, say, Husserl's "concrete multitude" consisting of the color red, Napoleon, and the moon. Is this entity a three? Does this thing have the property three? I do not think so. This set is not a three. What is true is that this set has the "property" of having three members. It is "three-membered." It is a triple. In this context, I shall concede that being three-membered or being a triple is a property of sets, just as being an elephant is a property of individual things. But the property of being a triple is not the same as the number three. To treat the number three as if it were a property of sets is to confuse the number with the property of being a triple.

As soon as we distinguish, as I think we must, between a number, on the one hand, and the "property" of having so-and-so many members (or the "property" of being exemplified by so-and-so many things), on the other, Cantor's view is stripped of its initial plausibility. Surely, from the fact that having three members may be conceived of as a property of sets it does not follow that the number three, by itself, is a property. The number three, as I pointed out earlier, is merely a part of that "property." This becomes obvious if we compare the "property" of having three members with the "property" of having three brothers. These are undoubtedly quite different properties, yet both contain the number three.

Having disposed of the view that numbers are properties of sets or of properties, we must next consider Frege's view that numbers are sets.

4) NUMBERS AS SETS: FREGE

Frege's view is contained in the famous "definition":

(F) The number which belongs to the concept F is the extension [Umfang] of the concept "equal [gleichzahlig] to the concept F."

(Frege, 1974, pp. 79–80)

There are a number of problems connected with Frege's use of the term 'extension' ('Umfang'), and I shall briefly allude to them. Firstly, Frege speaks of "value ranges" ("Wertverlaeufe") rather than sets, and this raises the question of whether the former differ from the latter and, if so, in what way. I shall take for granted, *in our general discussion of logicism,* that value-ranges are sets. But I must call attention to the fact that much in Frege speaks against this identification (see, for example, N. Cocchiarella, "Frege, Russell, and Logicism: A Logical Reconstruction"). And I shall presently offer an interpretation of Frege's peculiar brand of logicism which rests on a sharp distinction between value-ranges and sets. Secondly, there is the question of whether in the "definition" (F) Frege meant by 'extension' value-range. I shall assume that he did. It follows then that (F) asserts that numbers are sets. But this creates, thirdly, a most important philosophical problem for Frege's program. If numbers are sets, according to Frege's view, then arithmetic reduces to set-theory (and logic) and not, as Frege claims, to logic. Logicism, therefore, fails for this reason alone. Frege was aware of this objection. In the article cited earlier, for example, he says:

> Therefore if arithmetic is to be independent of all particular properties of things, this must also hold true of its building blocks: they must be of a purely logical nature. From this there follows the requirement that everything arithmetical be reducible to logic by means of definitions. So, for example, I have replaced the expression 'set', which is frequently used by mathematicians, with the expression customary in logic: 'concept'.

(Frege, 1984, p. 114)

There are two ways of looking at this and similar passages in Frege. It is natural to assume that Frege means to say that his "definition" could alternatively be formulated in terms of concepts rather than extensions of concepts, so that numbers turn out to be concepts and, therefore, logical rather than mathematical things. But this interpretation runs counter to Frege's whole approach. On the other hand, there is an "unnatural," rather Byzantine, interpretation which agrees well with the rest of his philosophy. I call it "Byzantine" because it rests on Frege's idiosyncratic view that 'the concept horse' represents, not a concept, but a so-called concept-correlate. Assume that concept-correlates are the extensions of concepts. Assume further that concept-correlates are Frege's value ranges. What Frege then claims, in the passage cited above and in similar passages, is that he could have said that the number of the concept F is *the concept* "equal to the concept F" rather than that it is *the extension of the concept* "equal to the concept F," bearing in mind that, according to his idiosyncratic view, 'the concept equal to the concept F' represents a concept-correlate (that is, an extension) rather than a concept. Either way, according to this interpretation, numbers turn out to be extensions, that is, value-ranges. And value-ranges, we must emphasize, are by Frege conceived of as logical rather than mathematical entities.

This point is so important that we must stay with it a moment longer. Frege, I submit, would have insisted that value-ranges are "constituted in their being" by the respective concepts. *It is this fact that characterizes them as "logical" things.* Sets, as conceived of by the mathematician, on the other hand, are "constituted in their being," not by concepts, but by their members (cf. Cocchiarella). Thus Frege's philosophy of mathematics requires a sharp distinction between value-ranges and sets. And his logicism demands that value-ranges, in distinction from sets, are "logical" rather than "mathematical" things. I do not think there are such things as Frege's value-ranges. But I do believe that there are sets. Hence, there is no possibility of "reducing" numbers to value-ranges, but there is the possibility of "reducing" them to sets. I shall therefore take this latter possibility seriously, and I shall pretend, contrary to fact, that Frege's "reduction" was meant to be a reduction to sets. Precisely speaking, and putting our discussion in a nutshell, Frege's logicism fails, first of all, not because he reduces numbers to sets, but because (as Russell's paradox proves) there are no value-ranges.

But it also fails for another reason. Frege calls (F) a "definition," but it is obvious that it is a description. It is an identity statement which may or may not be true. Most certainly, it is not a harmless abbreviation proposal, a mere stipulation for which the question of truth cannot arise. (F) amounts to:

(F') For any property f, the number of things which are f is (identical with) the set of all those properties which are similar to f.

Consider the number of planets, namely, the number nine. According to (F'), this number is the set consisting of all and only those properties which are similar to the property of being a planet. The number nine is described as a set of properties, namely, as the set of all and only those properties which are *exemplified by precisely nine things*.

Frege's view appears to be rather far-fetched. The number nine does not seem to be a set at all, to say nothing of a set containing such properties at the property of being a planet. How could one possibly arrive at such an outlandish view? Well, there are two straightforward ways. One could try to derive (F') from other perhaps more plausible statements. Or else one could try to argue for it directly by showing that this identity statement is true because the number and the corresponding set share all of their attributes (properties and relations).

Assume that 'A' is a mere conventional abbreviation for 'B'. If so, then 'A' represents whatever 'B' represents, and conversely. It follows that A is identical with B. Every abbreviation implies in this fashion a true identity statement. Is (F') of this sort? Is (F') simply a consequence of a harmless abbreviation? Obviously not. It seems to me to be obvious that the expression 'the number of planets' is not a conventional abbreviation for 'the set of properties which are similar to the property of being a planet'. It is preposterous to believe that there exists an implicit or explicit agreement among English-speaking people to use the phrase 'the number of F's' whenever they wish to talk about certain sets.

But perhaps (F') follows, not from an abbreviation, but from other true propositions. Consider the following two true equivalences:

(E₁) For all properties f and g: f is similar to g *if and only if* the set determined by the property of being similar to f is the same as the set determined by the property of being similar to g.

(E₂) For all properties f and g: f is similar to g *if and only if* the number of f's is the same as the number of g's.

Now, if you mistakenly think of these two equivalences as identities, then you may conclude that the right side of (E₁) is identical with the right side of (E₂), for both are then identical with: f is similar to g. And if you identify the right sides, then you get, in effect, Frege's "definition." But the right sides are not identical. We can only derive the following equivalence:

(E₃) For all properties f and g: the set determined by the property of being similar to f is the same as the set determined by the property of being similar to g *if and only if* the number of f's is the same as the number of g's.

And from (E₃) we cannot get by uncontroversial means to (F').

What, then, about a direct defense of (F¹)? We accept the law of the identity of indiscernibles as well as the law of the indiscernibility of identicals. Can we show that the number nine has the same attributes as the set of properties which are similar to the property of being a planet? I think that these two entities have quite different properties and stand in quite different relations to things. Numbers, for example, stand in arithmetic relations; sets do not. Nine is the sum of six and three, but the set of properties just mentioned is not the sum of anything. On the other hand, sets have members (elements); numbers do not. The set just mentioned contains as a member the property of being a pencil on my desk, since there are nine pencils on my desk at this moment; the number nine, on the other hand, has no members at all. Furthermore, sets form unions, numbers do not. The set of pencils on my desk is the union of the set of yellow pencils on my desk and the set of blue pencils on my desk. The number nine, by contrast, is not the union of anything. While numbers form one kind of structure, sets form an entirely different kind of structure.

There are, however, and this is a most important point, certain similarities between these two kinds of structures. This similarity is succinctly characterized when we point out that a certain portion of set theory and a certain portion of arithmetic are both "Boolean algebras." But this analogy between, say, the sum relation, on the one hand, and the union relation on the other, must not blind us to the fact that these are two different relations. We can no more add sets than we can eat them; and we can no more form the union of two numbers than we can join them in marriage. What we can add are the *numbers of the members* of two sets. A set which is the union of two nonoverlapping sets of two members each, for example, has four members because two members plus two members are four members. And two members and two members are four members because two plus two is four.

Our refutation of the view which we have attributed to Frege in the last few pages is straightforward: Numbers cannot be sets because arithmetic relations do not hold among sets. But there is an extremely popular response to this objection. Arithmetic relations, one claims, can be *defined* in set-theoretic terms. If this were true, then there really would be no arithmetic relations. And if there are no arithmetic relations, then they cannot hold among numbers. And if they do not hold among numbers, then they cannot distinguish between numbers and sets.

That arithmetic relations can be defined in terms of set-theoretic ones is a dogma for most mathematicians and many philosophers. Russell, to mention just one prominent example, maintains in the *Principles of Mathematics* that the "chief point to be observed is that logical addition of classes is the fundamental notion, while the arithmetic addition of numbers is wholly subsequent" (B. Russell, *Principles of Mathematics*, p. 119). Russell bases this claim on the following sort of "definition":

(R) m + n is the number of a class which is the logical sum of two classes u and v which have no common term and of which one has m terms, the other has n terms.

Notice, firstly, that Russell says that m + n "is the number of a class," but speaks of u as "having m terms." m + n, to be precise, is not the number of a class, but is the number *of terms* of a class. Secondly, it is obvious that (R) can be read either as an equivalence or as an identity. According to the first, it states that the number which is the sum of m and n is the same as the number of the class w *if and only if* w is the union of the two sets u and v. This is true, but implies that we are here concerned with two quite different relations. According to the second reading, (R) says that the number (sum) m + n is identical with the number of the members of the set w. This, too, is true; but it, too, does not show that the sum relation is the same as the "logical sum relation" among sets.

My case against the view that numbers are sets rests, in one sentence, on this contention. The sum relation among numbers is not identical with any relation among sets.

5) NUMBERS AS QUANTIFIERS

How one categorizes numbers depends on what categories one has available, that is, on one's ontology. I have argued that numbers are neither individual things, not properties, nor structures of certain kinds, nor sets. What categories remain? Well, there are relations and there are facts. I think that numbers are quite obviously not facts. I also believe that they are not relations, but hasten to add that there are plausible views which categorize numbers as relations, such as the one recently outlined by David Armstrong (see D. M. Armstrong, *A Combinatorial Theory of Possibility*, chap. IX: Mathematics, *manuscript*). If I am correct, then numbers do not belong to any one of the standard and familiar categories. And this suggests that they form a category of their own. What can we say about this new category? How shall we describe it? The so-called relational property of being exemplified by three things provides a clue, for it bears a striking resemblance to the "properties" of being exemplified by some (at least one) things, being exemplified by all things, being exemplified by nothing, being exemplified by almost all things, etc. This similarity suggests that numbers resemble such things as *all, some, almost all, no,* etc. These things are sometimes called "quantifiers," and we shall therefore say that numbers are quantifiers.

Unfortunately, the term 'quantifier' is not without ambiguity, and we must clarify our use. Firstly, according to our terminology, a quantifier is not a linguistic entity; it is not a sign or expression. Rather, it is what a certain expression represents. For example, 'all' is not a quantifier, but rather a word that represents the quantifier *all,* just as '3' is not a number but a numeral that represents the number 3. Secondly, we must distinguish between the quantifier (and the quantifier expression), on the one hand, and what such expressions as 'All things are such that', 'Some things are such that', etc. represent (and these expressions themselves), on the other. Some call the whole expression (or what it represents) a "quantifier." We do not. Only the word 'all', for example, represents a quantifier; the expression 'all things are such that' represents an entity that is quite different from this quantifier. In this expression there occurs, in addition to the word for the quantifier, a word that represents what is quantified, namely, 'things', and also a phrase that indicates the peculiar nexus which connects the quantified things with the rest of the state of affairs, namely, 'are such that'. Let us call the whole expression a "quantifier phrase." According to our analysis, we can then distinguish between three parts of a quantifier phrase: (1) the quantifier expression, (2) the expression for the kind of entity that is quantified, and (3) an expression for the characteristic nexus.

By calling numbers "quantifiers," we try to accomplish two things. Firstly, we describe what numbers do (in Dedekind's words: "Was sie sollen"): They quantify. Secondly, we also try to shed some light on their nature ("Was sie sind") by emphasizing their similarity to the well-known quantifiers of logic. For example, I hold that the sentences:

'There are four persons in this room', and

'There are nine planets'

represent facts of the form:

Four things (entities) are such that: they are persons and they are in this room, and

Nine entities are such that: they are planets.

One can easily represent these facts in a *Principia*-style symbolism.

What about statements like "Two persons plus two persons are four persons? We have already noted that this is an instance of the arithmetic truth that two plus two is four. It is also, but in a different sense, an instance of the law that two entities plus two entities are four entities. This law we can represent by:

'All entities are such that: two entities plus two entities are four entities'.

Our assertion about persons becomes:

All persons are such that: two persons plus two persons are four persons.

How shall we analyze the fact that Solon is one thing (rather than two things or three things)? I think that this fact amounts to:

One thing is such that: it is identical with Solon.

The assertion that Solon and Thales are two things becomes:

One thing is identical with Solon, and one thing is identical with Thales, and the former plus the latter are two things.

These examples show that numbers behave like the familiar quantifiers. We are in the fortunate situation that the behavior of the ordinary quantifiers is so well known that much light is shed on the category of number by pointing out that it encompasses the ordinary quantifiers. By the same token, though, whatever obscurity surrounds the ordinary quantifiers is bound to rub off on the numbers. Russell, at one point, offers an argument that there is no such thing as the quantifier *all*. It may further illuminate our view if we take a look at his argument. Russell states:

> If u be a class-concept, is the concept "all u's" analyzable into two constituents , *all* and u, or is it a new concept, defined by a certain relation to u, and no more complex than u itself? We may observe, to begin with, that "all u's" is synonymous with "u's", at least according to a very common use of the plural. Our question is, then, as to the meaning of the plural. The word *all* has certainly some definite meaning, but it seems highly doubtful whether it means more than the indication of a relation. "All men" and "all numbers" have in common the fact that they both have a certain relation to a class concept, namely, to *man* and *number* respectively. But it is very difficult to isolate any further element of all-ness which both share, unless we take as this element the mere fact that both are concepts of classes. It would seem, then, that "all u's" is not validly

analyzable into *all* and u, and that language, in this case as in some others, is a misleading guide. The same remark will apply to *every, any, some, a,* and *the.*

(Russell, 1964, pp. 72–73)

Russell argues here directly against our contention that 'all u's' is short for 'all entities which are u (are such that)', and that the latter represents a complex entity, involving the quantifier *all,* the variable *entity,* and the property *u.* According to him, 'all u's' is long for 'u's'. But this seems to be mistaken, for the plural can occur with many different quantifier expressions. In addition to 'all men', we have 'some men', 'several men', 'seven men', 'quite a few men', etc. The singular, on the other hand, occurs only with 'a', 'the', 'one', and 'no'. If the entity *all men* were the same as the thing *men,* then the entity *some men* would have to be the thing *some all men.* But there is no such thing. Of course, this is not to deny that we may speak of men being mortal rather than of all men being mortal. But this is possible, not because 'all men' simply means the same as 'men', but because 'men' means on these occasions what 'all men' usually means. As to how Russell's argument is to be applied to the quantifiers *every, any, some,* etc., I am at a loss.

It may be objected, in the spirit of well-established logical practice, that my example involving *some* in addition to *all* is gratuitous, for 'some' can be defined in terms of 'all'. There exists, therefore, only the quantifier *all,* and that quantifier reduces, according to Russell, to the plural of the respective property. Once again, we have run into the mistaken habit of reading an ontological reduction into a mere equivalence, for that is what the so-called "definition" consists in. As everyone knows, the following equivalence is true:

All properties f are such that: some things are f *if and only if* it is not the case that all things are not f.

But this equivalence does not show at all that the quantifier *some* (or, alternatively, the quantifier *all*) does not exist. Quite to the contrary, if this equivalence has any ontological significance, then it consists in showing that both the quantifier *all* and the quantifier *some* exist. It shows this by showing that certain facts involving the former are equivalent to certain facts involving the latter. According to our point of view, no quantifier is "ontologically reducible" to any other quantifier. All of the quantifiers so far mentioned, including the numbers, exist, but one can do logic with just a few of them.

6) THE EXISTENCE OF THE REAL NUMBERS

I have argued that natural numbers belong to the category of quantifier. What about the (positive) rational and irrational numbers? I have no doubt that the (positive) real numbers exist. Or, at least, I see no reason why one should believe otherwise. It is an axiom of my ontology, if you like to talk that way, that the real numbers exist. And if they exist, then obviously they also belong to the category of quantifier. I do not think that too many philosophers would disagree with me about the existence of the real numbers. However, many probably would be offended by my firm conviction that the rational and irrational numbers are not "constructed" out of the natural numbers. In my view, all of the real numbers are there, all of them "at once," the irrational numbers as well as the rational numbers, the rationals as well as the natural numbers. We must resist the fashionable talk about a piecemeal construction of the rational numbers out of the natural numbers, and of the irrational numbers out of the rational numbers. Such talk rests, once again, on a misconception of the ontological power of certain "definitions."

One customarily "defines" the rational numbers in terms of equivalence sets of ordered pairs of natural numbers. A relation R is "introduced by definition," as one so glibly says:

(D) [a, b] R [c, d] if and only if ad = bc.

(D) states that two ordered pairs of natural numbers stand in the relation R to each other if and only if the product of a and d is the same as the product of b and c. Of course, one cannot "introduce" a relation R, if there exists no such relation, and there is no reason to believe, in my view, that R exists. But even if it existed, (D) is a straightforward equivalence and as such does not "reduce" anything to anything. The true state of affairs is, rather, that the fraction a/b is that number which stands in the division relation to a and b. The fraction can be *described* as that number which stands in a certain arithmetic relation to two numbers. This number may be identical with the number which stands in the same arithmetic relation to two other numbers c and d. For example, the number which stands in the division relation to 1 and 2, namely, the fraction 1/2, is identical with the number which stands in that same relation to the numbers 2 and 4, namely, the fraction 2/4. One and the same number can be described in two different ways. Since division and multiplication are two sides of a coin, we get the following version of (D):

(D') The number which stands in the division relation to a and b is the same as the number which stands in that relation to c and d *if and only if* the number which stands in the product relation to a and d is the same as the number which stands in the product relation to b and c.

The fact that we can form the description expression 'the number which stands in the division relation to 1 and 2' does not guarantee, of course, that there exists such a number. If we believe that the fraction 1/2 exists, and of course we do, then our belief must be based on something other than our ability to form the expression. As usual, there are two obvious ways in which we can justify our belief in the existence of the fraction. We may claim that we are acquainted with the fraction; for example, that we perceive it. Or else we may try to present an argument which proves the existence of the fraction. I think we know that (some) fractions exist because we are indeed acquainted with them. We *see* the number 1/2, for example, when we see that only 1/2 of the pizza we bought for dinner is left, just as we see the color midnight blue when we see that our son's sweater is midnight blue.

Euclid's tenth Book contains a proof that the square root of two is not a rational number. From our pedantic but ontologically pure point of view, this means that a certain number, namely, the number which when multiplied with itself is two, is not identical with any number that stands in the division relation to two natural numbers. And this amounts to the surprising *discovery* that there are numbers which are neither natural numbers nor fractions. Dedekind's famous "definition" of the irrationals must be assessed in the light of our view that the irrational numbers were discovered and not created by definition. From this point of view, Dedekind, too, discovered something. What he discovered is that irrational numbers *can be described* as determining certain sets of rational numbers. For example, the square root of two divides all real numbers into two sets, namely, into those numbers which are smaller than it, on the one hand, and the rest of the real numbers, on the other. It can therefore be described as the smallest number of this latter set. Alternatively, we can think of it as dividing all the real numbers into the set of numbers which are larger than it is and the rest of the real numbers. In this case, we can describe it as the largest number of the latter set. In either case, though, we think of the square root of two as dividing up all of the *real numbers*. There is no "filling in the gaps between the rational numbers by postulating the existence of irrational numbers." We can no more "create" the irrationals than we can "create" the rationals, than we can "create" the natural numbers. Nor can we bring them into being by "postulating them." If we "postulate" that there are irrational numbers, then, if there are such numbers, our postulate is true. Otherwise, our postulate is simply false. Nothing could be further from the truth than Kronecker's aphorism that while the natural numbers are made by God, the rest of the numbers are our invention.

Much of what I have just said is in the spirit of Frege's philosophy of arithmetic. But not all of it. Frege, for example, points out that even if a concept does not contain a contradiction, we cannot conclude that something falls under it. Thus even if we could prove that the concept *square root of two* is without contradiction, we could not infer that there must be such a number. This observation corresponds to our insistence that the fact that we can form certain noncontradictory description expressions does not imply that these expressions describe something (Frege, 1974, pp. 105–107). Frege correctly goes on to argue that the mathematician can no more create numbers at will than the geographer can create continents at will. The mathematician, too, can only discover what is there and give it a name (Frege, 1974, pp. 107–108).

How then does Frege show that there are fractions or irrational numbers? How does he show, for that matter, that there are natural numbers? Frege faces a dilemma:

> How are complex numbers to be given to us then, and fractions and irrational numbers? If we turn for assistance to intuition [Anschauung], we import something foreign into arithmetic; but if we only define the concept of such a number by giving its characteristics, if we simply require the number to have certain properties; then there is still no guarantee that anything falls under the concept and answers to our requirements, and yet it is precisely on this that proofs must be based.
>
> (Frege, 1974, p. 114)

I do not think that Frege can escape from the horns of this dilemma, contrary to his own assessment of the situation. For our view, one of the two horns does not exist: We maintain that we know that certain numbers exist because we perceive them, and we do not consider this recourse to perception (Anschauung) an import of something foreign to arithmetic. Quite to the contrary, it is of the essence of our empiricism that knowledge of all entities of whatever kind, of their existence as well as their nature, must *ultimately* rest on perception or introspection.

In the end, Frege cannot but embrace rationalism in order to escape from the dilemma: numbers are presented, he maintains, not to the senses, but to reason:

> On this view of numbers the charm of work on arithmetic and analysis is, it seems to me, easily accounted for. We might say, indeed, slightly changing the well-known words: reason's true object is reason itself. In arithmetic, we are concerned with objects which are known to us, not through the medium of the senses as something foreign from the outside, but which are given immediately to reason to which, as its very own, they are utterly transparent.

(Frege, 1974, p. 115, my translation)

b) Acquaintance with Numbers

Our view that numbers are quantifiers may appear to cast a pall over our professed empiricism. If numbers are quantifiers, then surely they cannot be "sensible things." Quantifiers, if there are such things at all, traditional wisdom pronounces, are part of the most abstract furniture of the world, and abstract things, as everyone knows, are not sensible. It is a long-standing dogma of philosophy that all sensible things are spatio-temporal (concrete). Since quantifiers are not spatio-temporal, they cannot be sensible. Thus we seem to be forced into the arms of rationalism. As I have pointed out before, it is this dialectic that accounts for Mill's insistence that numbers are somehow perceptual structures. Nor can there be any doubt that it is responsible for Husserl's theory of eidetic intuition. Even Frege, as we shall see in a moment, was unable to resist its power. But it is a measure of his greatness that he added an important twist to that dialectic.

Powerful as the Platonic tradition is, its hold on the minds of philosophers can be assailed by a very simple and straightforward argument. Colors, I maintain, are abstract entities; they are not located in space and/or time. The color shade midnight blue, for example, has no spatial attributes: it has no shape, no size, and does not stand in spatial relations to other things. Nor does it have temporal attributes: it has no duration and does not stand in temporal relations to other things. If you do not agree with this categorization, then we have a disagreement that lies much deeper than the issue of rationalism versus empiricism. So, grant me for the moment that colors are indeed abstract things. But colors, I maintain, can be perceived. It is obvious, is it not, that we see with our very eyes that the sweater before us is midnight blue. It follows, therefore, contrary to the Platonic dogma and its Kantian refinements, that we perceive abstract entities, that is, things which are not spatio-temporal. I see only one way of avoiding this conclusion: You must deny that the colors which we see are abstract things. This is precisely what Husserl does. But he has to pay a dreadful ontological price: He has to invent a second sort of color, abstract colors, in addition to concrete colors. The colors we see, he holds, are concrete, individual things. But in addition, there also exist abstract, universal, colors, which we do not see, but which are grasped in eidetic intuition.

My strategy is to draw a parallel between the case I just made for colors and the case that can be made for certain (small) numbers. Numbers, like colors, are abstract things. Yet, like colors, they can be perceived. I appeal to the case of colors because it seems to me well suited to cast doubt upon the Platonic dogma that abstract things are not sensible. And as soon as this dogma is thrown into doubt, my view that numbers can be perceived will appear not only plausible, but inevitable.

When I claim that numbers can be perceived in precisely the same way in which we perceive colors, I do not mean to say, of course, that numbers belong to the same category as colors. Colors are properties (of individual things), while numbers are quantifiers. Rather, what I mean is that colors and numbers are presented to us in the *same kind of mental act,* for example, in an act of seeing. Nor do I wish to claim that a color or a number is ever presented to us in isolation, separate from all other things. We see colors when we see colored things, and we see numbers when we see numbered things. I see the color midnight blue when I see that my son wears a midnight blue sweater, and I see the number two when I see that there are two blue pencils on my desk.

As I just pointed out, colors and numbers are *categorially* different. But there is also the following important difference: While colors can only be seen, numbers can be seen, they can be heard, they can be felt, etc. Just as you can see that there are two pencils on the table, so can you hear that there are two dogs barking and you can feel two pains, one in each leg. In short, while colors are presented to us through just one sense, numbers are given to us through all of the senses.

I) THE SENSIBLE NATURE OF NUMBERS

Frege argues that number is not a sensible property like color (Frege, 1974, pp. 27–32). We agree that numbers are not properties and, therefore, could not be sensible properties. But Frege claims more, namely, that number, no matter to what category they belong, are not sensible. What convinces him is an argument that may be called "the argument from the lack of sense-impressions." In outline, the argument runs as follows. (1) Perception depends on sensations. (2) While there are color sensations, there are no number sensations. (3) Therefore, numbers, unlike colors, cannot be perceived. In support of (1), Frege says, for example: "When we see a blue surface, we have an impression of a unique sort which corresponds to the word "blue"; this impression we recognize again, when we catch sight of another blue surface" (Frege, 1974, p. 31). He then goes on to argue that there is no corresponding impression for the word "three" when we look, for example, at a triangle and see its three sides.

Frege gives two reasons for his contention that no sense-impression corresponds to the word 'three', but they come down to the same thing. Firstly, if we assume that something sensible corresponds to the word 'three', then that same sensible thing must be found also in three concepts. Hence, we should find something sensible, whatever corresponds to 'three', in something that is not sensible, namely, in concepts. "The effect would be," Frege says, "just like speaking of a fusible event, a blue idea, a salty concept, or a stringy judgment" (Frege, 1974, p. 31). Secondly, Frege asks how it is that we become acquainted with the number of figures of Aristotelian syllogisms. He states that it cannot be by means of our eyes, for what we literally see is at most certain symbols for the syllogistic figures, not the figures themselves. And how can we see their numbers, he asks rhetorically, if the figures themselves remain invisible?

Both of these considerations, I think, make the same point: Nothing sensible corresponds to the word 'three' because even nonsensible things can be three. Frege seems to take for granted that something sensible cannot be presented together with something nonsensible. Why does he take this for granted? Surely, the analogy to the blue idea misses its mark. A blue idea is impossible because ideas do not have colors. The problem is not that something sensible, the color, is supposed to be presented together with something nonsensible (the idea). A blue tone or a square with a pitch are just as impossible as a blue idea, even though we have here sensible things, namely, tones and pitches. We may agree with Frege that ideas (concepts) can be numbered, and that concepts are not sensible. But we fail to see how it follows that sensible numbers cannot be presented together with nonsensible concepts. The conclusion seems to be inevitable that Frege has fallen prey to the Platonic dogma, according to which the understanding contemplates the nonsensible forms and the senses acquaint us with the sensible individuals. The world is divided into two realms and the mind is split up into two separate faculties.

How deeply Frege is steeped in that unfortunate tradition can be seen from his conception of colors. Frege, we know, distinguishes between objective things and subjective (mental) things. This is his anti-Kantianism. But he does not escape completely from the Kantian spell. Objective things, he holds, divide into objects and concepts (more precisely: into objects and functions). The choice of the term 'concepts' betrays the Kantian influence, for concepts are nothing but properties; and while the word 'concept' has associations of subjectivity, no such connection with the mind adheres to the term 'property'. Is the color shade midnight blue, to go to the heart of the matter, an object, a concept, or else a subjective idea? Our answer is straightforward: It is a property and as such neither mental nor nonmental, neither subjective nor objective. Furthermore, it is a property both of mental things, namely, of sensations, and of nonmental things, namely, of perceptual objects. Frege's answer is not straightforward. It betrays all of the confusions of the Kantian tradition.

Frege distinguishes between blue as a sense-impression and as a concept. The color concept, what we would call the "property," he says, belongs to a surface quite independently of us. It consists of the power to reflect certain light rays (Frege, 1974, p. 31). The color concept, we are surprised to read, is not at all the property which we see with our eyes, but is a certain physical property of surfaces. Frege thus accepts the argument from physics and must suffer all of its catastrophic consequences. The color concept, therefore, is not sensible. What is sensible is the so-called color sense-impression.

But what, then, does the word 'blue' represent? What am I saying when I say that your sweater is midnight blue? In the *Foundations*, Frege seems to waver between two different answers. At times he seems to be saying that 'midnight blue' represents not the objective concept, but the sense-impression ("which we cannot know to agree with anyone else's," Frege, 1974, p. 36). But there are also many passages which seem to imply that all expressions purporting to represent subjective ideas in reality represent objective concepts. (This is also an essential premise of Frege's refutation of idealism. Cf. my *Reflections on Frege's Philosophy,* pp. 33–43.)

Color appears in Frege's philosophy either as a physical property of surfaces (which even a color-blind person could distinguish, Frege, 1974, p. 36), or else as a subjective sensation in the mind. The visible color of perceptual objects has disappeared from the world. Frege, like most philosophers of the last four hundred years, accepts unquestioningly the argument from physics. This comes as no surprise to us. But something else does. When Frege distinguishes between objects and concepts (functions), he applies this distinction only to the objective realm, not to the mind. But it is clear, as I have emphasized before, that a sensation, ontologically speaking, is just as much an object as a chair or the number two. And it is also perfectly obvious that this object has properties, that is, that it falls under certain concepts. Frege, we see, also makes the common mistake of thinking of the "color sensation" as being neither an individual nor a property. Or perhaps it would be more accurate to say that he simply never faces the question of whether it is an object or a concept.

To return to numbers, the number three, according to Frege, is not a sensible thing. There is no sense-impression as there is for the color midnight blue. But as soon as we distinguish, as we must, between a sensation and its properties, this claim is stripped of its plausibility. In what sense is there a sense-impression of the color? When we see a blue sweater, we experience under normal circumstances a blue sensation. We experience a sensation which has the same color as the sweater before us. The perceptual object shares the color with the sensation. The question, therefore, cannot be whether or not the number three is a sensation. The number three cannot be a sensation, just as the color cannot be a sensation. The question is, rather, whether or not sensations can be numbered, just as they can be blue. The answer to this question, I submit, is clear. Just as one may experience a *blue* sensation, so may one experience *two* sensations. When we look at the triangle of Frege's example and see that it has three sides, we experience three sensations (corresponding to the three sides), just as we experience a blue sensation if the triangle happens to be blue. (I do not wish to claim, of course, that these are all of the sensations which we experience, nor that we do not experience patterns of sensations rather than isolated sensations.) We conclude that, contrary to Frege's view, numbers are just as "sensible" as colors.

2) FREGE'S CONTEXT THESIS

In the *Foundations,* Frege's world divides into the realm of subjective ideas and the realm of objective objects and concepts. Numbers belong to the objective realm. How are we acquainted with them? Since numbers are not sensible things, according to Frege, it cannot be the senses that acquaint us with numbers. Thus it must be the understanding. Frege, as I said earlier, is forced to embrace rationalism. But I also said then that he adds a brilliant twist to the traditional dialectic.

When we look at a triangle, Frege says, we have a sense-impression that corresponds to the word 'triangular', but we do not have a corresponding sense-impression for the word 'three'; we do not see the three. Rather, we see "something upon which can fasten an intellectual activity of ours leading to a judgment in which the number three occurs" (Frege, 1974, p. 32). Frege is rather vague at this point. What precisely is it that we see? Is it the impression which we have? Or is it something else? If something else, what is it, and what is the difference, if any, between sensing, seeing, and judging? These important questions are not answered. But one thing is relatively clear: Frege claims that the number three appears as part of a *judgment*. From this remark and others, I have the impression that he distinguishes between the *experience* of subjective things, on the one hand, and *judgments* involving objective things, on the other. He holds that sensibility acquaints us with subjective things, while judgment is the eye that sees objective things. A color, for example, has both a subjective side and an objective side. It is a sensation in the mind and a concept in the objective world. The sensation is known through experience, that is, through sensibility. The objective concept, on the other hand, is known in a judgment. A number, in contrast to a color, is an objective thing (an object); there is no corresponding sensation. Hence it can only be known through judgment.

If judgment is the eye of the understanding, then it follows that all objective things are given to us within a context that is represented by a sentence; for judgments are expressed by sentences, not by words or phrases. This means that we shall not find the (objective) meaning (or referent) of a word, if we look for it outside of such a context. I believe that this is the point of Frege's famous principle, stated early in the *Foundations* (Frege, 1974, p. x.), that words have meaning only in the context of a sentence. Frege does not mean to subscribe to some kind of "meaning is use" doctrine as Dummett, for example, alleges (see M. Dummett, "Nominalism"). Rather, he claims that even though one can distinguish between different parts of the context represented by a sentence, these parts are never given separately to a mind. The only place where one finds the objective referent of a word is within the context of a judgment. Let us, for a moment, anticipate Frege's later distinction between the sense and the reference of a declarative sentence. In these terms, Frege claims that we are acquainted with objective things only by being presented with a whole thought, a thought which contains objective things—objects and concepts (functions)—as parts. (As I mentioned in connection with a discussion of Bolzano's "propositions," I think that the most fundamental flaw of Frege's ontology is his insistence that so-called thoughts are made up of senses rather than referents. This, of course, is a consequence of his view that a sentence refers to a truth-value. Cf. my *Reflections on Frege's Philosophy*, pp. 181–223.)

Objective things are presented to us in mental acts of judgment. Why does Frege hold this view? There are two clues in the *Foundations*. Firstly, he remarks that if one does not accept this view, then "one is almost forced to take as the meanings of words mental pictures or acts of the individual mind" (Frege, 1974, p. xxii). Secondly, he also says that only by adhering to his view can one "avoid a physical view of number without slipping into a psychological view of it" (Frege, 1974, p. 116). Let us try to reconstruct his train of thought.

Recall Kant's distinction between presentations, on the one hand, and judgments, on the other. Judgments, it is said, are based on presentations. Frege, I have just argued, changes this pattern. According to him, all presentations are mental. Acts of presentation acquaint us with nothing but subjective things. This leaves judgment as the only source of knowledge of objective entities. Thus Frege comes to hold that if we do not accept the view that objective things are presented in judgments, then they must be given through presentation. But if they are given in presentation, then they cannot really be objective; they must turn out to be "mental pictures or acts of the individual mind."

In order to understand Frege's thought behind the second quotation, we must again appeal to the Kantian foil. Presentations, according to Kant, divide into intuitions and concepts. Intuitions are particular (singular, individual), while concepts are universal (general). In this respect intutions and concepts resemble Frege's objects and concepts (functions). Now, Frege insists that numbers are objects rather than concepts. But this means, in Kantian terms, that they are intuitions rather than concepts. A Kantian would therefore conclude that if numbers are intuitions rather than concepts, they must be either "outer" or "inner" intuitions, that is, they must be either perceptual objects or else mental pictures. Frege argues that numbers are not perceptual objects (for example, against Mill). If he is correct, then they must be, according to the Kantian way of thinking, mental pictures. Frege tries to avoid this conclusion by arguing that even though numbers are "particular," they are not intuitions. They are neither "independent" outside objects nor "independent" inner pictures. Rather, they always occur dependently in certain contexts which are presented to judgment. In this fashion, I submit, he avoids "a physical view of number without slipping into a psychological one."

Frege's way out of the dilemma posed by the two alternatives that numbers are either individuals in the perceptual world or else individuals in the mind, becomes quite transparent in his later philosophy, which is centered around the category of thought. So-called thoughts (what a horrible misnomer!) are parts neither of the mind nor of the perceptual world. They are neither fish nor fowl. But they form the realm in which numbers dwell. They cannot be perceived; they can only be grasped by the understanding. This is the core of Frege's rationalism. But Frege, as we have just seen, adds what I earlier called a "twist" to the traditional rationalistic position: The eye of the understanding is propositional; it sees, not abstract things in isolation, but propositions (thoughts).

c) The Reduction of Arithmetic to Logic

I) THE IMPORTANCE OF DEFINITIONS

In the *Foundations,* Frege's aim is to make it "probable that the laws of arithmetic are analytic judgments and consequently a priori. Arithmetic thus becomes simply a development of logic, and every proposition of arithmetic a law of logic, albeit a derivative one" (Frege, 1974, p. 99). Frege contradicts Kant: Arithmetic is not synthetic, as Kant had proclaimed. How does Frege propose to show that arithmetic is analytic? A proposition is analytic, Frege explains, if and only if, in finding a proof for it, "we come only on general logic laws and on definitions, . . . bearing in mind that we must take account also of all propositions upon which the admissibility of any of the definitions depend" (Frege, 1974, p. 4). His task is perfectly clear: Frege must show that arithmetic propositions are really propositions of logic, and this can be achieved if it can be shown that the crucial arithmetic terms can be defined in logical terms.

Logicism stands or falls with the proper conception of definitions. In the *Foundations,* alas, there is no such conception. Instead, we find hints, allusions, and metaphors. In the last quotation, Frege speaks of propositions on which the admissibility of definitions depends. Assume for a moment that Frege were correct, that the number of F's is really the same entity as a certain extension. If this identity statement were true, then we could build a definition upon it. We could then conclude that a given numeral is just another sign for a certain extension, namely for the respective number. Schematically and in principle, assume that A = BC. Then we can of course use 'A' as just another expression for BC, and 'BC' as just another expression for A. Notice, however, that this is no longer true if 'A' or 'BC' are description expressions. From the fact that 'the number of F's describes the same thing as 'the extension of G', we must not conclude that these two expressions represent the same thing, that is, the same *description.* Rather, they represent different descriptions, but descriptions which describe the same thing (if Frege were correct). This is the vexing complication forced upon us by the existence of descriptions (and hence, of description expressions). If Frege thinks at this point of definitions as flowing from true identity statements in the manner just described, then his "reduction" of arithmetic to logic stands or falls with the truth or falsehood of the relevant identity statements. I have argued earlier that this particular and crucial identity statement is false.

But the *Foundations* also contains remarks to the effect that the crucial definitions are nothing but harmless abbreviation proposals. For example, on p. 78 he says: "The definition of an object does not, as such, really assert anything about the object, but only lays down the meaning of a symbol." In the same vein, we read in the *Grundgesetze:* "We introduce a new name by means of a *definition* by stipulating that it is to have the same sense and the same reference as some name composed of signs that are familiar" (G. Frege, *The Basic Laws of Arithmetic,* p. 82). On the whole, Frege is not too clear about the nature of definitions in the *Foundations.* He insists that definitions do not just specify concepts in terms of a list of characteristics, and then tries to illustrate their function by means of a geometrical example (Frege, 1974, pp. 100–101). Let concepts be represented by certain well-demarkated areas in a plane. A concept, defined by a list of characteristics (the "marks" of the concept), corresponds to an area which is common to all of those areas that represent the defining characteristics. No new line is drawn. We merely trace already existing lines in such a way that the new area, enclosed by the lines we trace, contains several of the original areas. For example, consider the two concepts (characteristics) *green* and *round.* We can introduce a new word 'ground' by stipulating that it shall be short for 'green and round', so that we can say 'A is ground' instead of 'A is green and round'. What we have done, in terms of the geometric picture, is to trace the lines which surround the two areas *green* and *round,* thus creating a larger area consisting of these two areas. That nothing new emerges in this way is obvious. In particular, it is clear that Frege's definition of the number of F's is not of this sort. Frege, therefore, wishes to contrast the "fruitful" definitions of the *Foundations* with these trivial conventions. The type of definition employed in the *Foundations,* he asserts, consists of drawing boundaries which did not previously exist. "What we shall be able to infer from it, cannot be inspected in advance; here, we are not simply taking out of the box again what we have just put into it" (Frege, 1974, pp. 100–101). But does this drawing of new boundaries not amount to the "creation" of concepts? And, surely, according to Frege's view, we can no more create concepts than we can create numbers. It took a while, as we shall see, before Frege fully realized that his reduction of arithmetic to logic requires a detailed analysis of the nature of definitions.

2) DETAILS OF THE REDUCTION

We know that Frege's attempt to reduce arithmetic to logic fails. It fails, for one, because extensions in Frege's sense do not exist. Rather, what there is that closely resembles such extensions are sets. But even if Fregean extensions existed, numbers are not identical with such extensions. If we try to improve on Frege's view by substituting sets for extensions, logicism does not fare any better. Firstly, numbers are not sets either. Secondly, even if they were sets, arithmetic would have been reduced to set theory rather than to logic.

But even though we know that Frege's philosophical goal cannot be achieved, we cannot but admire his ingenuity in regard to the details of the reduction. To exhibit this ingenuity, let us reconstruct Frege's steps from our point of view.

We start out with seven *abbreviations:*

(A_1) Let us agree to say for short 'the two-place relation R is *one-many*' instead of: 'the two-place relation R is such that for each second-place member of R there is exactly one first-place member of R which bears the relation R to that second-place member'.

(A_2) Let us agree to say for short 'the two-place relation is *many-one*' instead of: 'the two-place relation R is such that for each first-place member of R there is exactly one second-place member to which the first-place member bears the relation R'.

(A_3) Let us agree to say for short 'R is *one-one*' instead of: 'R is both one-many and many-one'.

(A_4) Let us agree to say for short 'the two-place relation R is a *correlator* between the two properties F and G (or between the two sets S_F and S_G)' instead of: 'the two-place relation R fulfills the following four conditions: (a) R is one-one, (b) the things which are F (which are members of S_F) are first-place members of R, (c) the things which are G (which are members of S_G) are second-place members of R, and (d) if any thing, say *a* is F (is a member of S_F), then the thing *b* which is related to *a* by R is G (is a member of S_G), and conversely'.

(A_5) Let us agree to say for short 'F and G are *similar* (S_F and S_G are similar) instead of: 'there exists a correlator between F and G (between S_F and S_G)'.

(A₆) Let us agree to say for short 'R is an *equivalence relation*' instead of: 'R is both symmetric and transitive'.

(A₇) Let us agree to say for short 'the property F is an *equivalence property with respect to R* (the set S_F is an equivalence set with respect to R)' instead of: 'F (S_F) fulfills the following two conditions: (a) R holds between any pair of things which are F (which are members of S_F), and (b) if any entity with the property F (any member of S_F) bears R to another thing, then the second entity is also F (belongs also to S_F)'.

Next, we have a number of true statements in which these abbreviations occur:

(T₁) If R is an equivalence relation, then the relational property of standing in the relation R to something (the set determined by this relational property) is an equivalence property (an equivalence set) with respect to R. (This follows from the fact that if R is both symmetric and transitive, then the relational property fulfills conditions (a) and (b) of (A₇).)

(T₂) Similarity is an equivalence relation. (This follows from the fact that it is symmetric and transitive.)

(T₃) The relational property of being similar to a given property (the set determined by the property of being similar to a given set) is an equivalence property with regard to similarity (is an equivalence set with regard to similarity). (This follows from (T₁) and (T₂).)

The following truths allow us to "connect" numbers with the abbreviations listed earlier:

(N₁) (a) There are o entities which are F (that are members of S_F) *if and only if* it is not the case that there is an entity which is F (which is a member of S_F).

(b) There is I entity which is F (which belongs to S_F) *if and only if* there is an entity e_1 such that any entity e_2 is F (belongs to S_F) if and only if e_2 is the same as e_1.

(c) And so on.

(N₂) (a) o is a number.

(b) I is a number.

(c) 2 is a number.

(d) And so on.

(N₃) Let N be any one of the natural numbers o, I, 2, etc., then:

(a) if there are N things which are F (which are members of S_F) and N things which are G (which belong to S_G), then F and G (S_F and S_G) are similar. (This follows from (N₁) and what we mean by 'similar'.)

(b) If there are N things which are F (which belong to S_F) and F is similar to G (S_F is similar to S_G), then there are N things which are G (which belong to S_G). (This, too, follows from (N₁) and the meaning of 'similar'.)

(c) If there are N things which are F (which belong to S_F), then there are N things which are G (which belong to S_G) *if and only if* F and G (S_F and S_G) are similar. (This follows from (a) and (b).)

(N₄) The "property" of there being N things with a given property (the set determined by the "property" of there being N things belonging to a given set) is an equivalence property (equivalence set) with respect to similarity. (This follows from (N₃), (c), and (A₇).)

(N₅) The set of sets which are similar to a given set S_F is the same as the set of sets which have the same number N of members as S_F. (This follows from (N₄) and (T₃).)

With these abbreviations and theorems at the ready, let us take another look at Frege's so-called definition. We shall assume that Frege's extensions are sets. And we shall also pretend for the time being that it makes sense to speak of the *property* of there being so-and-so many things which exemplify a certain property. In other words, we shall assume that numbers are properties of properties. If so, then it is true that a given "numerical property" U is coextensive with another property, namely, with the property of being similar to a certain property. Frege uses this fact, one may say, to get his definition: He identifies the numerical property with the set determined by the corresponding number. His definition, *after a fashion,* corresponds to our (N₅). But Frege reverses the order of introduction. He does not base (N₅), as I did, on certain statements about numbers. However, that does not really matter for my criticism. The fact remains that (N₅) is not a mere convention.

To round out the picture, let us briefly look at some steps of Frege's "reduction."

(1) Frege explains the expression 'the concept F is similar to the concept G' in the familiar fashion, corresponding to our (A₅) and the abbreviations that lead to it.

(2) He then "defines" the property of being a number as follows: "The expression 'N is a number' is to mean the same as the expression 'there exists a concept such that N is the number which belongs to it' " (Frege, 1974, p. 85).

Frege here treats his definition as a mere abbreviation proposal. But this appearance is deceptive. The word 'number' must always be taken in its ordinary and unproblematic meaning. With this ordinary meaning, it enters into the description expression 'the number which belongs to the concept F'. Since we understand this expression, we are in a position to decide whether or not Frege's so-called definition of the number of a concept is true. We are also in a position to decide whether or not Frege's "definition" of the concept number is *true;* for that "definition" is really an equivalence statement: All entities e are such that: e is a number *if and only if* there is a concept of which e is the number.

(3) Next, Frege proves that the number of F's is the same as the number of G's *if (and only if)* F is similar to G.

(4) He then "defines" individual numbers. The number o is "defined" as follows: "O is the number which belongs to the concept *not identical with itself*" (Frege, 1974, p. 87).

This corresponds to our (N₁), but differs from it importantly in that Frege mentions a definite "property" under which, as we know, nothing falls. This "property," in the spirit of the reduction, is conceived of as a "logical property." I would raise a minor objection: Identity, I think, is an ontological relation rather than a logical one. The law of self-identity, in my view, is an ontological rather than a logical law. It holds for all entities whatsoever.

(5) Next follows Frege's "definition" of the relation of immediate successor (in the series of natural numbers): "The expression 'there exists a concept f, and an object falling under it x, such that the number which belongs to the concept f is N and the number which belongs to the concept *falling under f but not identical with x* is M' is to mean the same as 'N follows in the series of natural numbers directly after M' (Frege, 1974, p. 89).

Here again we have a true equivalence statement rather than a linguistic convention.

(7) Finally, in sketching the proof for a certain theorem, Frege mentions the crucial "definition" of the ancestral relation of a relation R: "The proposition 'if every object to which X stands in the relation R falls under the concept F, and if from the proposition that d falls under the concept F it follows universally, whatever d may be, that every object to which d stands in the relation R falls under the concept F, then Y falls under the concept F, whatever F may be' is to mean the same as 'Y follows in the R-series after X'" (Frege, 1974, p. 92).

Frege mentions in passing that only by means of this "definition" is it possible to reduce the argument from n to (n + 1) to the general laws of logic. The "reduction" proceeds along the following line. Applying the general "definition" to the special case of the series of natural numbers, we discover that Y follows in the series after X if and only if Y has all the properties which (a) belong to X, and (b) are such that if they belong to any given number, they belong also to the number which follows in the series of natural numbers directly after the given number. Furthermore, it is also true that N is a natural number if and only if N is either the number 0, or else N has all the properties which (a) belong to 0, and (b) are such that if they belong to any number M, they also belong to whatever follows in the series of natural numbers directly after M. If one reformulates the principle of mathematical induction according to these "definitions," then the principle turns into the following truth:

If F is a property which (a) belongs to 0, and (b) is such that if it belongs to any number M, it also belongs to whatever follows in the series of natural numbers directly after M, then F belongs to everything which is either identical with 0 or has all the properties which (a) belong to 0, and (b) are such that if they belong to any object M, they belong also to whatever follows in the series of natural numbers directly after M.

After this brief survey of Frege's brilliant chain of "reductive steps," let us cast one last look at the principle of his reduction. As our example, we shall take his "definition" of 0:

(1) 0 = the number which belongs to the concept *not identical with itself.*
This is an informative identity statement. The number 0 is described as the number of a certain concept (property). Add to (1) the following proposition:

(2) The number of the concept *not identical with itself* is identical with the extension (set) of the concept of *being similar to the concept of not being identical with itself,* and you get:

(3) o = The extension (set) of the concept of *being similar to the concept of not being identical with itself.*

(3) describes the number o in purely logical terms, assuming that the notion of the extension of a concept is a purely logical notion. But in order to arrive at this description, we started with (1) which is not a *logical* truth, and we had to add (2) which, according to our view, *is not even true!* What Frege does in this case, from our point of view, is to start with a true description of the number o, add to this description the false assertion that the number is an extension, and conclude, mistakenly, that o is an extension. None of these three statements is a pure logical truth.

3) FREGE'S LATER THOUGHTS ABOUT DEFINITIONS

The so-called definitions of the *Foundations* are informative identity statements (or informative equivalences) and, as such, are not derived from harmless abbreviations. Like all such statements, they must either be shown to be true or else admitted as axioms. In the *Foundations,* Frege had as yet not developed his view about informative identity statements in terms of the distinction between sense and reference. It is clear that this view does not change the general picture which I have drawn of Frege's attempt to reduce arithmetic notions to logical ones. The dialectic remains the same. Definitions will serve Frege's purpose only if they are either straightforward abbreviation proposals or else identity statements derived from such proposals. Any other kind of statement, in particular, informative identity and equivalence statements, will not do.

It is not surprising, given Frege's high stakes, that he returned time and again to the question of what, precisely, the powers and limits of definitions are. For example, in a letter to Hilbert of 1900, Frege remarks: "In thinking about definitions, I have been tightening my requirements more and more, to the point where I have moved so far from the opinions of most mathematicians that communication has become very difficult" (G. Frege, *Philosophical and Mathematical Correspondence.* p. 45). But his most detailed attempt to describe the nature of definitions can be found in the unpublished manuscript *Logic in Mathematics* (probably from 1914) (In G. Frege, *Posthumous Writings*).

A genuine definition (eigentliche Definition), Frege says there, has the following characteristics: (1) It introduces a simple expression for a complex expression; (2) the simple expression receives the same sense as the complex expression; (3) such definitions are not really necessary for a system, since the new signs do not really add anything new, but merely allow for more manageable expressions; (4) after the simple expression has received its meaning (sense), the definition is transformed into an identity statement; (5) but this identity statement is tautological and does not extend our knowledge (Frege, 1979, pp. 207–208). Frege here describes what I have called "abbreviation proposals." (There is a difference between us, though, because I do not make his sense-reference distinction.) It is obvious, as I have emphasized time and again, that these definitions are ontologically harmless. However, Frege's so-called definitions in the *Foundations* and elsewhere are obviously not of this sort. And Frege comes close to admitting this fact when he says:

> Indeed, no truth must become provable by means of a definition which otherwise would be unprovable. Whenever something that purports to be a definition makes the proof of a truth possible, we do not have a genuine definition. Rather, this definition must contain something which must be either proven as a theorem or else acknowledged to be an axiom.
>
> (Frege, 1979b, p. 208; my translation)

Genuine definitions, according to Frege, must be distinguished from *logical analysis:*

> As little as it can be indifferent whether or not I analyze a body chemically in order to see what its elements are, as little can it be unimportant whether I undertake a logical analysis of a logical structure in order to learn what its components are, or leave it unanalyzed, as if it were simple, when in fact it is complex.
>
> (Frege, 1979b, pp. 208–209; my translation from the German)

Definitions, conceived of as instances of logical analysis, are far from harmless, for they make proofs possible which otherwise would have been impossible. The importance of such analyses can be seen if we recall Frege's treatment of the quantified propositions *All F are G, Some F are G,* etc. His analysis, far from being harmless or trivial, had the most far-reaching consequences for logic and ontology.

Frege concludes his investigation into the nature of definitions by distinguishing between two cases. Firstly, we may build up a sense from other senses and introduce a completely new and simple sign for the complex sense: "One could call this constructive definition (aufbauende Definition); but we shall simply call it definition" (Frege, 1979b, p. 210). Secondly, an expression may have been in use for some time, but we believe that its sense can be analyzed in such a way that we can more perspicuously represent this sense by a certain complex expression (with the same sense as the original expression). Frege thinks that it would be best not to speak in this second case of definition, because we are here dealing with an axiom: "In this second case, there remains no room for an arbitrary decision, because the simple sign already has a sense. One can only arbitrarily assign a sense to an expression which does not already have a sense" (Frege, 1979b, p. 210).

Let us take another look at Frege's "definition" of zero:

(Z) 0 = the number which belongs to the concept *not identical with itself.*

It is obvious that this is not a harmless abbreviation proposal or the result of one. Rather, the right side of (Z) is supposed to elucidate the ordinary meaning of '0'. Is it then an instance of logical analysis as understood by the later Frege? It appears so. An entirely new and different conception of the reduction of arithmetic to logic emerges in this case; for Frege gives us the following method of deciding whether or not a commonly used expression—in our case, 'o'—has the same sense as a complex expression arrived at after analysis—in our case, 'the number which belongs to the concept *not identical with itself*. We are to introduce a new sign, say '#', as an abbreviation for the longer expression, and ask whether or not this sign has the same sense as 'o'. Frege claims that we can avoid giving a direct answer to this question by rebuilding our system (of arithmetic, in our example), not using 'o', but using '#' instead:

> If we now succeed in this fashion to build the system of mathematics without needing the sign 'A' ['o'], then we can leave it at that and we do not need to answer the question: With what sense has 'A' ['o'] been used previously? This is the unobjectionable way of doing it. However, it may be convenient to use the sign 'A' ['o'] instead of the sign 'C' ['#']. But then we have to treat it as a newly introduced sign which had no sense before it was defined.
>
> (Frege, 1979b, p. 211; my translation)

A straightforward application of Frege's method is complicated by the fact that in (Z) we have, on the one hand, a name of the number zero and, on the other, a description expression for this number. According to Frege's sense-reference distinction, the name may be associated with any one of a great number of senses. Let us assume, however, that it does have the same sense as the description expression and, hence, also the same reference. But we shall pretend that we do not know that it has the same sense. Everything now depends on whether or not we succeed in building the system of arithmetic by using '#' instead of 'o'. But what is this system? Is it the system which, among other things, contains such truths as: 1 is the immediate successor of o? If so, how can we decide whether our new system contains this proposition? The new system will presumably contain the sentence: '1 is the immediate successor of the number which belongs to the concept *not identical with itself*, but does this sentence represent the proposition that 1 is the immediate successor of o? The only way to answer this question, it seems to me, is to decide whether or not 'o' has the same sense as the description expression. Thus we are back to our original question. Following Frege's instruction, we tried to avoid a direct answer to the question of whether or not 'o' has the same sense as the description expression by constructing arithmetic in terms of the description expression rather than the name. But then we are faced with the question of whether or not we have indeed constructed arithmetic rather than something else. And this question, it seems to me, cannot be answered unless we can first decide whether or not the name has the same sense as the description expression.

Within our view, naturally, the situation is quite different. Since 'o' does not have a sense, but only a reference, namely, the number zero, the question cannot be whether or not the name and the description expression have the same sense. However, for a description expression we must distinguish between the description which it represents and the thing which it describes. Obviously, the number is not identical with the description represented by the expression. Thus the question can only be: is the number zero the same as the thing described by the description? In this case, the answer is affirmative. (Z) is a true (informative) identity statement. Since (Z) is true, it is also true that since 1 is the successor of 0, 1 is the successor of the number of the concept *not being identical with itself*. But notice that on our view these propositions, though both true, are not the same. The state of affairs that 1 is the successor of 0 is not the same as the state of affairs that 1 is the successor of the number of the concept *not identical with itself*. Do we have a system of arithmetic if we replace the name by the description expression (and other names by other expressions)? The answer is obvious: As long as we talk in our system about the number zero, by means of whatever description expression, we are doing arithmetic. It does not matter how we describe the number, as long as we talk about it and not about something else. There are weird descriptions of zero and, hence, weird ways of saying that 1 is the successor of 0, but what is said, as distinguished from how it is said, is all that matters to the subject matter called "arithmetic."

In summary Frege's reduction of arithmetic to logic fails because numbers are not extensions. They are not extensions because, as Russell's paradox shows, there are no extensions. (But there are sets!) Even if there were extensions, numbers would not be extensions, because numbers are quantifiers. All of this assumes that if there were extensions, they would be "logical things." If we think of extensions as sets, constituted in their being, not by properties (concepts), but by their members, then the reduction fails for these two reasons: Firstly, once again, it is false that numbers are sets; secondly, even if they were sets, the reduction would at best reduce arithmetic to set theory, not to logic.

B. Systematic Considerations

ONE

███

Introductory Remarks

a) Three Fundamental Theses

In the *Foundations*, Frege raises and answers two questions:
 (1) What are natural numbers and how do we know them?
 (2) What is the nature of arithmetic truth?
His answers are:
 (1') Natural numbers are extensions of concepts, and these extensions are
 presented to us in certain judgments.
 (2') Arithmetic truths are analytic and, therefore, a priori.
I have explained that I disagree with both of Frege's answers. I argued that numbers are not extensions. Nor are they sets. Rather, they belong to a category of their own, the category of quantifier. Furthermore, certain natural numbers are presented to us in perception. We perceive these numbers in the same sense and just as directly as we perceive colors and pitches. In regard to Frege's second answer, I argued that arithmetic truths are synthetic, as Kant claimed. They are also a priori. But they are a priori, not in that they are "known independently of experience," but in that they are necessary and universal. We cut the connection with Kant's transcendental idealism by asserting that Kant's axiom is false that what is necessary and universal must be independent of experience. Thus, while we agree with Kant that arithmetic truths are necessary and universal, we insist also that they are "known empirically." This is our empiricism. We shall now go on to defend our answers to Frege's two questions against some more recent objections and to elaborate on these answers in the full light of contemporary philosophical wisdom.

But before we begin, I shall list some of our most basic assumptions. In philosophy, perhaps more than anywhere else, there is the danger that one loses sight of the woods in favor of the trees. The details of our view may obscure the philosophical framework within which it is developed. Nor could it be amiss to remind the reader that our view, like any other, rests on several metaphysical assumptions. Let me mention three such assumptions which are of special importance.

Firstly, we embrace the thesis of "semantic atomism." What a sentence represents, the state of affairs it is about, is determined in part by what the words in the sentence represent, and not the other way around. I pointed out earlier that this thesis is not contradicted by Frege's famous rule never to ask for the meaning of a word in isolation, but only in the context of a sentence. As I explained, Frege's claim is not that one must know what a sentence says before one can know what the words in it mean, but rather that acquaintance with abstract objects is propositional. It seems obvious to me that the opposing view has things upside down, as upside down as the verificationist view that the meaning of a sentence is its method of verification. It seems obvious to me that one has to know first what a sentence says, before one can think of how it is to be verified.

Secondly, we accept the thesis that truth is univocal: Statements of arithmetic (and of set theory and logic) are true (or false) in precisely the same sense in which statements of physics or botany are true or false. What distinguishes between a true statement of arithmetic and a true statement of botany is the subject matter: The former is about numbers, the latter is about plants.

Thirdly, there is the so-called "principle of acquaintance," the foundation of our empiricism. We know what there is by perception and introspection, or else by inference from these. The first alternative takes care of chairs, colors, and shapes, but also of (small) numbers and sets. The second accounts for our knowledge of elementary particles, black holes, and spin, but also for our knowledge of the higher infinites and of large sets. In particular, I claim that we know by acquaintance that there are certain numbers, and that we know by inference that there are others.

b) Apeirophobia

While I am at it, I may as well add some further, very general, observations. These ruminations are not meant to strengthen my view, but to put it in the proper perspective.

My view is free from apeirophobia, the horror of the infinite, which colored so much of what was written at the beginning of this century about the foundations of mathematics. I call it a phobia because, as Benacerraf and Putnam point out, there are few if any arguments against the infinite in the relevant literature (see *Philosophy of Mathematics,* ed. by P. Benacerraf and H. Putnam, p. 5). But it is clear that there are two worries about the infinite. The first is whether or not the notion of the infinite makes any sense; the second, whether or not there is such a thing, given that the notion does make sense.

How do we form the notion of the infinite? How do we come by it? I shall concede immediately that we are not acquainted with an infinity of things (with an infinite set of things). Here lies a fundamental difference between the notion of the number two, for example, and the notion of the denumerable infinite: while we perceive the number two, we never perceive the number aleph zero. But it does not follow that we have no notion of aleph zero, that we have no concept of it. We have notions of many things with which we are not acquainted. Such things we know, as Russell pointed out a long time ago, by description. Even though I am not acquainted with aleph zero, I can nevertheless describe it, as Frege does, as the number of natural numbers (G. Frege, *The Foundations of Arithmetic,* p. 96). Moreover, we have a notion of infinite numbers in general, that is, of infinite number: An infinite number is distinguished from a finite number in that only an infinite number is such that a set with infinitely many members has subsets which are similar to it. I trust that I do not have to go on. By now it may be conceded by everyone familiar with the technical aspects of set theory that there are descriptions of transfinite numbers.

But are these descriptions consistent? There used to be much to do about the question of whether or not the notion of an infinite number is consistent. Hilbert and his followers demanded a proof of its consistency. This demand, I submit, is an expression of apeirophobia. Why should one suspect the notion of the infinite to be inconsistent, unless one is unduly afraid of it? I find nothing in or about the notion of aleph zero that smells of inconsistency. Of course, in such matters, intuition is merely the first court of appeal. Who would have thought that there are properties, like the property of being a set (or of being a Fregean extension!), which do not determine sets? I do not wish to give the impression that my intuitions somehow *show* that the description of aleph zero is consistent. But I am not weary of it, and I am perfectly willing to accept it until a contradiction crops up.

Entirely different is the question of whether or not something answers to the description. Is there such a number as aleph zero? Of course, if the description is inconsistent, then there can be no such number. But the description may be perfectly consistent and yet not describe anything. It is also clear that if there are denumerably many things, then aleph zero exists. But are there? Hilbert argued that there are not, but I am not convinced (see D. Hilbert, "On the Infinite", pp. 136–37). Nor am I convinced that the world is finite. I simply have no firm opinion on this matter. But there are a few things I am relatively certain of. For example, if it is not the case that there are denumerably infinitely many things, then aleph zero does not exist, for numbers are numbers of things, just as colors are colors of things. If there were no olive green things, then the color olive green would not exist. If there were no five things (of any kind), then the number five would not exist. But even though it may be the case that aleph zero does not exist, we can still speculate about what would be the case if it existed. If there were such a number, for example, then it would be smaller than the number, if it existed, of the subsets of any set with aleph zero many members. The whole theory of transfinite cardinals can be treated in this fashion as being about things which may or may not exist, but which, if they do exist, behave just as described by the theory.

c) Intuitionism and Impredicative Descriptions

I have commented on Hilbert's concern about the consistency of the notion of the infinite and on what may be called "Russell's concern" about the truth of the axiom of infinity. In the literature, one finds a third worry, namely, the worry that certain "totalities" are not well-defined. Or perhaps it is more accurate to say that we find the suspicion that these totalities are not well-defined and, based on this suspicion, the view that statements about such totalities do not have a truth-value unless they can be proved or disproved in a certain way. Infinite totalities like the set of all natural numbers are under suspicion. I shall confess immediately that I do not fully understand the intuitionist's attitude, but I shall make a stab at explaining its source. It seems to me that this source is the belief that certain paradoxes are the result of a vicious circle, and that one can only avoid them by shunning so-called "impredicative definitions." Let us then briefly refresh our memory of how Russell at one time, and Poincaré consistently, diagnosed the trouble caused by certain paradoxes.

In my view, all of the so-called paradoxes—the logical, set-theoretic, and semantic ones—are nothing but proofs that certain things do not exist, (cf. my "Russell's Paradox and Complex Properties", and also *The Categorial Structure of the World*, p. 223–37). What makes these non-existence proofs paradoxical is the fact that they clash with our most basic intuitions. For example, it is fairly obvious that the color olive green is not olive green and that the property of being square is not square. What could be more self-evident, therefore, than that these two properties *share the property of not exemplifying themselves?* For, olive green does not exemplify itself and neither does the property of being square. But we can easily prove that this self-evident thesis is false, for we can prove that there is no such property as the property of not exemplifying oneself. The assumption that there is such a property, call it "F", leads to the conclusion that F is F if and only if F is not F. Or consider the property of being a set. That there is such a property cannot be doubted, for if it did not exist, then there would be no sets, and there are sets. Is it not also certain, indubitable, self-evident, that this property, like every other property we can think of, determines a set? Must there not be the set of all of those things which have this property, that is, which are sets? But we can prove that there is no such set. The assumption that this set exists, leads to a contradiction. What the paradoxes teach us, a lesson some refuse to learn, is that we must forever be ready to revise our most cherished intuitions about what there is.

The so-called semantic paradoxes are in this respect not different from the logical and set-theoretic ones. Consider Grelling's paradox. We assume that a predicate has a certain property, the property of being *heterological,* if and only if it does not have the property which it represents. The word 'long', for example, is heterological because it is not long. What about the predicate 'heterological'; is it heterological or not? It can easily be shown that it is heterological if and only if it is not heterological. From this consequence, I conclude that there is no such property as the property of being heterological. By now, I think, we are reminded of Russell's ramified theory of types and his short-lived attempt to blame the paradoxes on a vicious circle. I shall therefore be very brief; for our goal is not to revisit those ill-conceived attempts to get rid of the paradoxes, but to understand the intuitionist's notion of a totality that is not "well-defined."

It is customary to speak of "*impredicative definitions,*" but it should be obvious that one is dealing with impredicative *descriptions*. The difference in terminology may appear to be slight and inconsequential, but we must never forget that the word 'definition' carries with it an aura of convention, of mere stipulation, which is absent from the term 'description'. There are true and false descriptions, but most philosophers would hesitate to admit that there are true and false definitions. Now, Russell, as I remarked, at one point blamed a vicious circle for the paradoxes (see B. Russell, "Mathematical Logic as Based on the Theory of Types"). He observed that the paradoxes can be created by using descriptions which contain universal or existential quantifiers that range over the kind of entity to which the described thing belongs. Recall for example the description of the alleged property of not exemplifying itself: The f such that: for all properties g, g is f if and only if g is not g. This description mentions all properties g, and this is obviously a totality to which f itself belongs. Or consider the following description of the set of all sets: The set s such that: for all sets t, t is a member of s. Here the totality of all sets to which s itself belongs is mentioned.

Russell therefore suggested to cure us of paradox by banning all such "impredicative" descriptions. But this cure is almost as bad as the disease. It led Russell to the ramified theory of types and, hence, to the infamous axiom of reducibility. More to the point, it rested on the wrong diagnosis. Impredicative descriptions cannot be blamed for the paradoxes. Cantor's paradox, for example, cannot be laid at the doorstep of the description just mentioned, for it appears also if we describe the set s in a predicative way: The set s such that: everything which is a set is a member of it. This description is no more impredicative than the description of the set of all olive green things as the set such that everything which is olive green belongs to it. Nor does every impredicative description lead to paradox. Dedekind's impredicative description of the square root of 2, as far as we know, does not lead to paradox. Furthermore, the following description is impredicative: The person who is as tall or taller than any person in the room right now where I am working. Yet, this description actually describes a person and cannot, therefore, harbor a contradiction.

Our conclusion that impredicative descriptions cannot be blamed for the paradoxes is not surprising in the light of our own analysis of the situation. The paradoxes, I claimed, are straightforward nonexistence proofs which insult our most firmly held convictions. If this is correct, then there exists a proof that there is no such thing as the set of all sets. But, surely, the existence or nonexistence of this set does not depend on how we describe it, predicatively or impredicatively. If there is no such set, then there is no set to which all the things belong which have the property of being a set, nor is there the set such that all sets belong to it.

Russell does not explain clearly why he thinks that impredicative descriptions create paradoxes. He says: "In each contradiction something is said about *all* cases of some kind, and from what is said a new case seems to be generated, which both is and is not of the same kind as the cases of which *all* were concerned in what was said" (Russell, 1956, p. 61). A little later, he adds: "Thus all our contradictions have in common the assumption of a totality such that, if it were legitimate, it would at once be enlarged by new members defined in terms of itself" (Russell, 1956, p. 63). This is one place where our insistence that we are dealing with impredicative descriptions rather than definitions is of great importance. As soon as we abandon Russell's talk about impredicative definitions, we realize that there can be no talk about "generating a new case." We do not generate a thing by describing it. Nor can we "enlarge a totality" by describing something in terms of it. If we describe the square root of 2 as the least upper bound of the numbers whose square is at most 2, we do not "generate" or "create" that number. The square root of 2 is one of the numbers whose square is at most 2. It is not added to the totality of these numbers by our describing it.

Russell was not the only one who pointed the finger at impredicative descriptions. Poincaré announced that a definition is logically admissible only if it excludes all objects which are dependent on the notion to be defined (see H. Poincaré, "Les mathematiques et la logic,"). This sounds like nothing more than an injunction against circular definitions. But I believe that Poincaré had something else in mind. Before we get to what I take to be his point, we should ask: What does circularity have to do with paradox?

Everyone agrees that circular definitions are worthless. They do not accomplish what they are supposed to. But, granted that they are worthless, do they give rise to paradox? I do not see how they possibly could. It is not even *true* that impredicative descriptions are circular. The square root of 2 is the same as the number which is the least upper bound of the numbers whose square root is at most 2. One and the same number is described in two different ways. Let us say, for short, that two different features determine the same number. We could say that the two features have the same extension, that they are "equivalent." All the different descriptions of the same thing are of this sort: they involve equivalent features which determine the same thing. Now, if impredicative descriptions had to be shunned because they are circular, and if their circularity consisted in that they involve equivalent features, then all true identity statements with description expressions would have to be banned. Zermelo thought that this, indeed, is a consequence of Poincaré's criticism of impredicative descriptions: "Strict observance of Poincaré's demand [to exclude all impredicative definitions] would make every definition, hence all of science, impossible" (see E. Zermelo, "Neuer Beweis fuer die Moeglichkeit einer Wohlordnung," p. 191).

But Poincaré, as I hinted a moment ago, is not making the trivial point that circular definitions are worthless. I believe that something more interesting is on his mind, something that leads us back to intuitionism and ill-defined totalities. As I see it, the description of the square root of 2 as the least upper bound of certain numbers is to be banished because it involves the notion of number. The notion of the square root of 2 must be exorcized from the notion of all numbers before the latter can be used to describe the former; for the notion of the square root of 2 is somehow contained in the notion of all numbers. According to this line of reasoning, the notion of all numbers consists in part of the notion of the square root of 2. Therefore, in order to have the notion of all numbers, one must already have the notion of the square root of 2.

The set of all real numbers *contains* the square root of 2. But we are not talking about this set and its members. Rather, we are talking about certain notions, certain concepts, namely, the notion *all numbers* and the notion *square root of* 2. And what Poincaré claims, according to my interpretation, is that the former notion somehow consists in part of the latter. But this seems to me to be a mistake. Taking for granted that 'all numbers' is short for 'all things which are numbers', what this expression represents consists, among other things, of the property of being a number, but it does not contain the square root of 2 or the property of being a square root of 2. In order to have a notion of all numbers, to put it differently, one needs to have a notion of the property of being a number, but one need not have the concept of the square root of 2. Surely, there are many numbers you have never thought of, and yet you know perfectly well what you mean by 'all numbers'. Similarly, what such expressions as 'all sets', 'all properties', and 'all elephants' represent involve, among other things, the properties of being a set, of being a property, and of being an elephant. What they represent does not consist, in part, of the set of odd natural numbers, the property of being square, and the elephant Dumbo from the San Diego zoo.

It may be objected that we cannot acquire the concept of number without first acquiring the different concepts of all individual numbers. But this objection is so obviously misguided in regard to other notions that there is no reason to believe that it works for numbers. For example, we acquire the notion of olive green without having become acquainted with all of the olive green things in the world. Nor do we acquire the notion of an elephant by having thought of all individual elephants. How do we acquire these concepts? The answer is obvious. Some things are olive green, and on some occasion we notice that one of these things has this particular color. Similarly, some things are numbers; they have the property of being a number. The number two has this property, and so does the square root of 2. We acquire the concept of number by noticing, for example, that the number two is a number. A single act of perception is sufficient, just as in the case of olive green. Of course, we may have been in the presence of olive green things before, without perceiving that they were olive green or that olive green is a color. And we may have been in the presence of numbered things before, without perceiving how many of them there are or that their number has the property of being a number. What this shows is that it may take time before some property is perceived, not that we cannot perceive it. It is also clear that it may take a higher mental development to perceive such "higher" features as those of being a color, of being a number, or of being a set, than what is required for the perception of olive green, of the number two, and of the set of three pencils on my desk. But, again, this does not diminish the fact that such "abstract" properties can be perceived, and that they can be perceived in single acts of perception.

My reply to this last objection gives us a clue why an intuitionist may hold that impredicative descriptions are flawed and that ill-defined totalities are illegitimate. My reply assumes that there are such properties as the color olive green, being a color, and being a number. If we reject this ontological premise, then our reply to Poincaré will not do. If the word 'number' represents, not a property which many individual numbers share, but instead (as one says: commonly or indifferently) every individual number, then we could not possibly perceive what the word represents by perceiving an individual number. The view that 'number' is a *common name* of individual numbers rather than the proper name of the property of being a number may easily be taken to imply that we do not fully understand the word until we are familiar with all numbers. It may be taken to imply, to get back to our example, that we cannot fully understand 'number' in the description expression for the square root of 2, unless we are already familiar with the square root of 2. We are faced with the following dilemma: Either one knows the square root of 2, in which case one need not define it; or else one does not know it, in which case one cannot define it in terms of the notion of number, for one does not have this notion. In this manner, I suggest, the common name doctrine of "general terms" may lead to a rejection of impredicative descriptions. But if this is the source of the intuitionist's worry, then we need not share it, for the common name doctrine is quite obviously false. If it were true, then it would follow that we do not know what ordinary property words mean (represent). But we do know what they mean. The fact that we talk intelligibly about elephants, colors, and numbers, without being acquainted (in whatever fashion) with all elephants, all colors, and all numbers, reduces the common name doctrine to absurdity.

d) "Mengenfurcht" and "Mengenliebe"

The development of set theory is not only a monumental intellectual achievement, but also of great philosophical significance; for it amounts to nothing less than the discovery of an ontological category and its laws. This point needs emphasis. All too often, set theory is thought of as a branch of mathematics. In reality, it reaches far beyond mathematics. Of course, the most fascinating sets are infinite sets and, among these, sets of points and sets of numbers. But we must keep in mind that there are sets of peas and sets of pitches as well. The notion of a set, in short, is not a mathematical but an ontological notion, even though the most interesting sets are sets of mathematical things. (The situation is similar for relations: the notion of a relation is not a mathematical notion, even though some of the most interesting relations are relations among numbers.)

Set theory, to say it again, is nothing less than the theory of an ontological category. No wonder that its discovery and development met, on the one hand, with utmost suspicion and outright hostility and, on the other, with boundless enthusiasm. While philosophically-minded mathematicians often went so far as to suspect the very notion of a set, mathematically-minded philosophers soon elevated sets to the only category worthy of their attention. While the former blamed the set-theoretic paradoxes on the very notion of a set, the latter replaced properties by sets, relations by ordered sets, and, ultimately, philosophy by set theory. Both extremes are equally foolish. We must not succumb to "Mengenfurcht." But we must also beware of the laughable view that philosophy is nothing but applied set theory.

Benacerraf and Putnam remark that today "very few philosophers and mathematicians of any school would maintain that the notion of, say, an arbitrary set of real numbers is a completely clear one, or that all the mathematical statements one can write down in terms of this notion have a truth-value which is well-defined in the sense of being fixed by a rule—even a nonconstructive rule—which does not assume that the notion of an "arbitrary set" has already been made clear" (Benacerraf and Putnam, p. 15). I doubt that this is really true for mathematicians, as Benacerraf and Putnam claim. But be that as it may, it seems to me that the notion of an arbitrary set is no less clear than most notions in arithmetic, geometry, and physics. Ordinarily, we think of sets as being determined by properties, for example, by the property of being a planet that orbits the sun. But the existence of a set, we must constantly remind ourselves, does not depend on the existence of a "determining" property. The set whose only members are the color olive green, the moon, and Napoleon, exists just as truly as the set of planets, although it may well be the case that it has no "determining" property. And the axiom of choice, which I acknowledge without a moment's hesitation to be a truism, explicitly states that there are "arbitrary" sets (cf. Goedel's comment on the axiom of choice in his "What is Cantor's Continuum Problem," p. 259, footnote 2). No, neither the notion of a set nor the notion of an arbitrary set contains a confusion or ambiguity.

Nor do I share the peculiar view of those who hold, in Benacerraf's and Putnam's words, that "if we can show that a proposition is *undecidable* from the assumptions we currently accept, the question of its 'truth' or 'falsity' vanishes in a puff of metaphysical smoke" (Benacerraf and Putnam, p. 15). I call this view "peculiar" because it is hard for me to imagine that even the most "formalistically" inclined philosopher can fail to acknowledge after Goedel that truth is one thing, derivability quite another. Of course, if a proposition is undecidable from our current assumptions (axioms), then we do not know whether it is true or false. But it is silly to conclude from our ignorance that "since nothing else is relevant, the question of truth does not arise" (Benacerraf and Putnam, p. 15). Quite to the contrary, the question of truth becomes all the more pressing. As long as we do not merely play the game of trying to find out what follows from what, but are interested in truth at all, we must face up to the question of whether or not the proposition in question is true; for, if it is true, we must add it to our axioms, and if it is false, we must not. The situation is no different in set theory from what it is in geometry and physics. What would we think of a physicist who claims that the question of truth does not arise for what looks like a basic thesis of physics because he has just discovered that this thesis does not follow from the accepted assumptions of physics? Or what would we make of a geometer who declares that the question of truth does not arise for the parallel axiom since it is independent of his other axioms? Axiomatization is the servant of truth, not its master!

The situation in set theory (and arithmetic) is in this respect not different from the situation in physics or botany. In particular, there is no reason in the world why the continuum hypothesis should be treated differently from hypotheses in other fields of inquiry. Since it is independent of the standard axioms of set theory, the question arises naturally whether or not it is true and, hence, if true, should be added to the axioms. Considerations of the sort listed by Goedel suggest that the continuum hypothesis is false (Goedel, 1964b, pp. 266–68). If so, then it should of course be rejected. It would be comforting, needless to say, if we could discover a set-theoretical truth which is (a) independent of the standard axioms, and (b) together with these axioms implies the falsehood of the continuum hypothesis. We shall have to hope for such a fortuitous event.

It must have occurred to other philosophers that there is a certain irony to the fact that while philosophically-minded mathematicians often are leery of set theory, mathematically-minded philosophers substitute set theory for philosophy. If the notion of set is that unclear, that suspect, then it would surely be prudent not to treat set theory as if it contained the solutions to all philosophical problems. But if you look at the philosophical journals, you may conclude that a surprising number of philosophers cannot deal with a philosophical problem unless they have first transformed it into a problem of constructing some kind of set-theoretical model. Perhaps it is not too far from the truth that while some mathematicians live in dread of set theory because of its affinity to philosophers, some so-called philosophers worship it because of its distance from philosophy.

T W O

The Argument from Causal
Interaction

a) The Platonic Dogma

Past and present philosophers seem to agree that, whatever else may be true of numbers, numbers cannot be perceived. Steiner, for example, says that "No one today, however, upholds hard-core intuition—the direct intuition of mathematical objects, the first type of mathematical intuition mentioned above. No one, with the possible exception of Goedel on one reading of the passage quoted above, claims to having perception of individual numbers" (M. Steiner, *Mathematical Knowledge,* p. 131). If Steiner is correct, then there are at most two people who believe that we can perceive numbers, namely, Goedel and Grossmann. I must confess that I find the company congenial. However, I am not sure that Goedel really shares my view, for he does not speak univocally about perception in regard to numbers. The fact remains that the overwhelming majority of contemporary philosophers consider my view to be doubtful at best, absurd at worst. What accounts for this unanimity? What is responsible for this conviction?

It seems that the common view is based on a certain type of argument to the effect that we cannot perceive numbers because we cannot causally interact with them. I shall call this "the argument from causal interaction." Before we take a close look at it, let us locate it in the philosophical landscape.

Let us go backward, from the conclusion to the premises:
   (1) We cannot perceive numbers (and sets), because they are abstract things, that is, things that are not spatio-temporal.
   (2) Only spatio-temporal entities can be perceived.
Why can we not perceive abstract things?
   (3) Perception is a matter of causal interaction between the perceiver and the perceived object.
   (4) Abstract things cannot causally interact with anything; in particular, they cannot interact with perceivers.

The argument thus rests, firstly, on a certain view about causality, according to which abstract things cannot causally interact; and, secondly, on a certain view about perception, according to which perception is a matter of causal interaction between perceiver and perceived object. It must be emphasized that these two somewhat dubious views are combined for one and only one purpose, namely, to make premise (2) of the argument plausible. They are exhibited briefly, so to speak,

236

in order to defend (2), what I called earlier "the Platonic dogma," which otherwise would be nothing but an unfounded thesis. Of course, there is an easier way to defend (2): One could maintain that there are no abstract entities. But this would stand things on their heads, for we are here interested in an epistemological argument against abstract entities, and within this context it would be circular to assume that there are no such things. No, the reasoning goes the other way: If we cannot perceive abstract entities, one may reasonably doubt that there are such things.

I shall try to sever the connection between (3) and (4), on the one hand, and (1) and (2), on the other. In regard to (4), we obviously cannot here discuss the pros and cons of all of the theories of causality that have been proposed. In a nutshell, the question is: Does the causal nexus, whatever its nature may be, hold between concrete things (individuals) only? I do not think so. It seems to me that the most plausible theory of causality holds that causal relations obtain among states of affairs. But be that as it may, my purpose is to call your attention to the fact that the argument from causal interaction rests on a specific and, may I say, not too plausible view about the terms of the causal nexus. This reminder alone may suffice to shake your confidence in the argument.

But even if this specific view about causality were acceptable, a connection has to be established between it and perception. What does causality have to do with perception? Well, it is a piece of common-sense that our perceptions of green apples and multi-colored rainbows is caused by apples and rainbows. This belief is quite true. It may even help to explain, as some philosophers have claimed, the difference between true perception, on the one hand, and perception which, though veridical, is only true by accident, on the other (see, for example, H. P. Grice, "The Causal Theory of Perception"). But it does not show that we cannot perceive abstract things. Consider a simple example: I see that the pencils on my desk are yellow. Since this is not a hallucination, we believe that there are some pencils on my desk and that these pencils cause me to see that the pencils on my desk are yellow. This does not show, as I said, that I cannot see abstract things. Quite to the contrary! It seems to me to be certain that in this situation I see the color yellow. And since I believe that this color is an abstract entity, I conclude that I see in this situation an abstract entity.

This last argument reveals my strategy. I am convinced by it that (2) is false. Therefore, if (3) and (4) imply (2), I must conclude that either (3) is false, or (4) is false, or both are false. I propose to attack the argument by attacking (2) only, because I think it is easy to prove that (2) is false. That (2) is false follows immediately from the following two true propositions:

(a) We can perceive colors, shapes, pitches, etc.,

(b) Colors, shapes, pitches, etc. are abstract things.

No philosophical argument could possibly convince me that (a) is false. (b), however, is of a different sort. Arguments against (b) I would not just dismiss as being silly. How could I? What is at stake in regard to (b) is nothing less than the issue of the existence of universals. Fortunately, I need not go into this controversy, for two things are true in any case. Firstly, one cannot very well argue that there are no abstract entities because (2) is true, and then use this conclusion in order to argue that (2) must be true. Secondly, (2) must be false, it seems to me, if colors are abstract entities.

This second truth shows the weakness in our opponent's position. The question is: Can we or can we not perceive abstract things? Well, can we not perceive colors, and are colors not abstract things? If our opponent answers that we do not perceive colors, nothing more, I think, can be done to advance the dialectic of the two opposing views. Most likely, though, he will deny that colors are abstract things. All right then, what about shapes? We are told that they are not abstract either. And we get the same reply in regard to pitches. Are there then any abstract things at all, we ask, and if the answer is negative, as it most likely is, then the argument shifts from epistemology to ontology. The question is now: Are there abstract entities? It is clear that our opponent's answer to the epistemological question is based on his answer to the ontological one, and not the other way around. If numbers, in case they existed, were abstract things, and if there are, as a matter of fact, no abstract things, then it is obvious that we cannot perceive them, and the case is closed.

What else can our opponent do but rely on the ontological issue? But if he does, then the power of the color example becomes apparent. Surely, colors are abstract things; they are not located in space and time like the things which are colored. And is it not obvious that we see colors? Who could deny it? Who could think otherwise?

The case for the perception of numbers is as strong as the case for the perception of colors. Let us assume that you see, not that there are yellow pencils on the desk, but that there are two pencils on the desk before you. In this situation, I maintain, you see the number two just as in the earlier situation you saw the color yellow. And just as you may say that the yellow pencils on the desk before you caused you to have that perception, so may you say that the two pencils on the desk before you caused you to see that there are two pencils on the desk. If there had been three pencils on the desk instead, you would have seen that there are three pencils on the desk, just as you would have seen that there are blue pencils on the desk, had there been blue instead of yellow pencils on the desk before you. Under normal conditions, what there is in front of your nose determines, in the simple-minded way we are employing, what you see.

b) The Causal Theory of Perception

Steiner, trying to come to grips with the so-called causal theory of perception, considers the following version of if: (C) One cannot see an F, unless the F participates in an event that causes one to have *some* perceptual experience (Steiner, p. 118). And he goes on to argue that it is not obvious that (C) is true and, hence, that perception of abstract objects is impossible. I would like to argue along an entirely different line. First of all, it should be noted that Grice's version of the causal theory, as distilled in (C), is designed to distinguish between accidentally true perception and genuine veridical perception. Secondly, I do not think that the truth of (C) implies that one cannot perceive abstract things. Let us apply (C) to our pencil example: One cannot see a yellow pencil, unless the yellow pencil participates in an event that causes one to have some perceptual experience. At this point, we must recall one of our most basic assumptions—one of our "dogmas," if you wish—namely, that perception is propositional. This means that one cannot see a yellow pencil unless one sees some such thing as that this is a yellow pencil or that there is a yellow pencil on the desk. From our point of view, therefore, (C) becomes:

> (C') One cannot see that this is a yellow *pencil, in the veridical sense,* unless the fact that this is a yellow pencil plays somehow a causal role in one's seeing that this is a yellow pencil.

I think that this version of (C) is true. But it does not exclude the perception of abstract entities, for example, of colors. For the case of color, we have, corresponding to (C):

> (D) One cannot see a color, unless the color somehow participates in an event that causes one to have some perceptual experience.

Remembering our thesis that perception is propositional, we get:

> (D') One cannot see that this is a *yellow* pencil, *in the veridical sense,* unless the fact that this is a yellow pencil plays somehow a causal role in one's seeing that this is a yellow pencil.

I think that (D') is just as true as (C'). Finally, we can adapt (C) to the perception of numbers:

> (E') One cannot see that there are *two* pencils on the desk, *in the veridical sense,* unless the fact that there are two pencils on the desk plays somehow a causal role in one's seeing that there are two pencils on the desk.

(C), as I pointed out earlier, was formulated by Grice in order to avoid certain problems about perceptions that happen to be accidentally true. Assume that you are in bed, fast asleep, and dreaming that you are in your office. In your dream, you see that there are two yellow pencils on your desk. Assume also that there are two yellow pencils on your desk and that you saw yesterday, while you were sitting in your office, that there are two yellow pencils on your desk. Are you now, in your dream, seeing those yellow pencils on your desk? Phenomenally, what you see seems to be the same state of affairs that you saw yesterday, namely, the state of affairs that *there are two yellow pencils on this desk before me now*. Yet, you do not really see the pencils on your desk. How could you? You are not even in your office. You are merely dreaming that you are in your office. Grice's (C) is designed to distinguish between these two different seeings. In the first case, genuine seeing, the pencils on the desk actually cause you to see them; in the dreaming situation, they do not: They are miles away, your eyes are closed, etc. Similarly, in our version of Grice's explanation, the fact that there are two yellow pencils on the desk plays a causal role in the veridical case but does not play a role in the dreaming situation.

But does Grice's explanation work, not just for individual things like pencils, but also for abstract things like colors and numbers? One may argue that while you cannot see the pencils on your desk when you are asleep with your eyes closed, you can see the color yellow in your dream (see Steiner, p. 120). After all, while the pencils are miles away, in your office, the color yellow, since it is an abstract thing, is not located anywhere and, therefore, can never be "in your vicinity." One may therefore argue that (C) breaks down for abstract things: No causal interaction needs to take place; all that is required is that a phenomenal perception of the abstract entity occurs. But it would be a mistake, it seems to me, to conclude that you can literally and veridically see the color yellow with your eyes closed, just because it is not located in one place like individual things are. The case for properties is the same as the case for individual things: You can see neither the pencils on your desk nor their color when you are home in bed, fast asleep. But, of course, you may dream that you see the yellow pencils on your desk.

I have argued that we can see that there are two pencils on the desk just as we can see that there are yellow pencils on the desk. I have also argued that to see that there are two pencils on the desk is to see the number two, just as to see that there are yellow pencils on the desk is to see the color yellow. And finally I argued that the fact that there are two pencils on the desk must play a causal role in one's seeing that there are two pencils on the desk, just as the fact that there are yellow pencils on the desk must play a causal role, in the genuine case, in one's seeing that there are yellow pencils on the desk.

Let me put it more generally. Firstly, I hold that to perceive a pencil, a color, or a number is to perceive a certain fact; for example the fact that there are two yellow pencils on my desk. Secondly, I maintain that if one perceives, in the literal sense, a certain fact, then that fact must "play a causal role in one's perceiving it." Thirdly, I believe that such a perceived fact may contain, as constituents, both concrete and abstract things. The fact that this is a pencil, for example, consists not only of the individual pencil, but also of the property of being a pencil. The fact that there are two pencils on the desk contains, among other things, the number two.

c) Sets "Concreticized"

Philosophical fashions wash like waves over the philosophical seashore without being resisted. The argument from causal interaction is such a wave. When looked at more carefully, it turns out to be nothing more than the Platonic dogma in disguise. This dogma is mistaken. But dogmas do not yield to arguments. Nor are they well defended. Jubien, for example, takes for granted that one cannot perceive abstract things and concludes that, therefore, they cannot "be given by ostension": "Now apparently the method of ostension does not offer much hope given a deliberately platonist posture. For part of that position is that mathematical entities are not sensible" (M. Jubien, "Ontology and Mathematical Truth," p. 135). Jubien's remark calls to our attention yet another terminological matter.

What Jubien seems to have in mind when he mentions a "platonist posture" is ontological Platonism, that is, the view that there are abstract entities. But this Platonism must be distinguished from the Platonism mentioned in the second of his sentences, namely, the view that abstract entities are not sensible (cannot be perceived). In Plato, of course, these two views go hand in hand. But they need not be combined. My philosophy is a case in point: while I am a Platonist in the ontological sense, I reject what I have called the Platonic dogma, namely, the view that abstract things cannot be perceived. In order to avoid confusion, I shall call myself a realist (in regard to abstract entities), and also an empiricist (in regard to how we know those abstract things).

I wish to comment on another remark of Jubien's: "Although it seems to me possible that we have mathematical intuition in the sense of a clear, distinct, and perhaps immediate apprehension of certain mathematical verities, such an intuition does not presuppose any intuition of *objects* of the sort under consideration" (Jubien, p. 136). This view, I wish to point out, differs radically from the one I have outlined and advocated. I cannot be sure what mathematical verities Jubien has in mind, but the ones that come to my mind could not be apprehended without an intuition (perception) of mathematical entities. When I perceive that there are two apples on the table, I perceive (ipso facto) the number two. When I perceive that two apples plus two apples are four apples, I perceive (ipso facto) the numbers two and four. I also perceive, and this perhaps needs to be emphasized, the sum relation between those numbers. In short, these very simple "mathematical truths" can only be apprehended if one apprehends the mathematical things involved.

Among these mathematical things, as we must constantly remind ourselves, our opponents usually list sets, even though it is perfectly obvious that sets are no more "mathematical" than, say, relations are. There are all kinds of relations: There are spatial and temporal relations; there are relations among people; there are relations among color hues; and there are also arithmetic relations, for example, the sum relation. But the fact that there are arithmetic relations does not make the category of relations an arithmetic ("mathematical") one. Similarly for sets: There are all kinds of sets: There are sets of people, sets of color hues, and sets of numbers. The fact that there are sets of numbers, however, does not make the category of set a "mathematical" category, or sets in general mathematical entities. It is true, though, that sets, sets of people as well as sets of numbers, are commonly taken to be abstract things: They are not located in space and/or time. And this creates a problem for those philosophers who (a) accept some form of the argument from causal interaction, and (b) think of arithmetic as set theory. They must argue that this common view is mistaken, that sets are really concrete things.

Maddy is an example (see P. Maddy, "Perception and Mathematical Intuition"). She starts out by explaining the standard claim that sets, if they are abstract, cannot be "baptized by ostension," in distinction, for example, from gold. In the case of gold, so the familiar story goes, the Baptist looks at some samples of gold and announces that these, and all things like them, are gold. Maddy then asks why one should not be able to do the same thing with a set of books by announcing that "all the books on this shelf, taken together, regardless of order, form a set," and that this group and all other groups of things are sets? (Maddy, p. 167). Why not, indeed? As Maddy sees it, the objection to "this picture of set theoretic reference is that, while the gold dubber causally interacts with some samples, the set dubber interacts only with the members of some samples" (Maddy, p. 167). She goes on to argue that a realist may claim in response to this objection that the gold dubber has only interacted with a fleeting aspect of the pieces of gold, and that the same may be true for the set dubber. I am not sure that I understand what she has in mind. But another reply seems to me to be obvious. If it is granted that one can dub a *property* like gold, why should one be unable to dub a *property* like set? The property of being gold is just as much an abstract entity as the property of being a set. In order to dub gold, the dubber must interact with some lumps that have the property of being gold. He must perceive that certain lumps before him have this property. And this means that he must perceive the property gold. Similarly, in order to dub the property of being a set, the dubber must causally interact with some things that are sets. She must perceive that some things are sets. And this means that she must perceive the property of being a set. If one can causally interact with the property of being gold, why should one not be able to causally interact with the property of being a set?

There is a difference between the two cases, though, and I suspect that it is this difference which is thought to make a difference. Lumps of gold are concrete things, while sets are abstract things. In other words, while in the first case, the things that have the (abstract) property are concrete, in the second case, they are themselves abstract. Lumps of gold are located in space and time, while sets are not. One can literally point at lumps of gold, but one cannot literally point at examples of sets. I suspect that the view under discussion rests on the assumption that one can dub lumps of gold, but not sets, because the former but not the latter can be perceived by the dubber; and the former but not the latter can be perceived by the dubber, because the former but not the latter can causally interact with the dubber.

The example of the gold dubber suffers from an important ambiguity. It is not clear what it is that is being dubbed in the situation: Is it the lumps of gold or is it the property? In the background lurks the common-name doctrine and its nominalistic motivation. Is 'gold' a (common) name of the individual lumps, or is it a (proper) name of the property? If the former, then the dubber can be said to dub the individual lumps; if the latter, then she is dubbing the property by pointing at the lumps which have the property. Since I think that the common-name doctrine is false, I can only assume that the dubber is naming the property rather than the individual pieces of gold. I once heard a joke that makes my case against the common-name doctrine. A drunk, having been thrown out of a bar, lands on all fours on a piece of grass in front of the bar. He notices a grasshopper a few inches in front of his nose. "Do you know, little fellow," he addresses the grasshopper, "that they have named a cocktail after you?" The grasshopper looks at him very perplexed and says: "Oh, Irving?"

Can we dub properties of abstract things? Well, we can only name such properties if we can perceive that certain things have these properties. And we can only perceive that certain things have these properties if we can perceive these certain things. All depends, therefore, on the old question of whether or not we can perceive abstract things. And this question leads us back to the argument from causal interaction. That we cannot baptize sets (really: the property of being a set) follows from this argument. But the argument is not sound.

If it were sound, to look at it from another angle, then it would also follow that we cannot dub colors (the property of being a color). We can construct a case for colors that exactly parallels the case for sets. Assume that there are a number of differently colored and differently shaped pieces of cardboard on the table before you. The pieces are individual things, perceivable according to the Platonic dogma. But their colors and shapes are abstract things, in the same category with sets. The properties of being a color and being a shape are properties of these abstract things. If the argument from causal interaction were sound, then it would follow that you could not dub the colors (or the shapes). You could not perceive the colors and, hence, could not perceive that they are colors, just as you allegedly cannot perceive the sets and, hence, cannot perceive that they are sets. But surely, we are all familiar with the property of being a color (or with the property of being a shape), because we have seen that certain properties are colors, while others are, for example, shapes. And this shows, as far as I can see, that the argument from causal interaction as used in the dubbing case is not sound.

Maddy, on the other hand, accepts the argument. But she, too, wants to hold that we perceive (some) sets. Thus she is forced to maintain that some sets are concrete things, located in space and/or time. From our point of view, she turns abstract things into concrete ones, because she is under the spell of the Platonic dogma. Her argument revolves around perceiving three eggs in an egg carton: You see that there are three eggs left in an egg carton. According to Maddy, you "acquire the perceptual belief that there is a set of eggs before [you], that it is three-membered, and that it has various two-membered sub-sets" (Maddy, p. 179). This talk about "acquiring a perceptual belief" is a piece of jargon of which certain philosophers happen to be fond at the moment. We can safely replace it by straightforward talk about perception (or seeing, in our case). Maddy mentions the belief about the two-membered sub-sets because in her example, you are looking for two eggs for a recipe that calls for two eggs. I do not think that in this situation you see what Maddy thinks you see. When you see that there are three eggs left in the carton, you do not see a set of eggs, or any other set. You see precisely what you do see, namely, *that there are three eggs left in the carton.* I would argue, as we know by now, that you see, therefore, among other things, the number three and the property of being an egg. But you do not see a set. Not that you cannot see a set. But you typically do not see sets when you look for two eggs in an egg carton.

But let us go to the heart of the matter: Maddy maintains that the set of three eggs which you allegedly see "is located in the egg carton, that is, exactly where the physical aggregate made up of the eggs is located" (Maddy, p. 179). Shades of John Stuart Mill!

At this place, Maddy seems to distinguish between the physical aggregate and the set, but at other times she seems to identify the two. I hope that I do not misinterpret her if I assume from now on that the physical aggregate is not identical with the set. The dialectic, then, looks like this. Maddy holds that there is a spatial aggregate of eggs which is located within the egg carton. There also exists a set of eggs, in addition to the aggregate. This set is a concrete thing, just like the aggregate. It is located precisely where the aggregate is. Just as you can see the aggregate of eggs, so you can see the set. And you see it exactly where the aggregate is. Assume that one of the three eggs is located, not in the carton, but in the door of the refrigerator. In this case, the aggregate is different, the set is the same, and the set is now located differently, but again "where the aggregate is." If all three eggs are in the carton, then the set is in the carton; and if one of the eggs is in the door, then the set is not in the carton, but somehow spread out from the carton to the door.

I must admit that I do not know how to show that the set of eggs is not in the carton, as Maddy claims. Nevertheless, I cannot help feeling that it is a trick to locate the set wherever the aggregate is. It seems to me obvious that we do not see that the set is in the carton. To answer the question: Where is the set of three eggs? we are instructed to look where the eggs are that are members of the set. Since these eggs are located in space, they stand in certain spatial relations to each other. As a consequence, they form a spatial configuration, the aggregate mentioned earlier. This aggregate consists of the three eggs in their mutual relations. (I shall leave out temporal relations.) This aggregate is also a concrete thing; it, too, is located in space (and time). Thus we see with our eyes, looking into the carton, that the eggs are arranged in a certain way, forming a certain aggregate, and that this aggregate is in the carton. Having located the aggregate with our eyes, we are told that we have located the set of eggs: It is precisely where the aggregate is. According to our conception of sets, the set is not located anywhere. In particular, it is not where the aggregate is. What is true is, rather, that *the members of this set form an aggregate, and that this aggregate is located in the carton.* The trick works for all sets consisting of individual things, because all of these things form spatio-temporal aggregates.

A similar trick works for properties. The property gold, in my view, is an abstract entity; it is not spatio-temporal. According to another view, this property is universal in that it can belong to many different individual things, but it is also concrete (see D. Armstrong, *Nominalism and Realism,* Cambridge: Cambridge University Press, 1978). It is located in space (and time). Where is the property? Well, we are told, it is wherever there are lumps of gold. Thus this property is at many different places at once. In this case, too, we locate the property not directly, but by means of the lumps which have the property. If I want to know where the color olive green is, I am instructed to look for things which are olive green, to locate them, and then to conclude that the color is where the colored individuals are. In this case, too, the color is located by means of two facts: the fact that it is exemplified by certain things, and the fact that these things are located in space. In other words, the trick is accomplished because the property stands in a certain relation (exemplification) to things which are truly located in space.

My suspicion that trickery is at work is reinforced by the fact that the trick no longer works when the relation between the individual and the entity in question, the entity to be located, is not a one-one relation. Assume that point B lies between points A and C. Where is the relation of between? Obviously, it is not where any one of the points is. Nor is it located somewhere between points A and B. The trick no longer works, since the relation is "coordinated," not just to one individual thing, like a property is, but to three concrete things. But we have learned from Maddy's view how to overcome this obstacle: We must find an entity which (a) is located in space, and (b) is "associated" with the relation. We can then locate the relation wherever that entity is. Nor is it hard to find such an entity. The configuration (aggregate) of the three points will do. The relation *between*, we could claim, is located precisely where the aggregate is located which consists of the things that stand in this relation. As a result of this piece of legerdemain, we now have the set of the three points as well as the relation of being to the left of located in the same place, namely, where the configuration of the three points is. What convinces me that neither the set nor the relation is really located anywhere is the fact that their alleged location can only be specified in terms of the location of the three points. If they really were concrete things, then one would be able to determine their spatio-temporal positions directly, as we are clearly able to do in regard to the points A, B, and C.

d) Goedel on Mathematical Intuition

Of all the recent views about the nature of mathematical knowledge, Goedel's view comes closest to the one I am defending. But this proximity is due, not to a close resemblance between our two views, but rather to the distance that separates our two views from the rest of the field. (Maddy's position is an exception.) However, it is not possible to compare Goedel's view with ours in detail, for Goedel merely hints at his view. Nevertheless, it may be instructive to have a look at his view and to talk briefly about his commentators.

I am under the impression that two views actually appear in Goedel's papers. In the paper on Russell's mathematical logic, for example, we find the following remark:

> It seems to me that the assumption of such objects [classes and concepts] is quite as legitimate as the assumption of physical bodies and there is quite as much reason to believe in their existence. They are in the same sense necessary to obtain a satisfactory system of mathematics as physical bodies are necessary for a satisfactory theory of our sense perceptions and in both cases it is impossible to interpret the propositions one wants to assert about these entities as propositions about the "data", i. e., in the latter case the actually occurring sense perceptions.
>
> (K. Goedel, "Russell's Mathematical Logic," p. 220)

This passage, it seems to me, can be interpreted in two different ways. Interpreted in a way that is most congenial to my own view, Goedel claims that we need be no more suspicious of sets and properties than we are of perceptual objects; and that it is just as impossible to interpret statements about sets and properties as being really about other kinds of things, as it is to interpret statements about perceptual objects as being really about our sensations. Needless to say, this interpretation agrees fully with my sentiments. Properties, sets, and numbers, in my view, are just as much part of the furniture of the world as apples and electrons. Nor is it in the least plausible to claim that statements about sets are about anything but sets; statements about numbers, about anything but numbers; and statements about apples, about anything but apples. We must steadfastly reject the fashionable view which tries to snatch realism from the jaws of idealism by "constructing" numbers, sets, and perceptual objects out of other things. The *loci classici* of this view are Russell's *Our Knowledge of the External World* and Carnap's *Der logische Aufbau der Welt*.

The second interpretation, perhaps the more natural one, takes Goedel to be saying that just as perceptual objects must be *postulated* in order to have a satisfactory theory of perception, so mathematical entities have to be *postulated* in order to arrive at a satisfactory set theory (and arithmetic). What is implied by Goedel's view is that we are acquainted neither with perceptual objects nor with mathematical things, but that we have to postulate their existence in order to get adequate theories. Realism in regard to perceptual objects and in regard to mathematical entities is thus secured by postulation. This kind of realism is particularly popular among philosophers of science. The Gordian knot of the idealism-realism controversy, which has so vexed modern philosophy since Descartes, is cut with the sword of postulation. Whatever cannot be defended against the persuasive arguments of the idealist or skeptic is simply postulated. At times, one even finds astonishment that we bother to worry about such controversies, when a simple act of postulation will do the trick. Who does not remember the claim that such disputes are nothing but "Scheinprobleme"?

But we are not intimidated by our scientifically-minded colleagues. What is a "satisfactory" theory, we demand to know. One obvious answer will not do. It may be replied that, quite obviously, a satisfactory arithmetic, for example, must, among other things, deal with the arithmetic entities there are. In other words, it must be about numbers. And a satisfactory theory of perception must be about the perceptual things there are, that is, about perceptual objects. With this answer in mind, the view under discussion reduces to the truism that a theory of number must be about numbers, a theory of sets must be about sets, and a theory of perception must be about perceptual objects. Of course they must. But it is now assumed that we already know that there are numbers, sets, and perceptual objects, so that there may be theories about them, and the question is, precisely how we know this.

But talk about a "satisfactory" theory may take on a different meaning. What comes to mind is Russell's delightful example, which we discussed earlier, of the cat that walks from one corner of his room to the other. First, he sees it in one corner, then in the other, but he does not see it cross the room. Russell asks why we assume that there exists a cat that crosses the room, even if we do not see it, rather than assume that there are only the sense-impressions which Russell experiences when he sees the cat, first in one corner, then in the other. Why do we believe, in other words, that there are perceptual objects in addition to our sense-impressions? Russell's answer is: "Since this belief does not lead to any difficulties, but on the contrary tends to simplify and systematize our account of our experiences, there seems no good reason for rejecting it" (B. Russell, *The Problems of Philosophy*, p. 24). What Russell claims here is that a theory of our experiences is simpler and more systematic if we assume that there exist perceptual objects in addition to sense-impressions, and that this fact is our justification for believing in perceptual objects. But this is surely mistaken. We believe that there are apples and tigers, not because these beliefs fit a theory, but simply because we see apples and tigers. We believe that there are perceptual objects because we perceive them. As for the claim that this belief somehow simplifies and systematizes, the dialectic inevitably dissolves into pragmatic ambiguity, and we do not have the space here to pursue even one of its many sides. But it is clear that the only good reason for postulating perceptual objects or numbers, unless one is acquainted with them, is that one believes on other grounds that such things exist. According to our view, however, we are acquainted with perceptual objects and numbers, and, therefore, there is no need to postulate them.

Perhaps the analogy is supposed to be drawn, not between numbers and perceptual objects, but between numbers and physical objects; not between numbers and apples, but between numbers and electrons. Compare, for example, the following quite typical comment by George Berry:

> How then do we find out about this realm of extra-mental nonparticular, unobservable entities? Our knowledge of them, like our knowledge of the extra-mental, unobservable objects of the physical sciences, is indirect, being tied to perceived things by a fragile web of theory. In both cases—physics and logic—our hypotheses about the unperceived are tested by their success in accounting for the character of the perceived. Misreading this similarity, one might easily conclude that a faculty of non-sensory perception, call it 'intuition', is necessary to play a part in logic parallel to the role of sensation in physics.
>
> (G. Berry, "Logic with Platonism," p. 261)

I think that Berry's diagnosis is false. Those who appeal to some kind of "intuition" of logical or mathematical things, are not guided by the parallel which he describes. Rather, they want to draw a parallel between the perception of perceptual objects and the intuition of logical and mathematical things. It is at any rate true that some philosophers argue that numbers are like electrons: Neither numbers nor electrons can be perceived, yet we know that they exist, and we know this by inference. I admit that this is roughly true for electrons. They cannot be perceived, but their effects can, and from these effects, we can infer their existence by means of certain laws. But this case of inference is quite different from Russell's case of postulation. In the case of electrons, we maintain that they exist, period; not merely that the assumption of their existence simplifies or systematizes. We know that electrons exist in the same way in which Robinson Crusoe knew that Friday existed, because he saw his footprints in the sand. There is a fundamental difference between the way in which we know that there are perceptual objects and the way in which we know that there are physical objects. We know perceptual objects, not by inference from our sensations, as I have time and again emphasized, but because we perceive them. On the other hand, we know electrons, not because we perceive them, but by inference from what we perceive. Some philosophers, taking as their model our knowledge of electrons, mistakenly believe that our knowledge of apples is of the same sort. The question before us is this: Is our knowledge of numbers (and sets) like our knowledge of apples or like our knowledge of electrons? I am arguing that it is like our knowledge of apples: We perceive some numbers (and sets) just as we perceive apples.

Goedel, I said at the beginning, seems to hold, at different places, two different views. We have briefly discussed one of these two views, the one expressed in his article on Russell. We shall now turn to the other view. It is contained in the classic paper on the continuum hypothesis:

> But, despite their remoteness from sense experience, we do have something like a perception also of the objects of set theory, as is seen from the fact that the axioms force themselves upon us as being true. I don't see any reason why we should have less confidence in this kind of perception, i. e., in mathematical intuition, than in sense perception. . . .
>
> It should be noted that mathematical intuition need not be conceived of as a faculty giving an *immediate* knowledge of the objects concerned. Rather it seems that, as in the case of physical experience, we *form* our ideas also of those objects on the basis of something else which is immediately given. Only this something else here is *not*, or not primarily, the sensations. That something besides the sensations actually is immediately given follows (independently of mathematics) from the fact that even our ideas referring to physical objects contain constituents qualitatively different from sensations or mere combinations of sensations, e. g., the idea of object itself, . . . Evidently the "given" underlying mathematics is closely related to the abstract elements contained in our empirical ideas. It by no means follows, however, that the data of this second kind, because they cannot be associated with actions of certain things upon our sense organs, are something purely subjective, as Kant asserted. Rather they, too, may represent an aspect of objective reality, but, as opposed to the sensation, their presence in us may be due to another kind of relationship between ourselves and reality.

(K. Goedel, "What is Cantor's Continuum Problem?", pp. 271–72)

I think that this long excerpt contains a number of philosophical themes. It rings a series of philosophical bells. But not all of the tones harmonize with each other. The first paragraph starts with what seems to be the straightforward assertion that, in addition to ordinary perception, there is another kind of perception, "mathematical intuition," of mathematical things. Goedel seems to be saying, in Husserl's terms, that in addition to ordinary intuition, there is eidetic intuition, and that the latter is just as direct, just as immediate, as the former. The latter is a "vision," too, but a vision of what is abstract rather than concrete. Goedel defends the existence of this kind of intuition by pointing out that the axioms of set theory force themselves upon us as being true. The same, of course, could be said about the axioms of arithmetic. I have argued, in opposition to Goedel's (and Husserl's) view, that there is no second kind of intuition. There is no special kind of mental act which acquaints us with abstract or mathematical things. Perception alone, since it is propositional, acquaints us with both individual things as well as abstract entities.

As to Goedel's remark about the axioms, I believe that it applies to our view as well as to his. I have repeatedly claimed that just as we know that midnight blue is darker than lemon yellow by means of perception, so that this truth "forces itself upon us," so we know by perception that two things plus two things are four things, or that the set of fruit before us is the union set of a set of apples and a set of bananas, so that these truths, too, "force themselves upon us." Things are not quite that simple, when we turn to axioms, that is, to general facts. I can learn by means of perception that the sum of 3 and 2 is the same as the sum of 2 and 3, but I cannot learn by means of perception that this holds for all numbers. Similarly, I can learn by means of perception that there exists the union set consisting of the set of apples and the set of bananas, but I cannot learn in the same way that there exists a union set for any two sets. The truth of these axioms forces itself upon us in the same way in which all inductive truth forces itself upon us, namely, through the persuasion of its instances. Paraphrasing Goedel, we could say: Only because there is a perception (mathematical intuition) of the instances of these laws, are we forced, to whatever degree we are forced, to accept the laws.

Our understanding of Goedel's remark differs sharply from Chihara's (see C. Chihara, *Ontology and the Vicious-Circle Principle,* pp. 78–79). Chihara draws a parallel between the way in which, according to Goedel, the axioms of set theory force themselves upon us and the way in which conceptual truths about God, conceived of as the perfect being, may force themselves upon us, even if we are atheists. We do not see this parallel. In addition to the fact that hypothetical statements about God (God is a necessary being) are not laws, there is the difference that perception is lacking in the case of God but not in the case of set theory. An atheist may agree that if there is God, he is omniscient, but he would insist, in the same breath, that there is no perceptual evidence for God's existence in the first place. For sets, however, Goedel could and would insist that he is acquainted with sets and certain relations among them. The axioms of set theory force themselves upon him, not because of his concept of a set, divorced from all acquaintance, but precisely because he is acquainted with sets.

Returning to the rest of our quotation from Goedel, he considers next the possibility that mathematical intuition is after all not immediate, but mediated like the perception of perceptual objects. I take it that he adopts here, perhaps only tentatively, the position which we criticized a few paragraphs earlier, namely, the view that just as our knowledge of perceptual objects is a matter of inference from sensations, so our knowledge of mathematical things may be a matter of inference. If this interpretation is correct, then what I said earlier applies to Goedel's possibility.

But Goedel adds a Kantian theme to his considerations. He seems to be arguing that just as we are aware of perceptual objects by being directly acquainted with sensations, so we are indirectly acquainted with sets by being directly acquainted with something else. This something else, though, does not consist in sensations or, at least, does not primarily consist in sensations. And then he states that even in perception, something in addition to sensation must play a role. This is the Kantian twist which I just mentioned. As an example of the "something else" in perception,

Goedel mentions the idea of object. Without this idea, he may have reasoned, we could not possibly fashion out of the buzzing, booming confusion of our sensations the notion of a a perceptual object. What is given to the mind, in addition to raw sensations, are certain abstract elements, such as the property of being an object, and mathematical intuition is somehow based on such abstract elements. Goedel avoids the idealistic consequences of this view by pointing out that those abstract elements may not be purely subjective, as Kant concluded, but could be representing aspects of reality. (There occurs at this point also a hint of the infamous argument from causal interaction.) All of this is rather vague, so that we may feel free to interpret Goedel's statements in the spirit of our point of view. If we do, then we must purge them of talk about sensations in favor of talk about perception. Perception, we have repeatedly emphasized, acquaints us with abstract things, not just with individuals. The property of being an individual (perceptual) object, for example, is presented to us in perception, in addition to the individual things themselves. In short, what according to Goedel occurs on the level of sensation, occurs, according to our view, on the level of perception.

In the last sentence quoted from Goedel, he surmises that there may be a relationship other than causal interaction between us and reality. We know what this relationship is: It is the intentional nexus between a mental act and the state of affairs which is its object. When you see that there are two apples on the table in front of you, your mental act of seeing stands in a unique, noncausal, relationship to a certain fact. And this relationship obtains, in the case of perception, always between a mind (mental act), on the one hand, and an *abstract* thing, namely, a state of affairs, on the other. It is far from true that only concrete things can be perceived; it is rather the case that concrete things can only be perceived through the medium of abstract entities. Only as constituents of states of affairs do concrete things appear before the mind in perception.

This consideration may shed some light on the popularity among some philosophers of the causal theory of perception. The causal theory of perception is merely a part of a causal theory of knowledge. And the causal theory of knowledge is developed in opposition to a theory based on intentionality. The causal theory replaces the intentional nexus between mind and world with a causal connection. I suppose that there are many reasons for this rejection of intentionality. There exists an unfounded suspicion of the mental, an explicit or implicit materialism. Physics or physiology is to be preferred to "folk psychology"; philosophers without minds, to philosophers with minds. There is also a misplaced loyalty to science. Intentionality is unscientific, causality is not. Intentionality smacks of magic, causality does not. Finally, there is an unjustified aversion to abstract entities. Causality, one may mistakenly think, involves nothing but individual things in space and/or time. Allowing myself to stray from the straight and narrow path of detailed discussion, I venture the following sweeping diagnosis: Most recent views about the nature of mathematical knowledge are based on nominalism and physicalism, the twin ailments of analytic philosophy.

Mathematical Knowledge and Structure

a) Isomorphisms and Models

Among the furniture of the world, there is the category of structure ("whole"). A structure is a complex entity which consists of parts in relations to each other. It differs from a set because of the relations which it contains. It differs from a fact because of the relations in which it can stand to other things. These differences between structures, on the one hand, and sets and facts, on the other, are well-known, and I shall merely remind you of their most important features. Two sets are the same if and only if their members are the same. Two structures are identical, by contrast, if and only if (a) their nonrelational parts are the same, (b) their relations are the same, and (c) corresponding parts stand in corresponding relations. This clearly shows the difference between sets and structures. Facts differ from structures most strikingly in that they stand in such relations to each other as conjunction, disjunction, etc. Furthermore, there are negative facts, while there are no negative structures. These distinctions between structures, on the one hand, and sets and facts, on the other, are important because in my ontology sets, facts, and structures are the only complex entities (see my *The Categorial Structure of the World*).

The most interesting feature of structures is that they can be *isomorphic* to each other. Again, I shall be brief. We say of two structures S_1 and S_2 that they are isomorphic to each other if and only if the following is the case: There exists a relation R_1 and a relation R_2 such that: (1) R_1 is a one-one relation between the relations of S_1 called U_n and the relations of S_2 called V_n, (2) R_2 is a one-one relation between the members of the fields of U_n and the members of the fields of V_n such that: (3) if any n members form an n-tuple that stands in one of the relations U_n, then the members related to them by R_2 form an n-tuple that stands in the corresponding relation from V_n. Less precisely, two structures are isomorphic to each other if and only if their nonrelational parts are correlated one-one to each other, their relations are coordinated one-one to each other, and corresponding parts are coordinated by corresponding relations.

As ontologists, we must be much more careful than logicians and mathematicians and must call attention to the following two points. Firstly, there may not exist the relations R_1 and R_2, but merely the corresponding sets of ordered couples (sets of structures!). Just as there are sets which are not determined by properties—recall the axiom of choice—so are there sets which are not determined by relations. In case R_1 and R_2 do not exist, but the corresponding sets do, our explanation of isomorphism must of course be changed. Secondly, there exists no such relation as being isomorphic to something. To say that two structures are isomorphic to each other is a mere abbreviation of a longer story.

Isomorphisms are the delight of logicians and mathematicians. It would not occur to us, even for a moment, to begrudge or belittle this pleasure. Who but an insensitive worshipper of the humanities could be indifferent to the beauty and elegance of algebra? And yet, we cannot help but add a word of caution: In the hands of philosophically-minded logicians and mathematicians, algebra—the theory of structures—has caused endless confusion. It is the purpose of this chapter to try to dispel some of these confusions. Alas, I have no reason to expect that I shall succeed any better than Russell, Frege, and many others have in the past. There seems to exist a "mathematical set of mind" which simply refuses to acknowledge the true philosophical relevance of isomorphisms. Because of this mind-set, I shall have to repeat the obvious in the next few paragraphs.

Consider any nonempty set of things, which we shall call "elements," and certain relations between them such that the following ten *forms* are true:

(1) If a and b are elements, so too is a‡b.
(2) If a and b are elements, so too is a#b.
(3) There is an element x such that a‡x = a for every element a.
(4) There is an element y such that a#y = a for every element a.
(5) a‡b = b‡a for all elements a and b whose combinations are also elements.
(6) a#b = b#a for all elements a and b whose combinations are also elements.
(7) a‡(b#c) = (a‡b)#(a‡c) for all elements a, b, and c whose combinations are also elements.
(8) a#(b‡c) = (a#b)‡(a#c) for all elements a, b, and c whose combinations are also elements.
(9) There are at least two elements u and v such that u is not identical with v.
(10) If the elements x and y exist and are unique, then there is an element a such that (1) a‡ā = y and (2) a#ā = x.

A structure of this kind is called a "Boolean algebra." Boolean algebras are so interesting because a certain structure of numbers as well as a certain structure of sets are Boolean algebras. If we think of our elements as natural numbers, of ‡ as addition, # as multiplication, and if we take x and y to be 0 and 1, respectively, then the forms (1) through (9) turn into true laws of arithmetic. But we can also interpret the forms in a different way. This time we think of the elements as sets, of ‡ as the union relation, of # as the intersection relation, and of x and y as the null set and the universal set, respectively. We get again nine true statements about sets. For sets, we can even add form (10), taking ā to be the complement set of a. There is no straightforward interpretation of (10) for arithmetic. But, then, why should there be? Numbers are not sets. It is therefore not surprising that they do not behave in *every* respect like sets. It is remarkable enough that a structure formed from relations among numbers should be so much like a structure formed from relations among sets. You know, of course, that there is a third structure which is a Boolean algebra, namely, a structure formed from certain relations between states of affairs. We can interpret our elements to be states of affairs, ‡ is disjunction, # is conjunction, ā is the negation of a, and the two elements x and y are the two truth-values true and false, respectively. Upon this interpretation, the ten forms yield ten laws of "propositional logic."

Now for the obvious:

(1) *Forms* as such, containing in addition to familiar expressions also mere "place holders," are neither true nor false.

(2) Nor are they as such about any particular things and relations.

(3) Only after the forms have been turned into *sentences* by replacing the "place holders" with familiar expressions, can we speak of truth or falsehood.

(4) The resulting sentences are *about* the things and relations represented by the substituted familiar expressions.

(5) One and the same form may thus be turned into a sentence about numbers or a sentence about sets. Of course, these sentences make different statements.

(6) In the case of the forms for a Boolean algebra, there are at least three different interpretations of the first nine forms.

(7) We can express this fact by saying that (a certain part of) arithmetic is *isomorphic* to (a certain part of) set theory and (a certain part of) propositional logic.

(8) Or else we can say that the nine forms have three different *models:* an arithmetic model, a set theoretic model, and a propositional model.

(9) These models are not identical; only the forms are.

Fortified with these truisms, let us go back and inspect some of the historical roots of the philosophical confusions which, in my opinion, still flourish.

b) Dedekind's Notion of Number

The most common and serious confusion to which the discovery of isomorphisms has led is the belief that forms somehow "define" what they are about. Of course, they are not really *about* anything, since they are not sentences that make statements. How else, then, shall I put it? One believes that these forms somehow determine what the "place holders" represent. But place holders do not represent anything; that is why these shapes are called here "place holders." You can see how hard it is even to formulate the view we are about to criticize. Let us try again: One believes that the forms somehow define things for the place holders which, by themselves, do not represent anything. The technical term for this kind of "definition" is 'implicit definition'. The idea behind this kind of "definition" is at least as old as Poincaré and as young as Quine. In between, we can read about it in Hilbert as well as in Schlick. As a matter of fact, implicit definitions have been so popular that one can hardly open a book about the philosophy of mathematics without making their acquaintance. But it all goes back to Dedekind (see R. Dedekind, "Was sind und was sollen die Zahlen").

Dedekind gives four forms for what he calls "a singly infinite system N":

(1) R(N) is a part of N.
(2) N is the intersection I_0 of all those chains K to which the element I belongs.
(3) The element I is not contained in R(N).
(4) The mapping R is one-one.

The crucial place holders are 'N', 'I', and 'R'. It is understood that N is a kind of entity, I is one of the things of kind N, and R is a one-one relation. If we take N to be the natural numbers, I to be the number one, and R to be the relation of immediate successor, we get four true sentences about natural numbers. The first sentence, for example, says then that the immediate successors of natural numbers are themselves natural numbers; and the third sentence states that one is not the immediate successor of any natural number. But Dedekind's four forms can be interpreted in many other ways as well. For example, we may take I to be the number one as before, but interpret N to be just the odd natural numbers, and R to be the relation of being an immediate successor in the series of odd natural numbers. Once again, we get four true sentences. This time, these sentences are about the odd natural numbers. In a similar fashion, we can get four true sentences about all natural numbers divisible by ten. And so on.

One cannot but be impressed by Dedekind's brilliant insight into the nature of the progression of natural numbers. But Dedekind goes on to claim that his four forms somehow *describe* the natural numbers:

> If in the contemplation of a singly infinite system N, ordered by a mapping R, we disregard entirely the peculiar nature of the elements, retaining only the possibility of distinguishing them, and consider only the relations in which they are placed by the ordering mapping R, then these elements are called natural numbers or ordinal numbers or simply numbers, and the basic element I is called the basic number of R number series N.
>
> (Dedekind, p. 360)

I take it that Dedekind thinks of the four expressions as *forms* rather than *axioms* (true sentences); for he does not identify the natural numbers with any particular series of entities. Nor does he say that just any kind of entity which satisfies the forms is the series of natural numbers. Rather, he thinks of the natural numbers as a product of a *process of abstraction*. By means of this process, we obliterate all of the distinguishing characteristics of the various kinds of entities which satisfy the forms. Since the numbers are arrived at by such a mental process of abstraction, Dedekind thinks of them as creations of the mind: "In regard to this liberation of the elements from any other content (abstraction), one can justifiedly call the numbers a free creation of the human mind" (Dedekind, p. 360).

Dedekind is wrong. By means of abstraction, we do not arrive at the notion of natural number, but rather at the notion of progression. If we consider the series of natural numbers, we may notice that there are other things which also form such a series, for example, the series of numbers divisible by ten. And this realization may lead us on to notice that all of these different kinds of things have something in common, namely, that they form progressions. By abstracting from what distinguishes one progression from another, we arrive, not at the notion of some sort of "indefinite kind of thing" called "a natural number," but at the concept of a definite feature which definite kinds of entity share, namely, at the notion of (forming a) progression. By another process of abstraction, we may arrive at the notion of a Boolean algebra.

Dedekind, I said, is mistaken. But at least he does not claim that numbers are "whatever the forms say they are". He does not claim that the forms "implicitly define" the natural numbers. He saw, it seems to me, that there are different models for the four forms. However, it is clear that Dedekind's monumental achievement invites a conception of forms as definitions.

c) Implicit Definitions

1) POINCARÉ VERSUS RUSSELL

Our story of the enduring love affair between logicians and philosophers of science, on the one hand, and implicit definitions, on the other, begins with the classic dispute between Russell and Poincaré. In 1897, Russell published his *Essays on the Foundations of Geometry;* Poincaré, in the *Revue de Metaphysique et de Morale* of 1889, wrote a long review of Russell's work. Among other things, Poincaré raised the question of the definition of geometric terms. We cannot go into the details of Poincaré's criticism and Russell's reply to it. What is at stake, it must suffice to say, is the notion of definition. While Poincaré seems to request a definition of the primitive terms of the geometric axioms, Russell considers such a request absurd. The very notion of a primitive term precludes its definition. In particular, it would be absurd to think of the geometric axioms as definitions of the geometric terms which they contain.

I think there existed in that debate a certain misunderstanding between Russell and Poincaré; a misunderstanding invited by Poincaré's unfortunate use of the term 'definition' and by Russell's stubborn refusal to look beyond this use. What Poincaré really was asking for, it seems, was an *interpretation* of the primitive terms. What, he asked, is a straight line? Russell, of course, had an answer to this kind of question: What those terms represent, is given to us by acquaintance. Russell believes that it is undoubtedly by analysis of perceived objects that we obtain acquaintance with what is *meant* by a straight line in actual space. What made Russell reluctant to give this straightforward answer to Poincaré, we may surmise, is the fact that it was customary at that time to think of a straight line as an "ideal object," and of geometry as being about such "ideal objects." Kant's shadow still loomed menacingly over the philosophical scene. Ideal objects, not being a part of the perceptual world around us, were supposed to be given to "pure intuition." Poincaré put his finger on this sore spot when he guessed what Russell's answer to his question would be:

that there is no need to define [the primitive terms] because these things are directly known through intuition. I find it difficult to talk to those who claim to have a direct intuition of equality of two distances or of two time lapses; we speak very different languages. I can only admire them, since I am thoroughly deprived of this intuition.

(J. A. Coffa, *To the Vienna Station*, chap. VII)

We may agree with Poincaré that there exists no special faculty of intuition, no Kantian pure intuition, which acquaints us with those properties and relations. But this does not imply, as Poincaré seems to think, that we are not acquainted with them at all. What Russell should have said in reply to Poincaré is that we *perceive* with our very eyes that two lines are equal or unequal in length. Nor are these lines "ideal," whatever that may mean. We are talking about lines drawn with pencil or chalk on paper or a blackboard. We are talking about ordinary *perceptual objects*. The primitive terms of (Euclidian) geometry represent perceptual properties and relations, and geometry is about the individual things which have these properties and stand in these relations. What is involved is neither a mysterious faculty of pure intuition nor an obscure ideal object.

This straightforward answer to Poincaré's question, however, has seldom been given. The discovery of non-Euclidian geometry seems to have clouded rather than enlightened the minds of many philosophers. What could be more obvious than that 'straight line' means straight line, and that we explain to a child what property we have in mind by drawing a straight line with a pencil on a piece of paper? Why does anyone believe that this case is any different from explaining what property olive green is by showing the child an olive green piece of cardboard? Yet, Coffa says in his otherwise insightful book:

What was no longer a serious possibility circa 1900 was to conceive of acquaintance as playing the specific semantic *explanatory* role that it was supposed to play in the atomist picture of knowledge, whereby the construction of geometric theory would start with acquaintance, then proceed to a construction of claims and perhaps conclude with the testing of these claims.

(Coffa, chap. VII)

But this is precisely how geometry does proceed. In Goedel's words: "In geometry, e.g., the question as to whether Euclid's fifth postulate is true retains its meaning if the primitive terms are taken in a definite sense, i.e., as referring to the behavior of rigid bodies, rays of light, etc." (K. Goedel, "What is Cantor's Continuum Problem," p. 271).

What does Coffa think is the correct alternative to our view? In praise of Poincaré, Coffa says:

Poincaré's conventionalism is based on the idea that in order to understand geometry, one must stand Russell's argument on its head: since geometric primitives do not acquire their meaning prior to their incorporation into the axiomatic claims, such axioms do not express propositions in Frege's or Russell's sense.

(Coffa, chap. VII)

The so-called axioms of geometry, according to this view, are really implicit definitions of the primitive terms which they contain. Coffa sums up this view in these rousing words:

> Poincaré's point is, therefore, that all we can say about the meanings of geometric primitives is what geometric axioms say. Under these circumstances, the thesis of semantic atomism prevents those axioms from conveying any sort of factual (non-semantic) information. No wonder that they are neither analytic (in Kant's first sense) nor synthetic, since they are not propositions. No wonder either that they had always been regarded as extraordinary claims, endowed with a particular strong sort of truth. The error was to think that they convey a privileged sort of information, or information about some extraordinary domain. Their distinguishing feature is that they determine, to the extent needed in geometry, the meanings of geometric primitives; and the conviction that they are necessary emerges from the fact that we would be talking about something else or, better yet, meaning something different from what is intended, if we denied them. Geometric axioms are definitions disguised as claims, and what they define is the indefinables.
>
> (Coffa, chap. VII)

When we look at this approving description of Poincaré's view, the shortcomings of this view become all too obvious. Let us agree, for the moment, to use 'axiom' in a neutral fashion for whatever geometers call "axioms." Let us further assume that one of these axioms contains the expression 'straight line'. There are only two possibilities: Either this expression is the ordinary English phrase which means straight line, or else it is not. In the latter case, it is a mere "place holder," and we could have in its stead any other arbitrary expression. In the former case, the axiom is a true *sentence* of English. It says something about straight lines. In the second case, on the other hand, it is a mere *form*. In this case, it is not a sentence; it is neither true nor false. Nor does the form say anything about straight lines. Now, turn to Coffa's very first sentence. Coffa claims that the axioms say something about the meanings of geometric primitives, that is, in our example, about straight line. As we have just seen, this can only be true if we think of the axioms as English sentences. If we think of them as mere forms, then they do not say anything about anything and, in particular, they do not say anything about straight lines or the property of being a straight line. But turn now to Coffa's second sentence and you will find the exact opposite conception of the axioms. Coffa this time maintains that the axioms do not convey any kind of factual information. Now the axioms are treated as mere forms. Coffa seems to be unaware that he is working at one and the same time with two incompatible conceptions of the axioms. I think that we have here the basic confusion which spawns the notion of implicit definitions: Axioms are treated at the same time both as saying something about their primitives and also as not saying something about them. They are treated at the same time as axioms proper and also as mere forms. The charm of this confusion is that it allows one to switch back and forth between these two incompatible conceptions, just as the philosophical argument may require. When one argues that the axioms do not express propositions, one treats them as mere forms. When one argues that they define their primitive terms, that they say something about the meanings of these terms, one treats them as expressing propositions.

This confusion between treating an axiom as a mere form and treating it as a declarative sentence (an axiom) is neatly illustrated in a letter from Hugo Dingler to Frege:

> '2' and '3', too, are for me mere signs which acquire a "sense" only through the assumptions or axioms which one presupposes for them. The sentence '3 > 2' merely seems to have an independent sense, namely, when I work with the "presentation" [Vorstellung], as is the case on the pre-logical or pre-axiomatic level. Then '3', '>', '2' are . . . "popular concepts", that is, [they] are presentations abstracted from practical life with which the understanding works intuitively, as actually is the case in ordinary life for everyone everytime. For science, however, in the form to be aspired to, this condition cannot be ideal. The "presentations" which someone has when he sees the signs '2' and '3' should not, it seems to me, form the basis of science, but must be considered in their logically analyzed form. But then the sentence 3 > 2 is not an independent sentence, but merely a part of a—as you put it so nicely—sentence structure [Satzgefuege] which is based on a series of irreducible presuppositions or axioms. But then the difference between a > b and 3 > 2 is merely a matter of degree and not a matter of principle: both times, two signs are connected by '>', only that in one case there exist a few additional presuppositions about these signs. a > b thus constitutes only *one* presupposition, while 3 > 2 carries a whole group of presuppositions with it . . . Without these presuppositions, 3 > 2 is in no way different from a > b, for then '3' and '2' are completely arbitrary signs, just like any other.

> (My translation from the German. The letter appears in G. Frege, *Philosophical and Mathematical Correspondence*, pp. 23–25)

If one is allowed to treat the axioms of geometry at the same time both as forms and as true sentences, a number of traditional problems disappear, as Coffa indicates. Are the axioms of geometry analytic or synthetic? Well, they are not analytic like the truths of arithmetic, someone may reason. Are they then synthetic? How can they be? Surely they are different from the truths of botany! So, they cannot be analytic and they cannot be synthetic. Well, if they are mere forms, then it is perfectly obvious how we can escape from the threatening dilemma: Mere forms, since they do not represent propositions, are neither analytic nor synthetic. Are the axioms of geometry necessary? Well, they are not analytic, so the reasoning goes on. But they are obviously necessary in some sense. If the axioms are really definitions that say something about the primitives of geometry, then it is perfectly understandable how they can be necessary without being analytic: If we denied the axioms, we would not be talking about the primitives of geometry but about other things. For example, we could not mean straight line by 'straight line' if we denied that two points determine a straight line.

Wittgenstein, by the way, adds as usual his own twist to this confused conception. In a letter to Schlick, he writes:

> Does geometry talk about cubes? Does it say that the cube-form has certain properties? . . . Geometry does not talk about cubes but, rather, it constitutes the meaning of the

word cube, etc. Geometry says, e.g., that the sides of a cube are of equal length, and *nothing is easier* than to confuse the grammar of this sentence with that of the sentence 'the sides of a wooden cube are of equal length'. And yet, one is an arbitrary grammatical rule whereas the other is an empirical sentence.

(Coffa, chap. XIV)

Wittgenstein here supplants the notion of implicit definition by that of a grammatical rule. That is his peculiar twist.

2) HILBERT VERSUS FREGE

The second chapter of our story is about Hilbert and Frege: Hilbert conceives of the axioms of his celebrated *Grundlagen der Geometrie* as implicit definitions. Frege objects. Again, there can be no doubt in my mind that Frege is on the side of the angels. And, again, many contemporary philosophers of science have sided with Hilbert. Witness, for example, H. Scholz's assessment of the controversy:

> . . . no one doubts nowadays that while Frege himself created much that was radically new on the basis of the classical conception of science, he was no longer able to grasp Hilbert's radical transformation of this conception of science, with the result that his critical remarks, though very acute in themselves and still worth reading today, must nevertheless be regarded as essentially beside the point.
>
> (G. Frege, 1980, p. 31)

Contrary to Scholz, I think that Hilbert is confused and that Frege's remarks are precisely on target. (F. Kambartel is one of the few contemporary philosophers who reaches the same conclusion in his *Erfahrung und Struktur: Bausteine zu einer Kritik des Empirismus und Formalismus*.) In a letter to Hilbert of December 27, 1899, Frege makes all of the important distinctions between sentences, axioms, definitions, etc. and objects that the axioms of Hilbert's system do not, as Hilbert claims, define the geometric properties (point, line, plane) and relations (lies, between, parallel, congruent, etc.). In his reply, Hilbert mentions the three points on which he most fundamentally disagrees with Frege:

(1) Against Frege's insistence that an axiom, conceived of as a true sentence, *presupposes* an interpretation of its (non-logical) terms, Hilbert objects: "I do not want to assume anything as known in advance; I regard my explanation in sect. 1 as the definition of the concepts point, line, plane— if one adds again all the axioms of group I to V as characteristic marks (G. Frege, 1980, p. 39).

(2) But their disagreement goes much deeper than this. Frege thinks of axioms as true sentences. It follows then from the truth of the axioms that they do not contradict each other. Hilbert sees it differently: ". . . for as long as I have been thinking, writing and lecturing on these things, I have been saying the exact reverse: If the arbitrarily given axioms do not contradict one another with all their consequences, then they are true and the things defined by the axioms exist. This is for me the criterion of truth and existence" (Frege, 1980, pp. 39–40).

(3) Finally, Hilbert touches on the important topic of model construction. Frege had pointed out that Hilbert in one place had interpreted 'point' to be, not a geometric thing, but a pair of numbers, and he had complained that this leaves it unclear what Hilbert really means by that word. To this Hilbert replies: "But it is surely obvious that every theory is only a scaffolding or schema of concepts together with their necessary relations to one another, and that the basic elements can be thought of in any way one likes. If in speaking of my points I think of some system of things, e.g. the system: love, law, chimneysweep . . . and then assume all my axioms as relations between these things, then my propositions, e.g. Pythagoras' theorem, are also valid for these things. In other words, any theory can always be applied to infinitely many systems of basic elements" (Frege, 1980, p. 43).

The topics of this dispute have been discussed by quite a few philosophers. I shall merely add a few comments. Firstly, I think, as I said already, that Frege is correct on all three points. Secondly, it seems obvious to me that consistency neither implies truth nor existence. Thirdly, it is of course true that Hilbert's axioms, *when treated as forms*, allow for many different interpretations. But this very fact conflicts with Hilbert's first point, namely, that the axioms are definitions. We see that Hilbert treats the axioms sometimes as sentences (definitions) and sometimes as mere forms, thus creating the confusion which I pointed out earlier.

It must be mentioned that Frege clearly saw that there is still another way of looking at Dedekind's and Hilbert's axiomatizations of arithmetic and geometry, respectively (see Frege's letter to Hilbert of January 6, 1900; Frege, 1980, p. 43, and, especially, Frege's "Ueber die Grundlagen der Geometrie"). We replace the axioms by the corresponding forms, but with variables in place of the place holders. Then we consider those expressions which consist of a conjunction of the "axiom forms" as antecedent and a "theorem form" as consequent. If we close these expressions for the variables, we get a set of true sentences, namely, sentences of logic. If these truths of logic are properly instantiated, we arrive at true conditionals whose antecedents are the axioms of the theory. We have before us now a set of logical truths from which we can get, say, geometric truths, if we properly instantiate and separate the antecedents from the consequents. Needless to say, this whole process has nothing to do with definition. Nor does it turn geometry or arithmetic, properly understood, into logic.

Reading Hilbert's replies to Frege, one can fairly feel Hilbert's impatience with Frege's "philosophical quibbles." He shows an attitude quite common among philosophically inclined scientists. Things are really much simpler than philosophers tend to make them. We really need not worry about the nature of geometric points, lines, etc. and how we are acquainted with them. These objects, whatever they may be, are implicitly defined by the axioms of geometry. Nor need we torment ourselves about the nature of truth and existence. Consistency is truth and existence. Finally, the nature of geometry is an open book. Geometry is really a branch of logic; it consists of the set of propositions which state the implications from the axioms to the theorems (compare Russell's first sentence of the first chapter of the *Principles of Mathematics:* "Pure mathematics is the class of all propositions of the form 'p implies q' " . . .)

3) QUINE'S RESURRECTION OF IMPLICIT DEFINITIONS

After Frege's incisive criticism, one should have hoped that implicit definitions had been laid to rest forever. Alas, this hope is in vain. They still play the role of a *deus ex machina* on the philosophical stage. If your philosophical play is hopelessly entangled, implicit definitions to the rescue! (cf., for example, Schlick's attempt to stave off idealism by appealing to implicit definitions. M. Schlick, *Allgemeine Erkenntnislehre,* pp. 29–38).

Quine has recently argued that the axiomatic development of every synthetic theory can be replaced by an axiomatic development of the same theory whose true statements follow from the truths of arithmetic. He then claims that this alleged fact vindicates the view that axioms are implicit definitions (W. V. Quine, "Implicit Definitions Sustained").

Consider a set of chemical properties, C_i, of a certain theory of chemistry and let '$A(C_i)$' abbreviate the conjunction of the axioms of this theory. It is well known that one can also give an arithmetic interpretation of the axiom forms of this theory in terms of certain arithmetic properties K_i (see D. Hilbert and P. Bernays, *Grundlagen der Mathematik,* vol. 2, p. 253). Upon such an interpretation, we get the axioms $A(K_i)$. Quine now constructs a third interpretation in terms of properties F_i allegedly defined on the basis of both C_i and K_i. This construction proceeds in two steps. (1) The individual variables of the chemical and arithmetic theories must be allowed to range over both physical objects and natural numbers. This is achieved by what Quine calls "hidden inflation." We take an arbitrary element *a* of, say, the physical universe of discourse and extend the original interpretation of the chemical predicates to natural numbers by stipulating that the chemical properties belong to them if and only if they belong to *a*. Then we reinterpret the arithmetic predicates in a similar way. (2) The predicates 'F_i' of the third interpretation are defined as follows: '$F_i(x)$' is short for '$(A(C_i)$ and $C_i(x))$ or (not-$A(C_i)$ and $K_i(x))$'. (For the sake of simplicity, I only consider one-place predicates of the first level.) Now one can show that '$A(F_i)$' follows from the arithmetic truths '$A(K_i)$' alone. Hence it may be said that '$A(F_i)$' is true as a matter of arithmetic, that is, that it is an arithmetic truth. (Quine makes this point in terms of analyticity: If arithmetic is analytic, then '$A(F_i)$' is analytic.)

There are several things wrong with this construction and with Quine's conclusion. First of all, it makes no sense to *stipulate,* for example, that the inflated chemical predicates represent properties which belong to numbers if and only if they belong to an arbitrary physical object *a*. One cannot create properties as one wishes. One cannot just say: "Let there be such and such properties" and expect them to come into being. A contemplated property either exists or it does not exist. We can at best find out which is the case. There are certain chemical properties which may or may not belong to *a*. But these properties most certainly do not belong to natural numbers, and there is nothing Quine, or Dreben, or anyone else can do about it. At best, we may discover some properties—but we would hardly call them "chemical properties"—which belong to physical objects and which also belong to natural numbers if and only if they belong to a given physical object a. But I have no idea what these properties could be and seriously doubt that there are any.

There are also several things wrong with the definition of the predicate 'F_i'. Firstly, there is no reason at all to assume that 'F_i' represents a property (or some properties). From the fact that we agree to abbreviate an expression by a shorter one, it does not follow that the completely arbitrary sign 'F_i' is a predicate. Secondly, there is no guarantee whatsoever that the definiens represents a property (or properties). Quite to the contrary, since the definiens is a form, it could not possibly represent a property, as I have argued elsewhere (see my *Ontological Reduction;* and also "Structures, Functions, and Forms," pp. 11–32). In addition to these two objections, there is another difficulty. Quine's definition assures that the properties F_i—assuming that there are such properties—are coextensive with the properties C_i. But these two sets of properties are not the same. If we hold, as seems reasonable, that two theories may be distinguished, among other things, by the properties they attribute to things, then it follows that, contrary to Quine, '$A(C_i)$' is the axiomatic development of a chemical theory, but '$A(F_i)$' is not; for it mentions very queer properties—if we continue to assume for the sake of making a point that there are such properties—which are not chemical properties at all, but which happen to be coextensive with chemical properties.

Finally, that F_i and C_i have the same extension is not a mere matter of abbreviation, as one may be inclined to think from the definition given above. It depends on the chemical fact that '$A(C_i)$' happens to be true. For if we assume that '$A(C_i)$' is false, F_i will have the same extension as K_i instead. Thus we have in 'F_i' a group of predicates representing properties whose extensions depend on whether or not a certain chemical theory is true. And this fact clearly distinguishes the properties C_i from the properties F_i.

But what does all of this have to do with implicit definitions? It is not entirely clear to me why Quine thinks that his construction shows that implicit definitions are vindicated. Perhaps he reasoned as follows. To say that axioms are implicit definitions is to say, at least in part, that they are analytic, like ordinary kinds of definition. But we can show by means of the construction that axioms can be turned into analytic statements. Hence the conception of axioms as definitions is vindicated.

I think that Quine's construction shows, if it shows that much, that the "theory" '$A(F_i)$' can be deduced from '$A(K_i)$'. Thus, if the former were really a theory about certain things and their properties, it would be true as a matter of arithmetic. Let us agree, for the sake of the argument, that it would be an arithmetic theory. But how does this show that '$A(C_i)$' is an arithmetic theory? Of course, it does not show this if we are correct in our claim, contrary to Quine, that the chemical properties C_i are not the same as the properties F_i. But even if we assume, contrary to fact, that '$A(F_i)$' is an axiomatization of the same theory as '$A(C_i)$', this would merely mean that the chemical theory is true as a matter of arithmetic (whatever that may mean), but not that it is true as a matter of definition. The axioms '$A(F_i)$' would be comparable to arithmetic truths that follow from other arithmetic truths.

4) IMPLICIT DEFINITIONS AND TRUTH BY CONVENTION

Even if Quine's construction were sound, the desired analogy between definitions and axioms can only be drawn if we use the notion of analyticity as a verbal bridge. What is analytic, one must hold, is true by definition. Since Quine's construction seems to show that the axioms of chemistry, for example, are analytic, so one may reason, they are true by definition, that is, they are definitions. And this brings us back to the main point of our investigation, namely, the alleged analyticity of arithmetic. It is taken for granted by most recent and contemporary philosophers that arithmetic is analytic. What gives rise to this conviction is the "felt necessity" of arithmetic truths. To show that arithmetic is analytic, therefore, one must explain this necessity. Up to this point, there is general agreement. But now the views diverge. Frege and the logicists claim that the necessity of arithmetic is the necessity of logic, whatever that may be. A moment ago, we encountered a different strategy. Analyticity means, not reducibility to logic, but *truth by definition*. And since we can adopt any definition we feel like proposing, analyticity becomes *truth by fiat*. And since we can count on general agreement about our stipulations, analyticity turns out to be *truth by convention*. This is the refrain one hears time and again from analytic philosophers: Arithmetic is necessary, that is, analytic, because arithmetic truths are true by definitions, that is, by convention.

Quine's construction aims at making even the axioms of chemistry analytic. This, surely, is not in the spirit of making a sharp distinction between arithmetic, on the one hand, and the sciences, on the other. We must remind ourselves that Quine rejects the traditional and widely accepted distinction between analytic and synthetic truths. His defense of implicit definitions, therefore, kills two birds with one stone: It vindicates the conception of axioms as implicit definitions and, at the same time, breaks down the wall between arithmetic and the sciences. But if the axioms of chemistry are just as "analytic" as the truths of arithmetic, what happens to the "felt necessity" of the latter? Here is Quine's answer in a nutshell:

> There are statements which we choose to surrender last, if at all, in the course of revamping our sciences in the face of new discoveries; and among these there are some which we will not surrender at all, so basic are they to our whole conceptual scheme. Among the latter are to be counted the so-called truths of logic and mathematics, regardless of what further we may have to say of their status in the course of a subsequent sophisticated philosophy.

(W. V. O. Quine, "Truth by Convention," p. 342)

In part, we agree with Quine. We, too, reject the traditional positivistic analytic-synthetic distinction which rests on the conviction that while science is a matter of fact, mathematics and logic are not. We share Quine's view that science as well as mathematics and logic are made from one cloth. But Quine thinks that the cloth is woven from conventions, while we believe that it is woven from facts. While Quine argues, in the article about implicit definitions, that even chemistry can be made a matter of convention, we insist that even mathematics and logic are a matter of fact. Perhaps a better way of describing our difference is to say that while we both agree that mathematics and logic are as "empirical" as the sciences, 'empirical' means something quite different to Quine from what it means to us. The reason why we do not easily surrender the truths of mathematics and logic is that they are fundamental truths about the structure of the world.

d) Three Grades of Model Mania

I) MODELS AND CONSTRUCTIONAL DEFINITIONS

Axioms are not definitions; they do not define anything. But they may be said to describe the things which they mention. For example, Dedekind's third axiom says that the number 1 is not the successor of any natural number. It says something true about this number. It states one of the characteristics of 1. In this sense, it may be said to describe a feature of the number. But it does not define what '1' stands for. Quite to the contrary, we must know what '1' stands for in order to understand that the axiom says something about the number 1. To the question: What are numbers? one may therefore reply: Whatever the *axioms* say they are. But we must not confuse this answer with the quite different answer: Whatever the *forms* say they are. As I emphasized earlier, forms, in distinction from axioms, do not "say" anything.

But forms have models, and this fact has given birth to a whole branch of the philosophy of mathematics. It has even given rise to a new way of doing ontology. Quine, one of the main proponents of this approach, holds that one kind of entity is reduced to another kind of entity, if these two kinds yield isomorphic models for the same set of forms (see Quine's "Ontological Reduction and the World of Numbers" in W. V. Quine, *The Ways of Paradox*, New York: Random House, 1966; And see also N. Goodman, "Constructional Definitions" in *The Structure of Appearance*).

To be more specific, Quine holds that an ontological reduction has been achieved if one can specify a correlator between the individuals of the original theory and the individuals of the model such that all the properties (and relations) of the model are isomorphic to the properties (and relations) of the original theory. For arithmetic, represented by Dedekind's or Peano's axioms, there are many models which fulfill this condition. We mentioned earlier that the even natural numbers and the odd natural numbers yield models for the respective forms. But there are also progressions of sets which are models of those forms. For example, there is the "Zermelo progression" consisting of the empty set, the set whose only member is the empty set, the set whose only member is the set whose only member is the empty set, and so on. And there is also the "von Neumann progression," consisting of the empty set, the set whose only member is the empty set, the set consisting of the empty set and the set whose only member is the empty set, and so on. It follows from Quine's conception that the even natural numbers can be reduced to the odd natural numbers. It also follows that the progression of natural numbers can be reduced to either the Zermelo progression or to the von Neumann progression. But this shows clearly that Quine's notion of ontological reduction is an odd one. It does not bear on the question of what numbers are. Obviously, the natural numbers are not identical with the odd natural numbers. Nor are they identical with the Zermelo sets. Nor are they identical with the von Neumann sets. If we assume that Quine's method of reduction answers the question of what the natural numbers are, then the answer would be that they are both Zermelo sets and von Neumann sets, and since these two kinds of sets are not identical, the method is reduced to absurdity. According to our view, of course, the natural numbers are not identical with any of those other progressions.

If one admits, and Quine seems to admit it, that the different models for the Peano forms involve different domains of different entities, then there can be no question of "reducing" one of these domains to another. What philosophical sense could it possibly make to speak of "reducing" a line of ten elephants to the first ten natural numbers? Model construction reveals that very *different* kinds of entity can yield models for the *same* forms. It shows that very different kinds of thing can form isomorphic structures.

Quine and his followers concede that the natural numbers are not the Zermelo sets. But they are loath to part with the idea that model construction has something to do with ontological reduction. So they add a new wrinkle to the dialectic. Zermelo sets are not identical with the natural numbers, they claim, *but they can serve the same purpose* as the natural numbers: "Any objects will serve as numbers so long as the arithmetical operations are defined for them and the laws of arithmetic are preserved" (W. V. O. Quine, *Set Theory and Its Logic*, p. 81). And on the same page he claims that "We are free to take 0 as anything we like, and construe S as any function we like, so long merely as the function is one that, when applied in iteration to 0, yields something different on every further application". In another paper, Quine puts it this way: "Just so, we might say, Frege and von Neumann showed how to skip the natural numbers and get by with what we may for the moment call Frege classes and von Neumann classes." These classes, he continues, "Simulate the behavior of the natural numbers to the point where it is convenient to call them natural numbers . . ." ("Ontological Reduction and the World of Numbers," in *The Ways of Paradox*, pp. 199–207, p. 200).

But in what sense of "free" are we free, as Quine claims, to take 0 as anything we like and to construe S as any function we like, as long as the repeated application of S yields a progression? It seems to me that we are free to pick any first element and any one of several possible relations as long as we are not interested in the progression of natural numbers, but merely in a progression of whatever kind. Similarly, to say, as Quine does, that the progression of even numbers serves as a version of number can only mean that since the even numbers and the natural numbers both form progressions, it does not matter which one we consider, so long as we are only interested in a progression, but do not care what particular progression it is. And to say that we can skip the natural numbers and get by with Zermelo sets can only mean that we can pick the progression of Zermelo sets rather than the progression of natural numbers, as long as we are only interested in considering a progression of whatever sort. In short, as long as we are not interested in a particular progression, but only in the feature of being a progression, any example of a progression will do for the purpose at hand, just as any human being will do as an example, if we are merely interested in the property of being a human being. But just as there are many different human beings, irrespective of which one we select as our example, so there are many different progressions, irrespective of which one we consider. Zermelo sets and Frege sets both form progressions. They are alike in this respect. But this is the only sense in which the entities in the one domain "simulate" the behavior of the entities in the other domain. There is no reason whatsoever why we should deliberately confuse the one domain with the other. Zermelo is like Frege in that both are human beings, but we do not believe for a moment that this is a sufficient reason for confusing them with each other. Nor would it be convenient to call Frege "Zermelo", or conversely. Why, then, should it ever be convenient to call Zermelo sets anything but "Zermelo sets," and to call natural numbers anything but "natural numbers"?

Natural numbers form a progression, and so do many other kinds of things. To believe that for this reason alone the natural numbers should be reduced to or replaced by some other progression is as absurd as to believe that Frege should be reduced to or replaced by Zermelo, just because they are both human beings.

2) MODELS AND SEMANTIC ROLES

So far in this chapter, we have looked at two answers to the question of what numbers are. According to the first, numbers are whatever the axioms of arithmetic define them to be. According to the second, they are whatever we want them to be as long as we stick to things that satisfy the axiom forms of arithmetic. The next attempt to wring some kind of answer out of the fact that there are isomorphic models for the arithmetic forms is even more peculiar. It leads to the answer that numbers are not anything in particular:

> Any system of objects, whether sets or not, that forms a recursive progression must be adequate . . . That any recursive sequence whatever would do suggests that what is important is not the individuality of each element but the structure which they jointly exhibit . . . I therefore argue . . . *that numbers could not be objects at all;* for there is no more reason to identify any individual number with any one particular object than with any other (not already known to be a number) . . .
>
> The properties of being numbers which do not stem from the relations they bear to one another in virtue of being arranged in a progression are of no consequence whatsoever. But it would be only these properties that would single a number as this object or that.
>
> (P. Benacerraf, "What Numbers Could Not Be", pp. 69–70, my italics)

As I understand it, Benacerraf's argument has two parts. The first part is a straightforward argument from the existence of isomorphic models, and it goes like this. Any progression, no matter of what things it consists, "must be adequate" for the purpose of arithmetic. But that every progression "would do for the purpose of arithmetic" shows that what is important is the progression, not the elements of the progression. Therefore, arithmetic deals with progressions in general, and the numbers of arithmetic are not any individual, specific objects.

In this argument, we can distinguish three ingredients. Firstly, there is the pragmatic idea, which we have chastised before, that for the purposes of arithmetic any progression does equally well. This is simply not true. Any progression does equally well when our purpose is not to do arithmetic, but to consider the nature of progressions or, in other words, to consider progressions in general. Secondly, having conceived of arithmetic as being concerned with the nature of progressions rather than with the progression of natural numbers, Benacerraf concludes that arithmetic is concerned with the nature of an element in general, rather than with natural numbers. Thirdly and lastly, Benacerraf identifies the notion of an element of a progression with the notion of a number. The property of being a number is but the property of being an element of a progression. A number is anything that occurs in a progression. These numbers, of course, are definite things. What else could they be? But they are not elements of just one particular progression. They are not, for example, Zermelo sets, although Zermelo sets are numbers; and they are not von Neumann sets, although von Neumann sets are also numbers. But what about the progression of natural numbers, are they not numbers? Benacerraf's view seems to imply that while there are many progressions, there is no progression of natural numbers.

At this point, I think, the second of his two arguments is relevant. This argument rests on the quite amazing ontological fact that numbers have no properties, with the exception of the categorial property of being a number. What characterizes an individual number is not a set of properties, but rather a set of relations in which it stands to other numbers. What properties does the number two have? Well, it is an even number. But this means, of course, that it is divisible by two, that is, that it stands in the division relation to numbers. And similarly for all other alleged properties: They are one and all "relational properties."

But this does not mean, as Benacerraf seems to go on to argue, that numbers cannot be distinguished from other kinds of entities. First of all, there is the fact, for example, that elephants have properties which numbers do not have. Elephants eat peanuts, numbers do not. Secondly, and more importantly, the arithmetic relations among numbers suffice to distinguish numbers from all other kinds of things. What uniquely characterizes the numbers are the relations in which they stand to each other and to nothing else. Numbers and only numbers stand in the sum relation to each other; numbers and only numbers stand in the "successor relation" to each other, and so on. Neither elephants nor sets are sums of each other; neither elephants nor sets are "successors" of each other. Of course, sets stand in relations to each other which are *isomorphic* to the so-called successor relation. But these relations are not identical with the successor relation. Consider the Zermelo progression and the von Neumann progression of sets. The relations R_1 and R_2 which order these progressions are isomorphic to the successor relation. But they are different from each other and different from the successor relation. R_1 is the relation between a set and its singleton; R_2 can perhaps best be described as the relation which an element has to the set which has exactly it and all of its elements as elements. Neither one of these two relations is the relation which a natural number has to the next natural number. Thus what distinguishes between the Zermelo progression and the von Neumann progression; and between these two, on the one hand, and the progression of natural numbers, on the other, are the different, though isomorphic, relations that obtain between the elements of the progressions. For the rest, it is simply not true, as Benacerraf claims, that only properties could single out numbers from other kinds of things.

Let me quote another passage from Benacerraf:

> That a system of objects exhibits the structure of the integers implies that the elements of that system have some properties not dependent on structure. It must be possible to individuate those objects independently of the role they play in that structure. But this is precisely what cannot be done with the numbers. To *be* the number 3 is no more and no less than to be preceded by 2, 1, and possibly 0, and to be followed by . . . Any object can play the role of 3; that is, any object can be the third element in some progression.
>
> (Benacerraf, p. 70)

According to Benacerraf, the system of the natural numbers cannot exhibit the structure of the natural numbers; for the natural numbers cannot be individuated independently of the role they play in that structure. I take this to imply that there is no such thing as the system of natural numbers. In other words, Benacerraf argues that in regard to the Peano forms, for example, there exist all kinds of models except the model of the natural numbers. And this is so because numbers, in distinction from other things, have no properties *independent of structure*.

We hold that numbers are distinguished from all other kinds of things by the relations that hold among them. The question therefore becomes: Do numbers stand in certain characteristic relations which are independent of structure? And the answer, I submit, is clearly affirmative. Numbers and only numbers stand in the "successor relation" to each other. Is this not a feature which is independent of structure? What distinguishes one structure from another structure, *when both have the same structure,* may well be the fact that they contain different though isomorphic relations. From the fact that two structures share the same structure, it does not follow that they contain the same relations. And indeed, none of the structures which are isomorphic to the progression of the natural numbers contain the so-called successor relation. We see that Benacerraf's argument would be sound if isomorphic relations were identical. But they need not be.

So much for the exotic view that while there are many progressions, there is no progression of the natural numbers. In a recent article, it appears to me, Resnik has taken this view to its limits:

> The second [problem] arises from the fact that no mathematical theory can do more than determine its objects up to isomorphism. Thus the platonist seems to be in the paradoxical position of claiming that a given mathematical theory is about certain things and yet be unable to make any definite statement of what these things are.
>
> (M. D. Resnik, "Mathematics as a Science of Patterns: Ontology," p. 529)

How does Resnik arrive at the thesis that "no mathematical theory can do more than determine its objects up to isomorphism"? He does not tell us. One thing is certain, though; this thesis does not follow from the admitted fact that there are many *different* models for the axiom forms of arithmetic. Nor does it follow from any other set of facts, for it is false. From this false thesis, Resnik arrives at the view that: "The objects of mathematics, that is, the entities which our mathematical constants and quantifiers denote, are structureless points or positions in structures. As positions in structures, they have no identity or feature outside of structure" (Resnik, p. 530). What is a position in a structure? Perhaps Resnik holds the following view. The number three, for example, is the third position in many different structures. There are different structures, and these structures do consist of certain things. For example, there is the Zermelo progression and there is the von Neumann progression. In the Zermelo progression, the third position is occupied by the set whose only member is the set whose only member is the empty set; in the von Neumann progression, that position is occupied by quite a different set, namely, by the set which has two members: the empty set, and the set whose only member is the empty set. Although these two elements are quite different, they nevertheless occupy "the same position." A position, therefore, is some kind of property or feature which different things can share (relative to the structures in which they occur). But the number three is not just any position. It is the *third* position. Here we are confronted with the unanalyzed and unexplained (ordinal) notion of three. Why do we attribute this feature to the two sets mentioned earlier? Obviously, we do so by reference to a third progression, namely, the progression of natural numbers. The Zermelo set turns out to be that part of the Zermelo progression which is coordinated to the number three in the progression of natural numbers. And the same holds for the von Neumann set. What is common to these sets is not some kind of undefined property or feature that may be called "the third position," but rather that both sets are coordinated to the number three. But this explication of the notion of the third position implies, apparently contrary to what Resnik wishes to hold, that there exists the progression of natural numbers.

3) MODELS AND SEMANTIC NIHILISM

Resnik claims "that no mathematical theory can do more than determine its objects up to isomorphism." I assumed that this claim was based on the fact that there are isomorphic models for the arithmetic axiom forms, and then I pointed out that the claim simply does not follow from the fact. Let us now follow another, though connected, chain of thought. Consider the true sentence: 'This pen is blue at t_1' and its associated form: 'This f is g at t_n'. Obviously, there are interpretations of this form which are different from the original one and yield true sentences. For example, 'This book is green at t_1' happens to be true. Assume that we conclude that since there are many different "models" for this sentence form, the sentence determines its objects only "up to isomorphism." Would it not follow that we do not really know what the sentence is about "up to isomorphism"? And this would imply that we do not really know at all what the sentence is about. Hence we would have to conclude that we do not really know what any of our (declarative, true) sentences is about. I think that we have here a clear case of a *reductio* argument: If this is the consequence of our assumption that where there are models, there is indeterminacy up to isomorphism, then the assumption must be false.

I suspect, however, that there are philosophers who do not share my view and are willing to accept the conclusion. I suspect, furthermore, that this conclusion leads to a bundle of loosely connected thoughts which have been dubbed "the model theoretic argument against realism" (see H. Putnam, "Models and Reality,"). Whatever arguments there may be against realism, it seems obvious to me that they cannot possibly be based on the fact that certain forms allow for different models. But be that as it may, it is at any rate mistaken to believe that the sentence 'This pen is blue at t_1' "determines its objects only up to isomorphism." This sentence is about this particular pen, not about that book, and it says about the pen that it is blue (at t_1) rather than that it is green, or round, or sweet. Similarly for the axioms of arithmetic. The third Dedekind axiom reads: 1 is not the successor of any natural number. This axiom is about the number 1, not about 0 or Paris, and it says about this particular number that it is not the successor of any number, not that it is not the brother of any Spanish king.

Of course, the associated forms for the sentence about the pen and the axioms for arithmetic may be said to "determine their objects only up to isomorphism." Obviously, the form 'This f is g at t_n' does not tell us what it is about, for it is really not about anything. It is a form of something, of a sentence, that can be about something. It is a mere skeleton that needs to be fleshed out. Those who claim that the axioms of arithmetic do not determine their objects make the simple mistake, chastised in an earlier section, of confusing the axioms with their forms.

There is no reason why we should stop with the form 'This f is g at t_n'. Why not replace the rest of the words in this form by appropriate schematic letters? We may proceed, for example, to get the "pure" form: 'T f R g S t_n'. And this expression does not even determine its objects (the f's and g's) up to isomorphism. If one does not distinguish between the axioms of arithmetic, on the one hand, and all of the associated forms derivable from those axioms, on the other, one might as well conclude that the axioms of arithmetic do not even determine their objects up to isomorphism. One might as well conclude that they do not determine any objects at all.

In conclusion, let us look at one last argument for this sort of semantic nihilism (see Hockney's review of my *Ontological Reduction*, in *Philosophical Books*). We are to imagine a civilization whose entire arithmetic vocabulary consists of set-theoretical and logical items. These people speak a version of Zermelo arithmetic. Among them, there exists a person with my philosophical views called "Gro." Gro comes to hold that there is a special subcategory of the category of sets which he calls "sumbers" and which consist of the Zermelo sets arranged in the familiar way. Now, Gro assigns sumbers either (1) to the category of set, or (2) to the category of quantifier. According to Hockney, I cannot say in regard to alternative (1) that sumbers are really numbers and belong to the category of quantifier, since I hold that numbers are not sets. Quite so! On the other hand, if I claim that sumbers are just sets, and that there are other entities called "numbers," then Gro will reply, according to Hockney, that any fool can see that numbers are fictions, for no such entities are constituents of the states of affairs we perceive. The debate about alternative (2) proceeds presumably along the same lines. From this Hockney concludes that there are no means by which this argument can be resolved without giving up Gro's and my common principles; and these principles depend for their application on the view that it is clear what the constituents of states of affairs are. And from this he concludes further that these principles are useless, that there are no ultimate criteria which tell us to what our terms really refer, and that there is no unique answer to the question: What are numbers? The philosophical significance of constructional definitions consists, according to Hockney, in that they may be employed to display the range of legitimate ontological alternatives.

Hockney's chain of reasoning has several puzzling links. Firstly, it is not clear to me what he means by saying that the imagined civilization has an *arithmetical vocabulary*. Does this mean that those people use shapes like 'o', 'I', etc.—and that they make the corresponding noises—when they talk about Zermelo sets? I do not think so; for then a tribe of aborigines may be said, with equal justification, to be using a quantum theoretical vocabulary if the members of the tribe happen to use certain shapes and noises in order to talk about gum trees, rocks, and dingos. Rather, what must be meant is that the imagined civilization uses some other kinds of shapes and noises in order to talk about Zermelo sets. But since there is an isomorphism between the progression of natural numbers and the progression of Zermelo sets, one conceives of these shapes and noises as constituting an arithmetical vocabulary. However, this conception is odd at best and misleading at worst. Imagine a civilization that has an axiomatized theory of zoology, but no arithmetic. (If you cannot conceive of such a civilization, then I doubt that you can conceive of Hockney's civilization either.) Assume further that there is an arithmetical interpretation of the forms of that zoological theory. We could then say, following Hockney's strange usage, that the entire arithmetical vocabulary of this civilization consists of zoological terms. From our point of view, we would protest, of course, that this civilization has no arithmetical vocabulary at all, since its members never talk or even think about numbers. But we cannot prevent Hockney from using 'arithmetical vocabulary' in this bizarre fashion. And no philosophical harm need be done, as long as we constantly keep in mind just how strangely he uses this expression.

The civilization of zoologists, in my opinion, talks about animals, not about numbers. But of course there are numbers in addition to animals, and the animals of the theory merely "simulate the behavior of natural numbers" in that unproblematic sense which is explicated in terms of the arithmetic model of the forms of the zoological theory. Similarly, in regard to Hockney's civilization: Those people talk about Zermelo sets, not about numbers. There are numbers in addition and distinction to Zermelo sets, and Zermelo sets merely "simulate the behavior of the natural numbers." To this, Gro presumably replies that numbers are nothing but fictions, since they are never perceived as constituents of states of affairs. At this point, I find a second unclarity in Hockney's argument. We are not told whether or not the members of the imagined civilization perceive such states of affairs as that there are two tigers in the cage and that there are four pencils on the desk. Without this information, we simply do not know what to make of Gro's reply.

Let us assume that those people perceive, just as we do, that there are two tigers in the cage and that there are four pencils on the desk. Gro is then simply and plainly mistaken. He and his friends do perceive numbers, no matter how vigorously and stubbornly he may deny it. On the other hand, if we assume that Gro and his friends do not perceive such states of affairs, then we understand immediately why he does not believe us when we tell him that there are states of affairs involving numbers and, hence, that there are numbers. But what does this difference in our respective beliefs show? Surely not that there are no numbers. Otherwise, we could as easily prove that there are no tigers by merely imagining a civilization that does not perceive tigers, or that there are no philosophers by imagining a civilization that does not perceive philosophers.

What Hockney's argument is supposed to show, to remind ourselves, is that there is no way in which the debate between Gro and me can be resolved. This is the third obscure point. Does this mean that Gro may stick to his guns no matter what, even though he does see "numerical states of affairs"? Of course Gro may. But that would not prove anything. Does it mean that Gro's reply is just as reasonable as my view, provided that Gro cannot perceive numerical states of affairs? Gro is then certainly justified in being skeptical about the existence of numbers, just as someone who does not perceive tigers is justified in being skeptical about the existence of tigers. But this does not show that Gro's reply is just as reasonable, just as correct, as my view. If it did, then we could prove by the same sort of argument that it is just as reasonable to deny the existence of tigers, or of anything else, as it is to assert their existence. No debate about the existence of anything whatsoever could then be resolved.

This brings us to what Hockney calls the moral of his story, namely, that there are no ultimate criteria which tell us to what our terms refer, so that there is no unique answer to the question: What are numbers? Now, I do not care about *ultimate* criteria and *unique* answers. Ordinary criteria and plain answers will do. From this vantage point, I find Hockney's moral not just unclear, but downright incoherent. If we do not have criteria that tell us to what our terms refer, how do we know to what they refer? And if Hockney means to imply that we do not know to what they refer, how does he know that his imagined civilization talks about Zermelo sets? How does he know, for that matter, that he himself is talking about Zermelo sets rather than, say, von Neumann sets? How can he possibly distinguish between *different* (though "equally legitimate") models for the same axiom forms? And if there is no answer to the question: What are numbers? because we do not know to what our words refer, how could there be an answer to the question: What are tigers? Or does Hockney believe that there are no answers to any of these questions?

Looking back, it must surprise a philosopher of the next century that the discovery of isomorphic models gave rise to so much bad philosophy about the nature of mathematics. We just traced a path of misconceptions from implicit definitions to semantic nihilism.

FOUR

Mathematical Knowledge and Meaning

a) The Doctrine of "Empty Tautologies"

In our century, the Kantian challenge was accepted by the logical positivists and some outstanding philosophers who influenced them. Among the latter, Russell and Wittgenstein come to mind. Allow me to speak of "analytic philosophers" in order to group together those who professed to being positivists and also those who merely influenced the positivists or were influenced by them. In the hands of analytic philosophers, the Kantian challenge took a "linguistic turn," a turn every bit as fertile as Kant's "Copernican turn." Language became the medium through which philosophical problems are to be viewed.

Kant had argued this way: (1) arithmetic truths are necessary; (2) but they are not analytic; (3) therefore, there must exist a necessity not derived from analyticity. Analytic philosophers, by contrast, applied *modus tollens:* Since there is no necessity other than that of analyticity, either (1), or (2), or both, must be false. And since they could not convince themselves of the falsity of (1), they concluded that (2) must be false: Arithmetic truths must be analytic. This confronted them with a problem. They now had to find a notion of analyticity, according to which arithmetic could plausibly be said to be analytic. And this notion, ideally, should also cover logic. What they came up with was a "linguistic" or "semantic" notion of analyticity. This conception was never clear. Nor should we really talk about one notion, since there were several of them, which were often identified or even confused with each other. It is a hopeless task to try to untangle all of the themes that enter into the concept of "semantic analyticity." I shall have to be content with mentioning some of the main ingredients.

There is no necessity other than that of analyticity! This is the rallying cry of analytic philosophy. We could call it the "Humean dogma." Empirical matters of fact, according to the Humean tradition, are never necessary. This implies that arithmetic, since it is necessary, cannot be factual. But if it is not factual, then what does it say? The search for a satisfactory notion of analyticity is also a search for a satisfactory answer to this question. The dialectic revolves around two distinctions: Firstly, around the analytic-synthetic dichotomy and, secondly, around the factual-nonfactual distinction. The synthetic is of course identified with the factual; there is no problem here. The analytic must then be the nonfactual. But what *sense* can the nonfactual have? Does it not merely comprise nonsense? Metaphysics, many analytic philosophers held, is meaningless because it makes no factual statements. Now, if arithmetic and logic are analytic and, hence, nonfactual, how can they possibly avoid the fate of metaphysics?

We can therefore distinguish three interrelated problems that vexed analytic philosophers: (1) What kind of necessity is the necessity of arithmetic (and logic)? (2) What notion of analyticity characterizes arithmetic (and logic)? and (3) What meaning can nonfactual statements have?

The early Wittgenstein proposed a radical answer to these questions; an answer which influenced the later discussions of the logical positivists and their admirers. Let us briefly consider this answer, pretending, as we always must in the case of Wittgenstein, that there is a view to be studied rather than a mere web of loosely connected thoughts.

In the famous dialogue between Achilles and the Tortoise, Lewis Carroll has the tortoise argue that a valid inference can be drawn only after infinitely many tasks have been completed. Consider, for example, the familiar inference *modus ponens:*

(1) P,

(2) If P, then Q,

(3) Therefore, Q.

Carroll argues that unless we also assume:

(4) P and (If P, then Q), and

(5) If (P and (If P, then Q)), then Q,

we cannot infer Q. But even this will not do. We must further grant that (4) and (5) entail Q. And so on, *ad infinitum*. Now, it has often been pointed out that Carroll's formulation of the argument involves a temporal sequence of mental acts of granting certain premisses and that it is spurious for that reason alone. But it has also been claimed that if this appeal to time and psychology is removed, there remains a problem. Here is how Coffa sees the problem: "If the justification of the inference from (4) to (3) requires an appeal to the logical law (5), why don't we need to appeal to further logical laws in order to justify the inference from (4) and (5) to (3); and so on, *ad infinitum*" (J. A. Coffa, *To the Vienna Station,* chap. VIII).

The obvious solution to the puzzle is to point out that the inference is justified *without* an appeal to the logical law as an added premise. The inference involves premises (1) and (2) and nothing else. From (1) and (2) follows (3), and that is the end of the story. However, and this 'however' is all-important, we may ask why we accept this inference as valid and not, say, the inference from Q and If P, then Q, to P. In answer to *this* question, we cite the logical law:

(6) All p and all q are such that: If p is the case, and if p then q is the case, then q is the case.

We point out in defense of *modus ponens* that (6) is true or, equivalently, that it is a fact: It is a *fact* that all states of affairs are such that if p is a fact, and if p then q is a fact, then q is a fact. *That is the way the world is!* On the other hand, the corresponding sentence for our inference from Q to P is not true. There is no such fact. In short, the valid rules of inference are those which are based on logical laws, but these laws are not premises of the corresponding inferences.

All of this is fairly obvious. What it leads back to is the question after the nature of logical laws. I just claimed that logical laws are facts about the world. And this, of course, raises the question of how we discover and verify such facts. We could have saved ourselves the detour through Carroll's infinite regress argument and confronted the problem directly: What is the nature of the laws of logic? But there seems to persist a view among philosophers that the problem of the nature of logical laws is somehow infected by the regress argument. Wittgenstein, for example, seems to have thought that Carroll's argument showed something important about the nature of logic. What it shows, presumably, is that logic needs no justification. If I understand Wittgenstein correctly, he may have reasoned from the insight that the inference *modus ponens* needs no further premise to the conclusion that it needs no justification in terms of a logical law. Quite to the contrary. When we understand the premises of *modus ponens,* he holds, we also "see" the alleged logical law. The process is reversed: it is not the logical law which justifies the inference, but it is the inference which somehow calls our attention to the so-called logical law. Since we accept the inference, we accept the law; and not the other way around. Furthermore, the so-called logical law is not really a law, a fact, at all. Nor is its verbal expression a declarative sentence. If it were such a sentence, then it would say something; it would state a fact about the world. But this is not what logic is. Rather, logic "shows itself"; we recognize it *as soon as we understand language.* Logical sentences, contrary to what we have assumed, do not say anything about the world. In this respect, they are fundamentally different from other sentences:

If p follows from q, I can conclude from q to p. The mode of inference is to be understood from the two propositions alone. Only they themselves could justify the inference. "Laws of inference" which—as in Frege and Russell—are supposed to justify the inference, are senseless and would be superfluous.

(L. Wittgenstein, *Tractatus Logico-Philosophicus,* 5. 132)

From the correct premise that *modus ponens* does not require the relevant logical law as an added assumption, Wittgenstein concludes fallaciously that this law is "superfluous" and even "senseless." Of course, it is "superfluous" in the sense that it is not needed as an added premise, but it is not superfluous if we sort out valid inferences from invalid ones. And the logical law is certainly not "senseless." I think that we can now see more clearly how the infinite regress argument fits into Wittgenstein's view. As he conceives of the situation, the argument allows him to get rid of the logical law; first, by denying its importance, then by denying its very existence. Logic is dispensed with in favor of inferences, and what justifies the inferences is not logic, but our understanding of language.

The stubborn fact remains that logicians, and even ordinary people, talk about the laws of logic. No matter what Wittgenstein says, it is a fact that all states of affairs are such that if p is a fact, and if p then q is a fact, then q is a fact. Wittgenstein may try to sweep the laws of logic under the rug, but he can hardly hope to succeed using such a small rug. At the very least, he has to expand his view so that he can explain what these sentences of logic are about.

"My fundamental idea," Wittgenstein says, "is that the 'logical constants' do not represent anything" (Wittgenstein, 4.0312). It follows that there are no negative, no molecular, and no quantified facts. It also follows that logical sentences must connect with the world in a peculiar fashion. According to Wittgenstein, they *show* things, but do not *say* anything. It is not clear to me, even after reading a number of informed commentaries, how this distinction between showing and saying is to be understood. But we may possibly be enlightened if we consider what Wittgenstein has to say about identity.

Wittgenstein remarks: "Parenthetically, to say of *two* things that they are identical is nonsense, and to say of *one* that it is identical with itself says nothing" (Wittgenstein, 5.5303). Nothing could be farther from the truth. To say of two things that they are identical is not nonsense, but false. And to say of one thing that it is identical with itself is to say, not nothing, but that it is self-identical. It comes as no surprise, therefore, that Wittgenstein should arrive at the amazing conclusion that "expressions like 'a = a', and those derived from them, are neither elementary propositions nor otherwise meaningful expressions" (Wittgenstein, 4.243).

What moves Wittgenstein to the strange assertion that a false identity statement is nonsense and that a true one says nothing? He seems to think that this follows from the alleged fact that the false identity statement is a contradiction, and that the true identity statement is a tautology. He holds that tautologies, that is, the propositions of logic, say nothing (Wittgenstein, 5.142 and 5.43). Contradictions, on the other hand, have presumably no sense because they do not allow for any possible situation (Wittgenstein, 4.462).

From our point of view, a = a is not a *logical* truth. It is an instance of the *ontological* law of self-identity. (This law and its instances must be carefully distinguished from identity statements of the form: a is identical with the F.) Since it is an instance of an ontological rather than a logical law, it is true, not as a matter of logic, but as a matter of ontology. But this is a minor point. Our important disagreement with Wittgenstein concerns his claim that tautologies say nothing. The statement 'a = a' may be said to be trivial, and obvious, and even useless, but it cannot be denied that it says something, namely, something trivial, obvious, and useless. And there is no difficulty at all in stating what it is that the sentence says: It says that *a* is identical with itself. What holds for this statement of self-identity holds also for many instances of logical laws: They may be obvious and trivial, but they do say something. The tautology 'P or not-P' is obvious, trivial, and useless, but it says something, namely, that either P is a fact or else not-P is a fact. Similarly for contradictions. The contradiction 'P and not-P' may be saying something that is obviously and trivially false, but it does say something, namely, that both P is a fact and not-P is a fact. Tautological and contradictory statements, contrary to Wittgenstein's claim, make sense, are meaningful, and make true and false assertions, respectively.

We saw that Wittgenstein claims that some things cannot be said but show themselves. A case in point, and a relatively clear case, is identity. "Identity of object," he says, "I express by identity of sign, and not by using a sign of identity.

Difference of objects I express by difference of signs" (Wittgenstein, 5.53). In his "ideal" or "perspicuous" language, only one name occurs for every named thing, and every name is assigned to just one entity. One could therefore tell by the shape of an expression whether or not it represents the same thing as another expression, even if one does not know what thing the expression represents. Identity of objects thus "shows itself"; it is not stated in the "ideal" language. But what philosophical difference does this make? What philosophical insight follows? Whether the fact that a thing is different from another thing is *stated* in the language or merely *indicated* in some fashion or other, it remains a fact to be reckoned with. No linguistic operation can make this fact vanish from the world. There is Wittgenstein's *Tractatus* on my desk to the left of my typewriter. That is a fact. And it remains a fact if I do not state it as I just did, but merely "show it" by drawing a picture of the *Tractatus* to the left of a picture of my typewriter. Most importantly, the picture does not prove that there is no such thing as the relation of being to the left of, just as using different names for different things does not prove that there is no such thing as the relation of being different from each other (of being non-identical).

(Wittgenstein and many other philosophers fail to appreciate that there are facts involving identity which are not instances of the law of self-identity. For example, there are such "informative" facts as that Mozart is the composer of *The Magic Flute*. Not all identity statements, therefore, are trivial, obvious, and useless. Thus, even if we could argue from triviality to non-existence, it would not follow that there is no identity relation.)

Let us now return to logic proper. How does a tautology "show" what it does not say? And what, precisely, is it that is shown? I think that there is no answer to these questions in the *Tractatus*. But there is a theme that floats like a mist over the philosophical landscape inhabited by Wittgenstein and his admirers: Grammar somehow reflects the structure of the world. Language somehow shows by its structure what cannot be described by means of it, namely, the structure of the world. However, the negative side of Wittgenstein's view is relatively clear: Tautologies are not statements about the world; they say nothing about the world; they are not factual.

There is a third strand to Wittgenstein's early view. It centers around the notion of a truth table. Truth tables are thought to define the logical connectives out of existence, so that they vanish from the ontological inventory of the world (see Wittgenstein, 5.4 to 5.441). There seem to be two parts to Wittgenstein's argument against logical things; one explicit, the other merely hinted at.

In the first part, Wittgenstein argues that the "interdefinability" of the logical signs shows that these signs do not represent logical things. For example, the fact that 'if P, then Q' can be "defined" in terms of 'not' and 'or' is supposed to prove that the expressions 'if-then', 'not', and 'or' do not represent anything. If they represented logical things, so the argument goes, then what 'If P, then Q' represented would have to differ from what 'Not-P or Q' represented, since the former would contain the relation if-then, while the latter would not. But the "interdefinability" shows that what these two expressions represent is the same. Wittgenstein's point can be made most persuasively for negation. (1) If 'not' represented a logical entity, then 'P' and 'not-not-P' would have to represent different states of affairs, since only the latter represents a state of affairs which contains the thing *not*. (2) But these two sentences represent the same state of affairs. (3) Therefore, 'not' does not represent anything.

Wittgenstein's argument rests on a mistaken assessment of what "interdefinability" can yield. He assumes mistakenly that the interdefinability of, say, 'if-then' with 'or' and 'not' means that 'If P, then Q' and 'Not-P or Q' are merely two different expressions for the same thing (for the same state of affairs). But we are not dealing here with mere *abbreviations*, with mere linguistic conveniences. Rather, we are dealing with *equivalences*. The so-called definition is not of the form:

    (A) 'If P, then Q' is short for 'Not-P or Q',

but is of the form:

    (B) *If P, then Q* is a fact if and only if *Not-P or Q* is a fact.

And (B) follows, as an instance, from the logical law:

    (C) All states of affairs p and q are such that: *If p, then q* is a fact if and only if *Not-p or q* is a fact.

Thus we have, firstly, a logical law (a logical fact), and, secondly and automatically, an instance of this law. But neither from (B) nor from (C) does it follow that 'If P, then Q' and 'Not-P or Q' represent the same state of affairs: and only if one could show that they do, could Wittgenstein's argument be sound.

Since I hold that the conditional relation is not the same thing as the combination of negation and disjunction, I conclude that the two states of affairs are not the same. In the case of negation, it seems to me to be obvious—no doubt, as obvious as it seemed to Wittgenstein that the opposite was true—that P is not the same state of affairs as not-not-P. (That these two states of affairs are not the same does not *imply*, of course, that there must be infinitely many more states of affairs of the form not-not-not-not-P, etc.) Why am I so sure that there are "logical relations"? Well, if there were no such things, then one should be able to do logic without them, just as one is able to do zoology without unicorns. If the expressions for negation and the connectives were mere "syncategorematic signs," then one should be able to eliminate them. Otherwise, what is the point of calling them "syncategorematic"? Has anyone ever really seriously tried to get along without 'not', 'neither-nor', 'and', 'if-then', etc.? And yet, so many philosophers seem to believe that these expressions stand for nothing, are mere artifacts of language. Of course, we shall not permit any other way, straightforward or round-about, of depicting those relations or of "showing" what their expressions commonly represent. Nor shall we be impressed by the usual practice of "reducing" some of them to others. One single connective is as ontologically significant as a thousand of them, for it proves the existence of the sub-*category* of connective.

What these considerations show is that even if Wittgenstein had not mistaken true equivalences for abbreviations, his argument would still be unsound. Assume, for the sake of my point, that all connectives "reduce" to neither-nor. Even then we would be left with "irreducible" neither-nor sentences and the corresponding complex states of affairs. This is where the second part of Wittgenstein's argument makes its appearance. In order to eliminate the neither-nor relation and the corresponding complex states of affairs, one invokes truth-tables. The idea is to "define" 'neither-nor' in the familiar fashion by the truth table:

T, T: F

T, F: F

F, T: F

F, F: T (cf. Wittgenstein, 4.442).

This table does not contain the expression 'neither-nor'. Nevertheless, what it is supposed to convey is a certain proposition, namely, the proposition: The statement Neither P nor Q is true if and only if P is false and Q is false. (Equivalently: *Neither P nor Q* is a fact if and only if *P* is not a fact and *Q* is not a fact.) And this proposition clearly concerns the relation neither-nor. The truth table, we must keep in mind, is merely a convenient way of expressing a certain *proposition,* nothing less, and nothing more. It is not a definition, neither of the connective, nor of anything else. In general, truth tables are not definitions of the connectives, but are convenient ways of stating general truths about the existence of molecular facts as a function of the existence of their constituent states of affairs.

Wittgenstein's early conception of logic is rather obscure. When it is not obscure, so I have argued, it is mistaken. The laws of logic can be stated as any other laws can. The instances of logical generalities, tautologies, and contradictions are not empty and senseless, respectively. A tautology, far from saying nothing, says something that is necessarily (logical necessity!) true. A contradiction, far from being nonsensical, says something that is necessarily false. Finally, there is no truth to Wittgenstein's claim that there are no "logical things." The quantifiers and connectives are just as much part of the furniture of the world as elephants and spatial relations.

Since Wittgenstein's early views about the nature of logic are obscure if not clearly mistaken, one cannot but wonder why they had such a tremendous influence on the logical positivists. One explanation is that they promised to lift a heavy philosophic burden from their shoulders. Wittgenstein's views promised to exorcise the *synthetic a priori* from philosophy. As Schlick and others saw it, empiricism— their blend of empiricism—consisted in the rejection of the synthetic a priori. Carnap, in his intellectual biography puts it this way:

> Wittgenstein formulated this view in the more radical form that all logical truths are tautological, that is, that they hold necessarily in every possible case, therefore do not exclude any case, and do not say anything about the facts of the world.
> . . . he did not count the theorems of arithmetic, algebra, etc., among the tautologies. But to the members of the Circle there did not seem to be a fundamental difference between elementary logic and higher logic, including mathematics. Thus we arrived at the conception that all valid statements of mathematics are analytic in the specific sense that they hold in all possible cases and therefore do not have any factual content.

What was important in this conception from our point of view was the fact that it became possible for the first time to combine the basic tenet of empiricism with a satisfactory explanation of the nature of logic and mathematics.

(The Philosophy of Rudolf Carnap, pp. 46–47)

In Carnap's words: The true (valid) statements of mathematics are analytic because "they hold in all possible cases and therefore do not have any factual content." Might one not with equal force argue that the laws of zoology are analytic and without factual content, since they, too, hold "in all possible cases"? The only difference between (a) the laws of "sentential logic," (b) the laws of arithmetic, and (c) the laws of zoology is that the laws of (a) hold for all *states of affairs,* those of (b) hold for all *numbers,* and the laws of (c) hold for all *animals.*

b) Wittgenstein and Rules of Grammar

According to Kant, the a priori is the necessary. Arithmetic (and logic), everyone agreed, is necessary. But what kind of necessity attaches to arithmetic (and logic)? This is the most fundamental question of the Kantian challenge. Kant claimed that it is not the kind of necessity that arises from analyticity. The logical positivists and their friends rebelled: There is only one kind of necessity, they chanted, and analyticity is its source. But we must constantly keep in mind that, unless they were logicists in the Fregean mold, their notion of analyticity was suspect. We just saw that Carnap at one point thought of analyticity in terms of tautologies, taking a leaf from the *Tractatus.* The verbal bridge between the Kantian notion and this modified version of analyticity consists of the phrase 'lack of factual content'. One may mistakenly think that the new notion is the same as the old one, because according to either notion, analytic statements are supposed to lack factual content. From our point of view, the phrase 'lack of factual content' is much too vague to advance the philosophical dialectic.

However, analytic philosophers soon discovered a new kind of necessity and, therewith, a true alternative to Kant's doctrine of the synthetic a priori nature of arithmetic. This necessity is based on *meaning,* and this meaning emanates from *rules* (of grammar). In one of his lectures at Cambridge, Wittgenstein reputedly said that "To a necessity in the world there corresponds an arbitrary rule in language" (see Coffa, chap. XIV). As with most of Wittgenstein's aphorisms, this one allows for several interpretations. It seems not too far fetched, in the light of other things Wittgenstein said, to take it to mean that there is no independent necessity in the world, but only a kind of necessity which is a projection of grammar. The basic problem with this new notion is obvious. Either the rules of grammar are arbitrary, or else they are not. If they are, then the necessity of arithmetic and logic, such as it is, is merely a matter of convention. If they are not, then the question arises of what objective features of the world are reflected by these rules of grammar. And in this case, there are two plausible answers: The rules are either determined by the structure of the mind or else by the structure of the (nonmental) world. The first alternative is the Kantian view; the second yields our form of realism.

The basic idea of the semantic theory of the a priori is simple: A priori propositions are not really propositions at all, but are rules that determine the meanings of words. But though the idea may be simple, its development runs into a string of difficulties. Let us once again take a slight detour and return to Wittgenstein's early view on negation. He held that there is no such thing as negation; for if there were, then Not-not-P would have to be different from P. Around 1930, he argues that the law of double negation, to the effect that all p are such that not-not-p if and only if p, is not really a law, but a rule that constitutes the meaning of negation:

> There cannot be a question of whether these or other rules are the correct ones for the use of 'not' (that is, whether they accord with its meaning). For without these rules the word has as yet no meaning; and if we change the rules, it now has another meaning (or none), and in that case we may just as well change the word too.

> (See Coffa, chap. XIV)

And Ambrose's notes for 1932 contain the following remark: "The objection that the rules [of grammar] are not arbitrary comes from the feeling that they are responsible to the meaning. But how is the meaning of 'negation' defined if not by rules? not-not-p = p does not follow from the meaning of 'not' but constitutes it" (Coffa, chap. XIV). This is a relative of the view that certain sentences do not really represent states of affairs (propositions), but somehow "define" terms that occur in them. The difference is that Wittgenstein does not think of them as "implicit definitions," but as rules. But the strategy is the same: Certain perfectly normal sentences are separated from the rest and declared to be fundamentally different from other sentences in that they provide the meanings for their terms. These sentences are precisely those which, according to tradition, formulate a priori truths. The problem with this strategy is the obvious one that we need a principle of separation: How are we to distinguish between "ordinary" sentences and sentences which, though they look perfectly ordinary, are really definitions or rules in disguise? Why, for example, is the law of double negation not a true statement about (all) propositions, just as the law that whales are mammals is a true statement about all whales? Or is this latter law also a rule which constitutes the meaning of the word 'whale'? If so, what about the statement that John has blue eyes; does it constitute the meaning of 'John'?

The usual reply is that one can disagree about the color of John's eyes without disagreeing about the meaning of 'John', but one cannot dispute the law of double negation without disagreeing about the meaning of 'not'. But if one cannot dispute the law without a different meaning, then the law must somehow constitute the meaning of 'not' rather than rest on it. Acceptance of the law signals that one will follow the traditional rules for the use of 'not'. Let us cast this reply in the form of an argument:

(1) Whenever two people disagree about the truth of 'P', there are two possibilities:
   a) They mean the same by the expressions of 'P',
   b) they do not.
(2) If a) is the case, then they have a factual disagreement; but if b) is the case, they have a semantic disagreement.
(3) In the latter case, 'P' is not really a declarative sentence, but a rule for the use of certain words; and the disagreement shows that one person adopts the rule, while the other does not.

I think that it is obvious that (3) does not follow from the true premises (1) and (2). Nor can I think of any true assumptions from which (3) follows. But, then, I am of course convinced that (3) is false. Consider the law that all whales are mammals. Surely, one can find some persons who believe that whales are fish. Assume that Mary actually believes this. She disagrees with John about whether whales are mammals or fish. Do we have a factual or a semantic disagreement? Well, do they mean the same by 'whale' (or/and 'mammal' and 'fish'), or don't they? We ask Mary, showing her a picture of a whale, or taking her to the ocean. All her answers indicate that she means by a whale the same animal we have in mind. May we not conclude that she means by 'whale' the same as John does, but that she factually disagrees with him about whether or not these creatures are mammals? But what happens if an eager Wittgensteinian insists that there is really a semantic disagreement and, hence, that the law of zoology is not at stake? He brushes aside all of our tests with Mary and keeps insisting that she could not possibly mean the same by 'whale' as we do, because she believes that whales are fish. What she means by 'whale' is something that, among other things, is a fish and, hence, cannot be the same as what we mean by it. The apostle of Wittgenstein thus uses the existence of the disagreement between Mary and John as proof that it must be semantic in nature. But in doing so, I submit, he reduces his view to absurdity: Upon his criterion, any disagreement about the truth of a proposition becomes a semantic disagreement and there are no factual disagreements at all.

But let us assume that the Wittgensteinian concedes that the law about whales is a statement of fact rather than a rule for the use of 'whale'. Why does he believe that the law of double negation is different in character? Of course, the former is about whales, while the latter is about states of affairs; the subject matter is different. And of course, the law of double negation is much more general than the law about whales. And of course, we are much more certain, perhaps, that the law of logic holds. And of course, we cannot even imagine exceptions to the law of double negation, while we have no trouble imagining whales that lay eggs. But all of these differences do not add up to the difference between a factual and a semantic disagreement.

A direct defense of Wittgenstein's position is equally implausible. Is it really impossible for two logicians to disagree about the truth of a logical proposition? For example, must two logicians really disagree about the meaning of 'or' when they disagree about the law corresponding to disjunctive syllogism? I do not think so.

The recent history of logic, as well as of set theory, has shown beyond the shadow of a doubt that factual disagreements in these fields of inquiry do exist.

The plausibility of Wittgenstein's view rests on a specific notion of meaning, namely, meaning as use. Furthermore, 'use' must be understood in a very wide sense. This explains why Wittgensteinians so ferociously attacked the so-called "reference theory of meaning." Only by discrediting this theory could they hope to make room for their own method of philosophizing. Recall our example of the disagreement about whales. Mary and John, we shall assume, look at the same animal in the ocean, and they both agree that they are talking about that same animal "over there." John asserts that it is a mammal, while Mary insists that it is a fish. Surely they are talking about the same whale; they mean the same thing by 'that whale over there'. They are referring to the same whale. But meaning, the Wittgensteinian holds, is not reference. Meaning is use, and Mary uses 'whale' differently from John, for she adamantly asserts that this whale is a fish. This meaning of 'meaning' leads straightforwardly to the absurd conclusion that no two people can mean the same thing by an expression as long as they disagree about the truth of a sentence in which the expression occurs.

But the really important fallacy of Wittgenstein's line of reasoning hides somewhere else. Assume that two logicians disagree about the truth of the proposition associated with disjunctive syllogism:

(DS) All states of affairs p and q are such that: If *(p or q and not-p)*, then *q*.

Logician A believes that (DS) is true, while logician B believes that it is false. May not A say to B: "Well, I see what you are driving at. But, perhaps, we do not mean the same thing by 'or'. The 'or' I have in mind is such that (DS) is true"? Assume also that B agrees that they may have two different notions in mind. In that case, they should stop arguing whether (DS) is true or false; for, upon one notion it is true, and upon the other, it is false. The situation is similar to the one where one person insists that Paris is in France, while another insists that it is in Indiana. As soon as they discover that they are talking about different towns, they stop arguing. They now agree that a certain town named 'Paris' is in France, and that another town by the same name is in Indiana. Our two logicians could agree, similarly, that (DS) is true as long as 'or' means or_1, and false if it means or_2. But it does not follow from their agreement, and this is the important point I wish to make, that the respective sentences about Paris are rules rather than declarative sentences. From the fact that there was semantic disagreement, it does not follow that the sentences in question cannot represent states of affairs. Quite to the contrary. After the semantic confusion has been cleared up, both parties to the dispute will declare that the sentences are true and false, respectively. Of course, there is the other possibility that they agree that there is one and only one connective *or* and that, therefore, one of them must be mistaken about (DS). In this case as well, though, the disagreement is about a matter of fact.

What do the alleged rules of use have to do with grammar? Surely, someone who denies that whales are mammals, someone who says: "Whales are not mammals," does not speak ungrammatically. Nor is it a violation of grammar to assert that green is not a color or that a pencil is both blue all over and also not blue all over at the same time. We may say that the first is a denial of an a priori truth, and that the second is a contradiction, but neither is ungrammatical. Still, according to some passages in Wittgenstein, that green is a color is due to the "grammar of color words." It seems to me that just as his view rests on a vague notion that meaning is use, so does it depend on a diffuse notion of grammar.

But why should we not try to improve on Wittgenstein's idea and see where it may lead us? In order to have a relatively precise notion of grammar, let us consider the so-called formation rules for the artificial languages philosophers have constructed. These rules describe which strings of signs are well-formed or, as we may wish to say in our context, which strings of signs are grammatical. They correspond to the implicit rules of English grammar. For example, while the expression 'It is not the case that whales are mammals' is well-formed (grammatical), the expression 'It is not the case that apple' is not. The relevant formation rule may read like this: "A combination of 'not' with a whole sentence is well-formed, while a combination of 'not' with anything else but a sentence is not." The procedure is so well known that I shall not go into detail. What interests us is the origin of such rules of grammar. Why is 'Not-P' well-formed, while 'Not-F' is not (where 'F' is a property word)?

Our philosophy has an obvious and plausible answer: The rules of well-formedness reflect the ontological laws of the world. For example, it is a law of ontology that negation attaches to states of affairs and to nothing else. This is the reason why expressions of the form 'Not-P' are well-formed, while the negation of a property is not. If the world were different from what it is, although we cannot imagine such a difference, negation could combine with a category other than the category of state of affairs. This possibility must be distinguished, it should be added, from possible explications of the nature of negation within the framework prescribed by the just mentioned law of ontology. One must agree that negation "attaches" to states of affairs rather than to properties in isolation, for example, but that does not as yet imply that negation cannot be a relation between things and their properties. According to this view, negation exists in the form of negative exemplification. There are two indefinable, unanalyzable, relations between things and their properties, namely, positive and negative exemplification. I think that this view is mistaken, but its falsehood does not subtract from its intelligibility (see my *The Categorial Structure of the World*, pp. 356–57). And there are other possible categorizations of negation. The important fact is that the rules of grammar are not arbitrary, that they are determined by the laws of ontology, and that these laws lie even deeper than the laws of logic. The sentence 'This pencil is both blue and not blue all over at this moment' is perfectly grammatical, as I already pointed out, even though it states a contradiction, that is, a logical falsehood. In the artificial language of philosophers, both 'P and not-P' and 'P or not-P' are well-formed, even though the first represents a contradiction, while the second represents a logical truth (tautology).

Of course, Wittgenstein rejects this view. In regard to our example of negation and the apple, as we mentioned earlier, he is reported to have said:

You want to say that the use of the word 'not' does not fit the use of the word 'apple'. The difficulty is that we are wavering between two different aspects: (1) that apple is one thing or idea which is comparable to a definite shape whether or not it is prefaced by negation, and that negation is like another shape, which may or may not fit it:

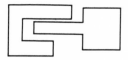

(2) that these words are characterized by their use, and that negation is not completed until its use with 'apple' is completed. We cannot ask whether the uses of these two words fit, for their use is given only when the use of the whole phrase 'not apple' is given. For the use they have *they have together*.

The two ideas between which we are wavering are two ideas about meaning (1) that a meaning is somehow present while the words are uttered (2) that a meaning is not present but is defined by the use of the sign. If the meaning of 'not' and 'apple' are what is present when the words are uttered, we can ask if the meanings of these two words fit; and that will be a matter of experience (i.e., of fact). But if negation is to be defined by its use, it makes no sense to ask whether 'not' fits 'apple'; the idea of fitting must vanish.

(Coffa, chap. XIV)

I do not waver between these two views. The first view seems to me to be correct. I would not describe it as Wittgenstein does, but in essence it is true that since 'not' represents negation rather than, say, the property of being sweet, and since 'apple' represents the property of being an apple rather than, say, the fact that there are apples, 'not apple' is not well-formed. It is not grammatical. It does not represent something that is *ontologically possible*. Why does Wittgenstein think that this view is to be rejected in favor of the second one?

'Not' and 'apple' have certain uses. For example, 'not' is used with sentences, if I may put it so, not with words. This is the very reason why we reject 'not apple' as ungrammatical: 'Not' is not used that way. But Wittgenstein goes on to argue that we cannot ask whether or not 'not apple' is ungrammatical, for whether or not it is ungrammatical depends, in part, on whether or not 'not apple' is ungrammatical. Thus the notion of something's being ungrammatical "must vanish." But I think that we have no difficulty in determining whether or not 'not apple' is ungrammatical. This is an open and shut case. And in general, the notion of well-formedness or of grammaticality makes perfect sense. Wittgenstein's argument must be fallacious. Specifically, it is not true, as Wittgenstein contends, that we can only decide whether or not 'not apple' is ungrammatical after we have already made up our minds whether or not it is ungrammatical. It is clear in what direction Wittgenstein's contention leads: If the issue can only be decided after it has been decided, then it can only be decided, if it can be decided at all, by fiat. We can only cut off the threatening infinite regress of having to find a reason for our decision before we find a reason for our decision, if no such reason is required in the first place, that is, if we can simply decree that the expression is ungrammatical. Wittgenstein's line of reasoning leads to the conclusion that whether or not an expression is ungrammatical is a matter of our choice, no laws of whatever sort restrict us.

What is the crucial step in this line of reasoning? Does the use of 'not' fit the use of 'apple'? Well, what is the use of 'not'? Surely, so Wittgenstein seems to argue, the use of 'not' involves, in part, the use of 'not' in connection with 'apple'. Thus to know the use of 'not', I must know how 'not' is used in combination with 'apple'. This means that I must know whether or not 'not' fits the use of 'apple', in order to know the use of 'not'. But now we are running around in circles: In order to know whether or not 'not' fits 'apple', I must know the use of 'not'; and in order to know the use of 'not', I must know whether or not 'not' fits 'apple'. The only way of breaking out of this circle, according to Wittgenstein, is to decree whether or not 'not' fits 'apple'. Only by means of a convention can we escape from the circle.

This line of reasoning resembles Poincaré's vicious circle accusation against impredicative descriptions. As I interpret Poincaré, he objects to the following description ("definition") of the square root of two: the least upper bound of the set of numbers whose square root is at most two. He objects to it because he thinks that it is circular. It is allegedly circular, because it uses the notion of number in general. The notion of the square root of two must be excluded from the notion of number in general before the latter can be used to describe ("define") the former. It is assumed that the notion of number in general somehow consists of the notions of individual numbers. It is assumed that one can have the general notion of number only if one already has the notion of the particular number which is the square root of two. Similarly, in Wittgenstein's argument it is assumed that one can have a notion of the general use of 'not' only if one already has the notion of a particular use. The use of 'not', it is assumed, somehow consists of all of the particular uses to which the word is put.

Ultimately, as I pointed out earlier, Poincaré's objection rests on the mistaken belief that we cannot acquire the notion of number without first acquiring the notion of every individual number. What is true is, rather, that we come by the notion of number, not by acquiring the notions of individual numbers, but by recognizing that something or other is a number. We come by the notion of the property of being an elephant, not by having met all of the individual elephants in the world, but by having seen one or two elephants. In summary, in order to acquire the notion of a property, it is not necessary to be acquainted with all of the things that have the property. Wittgenstein's argument contains the same mistake as Poincaré's. He assumes that the use of 'not' somehow *consists* of all of the particular uses to which the word is put. What is truly amazing is not that Wittgenstein should have arrived at a false conclusion, but that he should have made this particular assumption, for he talks constantly about the *rules* of grammar. The use of 'not', he ought to have realized, is given by such a rule. For example, the rule that 'not' can only occur within the context of a sentence decides that 'not' and 'apple' do not fit. Similarly, the formation rule that 'or' is a connective between sentences determines that 'or 7' is ill-formed. Wittgenstein has got it wrong when he argues that "if negation is to be defined by its use, it makes no sense to ask whether 'not' fits 'apple'; the idea of fitting must vanish." To the contrary, if negation is defined by its use, through the grammatical rules of English, then it makes perfect sense to ask whether or not 'not' fits 'apple', and the answer is then obvious.

The real question is, as I mentioned before, whether the rules of grammar conform to the laws of ontology or are arbitrary. I believe that the laws of ontology determine the rules of grammar, just as the laws of logic determine the rules of inference. Wittgenstein, on the other hand, seems to hold that the rules of grammar are somehow derived from the linguistic behavior of people, and that there can be no further question as to whether or not this behavior has to conform to anything. 'Not apple' is ungrammatical, not because of any feature of the world, but because people do not say "not apple", and we are not allowed to ask why they do not speak that way. The rules of grammar, after everything has been said, turn out to be conventions.

Wittgenstein presents an argument to the effect that nothing could justify the rules of grammar (see Coffa, chap. XIV). It goes like this: (1) A statement that justifies the grammatical rule governing 'not' would have to be of the form: Since negation only attaches to states of affairs, 'not' cannot be combined with anything but a sentence; (2) But for this statement of the rule to make sense, the part 'negation only attaches to states of affairs' must make sense; (3) It follows from bipolarity that the phrase 'negation *does not* only attach to states of affairs' must make sense; (4) But this is precisely what we are denying by our attempt to justify the grammatical rule; (5) therefore, if the rule could be justified, it could also be violated; (6) but it cannot be violated; (7) Therefore, it cannot be justified.

If this is indeed Wittgenstein's argument, then it clear that he goes wrong in step (4): We justify the grammatical rule, not by claiming that the sentence 'negation does not only attach to states of affairs' is *meaningless,* but by claiming that it is *false.* We justify the grammatical rule by claiming that the statement "Negation attaches only to states of affairs" is true, just as we justify *modus ponens,* not by claiming that a certain sentence is senseless, but by claiming that its negation is a law of logic.

I must hasten to add, as always when discussing Wittgenstein, that there are also numerous passages in which Wittgenstein seems to contradict the view that the rules of grammar are arbitrary. This inconsistency is most obvious in his discussion of mathematics. On the one hand, Wittgenstein, in agreement with our interpretation of him, says such things as: "The axioms of mathematics are sentences of syntax . . . The axioms are postulations of forms of expressions." On the other hand, he also states flatly that "set theory is false" (see Coffa, chap. XIV).

c) Analyticity and the Vienna Circle

I believe that it is fair to say that the logical positivists never developed a coherent and clear notion of necessity. Most of them agreed, however, on three things. Firstly, they insisted on a sharp distinction between analytic and synthetic statements. Secondly, they identified the necessary (the a priori) with the analytic.

Thirdly, they adopted Wittgenstein's dogma that the factual coincides with the synthetic. It must be said to their credit that Wittgenstein's distinction between what can be said and what can only be shown did not find wide acceptance. As far as the necessity of logic, arithmetic, and set theory is concerned, it was explained in a potpourri of ways. Nothing reveals their confusion about the nature of necessity and, hence, of the a priori, better than Ayer's treatment of this topic in his famous *Language, Truth, and Logic,* where he states the dilemma of the "empiricists" with admirable clarity:

> Where the empiricist encounters difficulty is in connection with the truths of formal logic and mathematics. For whereas a scientific generalization is readily admitted to be fallible, the truths of mathematics and logic appear to everyone to be necessary and certain. But if empiricism is correct no proposition which has a factual content can be necessary or certain. Accordingly the empiricist must deal with the truths of logic and mathematics in one of the two following ways: he must say either that they are not necessary truths, in which case he must account for the universal conviction that they are; or he must say that they have no factual content, and then he must explain how a proposition which is empty of all factual content can be true and useful and surprising.

> (A. J. Ayer, *Language, Truth and Logic,* quoted from
> *Philosophy of Mathematics,* P. Benacerraf
> and H. Putnam eds., p. 290)

As so often is the case, there is a way out of the dilemma. Our form of empiricism rejects Ayer's choice between necessity and factual content. The truths of mathematics and logic, we hold, have factual content *and* are necessary. Their necessity consists, not in their being devoid of factual content, but (a) in their being most general and (b) in the fact that their negation is unimaginable. Ayer chooses to be impaled by the second horn of the alleged dilemma. He cannot let go of the Wittgensteinian doctrine that a necessary truth must be devoid of factual content. Nor does he doubt that the truths of mathematics and logic are necessary. He must therefore explain how something so empty of all factual content can nevertheless be true, useful, and surprising.

But first Ayer tries to discredit the first of his two alternatives; the first of the two horns. He attributes this view to Mill, but we shall pretend that his objections are raised against us. The first objection is that "We may come to discover them [the truths of logic and mathematics] through an inductive process; but once we have apprehended them we see that they are necessarily true, that they hold good for every conceivable instance." (Ayer, quoted in Benacerraf and Putnam, p. 292.) Empirical generalizations, of course, are not of this sort. After we have discovered them, we do not see that they "hold good for every conceivable instance." If we substitute for Ayer's term 'conceivable' the word 'imaginable', we are in complete agreement with him. It is indeed true that the truths of mathematics and logic (as well as many other truths) are such that we cannot imagine them to be false, while the truths of science can be imagined to be false (if they can be imagined at all!). This is precisely one side of their necessity. But the fact that these truths are such that we cannot imagine them to be false does not imply that they are devoid of factual content. Rather, factual propositions can be divided into two large classes: Those that can be imagined to be false and those that cannot.

Next, Ayer argues that the truths of logic and mathematics must be necessary, and hence devoid of factual content, by giving examples of situations in which a law of mathematics or logic seems to be violated, but for which we decide, on second thought, to save the law. His point is that the laws of logic and mathematics are immune against falsification:

> And this indicates that Mill was wrong in supposing that a situation could arise which would overthrow a mathematical truth. The principles of logic and mathematics are true universally simply because we never allow them to be anything else. And the reason for this is that we cannot abandon them without contradicting ourselves, without sinning against the rules which govern the use of language, and so making our utterances self-stultifying. In other words, the truths of logic and mathematics are analytic propositions or tautologies.

> (Ayer, quoted in Benacerraf and Putnam, p. 293)

In this way, Ayer establishes a connection with analyticity: The truths of logic and mathematics are necessary because they are analytic. To be analytic is to be tautologous. To be tautologous means to be devoid of factual content: a tautologous proposition "holds for all cases and, therefore, says nothing in particular," as the incantation goes. By calling the truths of logic and mathematics analytic, Ayer really tells us no more than that they are devoid of factual content, whatever that may mean. But he also mentions the rules of language use. What then is it to be: Necessity explicated in terms of the "empty tautologies" of the early Wittgenstein, or necessity explicated in terms of the "grammatical rules" of the later Wittgenstein?

Ayer gives three reasons why we cannot abandon the truths of logic and mathematics: (1) We would be contradicting ourselves, (2) we would sin against the rules of the use of language, and (3) our utterances would become self-stultifying.

Assume that we gave up the truth (T) that two plus two is four and accepted that it is five instead. How would we be contradicting ourselves? Of course, if we believed both (T) and not-(T), we would believe a contradiction. But this is not the case. We have given up (T) and now believe not-(T) instead. Is not-(T) itself a contradiction? This question becomes: Is not-(T) a *logical* falsehood? I have argued in detail that arithmetic truths are not logical truths. Hence, while not-(T) is certainly an *arithmetic* falsehood, it is not a *logical* falsehood. I do not see, therefore, how we would be contradicting ourselves if we gave up (T).

Let us take a look at the second reason: If we accepted not-(T), we are told, we would sin against the rules of use of language. What are these rules? I cannot think of any plausible candidates that would not also either prohibit us from accepting that whales are not mammals, or else beg the question of why we never discard the truths of arithmetic. Moreover, if we really violated some rule of the use of language and did nothing else in our rejection of (T), then it must appear more rather than less mysterious that we do not easily give up arithmetic truths. For, nothing seems to be easier than to change our linguistic rules, and such changes occur all the time. On the other hand, if it were a matter of fact rather than of the rules of language that two plus two is four rather than five, then we should expect the most horrendous repercussions from any attempt to repeal this truth of arithmetic.

Ayer goes on to give a more precise explanation of analyticity and why analytic statements are incorrigible:

> Thus, the proposition "There are ants which have established a system of slavery" is a synthetic proposition. For we cannot tell whether it is true or false merely by considering the definitions of the symbols which constitute it. We have to resort to actual observation of the behavior of ants. On the other hand, the proposition "Either some ants are parasitic or none are" is an analytic proposition. For one need not resort to observation to discover that there either are or are not ants which are parasitic. If one knows what is the function of the words "either", "or", and "not", then one can see that any proposition of the form "Either p is true or p is not true" is valid, independently of experience.
>
> (Ayer, quoted in Benacerraf and Putnam, pp. 294–295)

Here then we have the test for analyticity: A proposition is analytic if and only if we "need not resort to observation to discover" that the proposition is true. (Notice that Ayer speaks of "validity," but I shall only say that *arguments* are valid (or invalid).) It is true that we need not consult experience to establish that the analytic proposition about ants is true: That it is true follows from the fact that it is an instance of a law of logic. But the same holds for synthetic propositions which are instances of the laws of nature: They also can be seen to be true without further observation. I know, for example, that the whale Walter is a mammal without "resorting to observation." We must therefore turn to the logical law itself. Ayer maintains, it seems to me, that we can see that this law is true, independently of experience, if we know the function of the connective words. But this claim is false. That all states of affairs (all propositions) behave in a certain fashion, that every one of them is such that either it is a fact or its negation is a fact, is just as much a fact about states of affairs and, hence, the world, as it is a fact about whales that every one of them is a mammal. In either case, the case of states of affairs and the case of whales, knowing the "function" of 'or', 'not', 'if-then', etc. is not to know the truth of the law. We know the function of 'not' and 'if-then' perfectly well without knowing on this basis alone whether or not it is not the case that all whales are mammals. We must know, in addition, something about whales in order to know whether or not they are mammals. And similarly in the case of states of affairs: We must know something about states of affairs before we can know whether every one of them is such that either it is a fact or else its negation is a fact.

We do not deny, of course, that there is a tremendous difference between a law of biology and a law of logic. Some laws are much more fundamental than others; they are much more general than others; they are much more pervasive than others; they are much more important than others. But they are facts, nevertheless. And it is a grave mistake to believe that they are devoid of factual content or that they tell us nothing about the world. The opposite is true: The laws of logic and mathematics have so much factual content and tell us such important things about the world that they serve as the very *foundation* for our more esoteric inquiries into the social structure of ant colonies.

Ayer argues that analytic propositions cannot be refuted because they have no factual content. Since they have no factual content, facts cannot touch them. We come to a different conclusion. The laws of logic and mathematics have factual content. They can therefore be refuted. But since they concern the most general features of reality, they can only be refuted by the most general facts about reality. This means that the tautology mentioned by Ayer cannot possibly be refuted by facts about ants. How could it be, since it is not about ants? But it would be refuted if states of affairs were other than they are.

Ayer argues that analytic propositions, even though they are devoid of factual content, can nevertheless give us new knowledge. They can be "useful" and "surprising" because they call attention to linguistic usage (Ayer, quoted in Benacerraf and Putnam, p. 295). Such propositions are not nonsense like the propositions of metaphysics. Where does this usage come from? It seems to be *fixed by definition,* as far as I can make out. The truth of an analytic proposition, Ayer says, follows simply "from the definition of the terms contained in it" (Ayer, quoted in Benacerraf and Putnam, p. 297). Does this mean that the truth of the law of excluded middle follows from the definitions of 'or' and 'not'? And how does the truth of a law follow from definitions? Let us be guided by a familiar example. Assume that we agree to use 'bachelor' as a convenient abbreviation for the much longer 'unmarried male of marriageable age'. Now, all sorts of truths will follow from our agreement. For example, it will be true by definition that all bachelors are males; and it will also be true that all bachelors are unmarried. These truths follow, it must be emphasized, from the abbreviation plus certain laws of logic. For example, that all bachelors are males follows from our abbreviation together with the law that if anything has properties F and G, then it has property F.

Can we make a parallel case for the law of excluded middle? What are the abbreviational agreements (definitions) for 'or' and 'not'? What is 'or' an abbreviation of? What is 'not' an abbreviation of? I cannot think of any plausible answers. The two cases are completely different. We may suspect that Ayer thinks of the truth-tables as definitions of the connective words, but we have already seen that the truth-tables do not represent linguistic conventions (abbreviations). Rather, they depict certain laws of logic. The truth-table for 'not', for example, depicts the law that all states of affairs p are such that if p is a fact, then not-p is not a fact, and if p is not a fact, then p is a fact.

We can see how precarious Ayer's grasp of the nature of definition is when we turn to his discussion of mathematics. He starts out with the standard positivist interpretation of geometry:

> We see now that the axioms of a geometry are simply definitions, and that the theorems of a geometry are simply the logical consequences of these definitions . . .

(Ayer, quoted in Benacerraf and Putnam, p. 297)

There is no sense, therefore, in asking which of the various geometries known to us are false, and which are true. Insofar as they are all free from contradiction, they are all true.

(Ayer, quoted in Benacerraf and Putnam, p. 298)

We conclude, then, that the propositions of pure geometry are analytic.

(Ayer, quoted in Benacerraf and Putnam, p. 298)

Take Poincaré's notion that the axioms of geometry are implicit definitions, combine it with Hilbert's identification of consistency with truth, and, presto, geometry is analytic! Of course, we can also convince ourselves along the same line that botany is analytic. Things are getting easier and easier. We may have thought that in order to decide whether or not geometry is analytic, we would have to decide whether or not the axioms of geometry are based on experience. Well, do we need observation in order to decide whether or not the axioms of geometry are true? What are these axioms about? Are they about chalk points, pencil lines, and triangles formed by light beams? If they are, then we must of course observe such points, lines, and triangles, just as we must observe whales in order to decide whether or not they are mammals. However, Ayer holds that these axioms are "not in itself about physical space" (Ayer, quoted in Benacerraf and Putnam, p. 297). And he hints that this follows from the discovery of non-Euclidian geometry. But how could it follow? How could the fact that a non-Euclidian set of axioms is consistent prove that a Euclidian set is not about "physical reality"? How could the discovery of non-Euclidian geometries possibly show that Euclidian geometry has no factual content? But we need not even use the discovery of non-Euclidian geometry in order to show that geometry is devoid of factual content and, hence, analytic. A shortcut is presumably available, as we saw a moment ago. We merely have to decree that the axioms of geometry are "definitions." What follows from these definitions is then true, not as a matter of fact, but as a matter of definition. What follows from these definitions is therefore analytic.

Things are no less confused when we turn from geometry to arithmetic:

> We see, then, that there is nothing mysterious about the apodeictic certainty of logic and mathematics. Our knowledge that no observation can ever confute the proposition "7 + 5 = 12", depends simply on the fact that the symbolic expression "7 + 5" is synonymous with "12", just as our knowledge that every oculist is an eye-doctor depends on the fact that the symbol "eye-doctor" is synonymous with "oculist".

(Ayer, quoted in Benacerraf and Putnam, p. 299)

No more talk about axioms being definitions. Ordinary numerical equations are now claimed to be true by definition. More precisely, they are said to be true because of the (fortuitous?) circumstance that language contains more than one expression for the same thing. One wonders why Ayer did not wave the magic wand of synonymy over geometry as well. That the inner angles of a triangle add up to two right angles could be claimed to be true "by definition" because the expression 'the sum of the inner angles of a triangle' is synonymous with 'two right angles'. But why stop with geometry? History, for example, is apodeictic, that is, devoid of factual content, that is, analytic, that is, a matter of synonymy. That Salzburg is the birthplace of Mozart is surely due to the fact that 'Salzburg' is synonymous with 'the birthplace of Mozart'; that Napoleon is the vanquished of Waterloo follows from the fact that 'Napoleon' is merely short for 'the vanquished of Waterloo'. Of course, I am jesting. Salzburg is correctly described as the birthplace of Mozart, and the number 12 is correctly described as the sum of 7 and 5, but neither the statement that Salzburg is the birthplace of Mozart nor the statement that 12 is the sum of 7 and 5 is analytic. And just as little as 'Salzburg' is an abbreviation of 'the birthplace of Mozart', just as little is '12' an abbreviation of 'the sum of 7 and 5'.

Nor is Ayer the only one who meets Kant's challenge by definition, so to speak. Lest I be accused of being unfair to Ayer, let me quote a passage from Hempel:

> For the latter [the proposition $3 + 2 = 5$] asserts nothing whatsoever about the behavior of microbes; it merely states that any set consisting of $3 + 2$ objects may also be said to consist of 5 objects. And this is so because the symbols "$3 + 2$" and "5" denote the same number: they are synonymous by virtue of the fact that the symbols "2", "3", "5", and "$+$" are *defined* (or tacitly understood) in such a way that the above identity holds as a consequence of the meaning attached to the concepts involved in it.

(C. G. Hempel, "On the Nature of Mathematical Truth," p. 368)

A little later (on p. 369), Hempel even claims that the transitivity of identity follows from the definition of identity.

Let us return to Ayer. It seems that Ayer has some misgivings about his short proof that arithmetic is analytic. There is the obvious objection that this proof leaves no room in arithmetic for surprises, for invention or discovery. He answers that "The power of logic and mathematics to surprise us depends, like their usefulness, on the limitations of reason. A being whose intellect was infinitely more powerful would take no interest in logic and mathematics." (Ayer, quoted in Benacerraf and Putnam, p. 300.) And in a footnote, Ayer quotes Hans Hahn: "An all-knowing being needs no logic and no mathematics." But Ayer's answer does not jibe with his analysis of arithmetic. If what he says about the equation $7 + 5 = 12$ is correct, then our limitations of reason have nothing to do with our interest in arithmetic. Nor is it the case that God can dispense with logic and arithmetic because he is all-knowing. No, if Ayer is correct, then our interest in logic and arithmetic is entirely due to our verbosity. If we could just stick to the practice of using no more than one expression for one thing, logicians and mathematicians would be unemployed. God's lack of interest in logic and mathematics would not be due to his superior intellect, but merely to the fact that he is laconic.

I have dwelt on Ayer's view because it reflects accurately, in my opinion, the logical positivist's response to the Kantian challenge. This answer, I submit, consists of a hodgepodge of unconvincing ideas. Arithmetic is claimed to be analytic, contrary to what Kant says, because (1) it consists of tautologies without factual content, (2) it follows from the rules of language (rules of grammar?), (3) it follows from definitions (it is a matter of synonymy), and (4) it consists of definitions. The unifying idea behind this conception of analyticity, if there is one, is that analytic propositions are trivially true because we make them true, and we make them true by manipulating language.

d) Conventionalism

The manipulation of language is clearly a conventional affair. Thus analyticity is ultimately a matter of convention. Ayer says quite explicitly that analytic propositions "simply record our determination to use words in a certain fashion. We cannot deny them without infringing the *conventions* which are presupposed by our very denial, and so falling into self-contradiction" (Ayer, quoted in Benacerraf and Putnam, p. 299; my italics). Conventionalism in logic and mathematics, we may say, is the unofficial view of logical positivism. I cannot discuss the many articles which have been devoted to this view, but it may shed light from yet a different angle on our own position, if we briefly consider Carnap's version of conventionalism and Quine's criticism of it.

What leads to conventionalism is the view that analytic statements are somehow true as a consequence of certain linguistic practices. The general idea is to view logic and arithmetic as games, played according to certain rules. Wittgenstein described it this way to his Vienna audience:

> Frege rightly opposed the view that the numbers of arithmetic are signs. The sign 'o' does not have the property that when added to the sign '1' it gives the sign '1' as a result. In this critique Frege is right. But he did not see what is justified in formalism, that the symbols in mathematics are not the signs, and yet they have no 'meaning' (Bedeutung). For Frege the choice is as follows: either we are dealing with ink-marks on paper, or else these ink-marks are signs of something, and what they represent is their meaning. That this is not a correct alternative is shown by the game of chess: here we are not dealing with the wooden pieces, and yet they do not represent anything—in Frege's sense, they have no meaning. There is a third possibility, the signs can be used as in a game.
>
> (Coffa, chap. XVII)

I do not think that Frege overlooked this third alternative. For him and for us, the crucial distinction is between ink-marks that represent something and ink-marks that do not; there is no third alternative. But we do not deny that ink-marks may be studied from two different points of view. Firstly, we may study their properties as ink-marks, for example, their chemical composition. Or, secondly, we may study the rules which someone has adopted for writing these marks down in a certain order. For example, it may be agreed never to write down a shape like 'o' followed by a shape like '+'. By adopting such rules, one may design an interesting game of writing down strings of ink-marks. But while Wittgenstein (and Carnap) think that arithmetic is a game of this sort, Frege and I do not. We do not overlook a third possibility; we are not being misled by false analogies; we are not being seduced by language. We straightforwardly deny Wittgenstein's (and Carnap's) contention that arithmetic is like chess: Chess is a game, arithmetic is not!

Carnap worked on Wittgenstein's idea with his customary technical skill and love of detail. The rules of the game are christened "syntax." The shapes of the signs of syntax matter as little as the shape of the rook matters in chess. All that matters are the rules for the use of the shapes. But if arithmetic is syntax, we protest, what happens to truth? Truth plays no role in chess, but it is of the essence of language. Well, analytic sentences are recognizable by their shapes alone, according to arbitrary rules of composition, and these sentences are supposed to represent the truths of logic and arithmetic. Why we select those particular strings of signs and these specific rules for their formation, *we must not ask*. This is a mere matter of convention. But why stop at the "logical" transformation rules? Why, indeed! Carnap clearly saw that the "syntactic" notion of analytic truth leads straightforwardly to a "syntactic" notion of truth in general:

> Wittgenstein continues: "And so also it is one of the most important facts that the truth or falsehood of non-logical sentences can *not* be recognized from the sentences alone". This statement, expressive of Wittgenstein's absolutist conception of language, which leaves out the conventional factor in language construction, is not correct. It is certainly possible to recognize from its form alone that a sentence is analytic; but only if the syntactical rules of the language are given. If these rules are given, however, then the truth or falsity of certain synthetic sentences—namely, the determinate ones—can also be recognized from their form alone. It is a matter of convention whether we formulate only L-rules, or include P-rules as well; and the P-rules can be formulated in just as strictly formal a way as the L-rules.

(R. Carnap, *The Logical Syntax of Language*, p. 186)

(But see also Carnap's later remark that "*truth and falsehood are not proper syntactical properties;* whether a sentence is true or false cannot generally be seen by its design, that is to say, by the kind and serial order of its symbols" Carnap, 1959, p. 216).

In this fashion, we can make any "synthetic sentence" true by virtue of its form alone and, hence, can turn it into an analytic sentence. The sentence 'All whales are mammals', for example, can easily be made true by convention and turned into an analytic sentence. Not everyone, however, was impressed by Carnap's surprising result. Schlick clearly saw the trick:

> When Carnap explains . . . that one can construct a language with extra-logical transformation rules by, for instance, including natural laws among the principles (i.e., they are considered as grammatical rules), then this way of putting things seems to me to be misleading in the same sense as is the thesis of conventionalism. It is true that a sentence (a sign sequence) which under the presupposition of ordinary grammar expressed a natural law can be made into a principle of language simply by stipulating it as a syntactical rule. But precisely by this device one changes the grammar and, con-

sequently, interprets the sentence in an entirely new sense, or rather, one deprives the sentence of its original sense. It is then not a natural law at all; it is not even a proposition, but merely a rule for the manipulation of signs.

(Coffa, chap. XIX, p. 30)

It is interesting that Schlick does not draw the next and obvious conclusion that as little as Carnap's P-rules are laws of nature, so little are his L-rules laws of logic. The syntactic transformation rules are also "merely rules for the manipulation of signs". We establish a connection with logic only if we acknowledge that these rules are not conventional, that they are not picked willy-nilly, but that they reflect the laws of logic.

It may be possible to interpret Carnap in such a way that he gives a *coherent* reply to Kant's challenge (see Coffa, pp. 32–33). As far as the object language is concerned, conventionalism rules: Whether or not one accepts, say, the axiom of choice, is not a matter of truth or of fact, but merely a matter of proposing the kind of language one wishes to use. There is no fact, no truth, that could be called "the axiom of choice." There really is no such thing, therefore, as accepting or rejecting the axiom of choice as being true. All one can do is either to incorporate or not to incorporate a certain string of signs into one's language, namely, that string which ordinarily is thought to express the axiom of choice. But, and this is where we have to interpolate, it is a fact, and not merely a matter of convention, that the so-called laws of logic, arithmetic, and set theory are a matter of convention in the manner just described. On the second level, therefore, there are facts. Now, if this is approximately Carnap's view, then our objection is that it is not true that the laws of logic, arithmetic, and set theory are a matter of convention.

As obvious as the failure of conventionalism is, to many analytic philosophers it seemed to be the only alternative to the dreaded Kantian doctrine of the synthetic a priori. Quine is a case in point. In his paper "Truth by Convention," he describes in detail how logic, mathematics, and even physics can be made "true by convention." One merely has to axiomatize the respective set of laws and treat the axioms as implicit definitions. The implicit definitions are said to be "true by convention." Quine's point is that logic and mathematics cannot be sharply distinguished from the sciences by claiming that the former are true by convention while the latter are not. He is taking the pragmatic point of view:

If in describing logic and mathematics as true by convention what is meant is that the primitives *can* be conventionally circumscribed in such a fashion as to generate all and only the so-called truths of logic and mathematics, the characterization is empty: our last considerations show that the same might be said of any other body of doctrine as well. If on the other hand it is meant merely that the speaker adopts such conventions for those fields but not for others, the characterization is uninteresting; while if it is meant that it is a general practice to adopt such conventions explicitly for those fields but not for others, the first part of the characterization is false.

(W. V. O. Quine, "Truth by Convention," p. 341)

In a style reminiscent of Carnap himself, Quine here rejects Carnap's claim that he can sharply distinguish between the a priori and the a posteriori or, what for the logical positivists is the same, between the analytic and the synthetic, between the merely conventional and the factual.

Quine's criticism is well taken. But there remains an obvious question: Is there then no difference at all between the a priori and the a posteriori? Is there no necessity attached to logic and mathematics? Are logic and mathematics completely on a par with the empirical sciences? Conventionalism, we agree with Quine, cannot capture the felt difference. But must we conclude that there is no difference at all? Quine cannot deny that there is a difference, but his aversion to metaphysics does not permit an ontological account of it. He turns it behavioristically into a "contrast between more and less firmly accepted statements" (Quine, 1964b, p. 342). "There are statements", he says, "which we choose to surrender last, if at all, in the course of revamping our sciences in the face of new discoveries; and among these there are some which we will not surrender at all, so basic are they to our whole conceptual scheme" (Quine, 1964b, p. 342). But this answer merely raises a further question: *Why* do we so stubbornly cling to the truths of logic and mathematics? A pragmatist has no answer to this question. Perhaps it makes no sense to him. However, Quine sees a way of combining his pragmatism with the Carnapian conventionalism:

> Now since these statements are destined to be maintained independently of our observations of the world, we may as well make use here of our technique of conventional truth assignment and thereby forestall awkward metaphysical questions as to our *a priori* insight into necessary truths. On the other hand this purpose would not motivate extension of the truth-assignment process into the realm of erstwhile contingent statements.

> (Quine, 1964b, p. 342)

Quine admits that there is a difference between the truths of logic and mathematics, on the one hand, and the truths of science, on the other. In contrast to Carnap—and in conformity to his pragmatism—he holds, however, that this difference is gradual. But the difference, though it may be gradual, exists, and we must ask in what it consists. Quine, as I said a moment ago, never addresses this question.

Carnap, we must emphasize, held fast to the analytic-synthetic distinction. However, in response to Quine's criticism of his conventionalistic explication of the distinction, he can do no better than point to his earlier distinction between changes in language and changes in truth-value:

> I should make a distinction between two kinds of readjustment in the case of a conflict with experience, namely, between a change in the language, and a mere change in or addition of, a truth-value ascribed to an indeterminate statement (i.e., a statement whose truth-value is not fixed by the rules of language, say by the postulates of logic, mathematics and physics). A change of the first kind constitutes a radical alteration,

sometimes a revolution, and it occurs only at certain historically decisive points in the development of science. On the other hand, changes of the second kind occur every minute. A change of the first kind constitutes, strictly speaking, a transition from a language L_n to a new language L_{n+1}.

(Coffa, chap. XX)

After all is said and done, the distinction between analytic and synthetic truths turns out to be based on nothing more than a blind belief that if we reject instances of the first kind, we are changing our language, while if we reject instances of the second kind, we are not. That this is not just the judgment of one who finds much of Carnap's philosophy unclear and even evasive can be seen from an interesting letter by Tarski to Morton White (see A. Tarski, "Letter to Morton White"). Tarski very cautiously endorses an empiricistic conception of logic and mathematics: "I would be inclined to believe (following J. S. Mill) that logical and mathematical truths don't differ in their origin from empirical truths—both are results of accumulated experience." Then he goes on to say: "I think that I am ready to reject certain logical premises (axioms) of our science in exactly the same circumstances in which I am ready to reject empirical premises (e.g., physical hypotheses) . . ." And Tarski concludes with this comment on Carnap's view:

Whether this description is true and adequate—I don't know. I have the impression that many people would agree with it. I think, e.g., that Carnap would agree. Nevertheless, he would claim that there is a fundamental difference between a change of logic and a rejection of a physical theory; for, he would say, in the first case we change the language, we begin to use the words in a new meaning, while in the second no such change occurs. Why? Well, this follows from his definition of meaning (which in turn is based on a definition of logical terms and logical truth). Of course, he is permitted to do so; he can accept whatever definition of meaning he wants; and perhaps I would find it also convenient to accept his definition. However, I don't see how such a definition can really affect the situation; if you define logical axioms as those which cannot be changed without the change of your whole language, then of course you cannot change them without changing the language—this is a truism (at least, in our present logic).

(Tarski, p. 32)

Bibliography

Adickes, E. *Kants Lehre von der doppelten Affektion unseres Ich.* Tuebingen: J. C. B. Mohr, 1929.

Armstrong, D. M. *Universals and Scientific Realism,* 2 vols. Cambridge: Cambridge University Press, 1978.

———. *A Combinatorial Theory of Possibility.* Manuscript.

Arnauld, A. *L'Art de penser; la Logique de Port-Royal.* Stuttgart: Fromman, 1965–67.

Ayer, A. J. *The Problem of Knowledge.* New York: Macmillan, 1956.

———. *Language, Truth and Logic.* London: Gollancz, 1958.

Beck, L. W. "Can Kant's Synthetic Judgments Be Made Analytic?" *Kant-Studien* 47 (1955):168–81.

Benacerraf, P., and H. Putnam, eds. *Philosophy of Mathematics.* Englewood Cliffs: Prentice-Hall, 1964.

Benacerraf, P. "What Numbers Could Not Be." *Philosophical Review* 74 (1965):47–73.

Berg, J. *Bolzano's Logic.* Stockholm: Almquist and Wiksell, n.d.

Bergmann, G. "Synthetic A Priori." In *Logic and Reality.* Madison: University of Wisconsin Press, 1964.

Berkeley, G. *A Treatise Concerning the Principles of Human Knowledge.* Indianapolis: Bobbs Merrill, 1957.

———. *Three Dialogues between Hylas and Philonous.* Indianapolis: Bobbs Merrill, 1965.

Berry, G. "Logic with Platonism." In *Words and Objections: Essays on the Work of W. V. Quine.* Ed. by D. Davidson and J. Hintikka. New York: Humanities Press, 1969.

Bollnow, O. F. *Das Wesen der Stimmungen.* Frankfurt: Klostermann, 1956.

Bolzano, B. *Rein analytischer Beweis des Lehrsatzes, dass zwischen je zwey Werthen, die in ein entgegengesetztes Resultat gewaehren, wenigstens eine reelle Wurzel der Gleichung liege.* In Ostwald's *Klassiker der exakten Naturwissenschaften,* No. 153. Leipzig, 1905.

———. *Wissenschaftslehre.* 4 vols., 2nd new printing of the 2nd ed. of 1929. Aalen: Scientia, 1981.

———. *Reine Zahlenlehre.* manuscript, from Berg, J., *Bolzano' Logic.*

Brentano, F. *Psychology from an Empirical Standpoint.* Transl. by A. C. Rancurello, D. B. Terrell, and L. L. McAlister. New York: Humanities Press, 1973.

Broad, C. D. *The Mind and its Place in Nature.* Paterson, N.J.: Littlefield, 1960.

———. "The Theory of Sensa." In *Perceiving, Sensing, and Knowing.* Ed. by R. J. Swartz, 85–129. Garden City: Doubleday, 1965.

Cantor, G. *Gesammelte Abhandlungen.* Berlin: Georg Olms, 1962.

Carnap, R. *Der logische Aufbau der Welt.* Berlin: Meiner, 1928.

———. *The Logical Syntax of Language.* Paterson, N.J.: Littlefield, 1959.

———. *The Philosophy of Rudolf Carnap. The Library of Living Philosophers.* Ed. by P. A. Schilpp. Evanston: Open Court, 1963.

Chihara, C. *Ontology and the Vicious-Circle Principle.* Ithaca: Cornell University Press, 1973.

Chisholm, R. M. *Perceiving.* Ithaca: Cornell University Press, 1957.

———. *Theory of Knowledge.* Englewood Cliffs: Prentice-Hall, 1966.

Church, A. *Introduction to Mathematical Logic.* Vol. 1. Princeton: Princeton University Press, 1956.

Cocchiarella, N. "Frege, Russell, and Logicism: A Logical Reconstruction." In *Frege Synthesized,* 197–252. Ed. by L. Haaparanta and J. Hintikka. Dordrecht: Reidel, 1986.

Coffa, J. A. *To the Vienna Station,* manuscript.

Cornman, J. W. *Perception, Common Sense, and Science.* New Haven: Yale University Press, 1975.

Dedekind, R. "Was sind und was sollen die Zahlen?" In *Gesammelte mathematische Werke.* Vol. 3. Braunschweig: Vieweg, 1932.

Descartes, R. *Meditations*.

Dummett, M. "Nominalism." *Philosophical Review* 65 (1956): 491–505.

Dunn, J. M. "A Truth Value Semantics for Modal Logic." In *Truth, Syntax, Modality*, 87–100. Ed. by H. Leblanc. Amsterdam: North-Holland, 1973.

Euclid. *Elements*. Transl. by Sir T. L. Heath. 3 vols. 2nd ed. Cambridge: Cambridge University Press, 1926.

Frege, G. *Translations from the Philosophical Writings of Gottlob Frege*. Ed. by P. Geach and M. Black. Oxford: Blackwell, 1960.

———. *The Basic Laws of Arithmetic*. Transl. and ed. by M. Furth. Berkeley: University of California Press, 1964.

———. "Ueber die Grundlagen der Geometrie," Part 2. In *Kleine Schriften*. Hildesheim: Olms, 1967.

———. *The Foundations of Arithmetic*. Transl. by J. L. Austin. Evanston: Northwestern University Press, 1974.

———. *Dialogue with Puenjer on Existence*. In *Posthumous Writings*, 53–67. Chicago: University of Chicago Press, 1979a.

———. *Posthumous Writings*. Chicago: University of Chicago Press, 1979b.

———. *Philosophical and Mathematical Correspondence*. Chicago: University of Chicago Press, 1980.

———. *Collected Papers on Mathematics, Logic, and Philosophy*. Oxford: Blackwell, 1984.

Gibson, J. J. "A Critical Review of the Concept of Set in Contemporary Experimental Psychology," *Psychological Bulletin* 38 (1941): 781–817.

Goedel, K. "Russell's Mathematical Logic." In *Philosophy of Mathematics*. Ed. by P. Benacerraf and H. Putnam. Englewood Cliffs: Prentice Hall, 1964a.

———. "What is Cantor's Continuum Problem." In *Philosophy of Mathematics*. Ed. by P. Benacerraf and H. Putnam. Englewood Cliffs: Prentice Hall, 1964b.

Goodman, N. *The Structure of Appearance*. 2nd ed. Indianapolis: Bobbs Merrill, 1966.

———. "Predicates Without Properties." In *Contemporary Perspectives in the Philosophy of Language*. Ed. by H. Wettstein, P. French, and T. Uehling. Minneapolis: University of Minnesota Press, 1978.

Grice, H. P. "The Causal Theory of Perception." in *Perceiving, Sensing, and Knowing*, 438–72. Ed. by R. J. Swartz. Garden City: Doubleday, 1965.

Grossmann, R. *Reflections on Frege's Philosophy*. Evanston: Northwestern University Press, 1969.

———. "Russell's Paradox and Complex Properties." *Nous* 6 (1972):153–164.

———. *Ontological Reduction*. Bloomington: Indiana University Press, 1973.

———. "Perceptual Objects, Elementary Particles, and Emergent Properties." in *Action, Knowledge, and Reality: Critical Studies in Honor of Wilfrid Sellars*. Ed. by H. N. Castañeda. Indianapolis: Bobbs Merrill, 1975.

———. "Structures, Functions, and Forms." Vol. 2 in *Studies on Frege*. 3 vols., Vol. 2, 11–32. Ed. by M. Schirn, Stuttgart: Fromman-Holzboog, 1976.

———. *The Categorial Structure of the World*. Bloomington: Indiana University Press, 1983.

———. "Nonexistent Objects Versus Definite Descriptions." *Australasian Journal of Philosophy* 62 (1984a):363–77.

———. *Phenomenology and Existentialism*. London: Routledge, 1984b.

Hegel, G. W. F. *Phenomenology of Spirit*. Transl. by A. V. Miller with analysis of text by J. N. Findlay. Oxford: Oxford University Press, 1979.

Hempel, C. G. and P. Oppenheim. "Studies in the Logic of Explanation." In *Readings in the Philosophy of Science*. Ed. by H. Feigl and M. Brodbeck. New York: Appleton, 1953.

Hempel, C. G. "On the Nature of Mathematical Truth." In *Philosophy of Mathematics*. Ed. by P. Benacerraf and H. Putnam. Englewood Cliffs: Prentice Hall, 1964.

Heyting, A. *Intuitionism, An Introduction*. Amsterdam: North-Holland, 1956.

Hilbert, D. *Grundlagen der Geometrie.* 7th ed. Leipzig: Teubner, 1930.

———. "On the Infinite." In *Philosophy of Mathematics.* Ed. by P. Benacerraf and H. Putnam. Englewood Cliffs: Prentice Hall, 1964.

Hilbert, D. and W. Ackermann *Principles of Mathematical Logic.* New York: Chelsea, 1950.

Hilbert, D and P. Bernays *Grundlagen der Mathematik.* Berlin: Springer. Vol. 1, 1934. Vol. 2, 1939.

Hockney, H. "Review of Grossmann's Ontological Reduction." In *Philosophical Books* 17 (1976):9–13.

Hughes, G. E. and M. J. Cresswell. *An Introduction to Modal Logic.* London: Methuen, 1968.

Hume, D. *A Treatise of Human Nature.*

Husserl, E. *Ideas.* Transl. by W. R. Boyce Gibson. New York: Collier Books, 1962.

———. *Logical Investigations.* 2 vols. Transl. by J. N. Findlay. New York: Humanities Press, 1970a.

———. *Philosophie der Arithmetik.* Vol. 12 of *Husserliana.* The Hague: Nijhoff, 1970b.

Jubien, M. "Ontology and Mathematical Truth." *Nous* 11 (1977):133–50.

Kambartel, F. *Erfahrung und Struktur: Bausteine zu einer Kritik des Empirismus und Formalismus.* Frankfurt: Fromman, 1968.

Kant, I. *Logik, gesammelte Schriften.* Berlin: de Gruyter, 1922.

———. *Prolegomena to Any Future Metaphysics.* Transl. by L. W. Beck. New York: Library of Liberal Arts Press, 1957.

———. *Critique of Pure Reason.* Transl. by N. Kemp Smith. New York: St. Martin's Press, 1965.

Kessler, G. "Frege, Mill, and the Foundations of Arithmetic." *Journal of Philosophy* 77 (1980):65–79.

Kierkegaard, S. *The Concept of Dread.* Transl. by W. Lowrie. Princeton: Princeton University Press, 1973.

Kitcher, P. *The Nature of Mathematical Knowledge.* Oxford: Oxford University Press, 1983.

Leibniz, G. W. *Discourse on Metaphysics.* In *Philosophical Papers and Letters.* 2 vols. Transl. by L. E. Loemker. Chicago: University of Chicago Press, 1956.

———. *The Leibniz-Clarke Correspondence.*

Locke, J. *An Essay Concerning Human Understanding.*

Maddy, P. "Perception and Mathematical Intuition." *Philosophical Review* 89 (1980):163–96.

Meinong, A. *Ueber die Erfahrungsgrundlagen unseres Wissens.* Berlin: Springer, 1906.

Messer, A. "Experimentell-psychologische Untersuchungen ueber das Denken." *Archiv fuer die gesamte Psychologie* 8 (1906).

Mill, J. S. *An Examination of Sir William Hamilton's Philosophy.* In *Collected Works.* Vol. 9. Toronto: University of Toronto Press, 1979a.

———. *A System of Logic.* In *Collected Works.* Vols. 7 and 8. Toronto: University of Toronto Press, 1979b.

Moore, G. E. *Some Main Problems of Philosophy.* New York: Macmillan, 1953.

———. "The Refutation of Idealism." In *Philosophical Studies,* 1–30. London: Routledge and Kegan Paul, 1970a.

———. "Some Judgments of Perception." In *Philosophical Studies,* 220–252. London: Routledge and Kegan Paul, 1970b.

Mueller, G. E. and F. Schumann "Experimentelle Beitraege zur Untersuchung des Gedaechtnisses." *Zeitschrift f. Psychologie* 45 (1889).

Mueller, G. E. "Zur Analyse der Gedaechtnistaetigkeit und des Vorstellungsverlaufs." Part 1. *Zeitschrift fuer Psychologie und Physiologie der Sinnesorgane.* Suppl. vol. 5. 1911.

Nagel, E. "Logic Without Ontology." In *Philosophy of Mathematics.* Ed. by P. Benacerraf and H. Putnam, 302–21. Englewood Cliffs: Prentice-Hall, 1964.

Poincaré, H. "Review of Russell's *Essays on the Foundations of Geometry*." In *Revue de Métaphysique et de Morale*. 1889.
——. "Les Mathematiques et la logique." *Revue de Métaphysique et de Morale* 14 (1906):294–317.
Price, H. H. *Perception*. London: Methuen, 1950.
Putnam, H. "Models and Reality." *Journal of Symbolic Logic* 45 (1980):464–482.
Quine, W. V. *Set Theory and Its Logic*. Cambridge: Harvard University Press, 1963a.
——. Two Dogmas of Empiricism." In *From a Logical Point of View*. New York: Harper and Row, 1963b.
——. "Implicit Definitions Sustained." *Journal of Philosophy* 61 (1964a):71–74.
——. "Truth by Convention." In *Philosophy of Mathematics*, 322–45. Ed. by P. Benacerraf and H. Putnam. Englewood Cliffs: Prentice-Hall, 1964b.
——. "Carnap and Logical Truth." In *The Ways of Paradox*, 100–125. New York: Random House, 1966.
——. *Philosophy of Logic*. Englewood Cliffs: Prentice-Hall, 1970.
Reid, T. *Essays on the Intellectual Powers of Man*. Cambridge: M.I.T. Press, 1969.
Resnik, M. D. "Mathematics as a Science of Patterns: Ontology." *Nous* 15 (1981):529–550.
Russell, B. *Our Knowledge of the External World*. London: Methuen, 1914.
——. *Introduction to Mathematical Philosophy*. London: Allen and Unwin, 1956a.
——. "Mathematical Logic as Based on the Theory of Types." In *Logic and Knowledge*, 59–102. Ed. by R. C. Marsh. London: George Allen and Unwin, 1956b.
——. *The Principles of Mathematics*, New York: Norton, 1964.
——. *The Problems of Philosophy*. Oxford: Oxford University Press, 1977.
Ryle, G. *The Concept of Mind*. New York: Barnes and Noble, 1949.
Sartre, J. P. *Being and Nothingness*. Transl. by H. E. Barnes. New York: Washington Square Press, 1966.
——. *The Transcendence of the Ego*, Transl. and with intro. by F. Williams and R. Kirkpatrick. New York: Farrar, Strauss, and Giroux, 1988.
Schlick, M. *Allgemeine Erkenntnislehre*. 2nd ed. Berlin: Springer, 1925.
Scholz, H. "Introduction to Frege's Philosophical and Mathematical Correspondence." In G. Frege, *Philosophical and Mathematical Correspondence*. Chicago: University of Chicago Press, 1980.
Sellars, W. *Science, Perception and Reality*. London: Routledge, 1963.
——. "The Structure of Knowledge." In *Action, Knowledge and Reality*, 295–347. Ed. by H. N. Castañeda. Indianapolis: Bobbs-Merrill, 1975.
Sergeant, J. *Solid Philosophy, Asserted against the Fancies of the Ideaists*. . . . London, 1697.
Simons, P. M. "Against the Aggregate Theory of Number." *Journal of Philosophy* 79 (1982):163–167.
Smith, B., ed. *Parts and Moments: Studies in Logic and Formal Ontology*. Munich: Philosophia, 1982.
Steiner, M. *Mathematical Knowledge*. Ithaca: Cornell University Press, 1975.
Tarski, A. "Letter to Morton White." *The Journal of Philosophy* 84 (1987): 28–32.
Twardowski, K. *On the Content and Object of Presentations*. Transl. by R. Grossmann. The Hague: Nijhoff, 1977.
Vaihinger, H. *Kommentar zu Kants Kritik der reinen Vernunft*. 2 vols. Berlin: Union Deutsche Verlagsgesellschaft, 1922.
Vesey, G. N. A. "Seeing and Seeing As." In *Perceiving, Sensing, and Knowing*, 68–83. Ed. by R. J. Swartz. Garden City: Doubleday, 1965.
Watson, R. A. *The Downfall of Cartesianism*. The Hague: Nijhoff, 1966.
Watt, H. J. "Experimentelle Beitraege zu einer Theorie des Denkens." *Archiv f. d. gesamte Psychologie* 4 (1905):289–436.
Whitehead, A. N. *The Concept of Nature*. Cambridge: Harvard University Press, 1964.

Wittgenstein, L. *Tractatus Logico-Philosophicus.* Transl. by D. F. Pears and B. F. McGuinness. London: Routledge and Kegan Paul, 1961.

Zermelo, E. "Neuer Beweis fuer die Moeglichkeit einer Wohlordnung." Transl. in *From Frege to Goedel. A Source Book in Mathematical Logic.* Ed. by J. v. Heijenoort. Cambridge: Harvard University Press, 1967.

Index